## Works in English by Czeslaw Milosz

*The Captive Mind*

*Postwar Polish Poetry: An Anthology*

*Native Realm: A Search for Self-Definition*

*Selected Poems by Zbigniew Herbert*
*(Translated by Czeslaw Milosz and Peter Dale Scott)*

*The History of Polish Literature*

*Selected Poems*

*Mediterranean Poems by Aleksander Wat*
*(Translated by Czeslaw Milosz)*

*Emperor of the Earth: Modes of Eccentric Vision*

*Bells in Winter*

*The Issa Valley*

*The Seizure of Power*

*Visions from San Francisco Bay*

*The Witness of Poetry*

*The Separate Notebooks*

# THE
# LAND
# OF
# ULRO

# THE
# LAND
# OF
# ULRO

## Czeslaw Milosz

TRANSLATED BY
LOUIS IRIBARNE

*Farrar · Straus · Giroux*
NEW YORK

The quotations from Oscar Milosz's *Ars Magna* and *Les Arcanes* are from Czeslaw Milosz's translation of selected works by Oscar Milosz (*The Noble Traveller*, Lindisfarne Press, 1984). All other translations of excerpts from Oscar Milosz's work are from the French by Louis Iribarne.

W. H. Auden's translation of Adam Mickiewicz's "The Romantic," copyright © 1956 by The Noonday Press, Inc.

Portions of this translation appeared in *Ironwood* and *Temenos*

Library of Congress Cataloging in Publication Data
Milosz, Czeslaw.
  The land of Ulro.
  Translation of: Ziemia Ulro.
  I. Title.
PG7158.M553Z3513  1984     809     84-8157

# Preface

DEAR READER, this book was not intended for you, and I feel you should be forewarned before you enter its bizarre tangle. When writing it, I indulged in a personal whim, dismissing in advance the idea of its publication in English. While other books of mine, such as *The Captive Mind* or *Native Realm*, took into account a Western audience, to whom I tried to explain the corner of Europe from which I come, this time I gave free rein to my meditations and didn't try to reach anybody in particular, except perhaps a few fastidious people able to read my Polish and belonging to the same circle of the literati.

Though the subject is philosophical and has nothing specifically Central European in it, my whole personal experience is involved in it, including my school and university years; my readings in Polish, French, and Russian; my fascination with certain poets unknown in America; and my quarrels with the milieu of literary Warsaw. That abundance of the exotic and the eccentric makes, I am afraid, for the book's difficulty.

My decision to write *The Land of Ulro* was an act of perfect freedom in the sense that I didn't aim either at pleasing, convincing, conquering, or seducing my contemporaries. It was as if I said to myself that a writer can afford to produce in his lifetime one maverick work. In a way, it was my rebellion against the reasonableness of my essayistic prose, in which I felt much more constrained than in my poetry. Perhaps my pleasure in digressing is sufficiently noticeable to compensate for a frequent recurrence of foreign names and for too many allusions to poets and critics unavailable in English translation. At least, such is my hope. I would have this book confirm the awareness of our common fate, wherever we live on our planet; even if we apply modes of thinking stemming from different traditions, we comment upon one universal civilization.

C.M.

1984

They rage like wild beasts in the forests of affliction
In the dreams of Ulro they repent of their human kindness.

—WILLIAM BLAKE

# THE
# LAND
# OF
# ULRO

# 1

WHO WAS I? Who am I now, years later, here on Grizzly Peak, in my study overlooking the Pacific? I have long deferred the telling of certain spiritual adventures, alluding to them until now only discreetly and grudgingly. Until I noticed that it was getting late—in the history of our shrinking Earth, in the history of a life—and that it was time to overcome my long-abiding distrust of the reader. That distrust can be traced back to my literary origins, to the distant thirties. Even in those days, as one who sensed the general drift of things, as a "catastrophist" who nonetheless pined for an age of "faith and fortitude"—as one of my early poems had it—there were few in whom to confide my hopes and fears. No doubt I was inhibited by certain class-inherited prejudices, resident in me as well, of the Polish intelligentsia, so that I was everywhere confronted by forbidden territory. The label "a young avant-garde poet" was, again, a significant source of misunderstanding: by and large, the avant-garde shunned those things with which I was, secretly, engaged. But since I had to belong somewhere, I conformed, often to the point of dissimulating. Thus was I given to many defense strategies, all the more as my attitude toward those monuments of wisdom towering in the universities and literary columns was one of sacred awe mixed with suspicion (maybe they were foundering, too), and nothing so favors arrogance and disdain as such an ambivalence. Not that I would condemn arrogance, as it can be a protection.

This partially explains my obsession with silence, the fear that if I spoke, no sound would escape from my mouth. One can well imagine the effect, on one so inhibited, of having one's gravest forebodings borne out; of wartime Warsaw and that postwar spectacle when suffering, by then routine, was to be experienced in even stronger doses, and how solitude and academic work could come to be a blessing. My work for foreigners has been of a practical, even pedagogic nature—I do not believe in the possibility of communing outside a shared language, a shared history—while my work in Polish has been addressed to readers transcending a specific time and place, otherwise known as "writing for the Muses."

I do not understand my life (who does?). Nor my books, and I shall not pretend to understand them. All bespeak a strenuous self-discipline—of which it can be said that those who lack it yearn for it, while those who have it to spare know how much is lost through it and long to be released from it, to proceed by impulse and the hand's own free momentum.

But to gain that freedom is to commune with a reader, hoping for some flicker of understanding in his eyes, believing that he is really communing with us, that we are joined by the same belief or at least by the same hope. I shall now assume such a reader; that a new audience, however few in number, is there. Among the readers of books, one in a

In their concrete analyses, however, classical functionalists have concentrated on issues or cases in which transformations in the environment, through differentiation and integration, triggered higher levels of adaptation of a system. As in the case of mainstream Marxism, functionalist theory construction has focused, with the exception of Eisenstadt's work, on the successful evolutionary pattern. Cases deviating from this type must appear as anomalies, rather than as instances of different evolutionary paths having their own logic.

The usefulness of functionalism for the explanation of the Argentine pattern of development would therefore be very limited. Even though functionalist theories can contribute to the conceptualization of the problem in terms of the variations in the international environment and the need to adjust to them, and, through their emphasis on the intended versus the unintended consequences of action, also to focus the researcher's attention on the key issue of elite rationality, they lack hypotheses to approach the phenomenon itself, that is, the reversal of Argentine development. The response to the collapse of the international order was an industrialization drive based on import substitution, or economic differentiation. But increased differentiation created a problem for system integration without providing, by itself, the resources for its solution. The integrative responses attempted by the state and the elite to the formation of the new industrial bourgeoisie and the new working class—expansion of the state control over the economy and the polity, the latter through corporatism and authoritarianism—were not adequate, as the decay of legitimacy and the high level of political instability indicate. And the overall consequence of differentiation has been, in the long run, the underdevelopment of Argentina, that is, a lower level of adaptation.

Understanding the logic at work in the Argentine case can be a step toward the development of a typology of evolutionary paths that would supersede simplistic binary stereotypes (developed-underdeveloped, dominant-dependent). Such logic is the result of concrete social processes, rather than the gradual unfolding of some essential force. What demands understanding is the interplay of objective constraints and "subjective" factors, the cognitive and ideological components of collective action. In the dis-

Evolution," *American Sociological Review* (1964), and *Modernization, Protest, and Change* (1966).

cussion above, I argued that the Argentine turning point is unlikely to have been an automatic effect of the transformations of the world economy between 1930 and 1945. But global structural and domestic infrastructural factors provided the constraints within which the different social groups interacted to produce the outcomes, underdevelopment in the economy and illegitimacy in the polity. But since, as I also stated, there was not a high level of class polarization during the period of the turning point, nor a realistic revolutionary threat, it is the behavior of the state and of the central fractions of the dominant class that appears particularly intriguing. Inasmuch as economic slippage and political illegitimacy are obviously against the interests of established elites, the question can be asked: were the outcomes under study solely attributable to structural constraints, or was there also a "subjective" factor, an element of choice by the elites or a segment thereof? If this was the case, elite false consciousness was at work.

I will show that the relationship between the Depression and the war and the reversal of development in Argentina was indirect. It was mediated by three factors: the autonomy of the state, distorted political knowledge, and peculiarities of the Argentine social structure. First, the structural changes in the world system produced economic and political threats to different groups and to the state, and they also led to the fragmentation of established elites. The joint consequence of these developments was the autonomization of the state. Second, the sector of the political elite in control of the state in the last stages of the war was driven by an unrealistic fear of revolution, not shared by economic elites. This fear was produced by a distorted image of the working class and by misinterpreted demonstration effects. As a consequence, the Argentine state resorted to a set of policies designed to thwart revolution. Third, the long-term consequences of these policies were stagnation and illegitimacy, owing to traits of the Argentine class structure that derived from the very "modernity" of the society.

My discussion will include both the role of structural constraints of different types and the rationality involved in the policies with which the segments of the elite in control of the state responded to the consequences of environmental transformations. Paraphrasing Theda Skocpol's remark about the state,[32] I think

32. Theda Skocpol, *States and Social Revolutions* (1979), pp. 24–33, and "Political Responses to Capitalist Crises: Neo-Marxist Theories of the State and the Case of the New Deal," *Politics and Society* (1980).

that ideology must be taken seriously. As the state is not just a transmission belt for infrastructural effects, ideology is not merely an emotional factor that distorts cognition or a mechanism for the rationalization, in the Freudian sense, of class interests. The hypostatization of the infrastructure-superstructure metaphor, as well as the recent concern with the role of ideology in the reproduction of social relations, lead to the consideration of ideology exclusively as an intervening variable between class position and behavior. But ideologies are also cognitive frameworks that control perception of the environment and the integration of cognitive contents, and that guide behavior. Ideology, thus, has independent effects, and the consistency between these consequences and the objective interests of the carriers is problematic, even for ruling classes and leaders of the state apparatus, whose propensities for higher levels of rationality are often taken for granted.

Elite responses to critical changes in the domestic or external environment are mediated by these cognitive frameworks, but neither the degree of development of productive forces nor the degree of social differentiation determine the objective consequences of these responses, and the higher the level of uncertainty, the greater the potential for divergence between intended and objective consequences. As Jürgen Habermas argues, ". . . there exists *a fortiori* no guarantee that a development in the forces of production and an increase in steering capacity will release exactly those normative alterations that correspond to the steering imperatives of the social system."[33] The imputation of rationality to state or elite behavior poses, in turn, another question: that of the sources of the cognitive framework that determines that behavior, and of changes in that framework. My analysis, in addition to ascertaining the causal weight of cognitive frameworks in elite choices, will endeavor to establish the processes by which the frameworks were generated.

33. Jürgen Habermas, *Legitimation Crisis* (1973), p. 13.

# 2 Is Argentina a Deviant Case? Resource Endowments, Development, and Democracy in Sociological Theory

The "Argentine question," the fact that a peripheral country such as Argentina has been underdeveloped since the war, is not surprising from the standpoint of the currently popular dependency and world-system approaches, but it is paradoxical in relation to a long-standing proposition in social theory. This proposition, a rare instance of theoretical convergence among theorists of different persuasions spanning two centuries, is that a society having a high land-labor ratio and a population shortage will develop an efficient capitalist economy and a democratic polity. Since the land and labor endowments of Argentina appear to fit these specifications, it is in connection with this hypothesis, often overlooked by contemporary sociologists of development, that Argentine economic and political evolution is enigmatic.

There is a school of thought in comparative sociology, beginning, as far as I know, with Adam Smith, that has attempted to explain the differences in the economic and political evolution of societies on the basis of quantitative and qualitative aspects of the resource endowment of these societies. More specifically, this approach has been an inquiry into the long-term effects of different characteristics of the supply of land and labor in agrarian social structures. The dependent variables have been the potential for a dynamic capitalist economy and/or for liberal democracy.

Arguments concerning these relationships were triggered by the differences within Europe and between European and other regions, which became evident in the late eighteenth and early nineteenth centuries. Observers at the time realized that all known societies could be ordered on a continuum representing potential for capitalism and liberal democracy. The American colonies that fascinated Smith and Tocqueville and the India that intrigued Marx were at the poles of this dimension. The problem was to under-

24

stand whether these variations represented qualitatively different paths of evolution, or were rather successive stages of a process common to all societies.

A brief survey of the argument linking land and labor endowments and long-term economic and political outcomes will support my contention about the theoretical significance of the Argentine case.

### The Classification of Societies in Adam Smith and Tocqueville

Adam Smith, on inquiring about the "causes of the prosperity of new colonies," concluded that "the colony of a civilized nation which takes possession either of a waste country, or of one so thinly inhabited, that the natives easily give place to the new settlers, advances more rapidly to wealth and greatness than any other human society."[1] The American colonies were the paradigmatic case but, well before their establishment, the historical record showed that new settlements in open spaces were more prosperous than colonies in which a more advanced population exploited the labor of a preexisting society. Smith compared the progress of the ancient Greek colonies, which in many cases "rivalled, and even . . . surpassed their mother cities"[2] with the relative backwardness of the Roman dependencies: ". . . the progress of no one of them seems ever to have been very rapid. They were all established in conquered provinces, which in most cases had been fully inhabited before."[3] Settlement colonies not only had a greater potential for economic growth, but they were also more likely to become egalitarian: in them, land was so cheap and abundant in relation to labor that salaries would be high and laborers would eventually have access to the land.[4] The society would tend, therefore, to become a homogeneous community of independent commodity producers.

Tocqueville dealt with the issue in a similar manner, but he paid greater attention to cultural factors, and emphasized democracy, rather than economic growth, as the main outcome associated with the "new country" situation.

1. Adam Smith, *An Inquiry into the Nature and Causes of the Wealth of Nations* (1937), pp. 531–32.

2. Ibid., p. 533.

3. Ibid.

4. Ibid., p. 532.

"Among the lucky circumstances that favored the establishment and assured the maintenance of a democratic republic in the
United States," he argued, "the most important was the choice of
the land itself in which the Americans live. Their fathers gave
them a love of equality and liberty, but it was God who, by hand-
ing a limitless continent over to them, gave them the means of
long remaining equal and free. . . ."[5] "In the United States, not legislation alone is democratic, for Nature itself seems to work for
the people."[6] A favorable land-labor ratio contributed not only to
prosperity but also to equality through the constitution of a society of middle class farmers: ". . . the soil of America rejected a territorial aristocracy; . . . to clear this untamed land nothing but the
constant and committed labor of the landlord itself would serve.
The ground, once cleared, was . . . [not] fertile enough to make
both a landlord and a tenant rich. So the land was . . . broken up
into little lots which the owner himself cultivated. [The English
colonies] . . . all from the beginning, seemed destined to let freedom grow, not the aristocratic freedom of their motherland, but a
middle-class and democratic freedom. . . ."[7]

Tocqueville also examined the consequences of the establishment of settlement colonies in North America and of exploitation
colonies in the Spanish and Portuguese empires, where European
settlers created forced labor systems:

> Modern nations have found in some parts of South
> America vast lands inhabited by peoples less enlightened
> than themselves, but those peoples had already taken
> possession of the soil and were cultivating it. The
> newcomers, to found their states, had to destroy or
> enslave numerous populations, and civilization blushes
> at their triumphs. . . . But North America was only
> inhabited by wandering tribes who had no thought of
> exploiting the natural wealth of the soil. One could still
> properly call North America an empty continent, a
> deserted land waiting for inhabitants.[8]

Both regions were rich in natural resources. However, they
evolved along different paths, both economically and politically:

5. Alexis de Tocqueville, *Democracy in America* (1969), p. 279.
6. Ibid., p. 280.
7. Ibid., pp. 33–34.
8. Ibid., p. 280.

"... where in the world can one find more fertile wildernesses, greater rivers, and more untouched and inexhaustible riches than in South America? Nevertheless, South America cannot maintain a democracy. ... Even if (the Spaniards) could not enjoy the same happiness as the dwellers in the United States, they ought at least to be the envy of European nations. Yet there are no nations on earth more miserable than those of South America."[9] The explanation for this difference is not to be found in physical causes, nor in the laws (Tocqueville noted that Mexico had adopted the same laws as the United States).[10] There must be some other reason, he concluded, and he found it in the "mores,"[11] by which he meant "the whole moral and intellectual state of a people,"[12] that is, culture, in both its evaluative and cognitive aspects. At this point, Tocqueville departed from all the other theorists I am considering here, who focused on land and labor as the main determinants, to the exclusion of other institutional and cultural factors.

### The Classification of Societies in Marx and Engels

The classical Marxist position on the economic and political consequences of the development of capitalism in contexts characterized by different supplies of labor and land can be summarized in five propositions.

The first is that precapitalist social structures have relatively static economies, characterized by simple rather than enlarged reproduction (accumulation). The extreme case is the stagnant type, represented by the "Asiatic mode of production," in which there is no division of labor in society: "These self-sufficing communities ... constantly reproduce themselves in the same form, and when accidentally destroyed, spring up again on the spot and with the same name—this simplicity supplies the key to the secret of the unchangeableness of Asiatic societies. ..."[13]

Second, the successful transition to the pure type of capitalism implies the destruction of precapitalist agriculture, be it the Eastern self-sufficient community or the Western forms based on relationships of personal dependence vis-à-vis a superordinate class

9. Ibid., p. 306.
10. Ibid., p. 307.
11. Ibid.
12. Ibid., p. 287.
13. Karl Marx, *Capital* (1967), p. 358.

(slavery and serfdom). This is a necessary condition for both self-sustaining economic growth and democracy. As Barrington Moore puts it in relation to the latter, and as a conclusion to his own research, ". . . getting rid of agriculture as a major social activity is one prerequisite for successful democracy. The political hegemony of the landed upper class had to be broken or transformed. The peasant had to be turned into a farmer producing for the market instead of his own consumption and that of the overlord."[14]

Third, a "pure" capitalist society, that is a society in which the capitalist relations of production are exclusive, is expected to have a dynamic, albeit fluctuating, economy and a liberal-democratic polity. Enlarged reproduction and the consequent increase in the organic composition of capital are the central logic of capitalism: in order to fight the tendency of the profit rate to fall and to compete with other firms, each capitalist is forced to convert surplus value into additional capital. The outcome is a continuous growth of productive forces (up to, of course, the point in which these forces "clash" with their capitalist integument). "Once given the general basis of the capitalistic system, then, in the course of accumulation, a point is reached at which the development of the productivity of social labour becomes the most powerful lever of accumulation."[15]

The affinity between pure capitalism and liberal democracy is presented more as an empirical association than as a causal argument, and it is subject to the important restriction mentioned before: the absence of a revolutionary threat. The equation "bourgeoisie = liberalism" seems to be founded on empirical observation and "explained" on the basis of the homology between the functioning of the market in a capitalist economy and the dynamics of liberal democratic institutions.

The fact that the economic interests of the capitalists could be protected under political forms other than the democratic state appears in Marxism as the exceptional case. For Marx and Engels, it is because of a revolutionary menace that the affinity between bourgeoisie and democracy breaks down in the "pure" capitalist society:

> At a certain point, which must not necessarily appear
> simultaneously and on the same stage of development

14. Barrington Moore, *Social Origins of Dictatorship and Democracy* (1966), p. 429.
15. Marx, *Capital*, p. 621.

> everywhere, [the bourgeoisie] begins to note that this, its
> second self [the proletariat], has outgrown it. From then
> on, it loses the power for exclusive political dominance.
> It looks for allies with whom to share its authority, or to
> whom to cede all power, as circumstances may demand.
> . . . These allies are all of a reactionary turn. It is the
> king's power, with his army and his bureaucracy; it is
> the big feudal nobility; it is the smaller Junker; it is even
> the clergy.[16]

More specifically, the activation of the proletariat is what leads to
a dictatorial regime: "the basic condition of modern Bonapartism
[is] an equilibrium between bourgeoisie and proletariat,"[17] and
". . . Bonapartism is . . . a *modern* [my emphasis, C.H.W.] form of
state which presupposes the abolition of feudalism."[18]

Fourth, "impure" capitalist societies are expected to deviate
from that model. In classical Marxism, structural heterogeneity
appears as a residue of precapitalist modes of production. Since
capitalist social relations imply both a market for commodities
and a market for labor (and hence what Marx calls "free labor"),
these residues involve not only self-sufficient agriculture, slavery,
and serfdom, but also independent commodity production without labor markets, that is, the cases of family farmers and artisans
who do not hire labor. Nowhere are capitalist relations of production generalized to the point of actual exclusiveness, but in the
most "modern" societies, precapitalist forms have negligible economic and social weight. It is the societies with large peasan-
tries—and usually this implies powerful landed elites—that are
structurally heterogeneous, even if capitalism is hegemonic. Germany and Russia in the nineteenth century were the obvious
models. These societies were expected to generate economic and
political structures different from those in truly modern countries
such as England. Marx noticed that mid-century France, while
more socially advanced than societies with feudal residuals, had
an economy that differed from the English standard. French industry was not central, and therefore the industrialists were not, like
their English counterparts, the hegemonic fraction of the

16. Engels, *German Revolutions*, pp. 8–9.
17. Engels, *The Housing Question* (n.d.), p. 72.
18. Engels, *German Revolutions*, p. 13.

bourgeoisie.[19] And Bonapartism was made possible by the existence of a large peasantry.[20] Analogously, Engels noted that it was the persistence of the Junkers that made the Bismarckian state possible.[21]

Fifth, it follows from the above propositions that the purest form of capitalism and, hence the form most prone to economic dynamism and liberal democracy is the one created *ex nihilo*, as in the American northern colonies. Marx defined colonies on the basis of two characteristics: "We treat here of real colonies, virgin soils, colonized by free labor."[22] In addition, land was also free, and this was conducive to economic growth: "The essence of the free colony . . . consists in this—that the bulk of the soil is still public property, and every settler on it therefore can turn part of it into his private property and individual means of production, without hindering the later settlers in the same operation. This is the secret . . . of the prosperity of the colony."[23] The absence of a feudal past also means that the bourgeoisie would have the monopoly of political power and establish what Engels calls a "durable reign."[24]

Finally, Engels distinguished between the "colonies proper, that is, the countries occupied by a European population," to which the foregoing analysis applies, and the typical underdeveloped case, "the countries inhabited by a native population, which are simply subjugated—India, Algeria, the Dutch, Portuguese, and Spanish possessions."[25] These were the societies impervious to change which, at least in the case of India, could only be set in motion by an external intervention that would disarticulate their structure: "English interference (in India) dissolved these small, semi-barbarian, semi-civilized communities by blowing up their economical basis, and thus produced the greatest, and to speak the truth, the only *social* revolution ever heard of in Asia," Marx wrote.[26]

Unlike Adam Smith and later the staple theorists, the classics of Marxism did not hypothesize positive links between a *shortage* of labor and economic growth and equality. They dealt with pop-

19. Marx, *Class Struggles*, p. 113.
20. Marx and Engels, *Selected Works* (1977), pp. 171–72.
21. Engels, *German Revolutions*, pp. 12–14.
22. Marx, *Capital*, p. 765n.
23. Ibid., p. 768.
24. Marx and Engels, *Works*, p. 394.
25. Ibid., p. 688.
26. Marx, *On Colonialism and Modernization* (1969), p. 93.

ulation in its quantitative aspect chiefly with reference to the "labor reserve army": one of the central principles of Marxian economics is the "fundamental law of capitalist accumulation," according to which capitalism necessarily produces a population surplus. This is the result of the increase in the organic composition of capital, and of technological innovation, and its function is to control the rise of wages. Eventually, this excess population is expected to have destabilizing consequences for the system.[27] They were also aware, in a context characterized by precapitalist relations of production, of a negative connection between scarcity of labor and social development and democracy. This instance was the "second serfdom" in eastern Europe, in the fifteenth and sixteenth centuries.

In Marx, precapitalist social relations always precede the development of capitalism, so that instances of structural heterogeneity appear as a transitional phenomenon. Trotsky's analysis of Russia as a case of "combined development" opened a different path, and contemporary analysts—the Latin American dependency theorists, Frank, and, most systematically, Wallerstein—have shown that traditional forms can be not only frozen by the development of capitalism but also be its product.[28]

### The Classification of Societies in Turner and the Staple Theorists

Both Frederick J. Turner and the staple theorists of growth examined the effects of a high land-labor ratio. Turner was especially concerned with the relationship between such a ratio and democracy, while the staple theorists' exclusive interest was the potential for economic growth and for social equality.

Turner connected the settlement of uninhabited lands with development and democracy. "Frontier" meant for him more than a favorable land-labor ratio: it was also a wild environment, some-

27. Marx, *Capital*, chap. 25. On this issue, see also Carlos H. Waisman, *Modernization and the Working Class: The Politics of Legitimacy* (1982), chap. 7.

28. See Samir Amin, *Accumulation on a World Scale: A Critique of the Theory of Underdevelopment* (1974); Cardoso and Faletto, *Dependency and Development*; Frank, *Capitalism and Underdevelopment*; Aníbal Pinto, *Tres ensayos sobre Chile y América Latina* (1971); Wallerstein, *World-Economy*; especially "The Rise and Future Demise of the World Capitalist System: Concepts for Comparative Analysis."

times referred to as "the forest," whose conquest transformed the settlers and shaped American culture and institutions. "The existence of an area of free land," he argued, "its continuous recession, and the advance of American settlement westward, explain American development."[29] The existence of open spaces was for him the determining factor of the pattern of economic evolution of the United States. It prompted the Homestead Act, the development of markets, migration, and other progressive trends. "But the most important effect of the frontier has been in the promotion of democracy here and in Europe; . . . the frontier is productive of individualism, . . . [and] the frontier individualism has from the beginning promoted democracy."[30] In a more radical statement of his views, which is in sharp disagreement with Tocqueville, Turner asserted that the availability of land was a more powerful determinant of democracy than the liberal political ideologies and institutions: "American democracy was born of no theorist's dream; . . . It came out of the American forest, and it gained new strength each time it touched a new frontier. Not the constitution, but free land and an abundance of natural resources open to a fit people, made the democratic type of society in America for three centuries while it occupied its empire."[31]

The staple theory of growth, derived from Harold Innis's work on Canadian development, focuses on the long-term economic and social consequences of the "open spaces" situation. In Melville H. Watkins' formulation, the theory applies to the atypical case of the "new country," which is characterized by "a favorable man/land ratio and an absence of inhibiting traditions."[32] Societies having these traits are expected to have a greater potential for economic growth and for the development of an egalitarian social structure than the standard settings, characterized by a large pool of labor and by premodern social relations and culture:

> [A favorable man-land ratio] . . . implies a relatively high standard of living which facilitates expanding domestic markets and substantial factor mobility. The fact that new countries do not start their development with population pressing against scarce resources gives them

29. Frederick J. Turner, *The Frontier in American History* (1920), p. 1.
30. Ibid., p. 30.
31. Ibid., p. 293.
32. Melville H. Watkins, "A Staple Theory of Economic Growth," *The Canadian Journal of Economic and Political Science* (1963); p. 143.

an enormous advantage over the typical underdeveloped country. Specifically, they have neither a large subsistence agricultural sector . . . nor a pool of cheap labour permitting industrialization to proceed with only limited impact on the incomes of much of the population.[33]

As for the lack of traditions, it means that these societies are likely to generate a modern culture, functional to development: ". . . institutions and values must be formed anew, and although there will be a substantial carry-over from the old world, the process will be selective and those transferred are likely to take a form more favourable to economic growth."[34]

In this tradition, Robert E. Baldwin's work on the production functions of different agrarian commodities is of particular interest. He compared the economic and social consequences, in a sparsely populated "new country," of specialization in two different types of export commodity: a plantation crop and a labor-extensive product such as wheat. His conclusion was that the second commodity, *ceteris paribus*, was more likely to produce "a faster and more balanced type of development" as well as a "more equitable distribution of income."[35] A plantation crop generates a society with a large pool of cheap, unskilled labor at the bottom, little entrepreneurial skill at the top, and a low potential for industrialization. Extensive agriculture, on the other hand, is more likely to lead to a society of middle-class farmers, which has favorable prospects for the growth of manufacturing.

## Two Models and the Argentine Case

The approaches I have reviewed in the foregoing discussion are convergent, and more complementary than contradictory. Two contrasting models emerge: the "colonies" without a precapitalist past and with a high potential for capitalist development and liberal democracy, and the traditional or structurally heterogeneous societies. If these models are applied to the agrarian societies outside the core of the world economy, they correspond to the "new country" or "open spaces" and to the "underdeveloped" types.

33. Ibid., p. 149.

34. Ibid., pp. 149–50.

35. Robert E. Baldwin, "Patterns of Development in Newly Settled Regions," *The Manchester School* (1956), p. 176.

The first is exemplified by the United States and the "lands of recent settlement," and the second by third-world societies, those in Latin America included. Table 2.1 summarizes the differences between the models with regard to land and labor supply, and to the expected long-term results of their evolution. Culture appears between brackets and both as a determinant and as an outcome because this is the only factor on whose causal status there is disagreement. For Tocqueville, it is an independent variable, whereas for Turner and the staple theorists it is a dependent one. In all cases, culture is expected to be functional to the economic and political outcomes.

According to this theoretical tradition, then, there is a bifurcation in the periphery: "colonies" having the right endowment of land and labor are expected to move to the core, while the settle-

*Table 2.1.*
*Types of Non-Core Agrarian Society.*

| Resource Supply Prior to Industrialization | Open Spaces or New Country | Underdevelopment (includes Latin America) |
|---|---|---|
| *Land* | | |
| Land-labor ratio | High | Low |
| Juridical status | Free | Appropriated |
| *Labor* | | |
| Quantity | Shortage (immigrant labor) | Surplus (native labor) |
| Social relations | Free labor | Nonfree labor, or mixed free-nonfree |
| (Culture) | (Functional to outcomes) | (Functional to outcomes) |
| *Long-Term Outcomes* | | |
| Economy | High levels of growth | Other |
| Society | Structurally homogeneous (traditional or precapitalist sector absent or small) | Structurally heterogeneous (traditional or precapitalist sector large) |
| | More egalitarian | Less egalitarian |
| Polity | Liberal democracy | Nondemocratic state |
| (Culture) | (Functional to other outcomes) | (Functional to other outcomes) |

ments based on surplus labor are doomed to evolve in such a way that their peripheral status is preserved or re-created. It follows from this line of argument that core/periphery status is not only a function of a country's position in the international system, as the standard versions of dependency theory imply, but also of the internal supply of land and labor.

These two types of colony are expected to produce in their development societies that resemble, in their structural characteristics, the two forms found in the European core since the Reformation and the age of revolutions: what Parsons called "the northwest,"[36] and southern and eastern Europe. The first group, typified by Britain, and considered by Marx as the model of capitalism, includes the societies in which precapitalist social relations were dissolved, the economy was dynamic, and a liberal-democratic state was established. The second case is that of the late developers, which produced "combined" social structures, backward economies, and polarized polities with a propensity for nondemocratic forms of state.

The questions before us are now two: to what extent does Argentina correspond to the "new country" type of peripheral society? If it does, why is it a deviant case?

36. Parsons, *Modern Societies*.

# 3 Images and Facts: Argentina Against the New Country and Latin American Mirrors

## Images: New Country or Underdeveloped Society?

The two models of peripheral society I discussed in Chapter 2 have been used for the characterization of Argentina. Three images have been influential at different points in time: they portray Argentina as a new country, as an underdeveloped, dependent society, and as a dualistic, structurally heterogeneous nation. The first of these images is based on the new country model, and the two others emphasize the external and the internal aspects of the underdevelopment type.

The representation of Argentina as a new country arose and became established in the period of ascent, particularly around the Centennial (1910), when politicians and intellectuals felt compelled to take stock of the massive changes that had taken place in the previous half century. The conception of Argentina as a typical Latin American country took root, predictably, during the decline. It became articulated by right-wing and later by left-wing intellectuals, and it gradually spread throughout the society, entering the mainstream of economic and political thought. The third representation, the dualistic one, is the oldest of all. It was the organizing principle of the ideology of the intellectual and political elites since the middle of the nineteenth century. This image persisted up to the present, through its combination with the other two conceptions. A "modernist" variety of dualism is usually combined with a new country image, while a "traditionalist" or nativist version is more consistent with the image of Argentina as an underdeveloped society.

### Structural Heterogeneity

There is, according to Tulio Halperin Donghi, an exceptional trait in Argentine history: the fact that the progress of the country since the 1870s can be ascribed in part to the implementation of a project formulated around the middle of the century by a group of intellectuals-politicians, Domingo F. Sarmiento and Juan B. Alberdi being the most influential ones.[1] The use of the term "project" should not, in my view, imply that the main dynamic forces in Argentine development were internal. As Juan Corradi put it, "for decades Argentines believed they were a chosen people. . . . Chosen they were, but not by deities. British imperialism had elected the pampas . . . to supply it with foodstuffs."[2] Still it is important to understand the role of internal factors. Argentine progress took place as a response to the expansion of the core of the world economy, but the definers of the "project," as Halperin emphasizes, understood the nature of the process, and aimed at accelerating and utilizing the trends which could integrate Argentina with that core.[3]

This "project" presupposed a dualistic view of Argentina. The philosopher José Ingenieros summarized Sarmiento's diagnosis and proposed solutions in this manner: "Sarmiento was obsessed by two basic ideas as an explanation for all the evils that have weighed on South America: (1) the Spanish heritage; (2) miscegenation (with the) Indians. . . . The social remedies appeared to him as the following two: (1) public education, (2) European immigration."[4] Alberdi's diagnosis was the same, but the solutions he emphasized were immigration and the establishment of what we would call an elite democracy. Both identified the littoral area centered in Buenos Aires with European immigration and culture, economic progress, and organized government, and the interior with Indian and Spanish population and culture, stagnation, and lawlessness. As Alberdi put it, "in America everything that is not European is barbarian."[5]

1. Tulio Halperín Donghi, "Prólogo," in idem, ed., *Proyecto y construcción de una nación (Argentina 1846–1880)*, (1980), p. xii.

2. Juan E. Corradi, "Argentina," in Ronald E. Chilcote and Joel C. Edelstein, eds., *Latin America: The Struggle with Dependency and Beyond* (1974), p. 309.

3. Halperín Donghi, "Prólogo," p. xiii.

4. José Ingenieros, "Las ideas sociológicas de Sarmiento," in Oscar Terán, ed., *Antiimperialismo y nación*, (1979), p. 334. See also Noé Jitrik, *Muerte y resurrección de Facundo* (1968); José Luis Romero, *A History of Argentine Political Thought* (1963), chap. 5; and Torcuato S. Di Tella, "Raíces de la controversia educacional argentina," in idem and Tulio Halperín Donghi, eds., *Los fragmentos del poder* (1969).

5. Juan B. Alberdi, *Bases y puntos de partida para la organización política de la República Argentina* (1946), p. 67. On Alberdi, see Jorge M. Mayer, *Alberdi y su tiempo* (1963); and Natalio R. Botana, *El orden*

The relationship between the sectors was conceptualized in three forms. First, as the coexistence, in the same territory, of two cultures, isolated from each other. In Sarmiento's words, "The inhabitants of the city wear the European dress, live in a civilized manner, and possess laws, ideas of progress, means of instruction, some municipal organization, regular forms of government, etc. Beyond the precincts of the city everything assumes a new aspect. . . . The people composing these two distinct forms of society do not seem to belong to the same nation."[6]

Second, the rupture was represented as a gap in time: "The only subdivision that the Spanish American man admits is into Littoral man and Interior or Mediterranean Man. This division is real and profound," wrote Alberdi. "The first is the fruit of European civilizing action in this century. . . . The other is the product of sixteenth-century Europe, the Europe at the time of the conquest. . . ."[7] Third, in the most precise formulation of the latent meaning, the cleavage was presented as a conflict between opposing forces and, more specifically, as internal colonialism. In Sarmiento's famous phrase, it is ". . . the struggle between European civilization and native barbarism, between mind and matter."[8]

It is important for our discussion of the incorporation of the working class into the political system to understand the image that different segments of the elite had of native and immigrant populations. Sarmiento compared Spanish colonies with those of other European countries. Unlike other colonizers, the Spaniards "incorporated the savages into (their) bosom; leaving to future times a bastard progeny, rebellious to culture. . . ."[9] In Spanish America, he argued, the population is the product of the fusion of the Spanish, Indian, and black races. The resulting culture is not conducive to progress, for none of its three components were either: "[this population] is characterized by love of idleness and incapacity for industry, except when education and the exigencies

---

*conservador* (1977), chaps. 1–3. For the differences between Alberdi and Sarmiento, see Natalio R. Botana, *La tradición republicana* (1984); Di Tella, "Raíces de la controversia"; and Romero, *Argentine Political Thought,* chap. 5.

6. Domingo F. Sarmiento, *Life in the Argentine Republic in the Days of the Tyrants* (1868), p. 14. On *Facundo,* see Jitrik, *Facundo.*

7. Alberdi, *Bases y puntos de partida,* p. 67.

8. Sarmiento, *Life in the Argentine Republic,* p. 24.

9. Domingo F. Sarmiento, "Educación popular," in Halperín Donghi, ed., *Proyecto y construcción,* p. 124.

of social position succeed in spurring it out of its customary pace;
... the American aborigines live in idleness, and show themselves
incapable, even under compulsion, of hard and protracted labor.
This suggested the idea of introducing negroes . . . which has produced such fatal results. But the Spanish race has not shown itself
more energetic than the aborigines, when it has been left to its
own instincts in the wilds of America."[10] The wilderness brutal-
izes: this anti-Turnerian thesis is the core of this image of Argentina. But Spanish civilization in general, both urban and rural, in
Europe and in America, is a barrier to progress: "The South American states belong to a race that lies at the bottom among civilized
peoples. Spain and her descendants appear today in the stage of the
modern world lacking all the qualities that the life of our epoch
requires," especially an aptitude for science and technology.[11]

Unlike Sarmiento, Alberdi did not believe that education could
change this mentality. In reference to the rural lower classes, the
gauchos, he claimed that not even after a century of the best educational system could they be a match for English workers.[12] The
solution could only be the replacement of the population through
mass immigration, preferably from countries other than Spain. In
a famous metaphor, he stated that it was through the fast method
of transplantation rather than through the slower procedure of
seeding that English freedom, French culture, and also European
and U.S. industriousness could be best transferred to the new
soil.[13] And the immigrants did come, albeit from other lands.

At the time of the Centennial, the project was largely accomplished, and Joaquín V. González, a distinguished politician and
scholar, could note with satisfaction: "The thought of the Constitution, which opened up Argentine soil so that men from all the
civilized world could come to till the land and build their free
home, [was realized]. Once the Indian had been extinguished by
war, servitude, and lack of adaptability to civilized life, the regres-
sive danger for the republic of the mix of their inferior blood with
the select and pure blood of the European race, the basis of our social and national ethnicity, disappears."[14] He was referring to the

10. Sarmiento, *Life in the Argentine Republic*, p. 11.

11. Sarmiento, "Educación popular," p. 123.

12. Alberdi, *Bases y puntos de partida*, p. 74.

13. Ibid., p. 13.

14. Joaquín V. González, "El juicio del siglo o cien años de historia argentina," in *Obras completas* (1936), vol. 21, p. 176.

nomadic tribes of the central plains and the south, for the northern periphery had been little touched by immigration, and its social structure and culture, albeit encompassing a small proportion of the population, were still of the modal Latin American type. The persistence of that sector was the "social base" of the nativist version of the dualist image, which otherwise would have been absolutely devoid of realism.

This modernist variety of dualism has remained up to now an important theme in Argentine ideology. Decades later, when most Argentines were already the descendants of the immigrants who arrived before the Depression, the myth of Creole barbarousness was still alive and well in Argentine culture, chiefly in its conservative segment (which is called "liberal" in the Argentine political vocabulary). However, a traditionalist or nativist version of the dualistic image also emerged. This version is the exact reverse of the modernist one: it implies the exaltation of the Creole population, and, in its right-wing variant, also a defense of traditional Catholic and Hispanic values, and an attack on liberalism and the other ideologies associated with European economic and political influence. This is an image of Argentina as a society whose genuine institutions and culture were threatened—or being destroyed—by the massive influx of alien individuals, institutions, and culture.

This fundamentalist image was articulated in the beginning of the twentieth century by several figures of the cultural establishment. Two of them were Manuel Gálvez, a prolific and popular biographer and novelist of right-wing nationalist sympathies, and Ricardo Rojas, a literary critic and educator, whose ideology was liberal-democratic. Both men, who were from the interior, deplored the erosion of traditional values brought about by the cosmopolitanism and particularly the "materialism" of the immigrants. Their solution was the "spiritualization" of the society, through the restoration of the Hispanic tradition. This fundamentalist discourse presupposed organicist conceptions of the society—the existence of a "national soul," and the like—as well as the reversal of Sarmiento's "intelligence versus matter" opposition. Now it was Hispanic, Creole culture that was endowed with a higher spirituality than the culture carried by the immigrants.

These intellectuals expressed the insecurity and fears of substantial segments of the native elites and middle classes, especially those from the periphery, in the face of the irresistible immigrant tide, which was dislodging them from business and some professions. In an internal replay of the nationalism of backward nations, they could only construct a positive identity through compensation, through a claim to a higher spirituality that would balance their apparently lesser material achievement.

As Gálvez wrote in a characteristic passage, "The immigrant, victorious . . . in the acquisition of fortune, has introduced in the country a new concept of life. He brought with him no purpose other than getting rich, and it was then natural that his exclusive respect for material values would infect the Argentines."[15] And the remedy lay in the values implicit in Hispanic culture: "Whether our country will have character and spirituality, this will depend upon the persistence of the element of good breed (*castizo*), that is, of the Spanish and Creole, in the definitive mix."[16]

The core of nativism was the glorification of rural society, especially that of the interior provinces, and of the culture that predated mass immigration. In a typical statement of this view, Rojas portrayed the gauchos and rural chieftains who participated in the war of independence as the genuine manifestation of the national spirit: ". . . the Argentine soul (*argentinidad*) vibrated then by instinct, and even if the illiterate gauchos and the violent chieftains (*caudillos*) did not discern doctrines well, it was they who served the essential destiny of our nationality."[17]

The counterpart of the exaltation of the native element was, in some cases, the devaluation of the immigrants. Carl Solberg has documented extensively the negative stereotypes of the various ethnic groups and of foreigners in different occupations that spread among elite circles at the turn of the century.[18] There were also instances of outright hostility toward the immigrants. José M. Ramos Mejía, an academic, presents an extreme case among influential establishment intellectuals. In a work with scientific pre-

15. Manuel Gálvez, *El solar de la raza* (1920), p. 14. On Gálvez, see Carlos Payá and Eduardo Cárdenas, *El primer nacionalismo argentino* (1978). See also Carl Solberg, *Immigration and Nationalism: Argentina and Chile, 1890–1914* (1970), chap. 6.

16. Ibid., p. 18.

17. Ricardo Rojas, *La argentinidad: Ensayo histórico sobre nuestra conciencia nacional en la gesta de emancipación, 1810–1816* (1916), p. 407. On Rojas, see Payá and Cárdenas, *El primer nacionalismo*; and Solberg, *Immigration and Nationalism*, chap. 6.

18. Ibid., chaps. 3–4.

tensions, he described the immigrant as biologically and culturally inferior to the native: "Any craniate . . . is more intelligent
than the immigrant just disembarked upon our shores. [He] is
something amorphous . . . his brain [is] as slow as that of the ox
next to whom he has lived. . . ."[19] But his progeny will be regener-
ated very slowly, in the new and more cultivated milieu: "The
first generation is often deformed and not very beautiful, up to a
certain age. It looks like the product of a rough mold; . . . his mor-
phology has not yet been modified by the chisel of culture. In the
second one, the corrections that the civilized and more cultured
life . . . have produced become apparent. . . ."[20]

This reversal of Sarmiento's formula culminated very dialecti-
cally in an attempt at synthesis. The resulting nationalism was an
attempt to transcend, in the realm of ideology, the low level of integration in the society. A typical example of this ideological enterprise was the construction, by Leopoldo Lugones, Carlos O.
Bunge, and other intellectuals, of the myth of the gaucho, a type
almost extinct by World War I, as the archetype of the national
soul. The previously despised rural mestizo of the plains was now
endowed with virtues such as wisdom, nobility, generosity, frank-
ness, and gallantry. This enterprise was successful to such a degree
that today in Argentine speech the word "gaucho," used as an ad-
jective, connotes all these qualities. Since the majority of the Argentines descend from Ramos Mejía's craniates rather than from
Sarmiento's and Alberdi's savages, induction into the Argentine
spirit had to be an achieved process, and the educational system
was charged with the beneficial task of regenerating the ox-
brained, through the generous infusion of the national soul. To
this effect, successive generations of educators and intellectuals
elaborated a panoply of ideological resources, ranging from what
must be one of the most overcrowded pantheons of national he-
roes, all of them predating immigration, to a naive literature that
develops, exemplifies, and confirms, when necessary, different
facets of the myth. In fiction, for example, this corpus ranges from
the gauchesque genre (novels, plays, and poetry written by urban
people, which idealize rural life and culture, with a focus on the
gaucho; Ricardo Güiraldes's *Don Segundo Sombra* is a good ex-

19. José M. Ramos Mejía, *Las multitudes argentinas* (1977), p. 205. See
also Solberg, *Immigration and Nationalism*, chaps. 3 and 6.
20. Ibid., p. 212.

ample) to the theme of assimilation of the immigrants, that is, their acquisition of the presumed national character (such as in Florencio Sánchez's play *La gringa*, or in Alberto Gerchunoff's *Los gauchos judíos*).

The nativist reaction to the transformation of the country was linked to an Argentine variety of manifest destiny, as could be expected on the basis of the material progress of the country until the Depression. Gálvez defined this destiny in terms of racial fulfillment. The fact that, contrary to Sarmiento's and Alberdi's expectations, most immigrants going to Argentina originated in Latin Europe, indicated for him that ". . . Latin Europe, poisoned with decay, begins to see in our Argentina the salvation of the race. . . . We possess the secret of energy. But ours will not be a barbarous and automatic energy such as the one that unceasingly boils in the United States of North America. Ours is and will be a harmonious energy, a force tempered with Latin elegance, and an intelligent impulse. . . ."[21]

These two versions of the dualistic image coexisted since the beginning of the twentieth century and fused with the other representations. The modernist variety has been always correlated with the new country image, and the traditionalist interpretation has been frequently associated with the underdeveloped, dependent image. The fact that these two contradictory, dualistic conceptions were established in different segments of the political and cultural elites contributes to explain elite strategies toward the middle and lower classes in the first half of the century. Neither the immigrant middle and urban lower classes, nor the largely Creole lower classes in the interior provinces who migrated to the cities after the Depression, were considered by the elite as full-fledged members of the national or, at least, the political community. The immigrants were welcomed as workers, tolerated as a middle class, and given civil rights, but they were not expected to participate in politics as an autonomous force, much less to attempt to wrestle power away from the only legitimate owners of the country. In addition, the Creoles were, for those subscribing to the modernist myth, an unwanted race to be pushed away or worse; for those supporting the nativist conception, the lower segment of an organic totality—whose controlling center, of course, was the elite.

21. Gálvez, *El solar de la raza*, pp. 57, 60.

## The New Country

There is now a considerable scholarly literature on the comparison between Argentina and the lands of recent settlement, with a focus on Australia. These works—see for instance, Héctor Diéguez, Guido Di Tella and Manuel Zymelman, John Fogarty et al; Carter Goodrich, Ruth Kelly, Theodore H. Moran, Arthur Smithies[22]—have been written mostly by economists and economic historians. Smithies states his subject as follows: "Argentina and Australia are both in the temperate latitudes of the Southern Hemisphere, both have endless expanses of agricultural land, but more than a third of their populations are metropolitan. Both have highly ambivalent feelings about the older and more populous Northern Hemisphere. They clearly invite comparison with each other."[23] The aim of this literature is to understand the divergent economic performance of Argentina and Australia. Observers in the beginning of the century, on the other hand, focused on the similarities between Argentina and open spaces, and described Argentina with the terms usually applied to these countries.

W. H. Koebel, a British writer, was typical among foreign enthusiasts. In a book published in 1910, he depicted the Argentine scene. In discussing investment opportunities, he argued that "there are probably few countries in the world that have offered so favourable a field for the operation of the capitalist as Argentina. So far as all-round progress is concerned, Canada almost alone can probably compare its forward strides with those of the Republic."[24] Focusing on the status of the working class, and probably ignorant of the intense class conflict at the time, he wrote: "So far as class hatred is concerned, in no country there is less evidence of this; very probably for the simple reason that in no other land has

22. Héctor L. Diéguez, "Argentina y Australia: Algunos aspectos de su desarrollo económico comparado," Desarrollo económico (1969); Guido Di Tella and Manuel Zymelman, Las etapas del desarrollo económico argentino (1973); John Fogarty et al., eds., Argentina y Australia (1979); Carter Goodrich, "Argentina as a New Country," Comparative Studies in Society and History (1964–65); Ruth Kelly, "Foreign Trade of Argentina and Australia, 1930 to 1960 (I)," United Nations, Economic Bulletin for Latin America (1965); Theodore H. Moran, "The 'Development' of Argentina and Australia," Comparative Politics (1970); Arthur Smithies, "Economic Growth: International Comparisons. Argentina and Australia," American Economic Review (1965).

23. Smithies, "Economic Growth," p. 17.

24. W. H. Koebel, Argentina: Past and Present (1910), p. 56.

the working man greater opportunities of advancement. Indeed ... it might be said that there is a millionaire's cheque-book in every artisan's toolbag."[25] Tenant farmers and landowners were also flourishing: "The working farmer ... is wont to rent his land and ... to thrive remarkably from the process. At the same time the financial return to the landowner is satisfactory, since it seldom amounts to less than ten per cent."[26] A liberal state presided over this general happiness: "One of the great merits attaching to the Argentine rule is the absolute freedom which its government extends to all. Liberty is no catchword here. . . . Indeed, it is a little difficult to dissociate freedom from the open, generous, sun-swept soil of the Republic."[27]

Inside the country, influential scholars and politicians agreed with that assessment. The nation had the basic traits of the lands of recent settlement, and thus it could be expected to evolve along similar lines. "Here we have neither castes, privileges, closed classes, a feudal complexion, nor historical injustices ... that would prevent individuals' free fullfilment ... according to their aptitude, their activity, their intelligence, and their work. . . . In this great democracy in the making there are no paupers. . . . The impermanence of individual bad economic circumstances is ... almost the rule among us. The rich of today were poor yesterday," argued Lucas Ayarragaray,[28] and Ernesto Quesada asserted that "Argentina [was reproducing] in the XXth century precisely the same march of the United States in the XIXth century."[29] Former president Carlos Pellegrini claimed that "this Republic possesses all the requisite conditions of becoming, with the passage of time, one of the greatest nations of the earth. Its territory is immense and fertile; . . . almost every climate is to be found within its limits, and consequently, it can yield all products. . . . It is governed by institutions more liberal than those of any other nation, especially in all that affects the foreigner. . . . Such are the causes of the prosperity of this country, . . . and as these causes are not acciden-

25. Ibid.
26. Ibid., p. 58.
27. Ibid., pp. 58–59.
28. Lucas Ayarragaray, *Socialismo argentino y legislación obrera* (1912), pp. 12–13, 18.
29. Ernesto Quesada, "La evolución social argentina," *Revista argentina de ciencias políticas* (1911), p. 653.

tal, but fundamental and permanent, they should produce in South America the same results as in the North."[30]

Consequences were also expected to radiate beyond Argentine borders. "Argentina is called upon to exercise hegemony in South America," wrote Eusebio M. Gómez, a jurist and academic, and to impose "a peaceful imperialism."[31] The manifest destiny theme, among expounders of the new country image, focused on the projection of economic and political power, and was usually devoid of the racial connotations it had among the nativists. Ingenieros connected this issue with the evolution of open spaces: "If Argentina and Australia continue with their very fast material development . . . they will eventually weigh in the world's political balance. If this is the case, the tutelage of the other South American and Oceanic countries will correspond to them. This evolution will convert them into new nuclei of imperialist activity." It was probable that these countries would "awaken to imperialism, and acquire a decisive influence on the affairs of the whole world. . . . (Argentina) is predestined by her territorial extension, fecundity, white race, and temperate climate to the exercise of the tutelar function among the other peoples of the continent."[32]

The Depression destroyed not only the extravagant imperialist designs, but also the more reasonable confidence in economic growth along the lines of the staples model. Their hopes dashed by processes whose nature they vaguely understood, and whose effects they could not control, Argentine politicians, ideologists, and scholars executed a dialectical leap, and the new country image converted into its opposite. The more the country slipped and the memories of progress faded with the passage of time, the more influential the representation of Argentina as a typical Latin American country became. The old image survived, but the circle of its beholders narrowed to where it became the patrimony of small groups of nostalgic conservatives. For the population at

30. Carlos Pellegrini, "Introduction" to Albert B. Martínez and Maurice Lewandowski, *The Argentine in the Twentieth Century* (1911), p. lii.

31. Eusebio M. Gómez, speech delivered in 1910, quoted by Miguel Angel Cárcano, in his *Sáenz Peña: La revolución por los comicios* (1963).

32. José Ingenieros, *La evolución sociológica argentina (de la barbarie al imperialismo)* (1910), pp. 98–101.

large, the echoes of that conception survive, only in a fossilized form, in the positivist ideology still alive in public education.

## Underdevelopment and Dependency

The content of this image is familiar. It conceives of Argentina as a society having a backward economy, whose development is blocked by imperialism. This blockage takes the form of extraction of wealth through trade gains and profit remittances. In the most complex forms of this representation, blockage is also due to the structure of the society itself, which was shaped in order to maximize exploitation, and transfer of wealth takes place through hidden mechanisms, such as unequal exchange. Imperialist power is exercised directly, through the presence of foreign firms, but the crucial mechanism in the relationship is the existence of an intermediary, the oligarchy, which excercises economic and political power for its own benefit and that of its foreign partners. As for the most important foreign power, it was Britain until World War II, and the United States thereafter.

The Left describes Argentina in these terms, and a statement like the following, in which Jaime Fuchs emphasizes the commonality between the country and the Latin American modal pattern, became commonplace: "The fact that our country has a greater capitalist development than others in Latin America does not invalidate the common traits in the economy of these countries: the agrarian structure with large property and backward relationships, and the dominance by foreign monopoly capital. These elements condition the . . . underdevelopment and the economic and social backwardness of our country, where the greater development of productive forces renders structural conflict more acute than in other countries."[33] A book by Jorge Abelardo Ramos, a popular left-wing writer, depicts Argentine society with terms such as "semicolonial or dependent (country)," an "oppressed nation," "a semicolonial country in a process of growth," "a backward country that struggles for liberation," etc.[34]

Argentines became aware of their dependency with regard to Britain when, as a consequence of the Depression, international trade broke down, and the system of imperial preferences was es-

33. Jaime Fuchs, *Argentina: Su desarrollo capitalista* (1965), p. 559.
34. Jorge A. Ramos, *La era del Peronismo* (1982), pp. 18, 20, 101, 142.

tablished in the Commonwealth. In order to secure a quota in the British market, Argentina had to grant the United Kingdom considerable concessions regarding trade and investment. The provisions of the agreement, the Roca-Runciman treaty of 1933,[35] as well as the terms in which the negotiations were carried out, were seen by significant segments of public opinion as indicative of a dependent and even colonial status. Also at that time, controversies surrounding the meat-packing industry and the transportation system of the city of Buenos Aires, both under foreign control, heightened sensitivity to the issue of imperialism in groups of the right- and left-wing intelligentsia.

Raúl Scalabrini Ortiz, a Radical intellectual with nationalist sympathies, was one of the most important propounders of this image of Argentina. He described this process of sudden awareness in *Política británica en el Río de la Plata (British politics in the River Plate)*, a book published in 1939, which became very influential in right-wing and some left-wing circles. "Until the year 1929, the Argentine Republic lived confident in the unlimited material magnitude of its future," the book begins,

> People and government floated in opulent optimism, far from any possibility of analysis, . . . and pride derived into vanity when we compared ourselves with the poorer South American republics. . . . But we believed we were acting on serious foundations. We saw our march forward palpable: the great packing houses erected on the shores of the rivers, the ports extending their cordial piers to overseas ships, the power plants punctuating the sky with their smoke needles. We saw the cities grow, the industries multiply. . . . [No one thought] that this visible exuberance might not be a truly Argentine wealth, and less so that this enormous power . . . could be an indication of weakness rather than of national energy. [No one thought about investigating] who were the owners of these power plants, of these railroads. Capital was an unimportant detail.[36]

35. On the Roca-Runciman pact, see Alberto Conil Paz and Gustavo Ferrari, *Política exterior argentina* (1964), chap. 1; Díaz Alejandro, *Essays*, pp. 98–99; Daniel Drosdoff, *El gobierno de las vacas, 1933–1956: Tratado Roca-Runciman* (1972); and the nationalist literature cited below.

36. Raúl Scalabrini Ortiz, *Política británica en el Río de la Plata* (1957), pp. 15–16.

Scalabrini did carry out such an investigation, and bitterly concluded:

> Everything material, venal, transmissible, or
> reproductive is foreign or is submitted to foreign
> financial hegemony. Foreign are the means of
> transportation and mobility. Foreign the manufacturing
> and marketing organizations. . . . Foreign the producers
> of energy, the power and gas plants. Under foreign
> domination are the internal means of exchange, the
> distribution of credit, the banking system. Foreign is a
> large proportion of mortgage capital, and foreign are an
> incredible proportion of the shareholders of
> corporations.[37]

This is an overstatement, but it represents the emotional response of somebody who suddenly discovers the inadequacy of the basic principles with which he and his contemporaries understand the nature of their society. Further, Scalabrini is also connecting foreign ownership with the reversal after the Depression.

Among right-wing intellectuals, the theme of economic dependency was linked to the other components of what was called nationalism: nativism and the critique of liberalism and communism from an authoritarian and corporatist perspective. One of the most influential books in that tradition was *Argentina y el imperialismo británico (Argentina and British imperialism)*, an attack on the Roca-Runciman pact, written by the Irazusta brothers in 1933. They blamed the oligarchy for having placed Argentina at the mercy of international capitalism and for the establishment of an "inhuman regime that consists of freedom for the foreigner and submission for the Creole."[38] "In a world converted to economic autarky, the internationalism of the oligarchs threatens to make us the last prey of world capitalism, [which is] persecuted or watched in the rest of the globe; the last field of maneuvres that anonymous and vagabond wealth, which in the last years has benefitted from abusive privileges [in our country], can avail itself of."[39]

A final example of the emergence of this image as a response to

37. Ibid., pp. 11–12.
38. Rodolfo and Julio Irazusta, *La Argentina y el imperialismo británico* (1933), p. 152.
39. Ibid, p. 156.

the Depression is a document put out by the right-wing organization The Argentine Guard, also in 1933. This diatribe was written
by Leopoldo Lugones, one of the leading intellectuals at the time.
In it, the Depression and the critique of foreign domination were
linked to the antiliberal and anticommunist theme, and also, in an
implicit reference, to the fascist example:

> The reduction and the growing disorganization of
> international trade . . . and the growing menace of the
> SECTS WITHOUT FATHERLAND . . . *socialism, communism,
> anarchism* . . . [who] are . . . FOREIGN ENEMIES [who] even
> in their own native country, have promoted this
> PATRIOTIC REACTION that ours experiences . . . and needs
> with double intensity, because it has suffered more than
> any other, perhaps, THE FOREIGN DEGENERACY OF
> LIBERALISM. . . . Our ideas, customs, laws and even
> sentiments have been *importation articles.* FOREIGN
> TRADE has dominated everything, even our morals,
> which for this reason are so low and confused. Nothing
> is our own except our existence, and even that is a
> COLONY UNDER THE LIBERAL ECONOMY; . . . [the country]
> can expect from abroad nothing but EXPLOITATION AND
> SERVITUDE.[40]

But both the extreme Right and the much less influential revolutionary Left were, prior to World War II, secondary strands. The
image of Argentina as similar to other Latin American countries
percolated very slowly into mainstream political discourse. In the
thirties, the major parties—Conservatives, Radicals, Socialists—
preserved the basic elements of the new country image, which
they tried to adapt to the new international situation. It was in the
forties, with Peronism, that this new representation of Argentina
entered standard discourse. Different formulations of the image
later spread to other parties to the point that this conception is
now linked to all types of economic and political platforms, except
economic liberalism, whose few supporters still conceive Argentina as a new country. Finally, the "Latin American" image en-

40. Cited in Federico Ibarguren, *Orígenes del nacionalismo argentino,
1927–1937* (1969), p. 188. On Argentine right-wing nationalism, see
Marysa Navarro Gerassi, *Los nacionalistas* (1968); and, for a partisan
account, Enrique Zulueta Alvarez, *El nacionalismo argentino* (1975).

tered academic discourse, by being articulated with the CEPAL doctrine in the fifties and sixties and with dependency theory in the seventies.

Thus, the images of Argentina were the correlate of the curvilinear evolution of the country: land of recent settlement during the period of ascent, underdeveloped society during the decline. To what extent are these images accurate? As we shall see, whereas Argentina differed in some respects from the new country model, it definitely diverged from the underdeveloped type.

### Argentine Land and Labor Endowments in a Comparative Perspective

We can now consider the adequacy of these images, by comparing Argentina with societies that are the classic examples of the new country and of the underdeveloped or Latin American models. It will also be useful to make some comparisons with European societies, especially those of the Mediterranean type.

#### Land

Argentine land-labor ratio is high, well within the range of open spaces, and much higher than in societies fitting the Latin American and Mediterranean types. In Table 3.1 I am using density in relation to agricultural land as a proxy.

But Argentina departs from some open spaces in relation to farm size, and from all of them in relation to the juridical status of the land when the mass of settlers arrived. Unlike the United States and Canada, but like Australia and New Zealand, Argentina's was a "big man's frontier," as Australia's has been called. Data on average sizes conceal the high degree of concentration of land tenure in the period of immigrant settlement: in 1914, just 2 percent of the farms had 5,000 hectares or more and they comprised 49 percent of the total area.

But the most important difference between Argentina and the open spaces model has to do with the pattern of land appropriation. When mass European immigration took place, Argentine land was not free, nor available for ownership by settlers. In most of the Pampean region, the central plains where temperate agriculture for export was concentrated, land was already appropriated by a preexisting elite and was only available for rent. The contracts

*Table 3.1.*
*Agricultural Density, Farm Size, and Land Tenure in Selected Countries around the Time of the Argentine Reversal.*

| Country | Agricultural Labor per Agricultural Area in Thousands of Hectares, ca. World War II | Average Area per Farm, in Hectares ca. 1930 | Tenants as Percentage of All Farmers, ca. World War II |
|---|---|---|---|
| United States | 20.6 | 63.5 | 31.7 |
| Canada | 17.8 | 90.6 | 12.9 |
| Australia | 1.3 | 290.5 | — |
| New Zealand | 10.2 | 206.0 | 25.9 |
| Mexico | 34.8 | 153.3 | — |
| Brazil | 62.4 | — | — |
| Spain | 111.9 | — | — |
| Italy | 429.5 | 6.3 | 23.8[a] |
| Argentina (1937) | 13.9 | 386.4 | 44.3 |

*Sources*: For Argentina, computations based on the agrarian census of 1937, except for data on agricultural labor used in the estimation of density in Column 1, which were taken from Naciones Unidas, *El desarrollo económico de la Argentina* (Mexico: United Nations, 1959), part 2. For the other countries, W. S. Woytinsky and E. S. Woytinsky, *World Population and Production. Trends and Outlook* (New York: Twentieth Century Fund, 1953).

*Note*: In the computation of agricultural area in Column 1, I included arable land and permanent meadows and pastures, and excluded forests and woodlands, unused but potentially productive land, and built-on areas and wasteland. 1 hectare = 2.471 acres.

[a] 1930.

were short-term, and their provisions basically protected the land-owner interest.[41] Big agrarian property was the economic power base of that elite, which was inextricably linked with the state apparatus. It was the homogeneous elite of the Pampean region that, in coalition with its counterparts of the interior, controlled the

41. See James R. Scobie, *Revolution on the Pampas: A Social History of Argentine Wheat, 1860–1910* (1964), pp. 58–60; Roberto Cortés Conde and Ezequiel Gallo, *La formación de la Argentina moderna* (1973), pp. 56–60; Horacio C. E. Giberti, *Historia económica de la ganadería argentina* (1961); Gastón Gori, *Inmigración y colonización en la*

state, and it was the action of the state that allowed the elite to acquire control of the soil through the waging of the Indian wars and the subsequent distributions and sales of public lands, and use it for profit, through the promotion of immigration, international trade, and foreign investment.

Land tenure was a function of the type of activity: the upper class was more likely to operate ranches than to cultivate the soil. When or where agriculture was more profitable than cattle raising, landowners preferred to lease their holdings to tenant farmers. In 1914, in the provinces and territories making up the Pampean region (Buenos Aires, Santa Fe, Entre Ríos, Córdoba, and La Pampa), 58 percent of the holdings devoted mainly to agriculture were managed by tenant farmers, 78 percent of whom were immigrants. But only 30 percent of the holdings mainly devoted to livestock were leased, and half of the tenants were Argentine-born. And 57 percent of all the livestock holdings were operated by the owners themselves.[42] For the agrarian elite and the state, the immigrants were only a necessary input—manpower—for the valorization of land; tenant farming, and allied forms such as sharecropping, were the ideal formula: the immigrants provided labor and management, and whatever improvements were necessary; the landowners reaped a substantial part of the profits without parting with their property, benefited from inflation, and kept all their options open, given the nature of the contracts, for future land use.

The situation changed over time, and in 1960 only 17 percent of the total agricultural area was operated by tenants, a proportion not very different from that of the United States (13 percent in 1969).[43] But the important point is that, when the immigrants arrived, the probability of acquiring land was very low. This explains why most settled eventually in the cities, in spite of the fact that the majority of them had been peasants in the country of origin, and of the strong probability that the availability of land was a "pull" factor in immigration to Argentina.

*Argentina* (1964); Jacinto Oddone, *La burguesía terrateniente argentina*, (1975); Ricardo M. Ortiz, *Historia económica de la Argentina* (1964), vol. 1, chap. 4; and Carl C. Taylor, *Rural Life in Argentina* (1948), chap. 8.

42. Argentine Republic, Comisión Nacional del Censo, *Tercer Censo Nacional* (1916–19), vol. 5. See Díaz Alejandro, *Essays*, pp. 154–59, and Giberti, *Historia económica.*

43. UCLA, *Statistical Abstract of Latin America* (1980), vol. 20, pp. 42–47.

*Labor*

In this area, Argentina not only fits the new country model, but in several aspects corresponds to the ideal type more than any other society in that category.

It differs from the typical Latin American country in two respects. First, Argentina did not have, at least until the 1970s, a large labor reserve. This was the case even before the growth of temperate agriculture toward the end of the nineteenth century, as Ernesto Laclau has shown.[44] Further, according to Carlos Díaz Alejandro, there was little or no surplus labor in the agrarian sector prior to 1930.[45] Latin American economies, on the other hand, have large labor surpluses, both in the traditional form of a peasantry and in the more "modern" one of an informal urban sector. Second, Argentina is, together with Uruguay, the only Latin American country whose population is constituted mostly on the basis of free immigrants from Europe. Darcy Ribeiro has called this type of population "transplanted peoples," while the typical Latin American forms are the "witness people," as in Mexico or Peru, where a small Spanish elite took control of a preexisting Indian society, and the "new peoples," as in Brazil or Chile, where relatively larger contingents of Europeans (and, in Brazil, Africans) fused with the native inhabitants.[46]

In the "great migration" from Europe, Argentina ranked second to the United States among recipient countries: from 1821 to 1932, it admitted 6.4 million, much less than the United States in the same period (34.2 million) but more than Canada (5.2 million), Brazil (4.4 million), Australia (2.9 million), Uruguay (.7 million), and New Zealand (.6 million).[47] The flow to Argentina was concentrated in a relatively brief period: from 1880 to 1930, 5.9 million immigrants landed (second- and third-class passengers only), and the net balance was 3.2 million.[48] Four characteristics of this

---

44. Ernesto Laclau, "Modos de producción, sistemas económicos y población excedente: Aproximación histórica a los casos argentino y chileno," *Revista latinoamericana de sociología* (1969).

45. Díaz Alejandro, *Essays*, p. 141.

46. Darcy Ribeiro, *The Americas and Civilization* (1971), pp. 79–87 and passim.

47. Woytinsky and Woytinsky, *Population and Production*, p. 72.

48. On immigration in general, see Roberto Cortés Conde, *El progreso argentino, 1880–1914* (1979), chap. 4; Gino Germani, *Política y sociedad en una época de transición* (1962), chap. 7; Solberg, *Immigration and Nationalism*, chap. 2; and Vicente Vázquez Presedo,

process are important for the comparison between Argentina and its open spaces and Latin American mirrors: the ratio of newcomers to the recipient population, the geographic concentration of the immigrants, their impact on the class structure, and their country of origin. The first and the last of these aspects determine a peculiarity of Argentina vis-à-vis all the other countries of recent settlement: a very high ratio of immigrants to the preexisting population in a situation in which most of them came from countries other than the original metropolis.

First, as Gino Germani, Carter Goodrich, and others have noted, the ratio of newcomers to the recipient population during the period of maximum impact (1880–1930), was higher in Argentina than in the United States, but lower than in other open spaces. In 1914, 30 percent of the Argentine population was foreign born, and the remainder, it is important to recall, included the native children of the immigrants, 91 percent of whom were, at the time of the census, 15 years or older. In the United States, on the other hand, the percentage of foreigners was never higher than 15 percent.[49] Australia and New Zealand had higher recorded ratios after the initial settlements were established (for instance, Australia had 53 percent in 1861 and New Zealand had 76 percent in 1864), but these resulted from flows originating almost completely in the metropolitan power, Britain.[50]

I mentioned above that the Argentine population in 1869, right before the massive inflow, was 1.7 million. But this figure already included a substantial immigrant component: 12 percent of that population was foreign born, and the percentage was 30 percent in what was then the nucleus of the economic and political core, the province and city of Buenos Aires, where 28 percent of the total population lived. The proportion of foreigners in the total jumped to 25 percent in 1895, reached its peak in the 1914 census, and was still 24 percent in 1930.

Second, most newcomers settled in the littoral region, so that the social and cultural cleavage between this region and the less populated periphery deepened. In 1914, 90 percent of all the foreigners lived in the littoral provinces and the wine-growing prov-

*El caso argentino: Migración de factores, comercio exterior y desarrollo, 1875–1914* (1971), chap. 3.

49. Germani, *Política y sociedad,* p. 198; Goodrich, "Argentina as a New Country," p. 86.

50. Torcuato S. Di Tella, *Sociología de los procesos políticos* (1985), pp. 340–44; Goodrich, "Argentina as a New Country," p. 86.

ince of Mendoza, which also had a dynamic economy. In that part of the country, which we can consider the core, lived 77 percent of the population at that time. Germani has calculated that foreigners in these provinces (excluding the city of Buenos Aires) were 51 percent of the population 20 years and older. In the city of Buenos Aires the percentage in that age group rose to a staggering 72 percent. However, the periphery was also affected significantly by immigration. In the non-core provinces, 20 percent of the population 20 years and older was foreign-born in 1914.[51] Finally, foreigners were concentrated in the cities: in 1914, almost 70 percent of them lived in urban areas;[52] they were half the population of Buenos Aires (size: 1.6 million), and 35 percent of the inhabitants in the other cities with a population of 100,000 and over.

Third, in 1914, foreigners accounted for almost half (47 percent) of the active population, but their share was larger in the urban than in the rural classes. They constituted 37 percent of the primary sector, 53 percent of the secondary, and 50 percent of the tertiary. In the secondary, they made up 66 percent of the proprietors in industry and 50 percent of the industrial personnel. In the tertiary, immigrants constituted 74 percent of the merchants, 51 percent of the employees, and 45 percent of the professionals.[53] But in the province of Buenos Aires, foreigners were 56 percent of those employed in the primary, and in the province and city they constituted 66 percent of the secondary and 62 percent of the tertiary.[54] The foreigners were, therefore, a very large proportion of the rural middle class and of all the urban classes, especially in the core area, where they made up the majority of the industrial bourgeoisie, the urban middle class, and the manufacturing workers. If we recall the demographic composition of the immigrant contingent, and the fact that mass immigration had begun a generation before the 1914 census was taken, it follows that a large proportion of the

51. Germani, *Política y sociedad*, p. 188; Oscar Cornblitt, "Inmigrantes y empresarios en la política argentina," in Di Tella and Halperín Donghi, eds., *Los fragmentos del poder*, pp. 396–401.

52. Cornblitt, "Inmigrantes y empresarios," p. 399.

53. Gustavo R. Beyhaut, Roberto Cortés Conde, H. Gorostegui, and S. Torrado, "Los inmigrantes en el sistema ocupacional argentino," in Torcuato S. Di Tella, Gino Germani, and Jorge Graciarena, eds., *Argentina, sociedad de masas* (1965); Germani, *Política y sociedad*, p. 191–95.

54. Calculation based on data in Cornblitt, "Inmigrantes y empresarios," pp. 402–4.

native minority of these classes was made up of the children of immigrants.

Fourth, unlike all lands of recent settlement except the United States, the majority of the immigrants going to Argentina originated in countries other than the original metropolis (Spain). Almost half were Italian, one third were Spanish, and most of the remainder were from other countries in Europe.[55] This heterogeneity implied an additional cultural cleavage between the elite and all the urban classes.

Germani did not think that this fracture had serious consequences for assimilation.[56] His argument was based on the obvious fact that there is little ethnic segregation in Argentina, and on the relative similarity between Spanish and Italian cultures. My impression is, however, that the implications of this situation for the evolution of the society as a whole have to be examined further. In the first place, the absence of a manifest assimilation question—given the ratio, processes of reciprocal rather than unidirectional assimilation ensued—does not imply that the ethnic fracture has not produced important "objective" integration problems, especially in the political sphere. Second, it is true that the bulk of the immigrants, the Spaniards and Italians, shared a Latin-Catholic culture and came from societies similar in important respects—low level of national integration, late unification, relatively low level of economic development vis-à-vis the Northwest; absence of the Reformation; absence of a successful "democratic" revolution, etc.—but the fact remains that the Italians, along with the other non-Spanish immigrants, carried a language, political traditions, and experiences different from those of the Spaniards and of the local population.

Finally, the origin of the immigrants presupposes further differences between Argentina and the open spaces and Latin American mirrors. In contrast to Argentina, open spaces, including the United States, received immigration originating mostly in northern and central Europe. Also, Argentina departs from the Latin American norm not only in that the majority of its population is of European origin, but also in that a large share, probably the majority, of the European component is of non-Iberian origin.

55. Vázquez Presedo, *El caso argentino*, pp. 95–117; Germani, *Política y sociedad*, p. 183; Goodrich, "Argentina as a New Country," p. 86.

56. Germani, *Política y sociedad*, pp. 197–210. Cornblitt, in "Inmigrantes y empresarios," is sensitive to this issue, as far as the bourgeoisie is concerned.

These four differences between Argentina and the new country and Latin American mirrors with respect to population had cumulative effects. The high ratio of immigrants to natives, the geographic and social concentration of these immigrants, and the fact that most of them were of non-Hispanic origin contributed to produce in sectors of the elite the belief that the lower classes were dangerous. As we will see, such an image, together with domestic and international factors of different types, was one of the causes of the reversal of Argentine development.

We may turn now to the question of the long-term outcomes of these inputs.

## Overview of the Reversal: Economy and Society

### Economic Development

Before the Depression, the image fitting Argentine economic development to that of open spaces appeared to have solid foundations.

The incorporation of the country into world markets as one of the largest exporters of grains and beef to European nations, especially to Britain, was a very rapid process. From 1890 to the outbreak of World War I, the area sown to wheat increased by 576 percent, and the one to corn by 308 percent.[57] From 1900 to 1929, the output of cereals and linseed increased by 441 percent, and the output of livestock by 241 percent.[58] In 1925, "a good but not exceptional year for agriculture, Argentina provided 66 percent of world exports of corn, 72 percent of linseed, 32 percent of oats, 20 percent of wheat and wheat flour, and more than 50 percent of meat."[59] Yields were well within the range of the lands of recent settlement. Table 3.2 indicates that, up to World War II, Argentina was comparable in this regard to other large producers with extensive agriculture. Even in the fifties (and sixties) its wheat yields were close to those of the United States and Canada, but those for corn had fallen substantially, due to the failure to keep up with

57. Ernesto Tornquist & Co., *The Economic Development of the Argentine Republic in the Last Fifty Years* (1919), p. 26.

58. United Nations, *El desarrollo económico*, vol. 1, p. 23.

59. Di Tella and Zymelman, *Las etapas del desarrollo*, p. 77; see also Vázquez Presedo, *El caso argentino*, chap. 4.

Table 3.2.
*Agricultural Yields before and after the Argentine Reversal (Ratios of Argentine Yields to Those of Other Countries of Extensive Agriculture, Quintals per Hectare, 1925–51).*

| Country | Wheat | | | Corn | | |
|---|---|---|---|---|---|---|
| | 1925–29 | 1934–38 | 1949–51 | 1925–29 | 1934–38 | 1949–51 |
| Australia | 1.21 | 1.23 | .92 | 1.21 | 1.22 | .73 |
| Canada | .69 | 1.38 | .86 | .84 | .72 | .42 |
| United States | .91 | 1.13 | .95 | 1.18 | 1.29 | .54 |
| (Argentina) | (8.6) | (9.8) | (10.1) | (20) | (18.1) | (12.8) |

*Source*: Computed on the basis of data in Colin Clark,
*The Conditions of Economic Progress* (London: Macmillan, 1960).

technological innovations—basically the adaptation of hybrid varieties—being introduced elsewhere.[60]

Argentine agriculture was—and still is—a high-productivity operation. In 1920, about 36 percent of the active population was engaged in agriculture, and it produced 30 percent of the GNP.[61] This product per worker ratio was very different from the typical Latin American and Mediterranean patterns. As Table 3.3 shows, even in 1960 countries like Brazil and Mexico had more than half of their active populations involved in agriculture, while Spain and Italy had 30 to 40 percent, but the agricultural share of the GDP in these economies was less than a fourth. This table also indicates that the overall composition of the Argentine labor force before the reversal resembled more those of the lands of recent settlement, including the United States, than those of Mediterranean and typical Latin American societies. It is only from the sixties onward that the latter types of society underwent the processes of urbanization and industrialization that allowed them to "catch up" with open spaces. In the late seventies, all the countries in the table had large industrial working classes, but Latin American na-

60. Díaz Alejandro, *Essays*, pp. 193–94; Richard D. Mallon and Juan V. Sourrouille, *Economic Policymaking in a Conflict Society: The Argentine Case* (1975), pp. 38–39.

61. United Nations, *El desarrollo económico*, vol. 1, p. 37, and ECLA data supplied in the statistical appendix of Díaz Alejandro, *Essays*, pp. 418–20, 428. See Cortés Conde and Gallo, *La formación*, chap. 3; and Vázquez Presedo, *El caso argentino*, chap. 4.

Table 3.3.
*Agriculture and Industry in Selected Countries during and after the Argentine Reversal (Percentage of the Labor Force in Agriculture and Industry, 1940–78; and Agricultural and Industrial Shares of GDP, 1960).*

| Country | Percentage of the Labor Force in Agriculture | | | Percentage of the Labor Force in Industry | | | Shares of GDP, 1960 | |
|---|---|---|---|---|---|---|---|---|
| | ca. 1940 | 1960 | 1978 | ca. 1940 | 1960 | 1978 | Agri-culture | Indus-try |
| United States | 18 | 7 | 2 | 32 | 36 | 33 | 4 | 38 |
| Australia | 16[a] | 11 | 6 | 35[a] | 40 | 34 | 14 | 42 |
| New Zealand | 20[b] | 15 | 10 | 26[b] | 37 | 35 | — | — |
| Argentina | 33[c] | 20 | 14 | 28[c] | 36 | 29 | 17 | 37 |
| Italy | 47[d] | 31 | 13 | 27[d] | 40 | 48 | 15 | 38 |
| Spain | 52 | 42 | 18 | 24 | 31 | 43 | 24 | 35 |
| Mexico | 65 | 55 | 39 | 13 | 20 | 26 | 16 | 29 |
| Brazil | 67 | 52 | 41 | 13 | 15 | 22 | 22 | 25 |

*Sources*: For 1940, except for Argentina, W. S. Woytinsky and E. S. Woytinsky, *World Population and Production: Trends and Outlook* (New York: Twentieth Century Fund, 1953); for 1940, Argentina, Carlos F. Díaz Alejandro, *Essays on the Economic History of the Argentine Republic* (New Haven: Yale University Press, 1970); for 1960 and 1978, World Bank, *Poverty and Human Development* (New York: Oxford University Press, 1980). For shares of GDP, World Bank, *World Tables 1976* (Baltimore: Johns Hopkins University Press, 1976).

*Notes*: "Agriculture" comprises agriculture, forestry, hunting, and fishing. "Industry" comprises manufacturing, mining, construction, and electricity and other utilities.

[a] 1947; [b] 1946; [c] 1940–44; [d] 1936.

tions still differed from the Mediterranean ones and from the lands of recent settlement in that they had large peasant reservoirs, that is, structural heterogeneity.

The development of agriculture and the intense process of urbanization in Argentina—by 1914 more than half the population was urban—spurred the expansion of manufacturing, construction, the power industry, and other activities in the secondary sector. The widespread image according to which Argentine industrialization began after the Depression is incorrect: Germani has estimated that already in 1895 over a fourth of the active population was in the secondary sector, including transport, and that the proportion in 1914 was close to a third.[62] Excluding transport, in 1910–14 it was 28 percent, which is not a very different picture from that of industrialized countries once the secondary sector has reached its top share of the labor force. Typical Latin American societies did not attain these levels of industrialization until the seventies, as Table 3.3 shows. In 1910–14, over 20 percent of the Argentine labor force was involved in manufacturing *strictu sensu*, and the proportion changed little up to World War II. And Argentine industry was not artisanal. In 1935, 59 percent of industrial workers were employed in firms having more than 50 workers and 21 percent in firms with more than 500.[63]

Much of manufacturing was a forward linkage of agriculture, both of the export type and of the industrial crops for the domestic market. There was, however, a substantial development of other branches. In 1914, foodstuffs—meat-packing, milling, etc.—and beverages accounted for over half of the value of manufacturing, but in 1930–34 that proportion had decreased to a third. Metals, vehicles, and machinery production, representing less than a tenth in 1914, were almost a fourth in 1930–34. In this latter period, chemicals and oil accounted for another tenth of the value.[64] Table 3.4 indicates, however, a first major difference between the industrialization of Argentina and that of the lands of recent settlement. Since the beginning of the century, its manufacturing product per capita has been about half of that in open spaces, and the distance has been maintained consistently during and after the Argentine industrialization spurt produced by the Depression and World War II. This table also shows, nevertheless, that Argentina had a higher manufacturing product per capita than Mediterranean countries even after the reversal. Italy caught up in the mid-fifties, and Spain even later, but typical Latin American economies were still lagging behind.

Until the Depression, the world economy had been the engine propelling Argentine expansion. After the war, the country did not

62. Gino Germani, *Estructura social de la Argentina* (1955), p. 129. See Vázquez Presedo, *El caso argentino*, chap. 5.

63. Data from the 1935 industrial census, supplied in the statistical appendix of Díaz Alejandro, *Essays*, p. 504.

64. Cortés Conde and Gallo, *La formación*, chap. 3; Di Tella and Zymelman, *Las etapas del desarrollo*, p. 101; Díaz Alejandro, *Essays*, p. 212; Adolfo Dorfman, *Historia de la industria argentina* (1970), chaps. 10–12; Eduardo Jorge, *Industria y concentración económica* (1970); Ortiz, *Historia económica*, vol. 2, chap. 8; and Vázquez Presedo, *El caso argentino*, chap. 5.

Table 3.4.
Net Value of Manufacturing Production per Capita before and after the
Argentine Reversal (Ratios of Argentine Value to That of Selected
Countries, 1913–55; Dollars of 1955).

| Country | 1913 | 1929 | 1937 | 1950 | 1955 |
|---|---|---|---|---|---|
| Australia | .45 | .58 | .49 | .48 | .41 |
| New Zealand | .56 | .61 | .54 | .53 | .45 |
| Italy | 1.08 | 1.12 | 1.17 | 1.45 | .97 |
| Spain | — | — | — | — | 1.38 |
| Mexico | — | — | 2.63 | 2.64 | 2.42 |
| Brazil | — | — | 4.20 | 3.63 | 2.90 |
| (Argentina) | (70) | (95) | (105) | (145) | (145) |

*Sources*: Computed on the basis of data in Alfred Maizels, *Industrial Growth and World Trade* (Cambridge; UK: Cambridge University Press, 1963).

reinsert itself into the reconstituted international system in such a way that external forces could lead to long-term growth. Rather, it turned inward. The share of the agrarian output consumed domestically increased, and manufactures, produced behind formidable protective barriers, could only be absorbed by the home market. The economy expanded, but only up to the limit allowed by internal resources and markets. This reorientation is the correlate of the divergence in paths between Argentina and the lands of recent settlement: it is after this shift that the country was overtaken by Mediterranean nations, and began to move closer to the Latin American pattern.

The arrest of Argentine economic expansion could not be easily apprehended by the people living through it because it was a discontinuous process taking place over two decades: traditional export agriculture stagnated at the outbreak of World War II and remained sluggish for a long period, while industry underwent what appeared to be a very intense spurt following the Depression and the war and then gradually became stunted. By the beginning of the fifties, the two processes converged. Since this was also the time in which Mediterranean countries began to catch up, the slippage of Argentina became evident at that point.

The Depression produced a drastic decline in the Argentine terms of trade, with the consequent contraction of imports. This and the exchange controls with which the government faced the crisis facilitated import-substituting industrialization. Argentine exports were also hindered by the formation of trade blocs, like the system of imperial preferences of the British Commonwealth, to which the government responded by seeking bilateral agreements such as the Roca-Runciman pact. Overall, the Argentine economy fared relatively well in the thirties: the volume of rural output and of exports declined very little, and manufacturing expanded. There was no substantial unemployment after 1934, and immigration even increased in the second half of the decade. While other nations stagnated or retrogressed, Argentina, like Australia, actually grew in the thirties.[65]

Agrarian stagnation began in the thirties: livestock production kept expanding until the end of the war, but the grain output reached levels that would not be matched again until the end of the sixties. The area planted with export crops also reached its peak in that period—Guido Di Tella and Manuel Zymelman have argued that the extensive occupation of the soil reached its limit in the interwar years.[66] In a replay of European enclosures centuries earlier, the more favorable terms of trade for livestock produced a shift in the use of Pampean land from grain to pastures. This was one of the factors facilitating the migration of labor into the cities, where the industries protected by the Depression and the war were surging.

After the war came the Peronist government (1946–55) with its pro-industry orientation. The agrarian policy of the regime—monopolization of exports by the state, domestic terms of trade favorable to manufacturing goods, the freezing of tenancy contracts, and higher rural wages—led to a sharp decline in rates of return. Perón modified some of these policies later, but during his regime the output of grains and beef declined by 10 percent. The most remarkable transformation of agriculture was its redirection towards the internal market. Domestic demand, which at the time of the Depression absorbed about half of the agrarian output, consumed about three-fourths of it after Peronism. Industrial growth and the high wages granted by the regime expanded demand at the same time that agrarian production stagnated or declined.

65. Aldo Ferrer, *La economía argentina* (1963), chap. 13; Di Tella and Zymelman, *Las etapas del desarrollo*, chaps. 3–4; Díaz Alejandro, *Essays*, chap. 2.

66. Di Tella and Zymelman, *Las etapas del desarrollo*, pp. 122–23.

This scissors effect is a potential brake on the development of lands of recent settlement, due to the peculiarity that, as economists often note in relation to the Argentine case, their export goods are also domestic staples. In typical Latin American countries, the output of the export sector, be it mining or labor intensive agriculture, is usually less sensitive to variations in the distribution of income. The consequence was a further difference with open spaces: the marginalization of Argentina from international markets. Its share of corn exports in world trade in 1950–54 was only 21 percent, a decline of 67 percent in comparison to 1934–38; the proportion for wheat 9 percent, a decrease of 53 percent, and its share of meat 19 percent, also a drop of 53 percent. Only in linseed did Argentina have still a large proportion of world exports (44 percent), but even this represented a decline of 35 percent with respect to the prewar level.[67]

Industry grew at a very fast rate after the Depression. Manufacturing employment in 1940–44 was almost 50 percent higher than during 1925–29, and in 1950 it had doubled.[68] In the early fifties the average share of manufacturing in the GDP was about 50 percent higher than that of agriculture. Industrialization was geared toward the local production of goods that could not be imported during the Depression and the war. In 1950, foodstuffs and beverages accounted for only a fifth of manufacturing employment, and the proportion was more or less the same for textiles and clothing or for metals, vehicles, and machinery. The comparison between the employment structure of Argentine industry in the postwar period and that of lands of recent settlement is instructive. As Díaz Alejandro has remarked, the Argentine employment profile around 1960 looked very much like that of the United States or Canada—the shares of metals, vehicles, and machinery were very similar.[69]

The difference between Argentine industrialization and that of other open spaces did not lie in the extent of industrialization as such, or in the range of branches developed, but in the type of goods produced: unlike Canada or Australia, Argentina focused on consumer goods. This is a second major divergence with the open

67. United Nations, *El desarrollo económico*, vol. 2, p. 48.

68. Ibid., vol. 1, p. 37. See also Díaz Alejandro, *Essays*, chaps. 2, 4; Ferrer, *La economía*, chaps. 14–15, Mallon and Sorrouille, *Economic Policymaking*, chap. 3; and Mónica Peralta Ramos, *Acumulación del capital y crisis política en Argentina (1930–1974)* (1978), pp. 62–78.

69. Díaz Alejandro, *Essays*, pp. 252–53.

spaces model, and it presents a similarity with the Latin American pattern of industrialization. Canada is not a good standard for comparison, due to the high level of integration of its economy with that of the United States, but Australia is. Ruth Kelly has shown that the industrialization of this country also proceeded along the lines of import substitution, but it was much more balanced, involving basic industries and producer goods of different types.[70] This was facilitated by the availability of iron and other minerals, which Argentina lacks or has in limited quantities.[71] However, the examples of Japan, the "new industrial countries" of East Asia, and several European nations show that this deficiency was not necessarily a major constraint.

The focus on consumer goods is indicated by the fact that textiles was the branch that contributed the most, in the thirties and forties, to the growth of manufacturing employment. From 1935 to 1950, its share of manufacturing employment increased by over a third, and in 1950 textiles and clothing represented over a fifth of the value of manufacturing.[72] Later, metals, vehicles, and machinery (in particular, the automobile industry) became the leading branches. These consumer goods were produced with imported machinery and intermediate inputs. In this lies the structural weakness of Argentine industrialization: if manufacturing cannot export, it depends for its expansion and at times for its survival on the foreign exchange generated by agriculture. Since this type of import-substituting industry expanded at the same time as agriculture was stagnating, the stage was set for blockage, if manufacturing could not attain international standards of price and quality. This is why the Peronist policy of protecting import-substituting industries regardless of their international competitiveness could only lead to stagnation. We can see now the nature of the new relationship that Argentina established with the international economy: from being the primary engine for growth, the world system became a potential brake.

From the fifties onward, the Argentine economy has been characterized by sharp cyclical fluctuations. Periods of industrial ex-

70. Kelly, "Foreign Trade," pp. 67–68.

71. Ibid., passim; John Fogarty, "Australia y Argentina en el período de 1914–1933"; and Ernst Boehm, "El desarrollo económico australiano a partir de 1930," in Fogarty et al., eds., *Argentina y Australia*.

72. Industrial censuses of 1935 and 1950. Data in Díaz Alejandro, *Essays*, p. 238; Di Tella and Zymelman, *Las etapas del desarrollo*, p. 100; Mallon and Sorrouille, *Economic Policymaking*, pp. 70–73.

pansion ended in foreign exchange crises and were succeeded by recessions. Agriculture has been growing after a long period of stagnation, but this sector is still incapable of supporting the massive concentration of labor and capital in a manufacturing establishment that still has a very limited ability to export. Significant steps toward the diversification of exports were taken in the late seventies, but Argentine industry could not sustain such a drive or spread it beyond a few firms. In that period, the over-valuation of the currency and the lowering of tariff rates led to massive bankruptcy in the least efficient branches of industry, rather than to a significant reconversion of the manufacturing sector. A previous experience in the export of manufactures took place during World War II, but it ended promptly when the international economy was reconstituted. This conflict between the primary sector and industry is a third difference between Argentine industrialization and that of the lands of recent settlement, and it shows a further similarity between Argentina and the Latin American pattern.

In conclusion, if Argentine agricultural development and extent of industrialization are in many respects comparable to those of open spaces, the specialization of its manufactures in consumer goods and the intersectoral relations in its economy resemble the underdeveloped model. These two "Latin American" traits acquired a decisive importance after the Depression. Eventually, they became a brake on the country's development.

### Dependency

In order to assess the level of dependency of the Argentine economy throughout this process of development, it is necessary to distinguish between trade dependency and the dependency based on the control of means of production by external actors. The first has always been relatively high, but decreasing since the war, and the second has been relatively low, but increasing. A third type, financial dependency, became paramount in the eighties.

As for trade, Argentina has always depended on the export of a few temperate agriculture products, and its transactions have been concentrated on a few markets. Both of these factors have been central in the shaping of the economic and social structure of the country.

Primary products accounted for 98 percent of the value of exports in 1925–29, and the proportion was still the same in 1950–

54.[73] Only in the late seventies manufacturing accounted for more than a fifth of the value of exports,[74] but this proportion included a large component of processed agriculture and livestock products, and much of the remainder could be exported because of bilateral agreements.

In relation to country concentration, it is well known that up to the end of World War II Britain received between one and two fifths of Argentine exports, and that from the fifties onward this relationship gradually dissolved. Continental European countries usually bought most of the balance, even though the United States became an important recipient of Argentine products after the war, matching or surpassing Britain in the early fifties. Links could never be very strong, however, because Argentina and the United States are competitors in the grain and beef markets. Complementarity with Europe also weakened gradually as the Common Market developed, forcing Argentina to reorient its exports. Since the late seventies, the Soviet Union became the most important trade partner, absorbing proportions comparable to those of Britain before the war. This new relationship has the potential to become long-term, due to the complementarity between the two economies, a prospect that would have major economic and political implications.

The impact of specialization and of trade concentration on the social structure has been a favorite theme among Argentine propounders of the Latin American image[75] and among dependency theorists more recently. From different perspectives, these authors have linked the economic, political, and cultural cleavage between the littoral and the interior to the type of insertion Argentina had in the world economy. Not only were the fruits of development concentrated in the grain and beef producing area, but the fact that Argentina imported its manufactures from Europe led to the ruin of handicrafts and small industries in the interior, thereby widening the gulf between the two regions. The foreign-owned railroads, which gathered export products from producing areas and transported them to the ports and which distributed European

73. United Nations, *El desarrollo económico*, vol. 1, p. 115.

74. United Nations, ECLA, *Statistical Yearbook, 1979*, p. 94.

75. See Ferrer, *La economía argentina*; Fuchs, *Argentina: Su desarrollo*; Irazusta, *La Argentina*; Jorge A. Ramos, *Revolución y contrarrevolución en la Argentina: Del patriciado a la oligarquía, 1862–1904* (1970); Ortiz, *Historia económica*, passim; Raúl Scalabrini Ortiz, *Historia de los ferrocarriles argentinos* (1958).

manufactures throughout the country, are usually presented as the agents of this process of dislocation. Since the tariff structure before the Depression was adapted to the Argentine position in the world economy, they argue, duties would have discouraged the development of manufacturing, even in the Pampean region. After the Depression, government policy would have identified the preservation of this "agro-export" structure with the national interest: the Roca-Runciman pact is presented by most of these authors as an instance of disprotection of home industries in order to save the British market for Argentine beef.

As for dependency based on the property of the means of production by external agents, another issue emphasized in the literature cited above is the fact that British and other foreign capital controlled the activities or services that made the functioning of the export economy possible. Most railroad lines and a major share of the meat-packing houses were British, American capital owned also a large proportion of the meat-packing industry, the grain exporting firms and the most important banks were foreign, Argentine products were carried by foreign ships, and so on. Foreign capital also controlled a big part of manufacturing and utilities. At the outbreak of World War I, almost half of the fixed capital in the country was foreign. This proportion was still a third at the time of the Depression,[76] and Felix J. Weil estimated that in 1940, 28 percent of all corporation profits were appropriated by foreigners.[77] The importance of foreign capital diminished after the war, when the Peronist government nationalized railroads and other holdings—in 1955, foreign capital was only 5 percent of total fixed capital[78]—but increased again with the expansion of the automobile industry and large-scale investment by multinational corporations in the sixties, to the point that in the early eighties most big firms are either government-held or foreign.

As for the nationality of capital, sterotypes held by the writers mentioned above are correct. In 1914, the value of British investment in Argentina amounted to 84 percent of the value of British investment in India, 77 percent of that in Australia, and 62 percent of that in Canada.[79] American investment was in the beginning

76. United Nations, *El desarrollo económico*, vol. 1, p. 28.

77. Felix J. Weil, *The Argentine Riddle* (1944), p. 123.

78. United Nations, *El desarrollo económico*, vol. 1, p. 28.

79. Vázquez Presedo, *El caso argentino*, p. 26. See also H. S. Ferns, *Britain and Argentina in the Nineteenth Century* (1960); and Jorge

also linked to the export economy, but after World War I it diversified to import-substituting industries producing for the internal market (durable consumer goods, metal and machinery, pharmaceutical industries). At the time of the Depression, American capital invested in Argentina was already larger than the British capital in areas other than railroads, and it became the largest after the fading of the British presence.[80] Continental European investment has also been significant, but the expansion of American corporations, especially from the sixties onward, made them the central foreign component.

The level of Argentine dependency, however, has to be assessed in a comparative perspective. It is true that, as far as commodity concentration is concerned, this level is high, as in other lands of recent settlement and in the typical Latin American countries. Nevertheless, and this is a theme emphasized in the staple theory literature, one of the distinguishing traits of the open spaces situation is the ability to shift the resource specialization according to changing market conditions. Argentina lacks the diverse resource base of Australia or Canada, due to its relative scarcity of minerals, but temperate agriculture provides access to a range of markets having some variability in their economic performance. Historically, Argentina shifted the relative proportions in its trade among grains, linseed, beef, wool, and similar products in response to price changes. This is, admittedly, a narrow range of variability, but it presupposes a much lesser degree of commodity concentration than the typical single-product economy that has existed in much of Latin America. For much of their contemporary history, countries such as Chile, Bolivia, Venezuela, Brazil, or Cuba had to rely on the export of a single commodity—copper, tin, oil, coffee, or sugar, respectively. Argentina never had such an exclusive specialization.

Second, in relation to country concentration, this was always high in Argentina, as in lands of recent settlement and in most Latin American countries. But this is also relative. Up to World War II Britain was the preponderant trade partner. Later the United States and, most recently, the Soviet Union occupied a central position. However, Argentine trade always had a considerable degree of diversification. In most years prior to the Depression, four or

Fodor and Arturo O'Connell, "La Argentina y la economía atlántica en la primera mitad del siglo veinte," *Desarrollo económico* (1973).

80. Jorge, *Industria y concentración*, pp. 91–100.

five other European nations absorbed a percentage of exports at least comparable to that of Britain, and in the mid-sixties the proportion of Argentine trade going to the most important partner was lower than those of Canada, Australia, New Zealand, and the twenty-one Latin American and Caribbean countries for which data are presented in the *World Handbook of Political and Social Indicators*.[81]

Overall, trade dependency diminished after the inward turn of the Argentine economy. Extensive industrialization based on the substitution of consumer goods may not be the most effective lever for long-term economic growth, due to the intersectoral conflict discussed above, but it reduced the dependency of the whole economy on the fluctuation of a few commodity markets. Autarky was not attained, but the impact of developments in the world system was cushioned by domestic diversification, even if this thin shield had a high cost in terms of misallocation of resources.

Third, as for the structural effects of dependency, it is true that incorporation into the international economy contributed to intensify the cleavage between the littoral and most of the interior, but it must be borne in mind that development is always "uneven" and that, in any case, an export sector based on labor extensive agriculture is more likely to spread the benefits of growth throughout the society than other types of resource-based economy. The argument was already made by Baldwin in relation to plantation crops,[82] and by dependency theorists in relation to the "enclave" situation that existed in Latin American societies specialized in mining.[83] The danger, at any rate, is not discontinuity per se, but the probability that uneven development becomes "combined" as well. In this connection, labor-extensive agriculture, by definition, does not require a large labor reserve, and thus it is unlikely to "freeze" or generate anew a precapitalist peasantry. Finally, there is no reason to believe that the handicrafts and traditional manufactures of the interior, left to themselves, would have evolved into modern capitalist firms. Probably, they would have just vegetated, for the society and culture of the interior at the turn of the century was a weak foundation for capitalist

81. Taylor and Hudson, *World Handbook*, pp. 369–71.

82. Baldwin, "Patterns of Development."

83. Cardoso and Faletto, *Dependency and Development*; Frank, *Capitalism and Underdevelopment*; Celso Furtado, *Economic Development of Latin America* (1970).

enterprise. In any case, the entry of foreign manufactures could not have been prevented, for free trade was the central principle of the world economy prior to the Depression, and Argentina could have never inserted itself into that economy without becoming an importer of manufactures. Also, this insertion did not prevent substantial industrialization in that period, as the record indicates.

Fourth, with regard to dependency based on the control of the means of production by foreign firms, this also has to be considered in a relative perspective. Land, especially the land of the Pampean region, was the strategic productive resource, and has always been in the hands of the domestic upper class. This distinguishes Argentina from the Latin American enclave situation, where in many cases the export sector was controlled by foreign firms. As for manufacturing, it is important to keep in mind that, even if most large private corporations—and presumably the most efficient as well—are foreign, small and medium size firms and the state sector still comprise most of manufacturing. At least in terms of shares of manufacturing employment, therefore, the sector of industry controlled by domestic actors is still much larger than the one under international control.

Thus, Argentina is certainly dependent, both in relation to trade and control of productive resources, but it is not more dependent than lands of recent settlement that industrialized successfully, such as Canada or Australia, and it is less so than the Latin American countries that developed on the basis of enclave export economies.

### Equality

To use a current distinction, the contrast between the new country and the underdevelopment models was formulated in the literature more in terms of equality of opportunity than of equality of outcome. Open spaces were expected to have a greater potential for access by the lower classes to satisfactory standards of living, and for social mobility in general, than underdeveloped societies.

There is no question that the Argentine record in these areas has been closer to that of the lands of recent settlement than to the Latin American pattern. Wages are a good indicator. On the basis of the income and productivity data we have seen, it is reasonable to assume that Argentine real wages were lower than in open spaces and higher than in Latin America. Since Argentina had a labor shortage and since there was a powerful "pull" factor in European emigration, it makes sense to presuppose that Argentine real wages were higher than in much of Europe. This latter point is corroborated by different fragments of evidence up to World War II, after which the relationship was reversed. Roberto Cortés Conde has estimated wage differentials with Italy from 1882 to 1912 and found Argentine wages higher in seventeen out of these twenty-two years.[84] Díaz Alejandro reports that, prior to World War I, wage rates in Buenos Aires for several categories of workers were higher than in Marseilles and, in most cases, than in Paris as well.[85] Furthermore, at the outbreak of World War II, the Armour Foundation estimated that unskilled urban wages, measured by their purchasing power, were higher in Argentina than in Germany, but lower than in the United States and Britain.[86]

But even after the slippage, standards of living and opportunities for social mobility remained higher in Argentina than in typical Latin American countries, and, in some cases, they were still within the range of lands of recent settlement. Table 3.5 indicates that, in terms of infant mortality rates, Argentina always lagged behind open spaces, but before the reversal its rate was lower than those of Mediterranean and Latin American countries. It is after the turning point that the former surpassed and some of the latter approached Argentine levels. As for nutrition, however, Argentina was and still is at the same level as open spaces, including the United States. The same is true for the supply of physicians (Table 3.6). Finally, in relation to access to higher education, the proportion of the population enrolled was, even in the sixties, higher than in Mediterranean countries. In the late seventies, that difference disappeared, but most Latin American nations were still behind.

Data on mobility are hard to come by. Available evidence, however, indicates that throughout the century upward mobility rates have been very high in Argentina, even after the slippage. Germani has estimated that, in 1914, two thirds of the members of the already large middle class had a manual origin. Taking the manual stratum as a basis, over a fifth of its members had moved to non-

84. Cortés Conde, *El progreso*, p. 265.

85. Díaz Alejandro, *Essays*, p. 41.

86. Armour Research Foundation, *Technological and Economic Survey of Argentine Industries* (1943), pp. 74–75.

Table 3.5.
*Standards of Living in Argentina and in Selected Countries (Ratios of Argentine Infant Mortality Rates and Nutrition to Those of Other Countries, 1911–81).*

| Country | Infant Mortality Rates (Deaths under 1 per 1,000 live births) | | | | Consumption of Meat per Capita | | Daily Calorie Supply per Capita |
|---|---|---|---|---|---|---|---|
| | 1911–19 | 1920–30 | 1941–49 | 1960 | ca. 1936 | ca. 1951 | 1981 |
| Australia | 1.91 | 2.16 | 2.56 | 2.75 | .89 | .96 | 1.06 |
| United States | 1.28 | 1.68 | 2.22 | 2.11 | 1.73 | 1.40 | .93 |
| Italy | .85 | .98 | .85 | 1.25 | 5.45 | 6.06 | .92 |
| Spain | .80 | .90 | .85 | 1.25 | — | — | 1.08 |
| Brazil | — | — | — | .43 | 2.15 | 3.55 | 1.35 |
| Mexico | — | — | — | .70 | 4.28 | 4.48[d] | 1.21 |
| (Argentina) | (124)[a] | (121)[b] | (82)[c] | (55) | (106.9) | (103) | (3,405) |

*Sources:* For infant mortality, 1911–30 and 1941–49, except for Argentina, W. S. Woytinsky and E. S. Woytinsky, *World Population and Production: Trends and Outlook* (New York: Twentieth Century Fund, 1953); for infant mortality, 1915–45, Argentina, Carlos F. Diaz Alejandro, *Essays on the Economic History of the Argentine Republic* (New Haven: Yale University Press, 1970); for infant mortality, 1960, World Bank, *Poverty and Human Development* (New York: Oxford University Press, 1980); for consumption of meat, Colin Clark, *The Conditions of Economic Progress* (London: Macmillan, 1960); for daily calorie supply, World Bank, *World Development Report 1984* (New York: Oxford University Press, 1984).
*Notes:* [a] 1915; [b] 1925; [c] 1945; [d] 1946–49.

manual occupations.[87] Immigrants' expectations were fulfilled, for rates among the foreign born were a third higher than in the native population. Data on foreign participation in different strata of the middle class have already been presented.

This picture approaches more closely the open spaces model than the underdevelopment pattern. After the slippage, the slowdown and, at times, the stagnation of the economy reduced the opportunities for expansion of the middle and upper positions, but

87. Gino Germani, "Movilidad social en la Argentina," appendix to Seymour M. Lipset and Reinhard Bendix, *Movilidad social en la sociedad industrial* (1963), p. 325.

Table 3.6.
*Higher Education in Argentina and in Selected Countries (Ratios of Argentine Supply of Physicians to that of Other Countries, and Enrollment in Higher Education, 1940–77).*

| Country | Physicians per 10,000 Inhabitants | | | Percentage of the Population Ages 20–24 Enrolled in Higher Education | |
| | 1940 | ca. 1966 | ca. 1977 | 1960 | 1976 |
| --- | --- | --- | --- | --- | --- |
| United States | .89 | 1.02 | 1.09 | 32 | 56 |
| New Zealand | 1.02 | .98 | 1.40 | 13 | 28 |
| Australia | 1.25 | 1.08 | 1.23 | 13 | 24 |
| Italy | 1.29 | .90 | .92 | 7 | 27 |
| Spain | 1.31 | 1.21 | 1.06 | 4 | 22 |
| Brazil | 5.48 | 3.87 | 3.21 | 2 | 12 |
| Mexico | 9.58 | 2.65 | 3.44 | 3 | 10 |
| (Argentina) | (11.5) | (14.66) | (18.87) | 11 | 29 |

*Sources:* For physicians 1940, W. S. Woytinsky and E. S. Woytinsky, *World Population and Production: Trends and Outlook* (New York: Twentieth Century Fund, 1953); for physicians 1966, Charles L. Taylor and Michael C. Hudson, *World Handbook of Political and Social Indicators,* 2nd ed. (New Haven: Yale University Press, 1972); for physicians 1977 and for enrollment World Bank, *Poverty and Human Development* (New York: Oxford University Press, 1980).

the existence of a mass system of higher education provided a continuous flow of claimants to these positions. At the same time, processes such as concentration of capital, and more recently the relative opening of the economy and the contraction of the domestic market, must have produced substantial downward mobility. In the same study quoted above, Germani supplied information for a representative sample of family heads in Buenos Aires in 1960–61. When socioeconomic status was trichotomized, over 40 percent of all the individuals in the middle and upper strata were found to be upwardly mobile, and close to a similar proportion of the lower stratum had moved down.[88] Again, this pattern is not consistent with the rigid nature of society in the underdevelopment model.

88. Ibid., p. 340.

Finally, a comment on equality of outcome. In relation to income distribution, Argentina in the seventies occupied an intermediate position between "developed" and "underdeveloped" countries. Overall, it was less egalitarian than open spaces and Mediterranean nations, even though the share of household income held by the lowest quintile was similar to that of the United States or France.[89]

The picture with respect to equality is thus consistent with the pattern of economic evolution we have considered above. Argentina was, before the turning point, much closer to the open spaces model than to the Latin American one. After the slippage, the country began to veer in the opposite direction, but mass higher education kept producing upward mobility, and standards of living continued being relatively high.

### Structural Heterogeneity

This was another outcome of the different endowments of land and labor. In the world of ideal types, the open spaces situation was expected to lead to a society in which capitalist social relations are generalized to the point of exclusiveness, whereas underdeveloped societies would be more likely to articulate a "modern" and a "traditional," or precapitalist, sector, in a pattern of combined development. In this respect, Argentina has also been much closer to the lands of recent settlement than to the typical Latin American model, but the informal sector has been growing since the turning point.

The processes of expansion of temperate agriculture, immigration, and urbanization involved the extension of production based on free labor. Unlike Brazil and other Latin American countries, Argentina constituted what Celso Furtado has called a "unified labor market," in which extraeconomic coercion was absent.[90] It is important to note that tenant farming was a fully capitalist activity. The claim by some writers that it was a "semi-feudal" trait[91] is incorrect, for farmers were not tied to the soil, and they were producing for the market. In fact, farmers were agrarian capitalists

89. World Bank, *Poverty*, pp. 84–85.

90. Celso Furtado, "Development and Stagnation in Latin America," in Irving L. Horowitz, ed., *Masses in Latin America* (1970).

91. Fuchs, *Argentina: Su desarrollo*.

who hired outside labor, and tenancy, rather than being a "survival" of traditional social relations, developed in response to market conditions. As for the Argentine periphery, much of it, especially in the south and parts of the northeast, is of the frontier type, and thus fits the open spaces model. But the northwest (13 percent of the population in 1914, 11 percent in 1960 and also in 1980[92]) contained, and still contains in the most traditional provinces, areas of minifundio and even pockets of subsistence agriculture. These, as well as the family farms in these and other areas that do not require nonfamily labor, depart from the "pure" type of capitalist enterprise, which involves linkage to both the commodity and the labor markets. This is, in any case, a small traditional periphery.

The urban counterpart of this situation is the informal sector, in particular the artisans and the unskilled "independents" in the tertiary. As Miguel Murmis has remarked, the persistence of a large proportion of these "independents" in Argentina indicates departure from classical capitalism,[93] and Juan M. Villarreal has shown not only that their proportion has not declined over time, but that it has increased very sharply since the turning point. From 1947 to 1970, the percentage of "independents," other than family labor, in the active population grew by 128 percent, and, in the latter date, they were 16 percent of the labor force.[94] The process intensified in the seventies, due to the economic policy carried out toward the end of the decade. As I stated above, a decrease of the effective protection to manufacturing led to a large-scale reduction of industrial employment. This had a ripple effect throughout the economy. In 1980, the "independents" were almost one-fourth of the labor force. Most of them had low-productivity jobs in commerce and services.[95] One social consequence of the slippage, then, is the marginalization of a growing proportion of the population from capitalist social relations. Also in its social structure

92. Provinces of Catamarca, Jujuy, La Rioja, Salta, Santiago del Estero, and Tucumán.

93. Miguel Murmis, "Tipos de capitalismo y estructura de clases: Elementos para el análisis de la estructura social de la Argentina," in Miguel Murmis et al., *Tipos de capitalismo y estructura de clases: La formación de la sociedad argentina, 1500–1800* (1974).

94. Juan Villarreal, *El capitalismo dependiente: Estudio sobre la estructura de clases en Argentina* (1978), pp. 60–61.

95. Data in *Clarín económico* (Buenos Aires), July 8, 1984.

Argentina is becoming Latin American: a substantial labor reserve is forming.

The overall balance of this comparative analysis of Argentine economy and society is that the country switched developmental tracks. Before the Depression, it was much closer to the lands of recent settlement than to the Latin American nations in almost all respects: the overall level of development, the organization of agriculture, the extent of industrialization, the level and type of economic dependency, the degree of equality of opportunity, and the absence of structural heterogeneity. Since the fifties, the situation of Argentina has changed. Nowadays, the country's agriculture is still very productive, its economy is relatively less dependent because of its greater diversification, its standards of living are relatively high, and mass higher education sustains social mobility. But the country slipped in relative terms. It increased its distance with the open spaces model, was overtaken and surpassed by Mediterranean societies, and begins to take on the characteristics of underdevelopment: a sluggish or stagnated economy, an inefficient manufacturing sector, social blockage, and a substantial segment of the labor force in the informal sector.

Let us see how this change of evolutionary paths has affected the political system.

## Overview of the Reversal: Society and Politics

### Arrested Democratization

Earlier I characterized the period 1880–1930 as an expanding liberal democracy. This label presupposes an evaluation of the oligarchic regime that existed until World War I as one closer to the open spaces pattern than to the modal Latin American type.

The Argentine polity, when the country became a major exporter, was a typical Whig democracy, similar in its basic traits to its counterparts in many agrarian societies in Europe and Latin America. First, since the mass of the population was not mobilized, the elite and some sectors of the middle classes were initially the only participants. Second, given that the various factions or parties represented different segments of the elite, pluralism, or toleration of dissent, had a relatively narrow range in terms of the diversity of interests actually in contention.

What distinguishes evolving liberal democracies from preindustrial exclusionary regimes is their response to mobilization. The development of capitalism and the industrial and educational revolutions bring new political forces to the fore: the industrial bourgeoisie, other urban middle-class sectors, and the working class. Elite responses can be triggered by the mere formation of these new classes or can be a reaction to their mobilization. In *Modernization and the Working Class,* I have classified these responses into three elite strategies: inclusion, which is the extension of the right to participate in the polity as an independent political force; exclusion, which is the denial of that right; and co-optation, which is an intermediate form consisting of participation under the control of the elite or of the state apparatus, usually on the basis of corporatist mechanisms. Elements of two or even of the three strategies are present in most societies, especially in the early stages of industrialization, but some patterns emerge. In early industrializers and in lands of recent settlement, the predominant elite strategy has been inclusion, while in Mediterranean and most Latin American latecomers to industrialization elites have been prone to exclusion and co-optation, so that for much—or most—of their history as industrial societies these countries have wavered between authoritarian and corporatist regimes.[96]

As far as Argentina is concerned, the inclusionary aspect of the elite response to the mobilization of the middle and working classes before 1930 is indicated by the toleration of peaceful opposition by the Radical and Socialist parties, which represented these new social forces; by the Reform of 1912, which enfranchised the native middle classes; and by the transfer of political power to the Radicals in 1916. A secondary element of exclusion existed, but it was usually triggered by the violent activities of the Anarchists.[97] Policies such as the suspension of constitutional

---

96. Waisman, *Modernization,* chaps. 2 and 5.

97. For discussions of the oligarchic state, see Botana, *El orden conservador,* and two classical works: José N. Matienzo, *El gobierno representativo federal en la República Argentina* (1917); and Rodolfo Rivarola, *Del régimen federativo al unitario* (1908). The origins of the state are examined in Oscar Oszlak, *La formación del estado argentino* (1982); and the party system is discussed in Karen L. Remmer, *Party Competition in Argentina and Chile: Political Recruitment and Public Policy, 1890–1930* (1984). For general analyses of politics and society in the period 1880–1930, see Ezequiel Gallo and Roberto Cortés Conde, *Argentina: La república conservadora* (1972); Darío Cantón et al.,

guarantees through the state of siege and the persecution of terrorists (but also of labor militants and of leftwing activists) through
the laws of Residence and of Social Defense were applied, but spar-
ingly, in comparision with other societies.[98] In fact, it would be
the Radicals, rather than the administrations representing the
Conservative oligarchy, who responded to labor mobilization, in
isolated instances, with large-scale repression.

As for participation, it was restricted by the initially low level of
mobilization among nonelite classes and strata, but also by fraudulent electoral practices—which covered the whole range, from
the buying of votes to the falsification of results.[99] These practices
disappeared or were minimized, however, with the Reform of
1912.

The mobilization of the middle and lower classes presented
challenges that, for different reasons, could be met by the oligarchy without altering the existing distribution of wealth and
power. The Radicals, with an elite leadership and a mass base including large segments of the middle classes, staged several armed
revolts at the turn of the century. Their demands, however, were
totally consistent with continued oligarchic rule. Their central
goal was the extension of electoral participation, through the
"universal" and secret manhood suffrage, and nothing in their diffuse economic and social doctrine could be construed as antagonistic to the status quo.

Labor mobilization was intense in the first decade of the century
and, because of the Anarchist presence, was coupled with a significant amount of violent activity. But this mobilization did not represent a high level of threat to oligarchic rule either, for three rea-

---

*Argentina: La democracia constitucional y su crisis* (1972); Gustavo
Ferrari and Ezequiel Gallo, eds., *La Argentina del ochenta al centenario*
(1980); Marcos Giménez Zapiola, ed., *El régimen oligárquico:
Materiales para el estudio de la realidad argentina (hasta 1930)* (1975);
and David Rock, *Politics in Argentina, 1890–1930: The Rise and Fall of
Radicalism* (1975). See also Juan E. Corradi, *The Fitful Republic:
Economy, Society, and Politics in Argentina* (1985), chap. 2; Eduardo
Crawley, *A House Divided: Argentina 1880–1980* (1984), chaps. 1–3;
Gilbert W. Merkx, "Political and Economic Change in Argentina from
1870 to 1966" (1968), chaps. 4–6; and David Rock, *Argentina 1516–
1982: From the Spanish Colonization to the Falklands War* (1985),
chap. 5.

98. See Rock, *Politics in Argentina*, p. 83.

99. See Botana, *El orden conservador*, pp. 174–89; Darío Cantón,
*Elecciones y partidos políticos en la Argentina* (1973), chap. 1.

sons. In the first place, the central themes of workers' protest were conventional bread-and-butter issues and opposition to repression. As such, they could be controlled by political reform and the institutionalization of the labor conflict, two measures that were feasible in the existing economic and political structure. Second, the distribution of forces in the labor movement—Socialists and Anarchists—presented an ideal context for the application of carrot-and-stick elite strategies. The inclusion of the Socialists, who were convinced supporters of free trade and liberal democracy, could only strengthen existing institutions. And the exclusion of the Anarchists was facilitated by two traits of their ideology: concentration on immediate demands and rejection of participation in the existing state. Finally, most workers were foreign, a fact that facilitated elite strategies, as we will see below. Thus, Socialists and Radicals were incorporated into the system, and government intervention in labor disputes grew during the period, especially after the transfer of power to the Radicals. The use of force by this party (there were two major incidents, which I will discuss in Chapter 7) was more a reflection of panic and of a lack of capability for riot control than of a systematic policy of persecuting the labor movement.

The oligarchic regime has to be evaluated in a comparative perspective. Certainly, it did not rank very high on the democratic scale, but it would not make any sense to place it in the same category with contemporary authoritarian polities such as Bismarckian Germany or the extreme case of Czarist Russia. The crucial issue is that the Argentine elite did extend participation to the new classes generated by development, and it was willing to abide by the norms of the liberal democratic game, which included losing control of the government, as long as its basic economic interests were not endangered. Elites in many late industrializers were not so inclined.

The peculiarities of Argentine political evolution are related to two traits that, as we have seen, distinguish Argentina from lands of recent settlement and from the typical Latin American society. Unlike open spaces, it had a landed upper class that controlled the state apparatus, and unlike the modal Latin American setting, its population included a high proportion of immigrants. In the specific conditions of Argentina, the second trait was conducive to democracy, while the first one was not.

The immigrant presence contributed to democratic development not because of the culture carried by the foreigners, but because their sheer weight and marginality to the society allowed
the elite to reconcile the ideal norms of democracy with the reality
of its control of the state. Two traits of this immigrant contingent
in the beginning of the century are important for the understanding of how "cheap" political reform was for the elite. In the littoral, where the bulk of the population was concentrated, 50 to 70
percent of the males over twenty years old were foreign-born,[100]
and in the whole country only 1.4 percent of the foreigners had become Argentine citizens in 1914.[101]

The reasons for the latter are complex. First, according to an observation by the disappointed Sarmiento, which all commentators
have accepted as the standard explanation, immigrants were interested in getting rich—"making it in America"—rather than in becoming citizens of the new nation. Second, Solberg has shown that
naturalization involved complex bureaucratic procedures, which
the elite was not interested in simplifying.[102] Third, as Oscar
Cornblitt has remarked, until the Radicals came to power, Argentine parties did not develop the urban machines that were a central
mechanism for the political assimilation of immigrants in the
United States. But the Radicals, South American virtuosi of the
machine variety of politics, were not oriented toward the foreigners.[103] Fourth, the immigrants going to Argentina lacked a tradition of autonomous political participation. And finally, Pellegrini,
Koebel, and others correctly described the extent to which foreign
residents were granted civil rights. As political rights were not
very meaningful before the Reform of 1912, few immigrants experienced either the need or the inducement to become citizens.

These peculiarities of the foreign population permitted the elite
to legitimize the exclusionary aspects of its response to the mobilization of the lower classes. Since most industrial workers were
foreign-born, agitators and organizers could be deported, that is,
excluded permanently, a treatment not applicable to citizens in a
democratic polity. Also, the immigrant presence allowed the elite
to live up to the ideal of universal manhood representation with-

100. Germani, *Política y sociedad*, p. 225.
101. Cornblitt, "Inmigrantes y empresarios," p. 417.
102. Solberg, *Immigration and Nationalism*, p. 83.
103. Cornblitt, "Inmigrantes y empresarios," pp. 419–29.

out, as Peter Smith notes, enfranchising the lower classes.[104] The Reform of 1912 established an universal, secret, and compulsory ballot, on the basis of new and complete rolls. However, in the 1916 election, won by the opposition Radicals, voters were, in the most important districts, no more than 9 percent of the total population and only 30 percent of the males over 18.[105]

This is not to imply that the Reform was meaningless. It is true that the elite yielded to mobilization because it expected to win under the new rules. (To this end, a faction of the oligarchy tried to organize a "modern" Conservative Party in order to compete with the Radicals.) It is also true that in supporting the Reform some elite leaders had a hidden agenda: they expected, very reasonably, that participation would deflect labor militancy. Finally, there was some apprehension about Radical revolts, even though it would be an overstatement to claim that the 1912 law was a fearful reaction to the mobilized masses.[106] In spite of all these factors, the Reform was a genuine leap in the dark, even if a deferred one. The elite was aware that, in one to two decades, the children of the immigrants would join the electorate and the whole male population would then be enfranchised.

We may now turn to the other Argentine peculiarity vis-à-vis open spaces: the existence of the landowning oligarchy itself. The local upper classes, both in the littoral and the interior, were constituted as political forces and laboriously developed norms for their interaction before the constitution was adopted and applied. The half century from independence to national organization is usually seen as one of "anarchy," but the counterpart of the protracted conflict among the provinces was the gradual development of a consensus about the institutions of the new nation. In social terms, this meant the emergence of a relatively homogeneous national ruling class out of a contentious set of local ones.

The massive and swift transformation in all spheres of life that followed the establishment of democratic institutions had contra-

104. Peter H. Smith, "The Breakdown of Democracy in Argentina," in Juan J. Linz and Alfred Stepan, eds., *The Breakdown of Democratic Regimes: Latin America* (1978), and Smith, *Argentina and the Failure of Democracy* (1974), pp. 16, 23, 90–92.

105. Botana, *El orden conservador*, p. 328. See also Cantón, *Elecciones y partidos*, chap. 2.

106. On the Reform, see Botana, *El orden conservador*; Cantón, *Elecciones y partidos*; Rock, *Politics in Argentina*; and Cárcano, *Sáenz Peña*.

dictory effects on legitimacy. The organization of the export economy, foreign investment, and mass immigration showed the effectiveness of the elite, enhancing the legitimacy of the *social* order, and converted the elite into a hegemonic force. In the long run, however, the transformation undermined *political* legitimacy. This was due to the fact that these economic and social processes triggered mobilization before the new political institutions could attain a high level of legitimacy among the different social groups, the established elite in particular. Such a level of legitimacy implies an acceptance that is automatic rather than deliberate, emotional rather than rational. Only in that situation, social and political forces, and especially the elites, develop stable conceptions of the general interest as a product of impersonal institutions, binding on all social groups, even when that general interest differs from, or is in contradiction to, particular interests. The attainment of this sort of legitimacy presupposes at least two conditions, efficacy and time,[107] the second of which was missing in the Argentine case.

The Argentine upper class was not deeply committed to democratic norms, as Robert Dahl, Darío Cantón and others have remarked.[108] However, such a commitment is not an intrinsic attribute of a social group nor its absence just a deficiency of the educational system. The institutionalization of liberal democracy was thwarted. The lapse of time between the establishment of the new institutions and the appearance of fresh claimants to power was so brief that the outcome was natural. As long as it had no intense conflicts with these new forces, the oligarchy was willing to enfranchise the middle classes and even to transfer power to the party representing them. It could also tolerate peaceful labor opposition. But once its basic interests were in danger, the agrarian elite revoked its support for liberal democracy and seized control of the state.

Until 1930, all social and political forces, except for the Anarchist faction of the working class, coincided in supporting the basic characteristics of Argentine society and its insertion in the world economy. Since most manufacturing was a forward linkage of agriculture, there was no conflict between agriculture and in-

107. See Samuel P. Huntington, *Political Order in Changing Societies* (1968), chap. 1; Juan J. Linz, *The Breakdown of Democratic Regimes: Crisis, Breakdown, and Reequilibration* (1978), chap. 2; and Seymour M. Lipset, *Political Man: The Social Bases of Politics* (1963), chap. 3.

108. Cantón, *Elecciones y partidos*; Dahl, *Polyarchy*, pp. 133–36.

dustry. Foreign capital was combined or allied with domestic rural and urban capital, so there was no contradiction between them. Also, since the well-being of the middle and working classes depended upon the export economy, vertical cleavages were moderate in contents, in spite of the occasional use of violent forms of action. Except, again, for the Anarchists, conflicts involving interest groups and political parties were exclusively of a secondary or nonantagonistic nature. Thus, the oppositions between the littoral and interior elites, breeders and fatteners, cattlemen and meat-packers, domestic and foreign capital, landowners and tenant farmers, the agrarian elite and the urban middle class, capitalists and workers, and Conservatives and Radicals or Socialists were all consistent with the hegemony of the agrarian upper class. These were conflicts over participation in decision making, or distribution of the surplus, rather than over property or the nature of political institutions. Thus, when the Radicals were in power from 1916 to 1930, their opposition to the Conservatives was exclusively of a political nature. Smith points out that the Radicals departed from the Conservative tradition of government by consensus and moved toward competitive decision making.[109] In addition, as Smith and Anne Potter contend, they aimed at weakening the Conservatives' local power base, through the systematic intervention of the federal government in provincial administrations.[110] Nevertheless, as David Rock argues, the Radicals limited themselves to administering the existing economic and social order. They did not attempt to introduce any major changes in the structure of Argentine society or in its location in the international economy.[111]

However, when the Depression hit Argentina, elite hegemony was endangered. Not only did the position of the country in the international system have to be renegotiated, but the consent of subordinate classes could erode as the domestic conflict took the appearance of a zero-sum game. In this situation, the upper class turned away from democracy, more in order to face the critical situation than to restore the premobilization oligarchic state.

109. Smith, *Failure of Democracy*, pp. 93–94, and "Breakdown of Democracy."

110. Ibid., and Anne L. Potter, "Political Institutions, Political Decay, and the Argentine Crisis of 1930" (1978), and "The Failure of Democracy in Argentina, 1916–1930: An Institutional Perspective," *Journal of Latin American Studies* (1981).

111. Rock, *Politics in Argentina*.

There is no question that the Depression was followed by an oligarchic restoration, but this does not mean that the Depression itself was the main cause of the coup of 1930, the event that marked the end of the process of democratization. This is still a debated issue. Smith has challenged the traditional interpretation, according to which there was a direct link between the economic crisis and the coup. He asserted that the important repercussions of the Depression appeared only after the coup. Instead, he explained the coup by the Radicals' refusal to abide by the Conservative tradition of power sharing. The ensuing separation between economic and political power would have led the agrarian elite to withdraw legitimacy from the democratic institutions and seize power by force.[112] In opposition to Smith, Rock and Solberg restated the traditional interpretation, arguing that, even before the overthrow of the Radical government, the economic situation had deteriorated significantly and that the seriousness of the situation was already manifest to the economic and political elites.[113]

My own view was stated above. Regardless of the specific determinants of the coup as such, there was a causal connection between the Depression and the establishment of nondemocratic regimes *after* the coup. I think that the breakdown of democracy was not caused by the Depression itself, but by *its timing*. The crisis took place when the norms of liberal democracy were being institutionalized. Power had been transferred from the Conservatives to the Radicals, but the different social and political forces were just beginning to develop shared norms for their interaction. These groups granted legitimacy to the social order and to the political system, but it was still a pragmatic, tentative, contingent type of legitimacy. In such a situation, the Depression, which affected the basic interests of all the groups in the society, put an end to the process of democratization. Delegitimation did not begin at the bottom of the social structure, but at the top. Apprehensive about the effectiveness of democratic rules for the protection of its economic interests and its hegemony over other social forces, the agrarian upper class and its Conservative Party inaugurated a period of rule on the basis of force, fraud, and proscription.

112. Smith, "Breakdown of Democracy."
113. Rock, *Politics in Argentina*, chap. 11; and Carl E. Solberg, *Oil and Nationalism in Argentina* (1979), chap. 5. See also Carlos A. Mayo et al., *Diplomacia, política y petróleo en la Argentina* (1976).

### The Non-Democratic State

The coup of 1930 did not lead to a stable authoritarian regime, for the elite faction, which in Argentina's Orwellian political discourse is called "liberal," prevailed over the "nationalist" one, and proscriptive democracy was then inaugurated. The organizations and procedures established by the Constitution were reinstated, but the majority party, the Radicals, were excluded from elections. The means employed were not only the conventional one, electoral fraud, but also outright banning. Also, Communists and other leftists were repressed. In spite of this, the regime that existed until 1943 was a limited democracy, for there was a significant degree of pluralism and, in general, of political and ideological contestation.[114]

Given the contradiction between the ideal norms of democracy and the actual operation of the regime, political legitimacy floundered—this period is commonly called "the infamous decade"—but social legitimacy declined more slowly. In spite of the cumulative impacts of the political and economic crises and of the polarization in world politics, mass-based radicalism did not develop. The revolutionary Left remained small, but right-wing nationalism, a diffuse movement whose ideology combined traditionalist Catholic doctrines, authoritarianism, and fascist themes, developed significant followings within intellectual, military, and religious circles. Thus crystallized what can be called the antiliberal pole in Argentine politics, for the core of its ideology was the rejection of both economic and political liberalism. It would contribute, from the thirties onward, ideas, activists, and officials to exclusionary regimes and to Peronism.

The social order was still legitimate in the thirties because it could still borrow from the "capital of trust," to use Blondel's expression, accumulated over two generations of satisfactory performance.[115] And this capital was "well distributed," for it had

114. On this period, see Alberto Ciria, *Partidos y poder en la Argentina moderna (1930–1946)* (1964); the contributions to Mark Falcoff and Ronald H. Dolkart, eds., *Prologue to Perón: Argentina in Depression and War, 1930–1943* (1975); and Cantón et al., *Argentina*. See also Corradi, *Fitful Republic*, chaps. 3–4; Crawley, *A House Divided*, chap. 4; Merkx, "Political and Economic Change," chap. 7; and Rock, *Argentina 1516–1982*, chap. 6.

115. Jacques Blondel, *Comparing Political Systems* (1972), chap. 4. See also the discussion of legitimacy as capital in Waisman, *Modernization*, chap. 2.

reached precisely the potential mass base for radicalism: the immigrant working class. The Anarchist rhetoric of a large segment of the labor movement up to World War I reflected more the strains of the transition into the industrial world and of the assimilation into the new society than an articulate opposition to the social order. Such an opposition would have been surprising, given the intense social mobility that existed in the country.

However, social legitimacy would eventually be undermined by the commitment, in the thirties and forties, of a large proportion of the country's capital and labor to a noncompetitive form of manufacturing. Import substitution, which began in the thirties as a response to the Depression and became permanent in the forties as a consequence of extreme protectionism, in the course of time sapped legitimacy for two reasons. First, it generated two new classes whose interests were incompatible with the hegemony of the agrarian upper class. These classes were the new bourgeoisie, large but weak, and its workers, who, in the forties and fifties, would develop a powerful labor movement. These two classes were oriented to the internal market, but needed, as we saw above, the foreign exchange generated by agriculture. Second, the institutionalization of extreme protectionism contributed, in the long run, to the erosion of legitimacy among all social classes, because it eventually led to lower growth rates, and thus to a decrease in the level of perceived efficacy of the social and political order.

The thirties and early forties were also a period of intense social mobility. The new bourgeoisie was recruited from the middle and working classes and the new proletariat from the rural lower class. The secondary sector was thus fragmented along economic and cultural lines. Old and new bourgeoisie were mostly of immigrant origin, but the old segment included a larger proportion of older Argentines, controlled larger and more efficient firms, and was tied with the agrarian elite and foreign capital. In the working class, there was a cultural gulf between the older immigrant segment and the new creole one.[116] The essence of Peronism was pre-

116. See Miguel Murmis and Juan Carlos Portantiero, *Estudios sobre los orígenes del peronismo* (1971); Gino Germani, "El surgimiento del peronismo: El rol de los obreros y de los migrantes internos," and Tulio Halperín Donghi, "Algunas observaciones sobre Germani, el surgimiento del peronismo, y los migrantes internos," en Manuel Mora y Araujo and Ignacio Llorente, eds., *El voto peronista* (1980).

cisely the attempt and failure to incorporate these new social forces through a corporatist state.[117]

The military coup of 1943, out of which sprang Peronism, is in my view the watershed in Argentine economic and political development.[118] The regime that came to power in 1930 had modified the nature of the polity, and the economic policies followed by the agrarian elite after it had regained control of the state apparatus led to significant changes in the society. However, it was the authoritarian regime established in 1943 and its successor constitutional administration headed by Perón that reoriented the Argentine economy inward and the Argentine state downward, that is, in a corporatist direction. Unlike the changes that took place in the thirties, these shifts were irreversible: they transformed the social structure and the state, and altered the position of Argentina in the international system. I will argue in this book that it was as a consequence of this reorientation of economy and state that Argentina switched developmental tracks, and veered toward the modal Latin American pattern of evolution.

Labor was the core of the Peronist social base. This distinguishes Peronism from European fascism, whose social base was the petty bourgeoisie, and also from other Latin American popu-

117. For interpretations of Peronism, see two articles by Eldon Kenworthy: "The Function of the Little-known Case in Theory Formation, or What Peronism Wasn't," *Comparative Politics* (1973), and "Interpretaciones ortodoxas y revisionistas del apoyo inicial del peronismo," in Mora y Araujo and Llorente, eds., *El voto peronista*. Corporatism is used here in the sense of Schmitter's state corporatism and Stepan's inclusionary corporatism. See Phillippe C. Schmitter, "Still the Century of Corporatism?" in Frederick B. Pike and Thomas Stritch, eds., *The New Corporatism* (1974); and Alfred Stepan, *The State and Society: Peru in Comparative Perspective* (1978), chap. 3. On the meanings of corporatism, see David and Ruth B. Collier, "Who Does What, To Whom, and How: Toward a Comparative Analysis of Latin American Corporatism," in James M. Malloy, ed., *Authoritarianism and Corporatism in Latin America* (1977).

118. For analyses of this regime, see Ciria, *Partidos y poder;* Enrique Díaz Araujo, *La conspiración del 43* (1971); Ruth and Leonard Greenup, *Revolution before Breakfast (Argentina, 1941–1946)* (1947); Gontrán de Güemes, *Así se gestó la dictadura: El G.O.U.* (1956); Ray Josephs, *Argentine Diary: The Inside Story of the Coming of Fascism* (1944); Robert A. Potash, *The Army and Politics in Argentina, 1928–1945: Yrigoyen to Perón* (1969); Alain Rouquié, *Pouvoir militaire et société politique en République Argentine* (1978); and the general discussions in Corradi, *Fitful Republic*, chaps. 3–4; Crawley, *A House Divided*, chaps. 4–5; Tulio Halperín Donghi, *Argentina: La democracia de masas* (1972), chaps. 1–2; and Rock, *Argentina 1516–1982*, chap. 4.

list movements, whose working-class component was less central.[119]

As for the institutional features of the Peronist constitutional administrations of 1946–55, they were closer to those of the high-participation democratic model than in any government Argentina had had since the collapse of the liberal state in 1930. Elections were held regularly, and the opposition was tolerated. Transgressions against pluralism, however, were very important. Opposition leaders and activists were often persecuted, and freedom of the press was systematically curtailed. The police state instruments, which had developed earlier (control of political activity by the police, almost unlimited power to search and detain, the use of torture) were institutionalized.

Cleavage lines under Peronism were clear. In its inception, the regime was an alliance among labor, the new industrial bourgeoisie, and a sector of the state (the military, the church). Against the regime were most of the agrarian upper class and the "older" bourgeoisie and considerable segments of the middle classes, together with liberal and leftist parties and organizations.

The economic policies of the regime corresponded to this cleavage. Perón transferred surplus from agriculture to manufacturing through the nationalization of exports and the control of domestic terms of trade. He also nationalized railroads and utilities and further improved the standard of living of the working class through protective legislation and large wage increases. Agriculture was reoriented toward the domestic market, and noncompetitive manufacturing was not only preserved but expanded. The regime's central goal was employment; thus the long-term viability of industries geared toward captive markets and kept alive by impregnable tariff barriers was not a consideration.[120] However, these

119. For discussions of the Peronist regime, see George I. Blanksten, *Perón's Argentina* (1953); Antonio Cafiero, *Cinco años después* (1961); Alberto Ciria, *Perón y el justicialismo* (1972); Carlos S. Fayt, ed., *La naturaleza del Peronismo* (1967); Félix Luna, *Perón y su tiempo*, vol. 1, *La Argentina era una fiesta, 1946–1949* (1984); Pierre Lux-Wurm, *Le peronisme* (1965); Frederick C. Turner and José E. Miguens, eds., *Juan Perón and the Reshaping of Argentina* (1983); and Peter Waldmann, *El peronismo, 1943–1955* (1981). For general overviews of the period, see Corradi, *Fitful Republic*, chap. 6; Crawley, *A House Divided*, chaps. 6–9; Halperín Donghi, *Argentina*, chap. 3; Merkx, "Political and Economic Change," chap. 8; and Rock, *Argentina 1516–1982*, chap. 7.

120. On Perón's economic policies, see Díaz Alejandro, *Essays*, chap. 2; Ferrer, *La economía*, chaps. 15–17, and *Crisis y alternativas de la política económica argentina* (1980); Mallon and Sorrouille, *Economic*

policies had limits. There were no significant expropriations of land or industrial capital, and Perón shifted to a more moderate course when it became evident, after a few years, that his antiagrarian policies were leading to a reduction of output and exports.

The Peronist regime shows what I called elsewhere the intrinsic weakness of corporatism.[121] It can be more properly considered its contradiction. In order to control the new industrial bourgeoisie and the working class, Perón had to organize these classes—with the corporatist's expectation, of course, that the new organizations would be the transmission belt for state power. But such a plan, to be workable, would have required continuous redistribution, that is, the steady transfer of surplus to these growing urban sectors. When stagnating tendencies appeared, toward the end of the forties, transmission belts à la Lenin became organizational weapons à la Selznick. The conflict between the powerful labor movement and the weak bourgeoisie surfaced; the segment of the latter supporting the regime distanced itself and finally left the coalition. Workers accepted corporatist controls for as long as their welfare improved, but they became an autonomous political force when their standard of living stagnated or began deteriorating. Thus, following the failure of the corporatist attempt, labor became a much stronger power contender than it would have been without state-controlled organization. The corporatist weapon backfired. From then on the unbound proletarian ghost haunted Argentine elites, and their attempts to banish or to harness it have ended in failure.

Conflict in post-Peronist Argentina has largely been a contest for the distribution of the surplus, the main players being labor, industrialists, agrarians, and the armed forces. The latter usually acted as the political party for other social groups, the propertied classes in particular. Guillermo O'Donnell, Lars Schoultz, and Gary Wynia have described this game very well.[122] In the Argen-

---

*Policymaking,* chap. 1; Peralta Ramos, *Acumulación,* pp. 79–101; and Gary W. Wynia, *Argentina in the Post-War Era: Politics and Economic Policymaking in a Divided Society* (1978), chap. 3.

121. Waisman, *Modernization,* pp. 22–23, 65–66.

122. Guillermo A. O'Donnell, *Modernization and Bureaucratic Authoritarianism: Studies in South American Politics* (1973), and "Permanent Crisis and the Failure to Create a Democratic Regime: Argentina, 1955–66," in Juan J. Linz and Alfred Stepan, eds., *The Breakdown of Democratic Regimes: Latin America* (1978); Lars Schoultz, *The Populist Challenge: Argentine Electoral Behavior in the Postwar Era* (1983); and Wynia, *Argentina.* See also Oscar Braun, *Desarrollo del capital monopolista en la Argentina* (1970); Adolfo

tine structural context, no social force could replace the agrarian upper class as the hegemonic group. From the fall of Peronism in 1955 to the reestablishment of democracy in 1983, the country was under exclusionary regimes, except for the Peronist swan song in the mid-seventies. For most of the period, these regimes were military dictatorships of the type that O'Donnell calls bureaucratic-authoritarian.[123]

The coup that overthrew Perón was an attempt to restore the power of the agrarians, but the structural changes that had taken place in the forties and fifties rendered a project of this sort unworkable. From 1958 to 1966, weak regimes of limited democracy tried vainly to govern in the face of continous threats of military intervention and on the basis of the exclusion of the largest party, the Peronists. From 1966 to 1973, and from 1976 to 1983, military regimes, the second of which was highly coercive for Argentine and Latin American standards, eventually triggered the active resistance of the middle and lower classes. Naive and unsophisticated military rulers found that, contrary to their expectations, the forcible suppression of dissent, rather than facilitating effective government, led to the erosion of whatever passive acceptance their administrations had had in the beginning. The brief Peronist interlude of 1973–76 collapsed, for the old corporatist design was of no use with autonomous working class and industrial bourgeoisie and without a surplus available for redistribution.

Post-Peronist Argentina, with its strong interest groups contending for the surplus in an unstable and sluggish economy, is the perfect embodiment of Samuel Huntington's praetorian society.[124] All kinds of means have been used in this conflict, but the

---

Canitrot, "Teoría y práctica del liberalismo: Política anti-inflacionaria y apertura económica en la Argentina (1976–1981)," *Estudios CEDES* (1981); Marcelo Cavarozzi, *Autoritarismo y democracia (1955–1983)* (1983); Corradi, *Fitful Republic*, chaps. 6–10; Crawley, *A House Divided*, chaps. 10–23 and Epilogue; Liliana De Riz, *Retorno y derrumbe: El último gobierno peronista* (1981); Halperín Donghi, *Argentina*, chaps. 4–5; Merkx, "Political and Economic Change," chap. 9; Guillermo O'Donnell, *1966–1973: El estado burocrático autoritario* (1982); Peralta Ramos, *Acumulación*, pp. 102–440 ; Rubén M. Perina, *Onganía, Levingston, Lanusse: Los militares en la política argentina* (1983); Rock, *Argentina 1516–1982*, chap. 8; and Peter Snow, *Political Forces in Argentina* (1979).

123. O'Donnell, *Modernization*. See also the essays in David Collier, ed., *The New Authoritarianism in Latin America* (1979).

124. Huntington, *Political Order*.

lesson the military taught the other groups, that power grows out of the barrel of a gun, slowly percolated throughout the society, and mobilization gradually took on violent forms. Working class protest used conventional means—waves of strikes, seizure of plants, and others—but the mobilization of the middle class, especially of students and the intelligentsia, culminated during the seventies in urban terrorism and guerrilla warfare. This, in turn, triggered a much more violent and arbitrary repression carried out by the armed forces, another segment of the middle classes.

In 1983, as a consequence of the catastrophic failure of its foreign and domestic policies, the military regime established in 1976 collapsed, and transferred power to a civilian administration. Transitions like this had taken place before, but this time it was the first since 1930 that an elected government committed not only to majority rule but also to the toleration of dissent and the institutionalization of civil and political rights came to power. Whether the cycle of instability can be broken in a country with a stagnated economy, highly mobilized social forces, and a military and security apparatus still imperfectly controlled by the government is as yet an open question.

The period from 1930 to 1983 is, then, one of erosion of political and social legitimacy. I argued above that the initial breakdown of democracy was more a consequence of the lack of time for its institutionalization than of its inefficacy. But the subsequent decay of legitimacy was due to the perception, on the part of different social forces, that the organizations and procedures established by the liberal constitution were not the most effective mechanisms for the pursuit of their interests. And time without efficacy does not lead to institutionalization. Thus, post-Peronist Argentina became ungovernable, in spite of the authoritarian facade of its polity for most of the period. As this combination of disorder and dictatorship corresponds to the stereotype of the underdeveloped society, it is understandable that this kind of image appears to most Argentines as the adequate representation of their reality.

The political development of Argentina, thus, is a correlate of its economic evolution: expanding liberal democracy up to the Depression and prevalence of nondemocratic forms of state ever since. Before the Depression and the war, Argentine political evolution was closer to that of new countries than to the Latin American modal pattern. Today, there is no question that the country's polity belongs fully in the Latin American type.

Economy and polity interact, but the reciprocal effects, which before the turning point were favorable to both growth and democratization, now form a vicious circle that perpetuates economic sluggishness and political instability. A correlation of this sort is not yet an answer for the question I asked in the beginning, that is, why Argentina has failed to couple an industrial society with a stable liberal democratic polity. The materials discussed in this chapter, however, suggest a series of potential explanatory factors. I now turn to their analysis.

# 4 In Search of Argentina: The Adequacy of Various Factors for the Explanation of the Reversal

This chapter reviews different hypotheses in order to assess their applicability to the Argentine case. I examine the possible role of cultural, socioeconomic, and political factors as determinants of the reversal of development in the country. I consider the validity of bivariate relationships for the elucidation of a process that calls for a multivariate explanation, but this is the most systematic procedure that can be followed. Only by isolating each factor is it possible to assess its plausibility as a determinant and to hypothesize about its interrelationship with other factors.

This review substantiates the statement I made in Chapter 1; that is, the Argentine question cannot be easily accounted for by theories of democracy and dictatorship. Culture and dependency, apparently the most plausible causal factors, do not provide per se a satisfactory explanation for this reversal and similar results obtain by hypotheses based on characteristics of the social structure and the political system and on sociopolitical processes such as mobilization.

I conclude that the immediate causes of Argentina's failure to establish an industrial democracy are social and political. The reversal of Argentine development can be understood in terms of an institutionalization hypothesis: it was the effect of the transformations that took place in the social structure as a consequence of two policies followed during and after World War II. These policies were, in the economy, radical or absolute protectionism for import-substituting manufactures, and, in the polity, an inclusionary corporatist strategy toward the working class. They represented a shift from the previous pattern of limited or contingent protectionism and an exclusionary elite strategy. The shift took place after the military coup of 1943, and the process of institutionalization was completed during the subsequent Peronist administration.

### The Cultural Factor

Before analysis, culture appears to be a plausible explanation for the Argentine reversal. Cultural characteristics are the most obvious contrast between Argentina and the lands of recent settlement. In addition, there is a large body of literature, beginning at least with Tocqueville, which focuses on cultural factors as determinants of differences in levels or types of economic and political development.

I already stated my central objection to a cultural argument for the explanation of the Argentine case: since culture changes more slowly than other parts of a society, it is not likely to account for a rapid reversal of economic and political development. A cultural explanation for the Argentine pattern of evolution would have to contend with the fact that values that proved to be appropriate for economic and political development up to a certain point turned dysfunctional afterward. However, a more sophisticated cultural argument, which takes this objection into consideration, can still be formulated. It too seems implausible, as I will show.

Let us begin with the evaluation of the most familiar type of cultural argument. As we saw, Tocqueville explained the institutional contrasts between the United States and the former Spanish colonies on the basis of the cultural differences between the two types of society. However, it is Weber's and Troeltsch's classical analyses of Catholicism that have inspired, in many cases through the Parsonian rendering, the standard culturalist interpretation of "Latin" (American and European) economic and political backwardness. This interpretation became established in the sixties, and it still underlies, usually as a latent assumption, most non-Marxist contemporary research on development.

Talcott Parsons, in *The Social System*, used Spanish American society as an example of his "particularistic-ascriptive" pattern. (His source for that attribution seems to have been Florence Kluckhohn's early research.) He described that culture as inconsistent with performance and instrumental orientations, a point developed later by David McClelland. He also depicted Spanish American society as hospitable to the establishment of authority, and hence susceptible to dictatorial government.[1] John Gillin's description of the values held by the "Latin American middle segments" is a typical reverberation of a theory of this type. In a series of sweeping generalizations, he lists values such as personalism, familism, hierarchy, materialism of a "tangible" type, fatalism, and so on.[2] These are orientations hardly compatible with those of the ideal-typical participant in a liberal polity or a capitalist economy.

Culturalist explanations of Latin American economic underdevelopment are commonplace—see for instance McClelland's argument about the weakness of achievement orientations in Latin American culture,[3] or Karl Deutsch's characterization of the "Hispanic-Muslim complex" as the embodiment of the counterindustrial tradition.[4] Another popular theme is the alleged incongruity between Catholic-Hispanic culture and the institutions of liberal democracy. What Alfred Stepan characterizes as the "organic-statist" conception of the state,[5] which developed in Counter-Reformation Spain and still percolates in much of contemporary Catholic social thought, has been held responsible by many authors for the antiliberal nature of Latin American political institutions. Thus, Richard Morse argues that the Thomist-Suarezian conception of society, whose central principles are organicism and patriarchalism, corresponds best to the patrimonial state. This congruity would explain the gravitation of Latin American politics toward that ideal form.[6] And Howard Wiarda explains the Latin American propensity to corporatism by a transfer from Iberian culture. This "distinct tradition," which has maintained its central principles since the conquest, would constitute a specific path

1. Talcott Parsons, *The Social System* (1964), pp. 198–99.

2. John P. Gillin, "The Middle Segments and Their Values," in Robert D. Tomasek, ed., *Latin American Politics*, (1966), pp. 23–40; Gillin, "Ethos Components in Modern Latin American Culture," in Dwight B. Heath and Richard N. Adams, eds, *Contemporary Cultures and Societies of Latin America* (1965), pp. 503–17.

3. See his analysis of Brazilian and Mexican data, in David C. McClelland, *The Achieving Society* (1967), pp. 217–21, 226–28, 241–45, 287–89, 406–11.

4. Karl W. Deutsch, "Imperialism and Neocolonialism," *Papers of the Peace Science Society (International)* (1974).

5. Stepan, *State and Society*, chap. 1.

6. Richard M. Morse, "The Heritage of Latin America," in Louis Hartz, ed., *The Founding of New Societies*, (1964).

of political evolution that he terms "a fourth world of development."[7]

Echoes of this line of argument are found in the literature on Argentina. Tomás Fillol's work is a radical example. He contends that cultural factors are the critical barrier to Argentine economic development. He describes the Argentine "national character" in terms of Kluckhohn's conceptual scheme. Among the orientations inhibiting capitalism, he lists a conception of human nature that he defines as being composed of good and bad, subjugated to external nature, directed toward present time, and concerned more with "being" than "doing" or "accomplishing." Also, "need aggression" and "need dependency," which are conducive to unruly behavior and to submission to strong authority, would be widespread in the "need structure" of the Argentine population.[8] More limited cultural arguments are common. For instance, Guido Di Tella, in trying to understand the differences between Argentine and Australian development, points to the Mediterranean cultural base. If both Spain and Italy, Argentina's "original fatherlands," have fared poorly as industrial economies, he argues, there are no reasons to expect their South Atlantic offshoot to do better.[9]

A detailed evaluation of these arguments is not necessary for my analysis, for I have pointed out already the basic problem with a strict culturalist hypothesis: its lack of fit with a curvilinear pattern of economic and political development, such as that of Argentina. One can speculate sensibly about the incompatibility between Hispanic values and capitalism or liberal democracy, but

7. Howard J. Wiarda, "Social Change, Political Development, and the Latin American Tradition," in idem, ed., *Politics and Social Change in Latin America: The Distinct Tradition*, (1974), pp. 3–22; "Social Change and Political Development in Latin America: Summary, Implications, Frontiers," ibid., pp. 269–92; "Towards a Framework for the Study of Political Change in the Iberic-Latin Tradition: The Corporative Model," *World Politics* (1973); and "Corporatism and Development in the Iberic-Latin World: Persistent Strains and New Variations," in Pike and Stritch, eds., *New Corporatism*, pp. 3–33. See also his other essays on the subject in his *Corporatism and National Development in Latin America* (1981).

8. Tomás R. Fillol, *Social Factors in Economic Development: The Argentine Case* (1961), pp. 5–26.

9. Guido Di Tella, "Controversias económicas en la Argentina, 1930–1970," in Fogarty et al., eds., *Argentina y Australia*.

such interpretation is still inconsistent with the Argentine pre-Depression record.

I said above that a more elaborate hypothesis, which makes allowance for this fact, can be advanced. The foregoing argument assumes that "values" are relatively stable and congruent with the institutional arrangements which, to a large extent, manifest them. But it is possible to think that rapid environmental changes may cause this congruity to decline—perhaps as a short-term maladjustment only—so that the efficacy of these "values" to reconcile generalized standards of evaluation with adaptive exigencies may decline. Thus, the Latin-Catholic-Hispanic value complex could have been consistent with economic growth and an expanding liberal democracy up to a certain point (the Depression? large-scale industrialization? the incorporation of the working class into the political system?) and have become incompatible afterward.

Hypotheses of this sort are frequent in the literature. For instance, Seweryn Bialer explains the Soviet economic slowdown in the seventies by the fact that the preexisting ideological framework and its corresponding institutions were only conducive to an extensive type of growth, one based on the mobilization of additional productive factors. Once all the available land, labor, and capital have been committed, further growth can only be of an intensive nature, that is, growth based on the increased efficiency of the already mobilized factors. He contends that Soviet ideological frameworks and institutional arrangements are inadequate to lead such a shift.[10] In relation to Argentina, an argument of this type was suggested by Carter Goodrich: ". . . attainment of wealth and eminence as a pastoral economy required less modification of the older Spanish traditions than does the creation of a fully industrial society . . . ; the more complex demands of a diversified manufacturing economy appear to call for much greater institutional adjustments. . . ."[11] The proposition focuses on economic outcomes—presumably, political dislocation would also follow from the economic breakdown—and on elites as the strategic actors. This is a familiar theme. The "aristocratic motivations" of the traditional economic elite have been emphasized by Jacques Lambert with reference to Latin America in general, and by Felix Weil in

10. Seweryn Bialer, "The Harsh Decade: Soviet Policies in the 1980s," *Foreign Affairs* (1981).

11. Carter Goodrich, "Argentina as a New Country."

relation to Argentina.[12] And several authors have pointed out the differences between the Latin American industrial bourgeoisies and the ideal-typical capitalist class.[13]

A priori, the hypothesis makes sense. It can be argued that the export-led type of growth, which prevailed until the Depression, was "easy" for the Argentine upper class, and that it did not require a break with its allegedly traditional values. Pampean land assured a differential rent; agriculture and livestock production required little technology; the immigrants furnished ample and willing labor; Britain and other European trade partners provided secure markets and contributed capital and technical skills for the development of railroads, sea transportation, and grain-trading firms; the government guaranteed law and order, protective legislation, and financing through the National Bank, and so on. Manufacturing, on the other hand, requires a cultural revolution. It calls for considerable managerial skills, for a complex and changing technology, for coming to terms with an assertive labor force, and, if industry is going to lead the growth of the whole economy in a sustained manner, for conquering foreign markets in competition with producers in relation to whom Argentine capitalists are at a comparative disadvantage. The fraility of Argentine hothouse manufacturing, with its difficulty in transcending the level of the family firm producing with antiquated technology, and with its inability to exist without formidable tariff barriers and to penetrate foreign markets, seems to confirm a hypothesis of this type.

The obvious shortcoming of a "Hispanic" argument like this for the Argentine case is that it does not take into account the major difference between Argentina and the standard "Hispanic" countries: the immigrant origin of the majority of the population, to-

12. See Jacques Lambert, *Latin America: Social Structures and Political Institutions* (1974), pp. 98–102; and Weil, *Argentine Riddle*, chap. 3.

13. See, inter alia, Stanley M. Davis, "United States vs. Latin America: Business and Culture," in idem and Louis W. Goodman, eds., *Workers and Managers in Latin America* (1972); Filloll, *Social Factors;* Gillin, "The Middle Segments"; Seymour M. Lipset, "Values, Education, and Entrepreneurship," in idem and Aldo Solari, eds., *Elites in Latin America* (1967); W. Paul Strassmann, "The Industrialist," in John J. Johnson, ed., *Continuity and Change in Latin America,* (1964); Rock, *Argentina 1516–1982;* Véliz, *Centralist Tradition,* chap. 12. For more structural analyses, see Fernando H. Cardoso, *Ideologías de la burguesía industrial en sociedades dependientes (Argentina y Brasil)* (1971); and José Luis. de Imaz, *Los que mandan (Those Who Rule)* (1970), chaps. 7–8.

gether with the fact that most immigrants were of non-Hispanic origin. However, it is still possible to circumvent this issue, by giving the hypothesis a Harzian twist.[14] Since most immigrants came from peasant, that is, traditional Catholic-Latin backgrounds, Italy and Spain would have transferred a portion of what Louis Hartz calls their feudal or backward "fragment" to Argentina. Once there and in interaction with the equally backward native population, which was itself a traditional fragment of imperial Spain, their presence would have reinforced the antimodern tendencies and contributed to blocking the transition to an industrial democracy. The mix would not have contained the stimulus for cultural evolution, for the "feudal fragment," when detached from its original whole, lapses into immobility, as Hartz puts it. An interpretation of this sort has not been specifically advanced for Argentina, as far as I know, but it is a logical addendum to the modified cultural argument for the case of a "new country."

I remain skeptical for a variety of reasons. The first one is that most types of manufacturing in which Argentine industrial capitalists are involved are not much more complex, in terms of the entrepreneurial skills required, than the modern large-scale temperate agriculture that the "oligarchy" and tenant farmers operated prior to the reversal. Organizational and technological characteristics of the productive units may be different, but I do not think there is a qualitative difference in terms of complexity. Moreover, some of the factors that facilitated agricultural success are available, in an equivalent form, to the industrialists: a secure demand (in this case, the captive home market), the option to specialize in activities based completely on domestic inputs; to obtain needed capital, technology, managerial skills and even, under certain conditions, access to foreign markets, through the association with foreign capitalists; the availability of favorable economic policies and, in general, governmental support; and even the ability to contract out cumbersome or less profitable activities, through vertical integration with a "lumpen-capitalist" sector.

Secondly, neither the economic behavior of the agrarian upper class nor that of the industrial bourgeoisie, including its segment developed after the Depression, have expressed "traditional" or

14. Louis Hartz, "A Theory of the Development of the New Societies," in idem, ed., *The Founding of New Societies.*

otherwise anticapitalist attitudes. There is no trace in their mentality of what the propounders of a culturalist argument call "traditional Spanish values."

It is true that the core stratum of the agrarian elite has considered itself an aristocracy, affected a noble lifestyle, established paternalistic relationships with their employees, and so on. But this does not imply that the *economic* behavior of that upper class was controlled by precapitalist values. The agrarian elite is a gentrified bourgeoisie, like any other old bourgeoisie, agrarian or industrial, especially after "newer wealth" comes to the fore. Its members may have lived in palaces and regarded nonlanded types of business with disdain, but their mentality was modestly Weberian. In order to maximize their profits, they were ready to vary the size of their output, or to shift from commodity to commodity, in response to market signals. They also introduced technological innovations, especially in livestock raising. And their preference for tenancy contracts in agriculture reflected rational, maximizing behavior, given their monopoly of land and the availability of immigrant labor.

The economic behavior of the Argentine industrial bourgeoisie (incidentally, the least "Hispanic" social class in terms of ethnicity) since Peronism can best be understood as a rational adjustment to the economic environment in which this class operates. Attachment to the domestic market, reluctance to introduce the most modern technology, and resistance to expand in order to integrate production or to take advantage of economies of scale are instances of profit-maximizing behavior in a context characterized by the presence of a captive market, hyperinflation coupled with a very unstable economic policy, and the existence of domestic opportunities for diversification. The central trait of the Weberian ideal-type capitalist behavior is the orientation toward the maximization of profits through production. Neither risk taking nor the introduction of technological innovations are intrinsic components of capitalist rationality: these are courses of action capitalists are forced to follow, because of environmental constraints, in order to protect their assets or maximize profits.

Wherever there is blanket protection, as in Argentina, rational capitalist behavior will be oriented to the expansion of the output until the market is saturated. After this point has been reached, domestic diversification in the protected ground is likely to be preferred to the riskier expansion into foreign markets. Further, monetary and exchange policies fluctuate so quickly in an unstable polity such as Argentina's that committing a large amount of resources to the importation of expensive technology or to production for export is not rational. This behavior is not specific to domestic capitalists: multinationals operating in the Argentine environment adapt to it as well.

Third, if the economic behavior of the ruling classes, both agrarian and industrial, fits the model of capitalist rationality, their political behavior, as well as that of labor, has been equally "modern": they have pursued eminently instrumental goals, such as wealth and power.

This is clear in the record since the Depression. As we will see, the policies leading to the commitment of a large proportion of the country's resources to a noncompetitive form of manufacturing after World War II were the outcome of a political process in which the different social classes contended for the surplus and the maintenance or improvement of their power positions. Since Peronism presided over this transformation, and its ideology was corporatist, the issue of the relative weight of traditional values in the support for Peronism can be raised. This will be examined further, but it is important to note, in connection with this discussion of culturalist arguments, that support for corporatism among labor and the new bourgeoisie created by import substitution was pragmatic and contingent. They supported it because it suited their economic and political interests better than liberalism, which was dominant among the agrarian elite and the middle classes subordinate to the export-led framework of development. And the groups supporting Peronism were not bound to it by traditional forms of legitimacy; support was contingent upon performance, in terms of the protection or advancement of group interests.

Likewise, the spread of corporatism in a segment of the intellectual and state elites was less the result of a cultural continuity with colonial thought than of the very modern process of empathy. The dominance of positivism and liberalism, since the large-scale incorporation of the country into the world economy and the population transplant, had weakened, at least in the core area where three-fourths of the population was concentrated, the linkages with traditional ideologies. Antiliberal orientations, which reflected Catholic-corporatist doctrines, were a secondary strand in Argentine culture prior to the reversal. Both the nativists, fearful of mass immigration, and the nationalists, resentful of the country's dependent status, could delve into that ideological repository in their search for a language in which their anxiety and frustration could be articulated. The existence of these ideas contributed to the development of nationalism and of Peronism, but the development of corporatism owed more, I will argue, to demonstration effects: the apparent success of fascist and authoritarian regimes in controlling social conflict. Thus, the emergence of antiliberal trends after the Depression was not the actualization of latent contents in the country's culture or the resurgence, after a liberal-positivist interlude, of the authentic ethos of that culture. Rather, it was the product of an ideological re-orientation by segments of the elites as a consequence of the Depression and the ensuing breakdown of the international economic and political order.

Fourth, European immigration to Argentina was not the displacement of a "feudal fragment." At least a large minority originated in the areas that were currently or would soon become the cores of industrial development in their countries, and the majority did not belong to the backward regions of Spain and Italy. Most Spanish immigrants were from Galicia and other depressed areas, but a sizable minority came from Catalonia and the Basque country, that is, the North, in the geographic and economic senses.[15] About half of the immigrants were Italian, and about half of them were from the advanced North. For instance, from 1876 to 1914, 46 percent of the Italian immigrants originated from the Piedmont, Liguria, Lombardy, Venice, Emilia and Tuscany.[16] (This contrasts with the Italian immigration to the United States, which was mostly from the South.)[17] The remaining immigrants were mostly from other European areas (the largest contingents were French, German, and east European Jewish); thus they had not been socialized into the type of values to which the "Hispanic" and the other culturalist hypotheses specifically refer. The net result is that a large proportion of the immigrants (probably the ma-

15. See data from Dirección General del Instituto Geográfico y Estadístico, *Estadística de la emigración e inmigración de España, 1882–1890* (1891); and *1891–1895* (1898), supplied in Vázquez Presedo, *El caso argentino*, p. 106.

16. Based on data from Commissariato Generale dell' Emigrazione, *Annuario Statistico della Emigrazione Italiana 1876 al 1925* (1926), supplied in Vázquez Presedo, *El caso argentino*, p. 98. See also Herbert S. Klein, "La inmigración italiana a la Argentina y a los E.E.U.U." *Desarrollo económico* (1981).

17. See Scobie, *Revolution on the Pampas*, pp. 29–30; and Vázquez Presedo, *El caso argentino*, pp. 100–101.

jority) did not originate in the depressed peripheries of Spain and Italy. Many of them had very traditional backgrounds, but I do not think it would be appropriate to characterize globally these immigrants as a "feudal fragment."

In addition to the difficulty in explaining a curvilinear pattern of economic and political development, there are other, more general reasons for the inadequacy of the culturalist interpretation of "Latin," Spanish, Latin American, or Argentine evolution.

First, this conventional interpretation is often based on a neo-Platonic conception of values, which has not been a very productive tool for the understanding of social processes. Rather than considering values as a dynamic product of the collective experience of the individuals who are their carriers, this conception defines values as reified abstractions, which are assumed to be relatively constant entities (the use of the genetic code as a metaphor by Parsons is revealing in this regard). They are assumed to be separate from the empirical social world and yet connected with it through the process of institutionalization (in fact, a process of reflection, in which social structures are treated as the manifestation of underlying values).

Second, this line of reasoning is questionable from a methodological point of view. Most authors discussed above attribute values to populations on the basis of one or more of the following operations: impressionistic observation, generalization from observation at the microscopic level, and the risky assumption that the systematic doctrines that underlie religious, economic, or political institutions do reflect or correspond to the values actually held by the population participating in these institutions. The second of these shortcomings is especially serious in relation to a structurally complex and culturally heterogeneous society such as Argentina. The assumption that cultural traits are uniformly distributed in a population of this type is untenable.

Third, the organicist-corporatist strand, clearly an obstacle to liberalism and modern culture, is a central component of Hispanic-Catholic social and political thought, but it was not the dominant one at all times and in all places. This point is made by Stepan, who is skeptical of the explanation of Latin American corporatism on the basis of cultural continuity.[18] The Spanish political tradition included also liberal and radical components. More-

18. Stepan, *State and Society*, pp. 52–53.

over, Latin American culture was influenced by continental philosophical and political doctrines, and in many of these societies, Argentina included, positivism, liberalism, and varieties of socialism became more important than the Thomist or Suarezian tenets. In any case, the hegemonic intellectual and political elites, prior to the reversal, looked down upon Spanish cultural influences and were oriented toward French and other European trends. In addition, it is not obvious that the cultural continuity argument can be applied in a straight manner to Argentina, whose society and culture are less "Hispanic" than those of other countries in the region.

Fourth, the interpretations discussed above overlook the complexity of the Catholic heritage, at least as far as political effects are concerned. Certainly, those Latin-Catholic societies that reached substantial levels of industrialization and urbanization have been prone to authoritarian and corporatist regimes, but most of them also developed a substantial revolutionary political strand (Anarchism and later Communism). I noted elsewhere that most mass Communist parties in the West have arisen in Latin-Catholic countries (Mediterranean Europe and the Southern Cone).[19] It can be argued that this radicalism developed as a secular response to traditional authoritarianism, but left-wing strands of Catholicism (theology of liberation and the like) also developed and spread primarily in Latin-Catholic countries.

Fifth, there is substantial evidence disconfirming the proposition that establishes a negative correlation between Latin culture and liberal democracy. Relatively stable, mass democratic institutions existed for long periods in Italy, Chile, Venezuela, and Costa Rica, and the postauthoritarian regimes in Spain and Portugal seem to be secure. As far as Argentina is concerned, we have already seen that it had an expanding liberal democracy during the process of industrialization and urbanization. France, if included in the "Latin" category would, of course, provide another negative case. (The status of this country in relation to these culturalist arguments is, by the way, unclear. Parsons, for one, excluded it from the Latin-Catholic type, with the justification that France "almost went reformed.") The exclusion of France makes sense, but it implies that the meaning of "Latin-Catholic" has to be specified further; it does not refer to a type of culture in general, but to the cul-

19. Waisman, *Modernization*, p. 41.

ture of a group of societies that followed a particular developmental path, characterized by the absence of the three great revolutions, religious, political, industrial, which transformed the European Northwest.[20]

Sixth, if this is the case, then it is not clear whether the independent variable in these arguments is culture as such or the structural background in which that culture evolved. In some of the works discussed above, the causal status of the "cultural" variables is questionable. Dialectics aside, it makes more sense to treat some of them as dependent variables, in relation to their structural context, than as independent ones. Are not a "tangible materialism"–for instance, the tendency to invest in real estate rather than in securities—or a "present-time orientation" the logical correlates of highly inflationary economies, or a hierarchical orientation and "need aggression" the cultural counterpart of dictatorial or polarized political institutions?

It should be clear that neither my objections to the culturalist argument, nor my rejection of its application to the specific question at issue, the Argentine reversal, imply a dismissal of the causal weight of preindustrial culture on the economy and politics of industrial societies, or a rejection of the proposition that the organicist corporatist tradition is a hindrance to democracy. My point here is that this tradition did not block dynamic capitalism and democratization prior to the reversal, and that it could not have caused the economic and political decline.

### Economic and Social Hypotheses

The Argentine reversal cannot be explained either by economic or sociopolitical hypotheses that are standard in the literature. The reversal was not directly caused by the country's location in the international economy, by its level of development or its preindustrial class structure, by an excess of political mobilization, or by deficiencies of representative mechanisms.

Arguments focusing on the economic or political consequences of Argentina's peripheral status in the world economy are commonplace, either in the form of the classical theory of imperialism

---

20. Talcott Parsons, *The Evolution of Societies* (1977), chaps. 7–8 (also, personal communication in the early seventies); Véliz, *Centralist Tradition*, pp. 3–5.

or in the more recent one of dependency theory. In a typical statement, Milcíades Peña discusses the "relationship between the imperialist metropoles and the ruling classes in a backward and semicolonial country such as Argentina," and concludes that "both have in common a fundamental economic interest consisting in maintaining . . . the structure of property relations that constitutes the source of their super-profits, that is, the combined type of development, the backwardness of the country."[21] Similarly, Jaime Fuchs asserts that "the landowning oligarchy as well as imperialist capital were interested in maintaining such backwardness, in order to avoid by all means capitalist development in the country, which could establish a domestic and independent foundation for the economic process."[22] He also states that economic backwardness and nondemocratic forms of government are the consequence of the "deformation" of capitalist development by the central presence of foreign capital and the survival of latifundia.[23]

These are versions of the primitive dependency argument, according to which an inexorable (and unexplained) logic in the world economy consigns peripheral countries to permanent backwardness and, in some renditions, also to military rule. Oscar Braun carried out a more complex analysis at the heyday of dependency theory. He argued that "the essential characteristic of dependency" is the fact that, "given capitalist relations of production and distribution, the global growth rate of the economy is limited by the rate of growth of available foreign exchange."[24] Since tariff barriers restrict the access of exports from dependent countries to imperialist markets, stagnation ensues. The "hegemony" of foreign capital is another consequence: the blockage of productive forces "facilitates the penetration of imperialist capital in dependent countries, for the latter are forced to receive it in order to compensate in part—and for a brief period—for their lack of

21. Milcíades Peña, *La clase dirigente argentina frente al imperialismo* (1973), p. 7.

22. Fuchs, *Argentina: Su desarrollo*, p. 524.

23. Jaime Fuchs, *Argentina: Actual estructura económico-social* (1981), pp. 297–305.

24. Oscar Braun, *Desarrollo*, p. 15. See also idem and Leonard Joy, "A Model of Economic Stagnation: A Case Study of the Argentine Economy," *Economic Journal* (1968).

foreign exchange."[25] At least in the case of Argentina in the sixties, repression was another result of dependency: this hegemony (a term he used in the sense of "preponderance") was coercively implemented by an authoritarian regime whose main base was a coalition of monopoly capital and the military.[26]

The arguments advanced by these authors do not explain the Argentine reversal (although Braun's description of basic aspects of the economic and social structure *after* the reversal is accurate). The country's failure to become an industrial democracy cannot be attributed, in a direct causal link, to its location in the international economy, for societies similarly placed in the beginning of the century, the lands of recent settlement, have had different types of economic and political evolution. And the Argentine reversal cannot be a direct effect of the degree of dependency, for we have seen that both trade and capital dependency decreased at the time the country switched developmental tracks. Further, it would be unwarranted to claim that the reversal of economic or political development in Argentina was a long-term consequence of dependency *as such*. Argentine development was externally induced and dependent throughout, but no evidence supports the proposition that an evolution of this type is inherently self-limiting (a statement that would make sense, however, in relation to the consequences of autarkic industrialization, which leads in the long run to the massive misallocation of resources and thus to low growth rates).

For it was autarkic industrial policy, rather than dependency, that led to the stagnation of Argentina. The argument that imperialism necessarily produces backwardness is not tenable. Tony Smith's strong denunciation of this simplistic dependency proposition is justified.[27] The proposition is even less plausible when it refers to manufacturing. Peter Evans, a sophisticated dependentist, has shown, for the case of Brazil, how a constellation of structural constraints may impel sustained growth of the manufacturing sector under the aegis of a coalition involving the domestic bourgeoisie, foreign capital, and the state.[28] Dependent de-

25. Braun, *Desarrollo*, p. 19.

26. Ibid., p. 25.

27. Smith, *Pattern of Imperialism*, p. 50.

28. Peter B. Evans, *Dependent Development: The Alliance of Multinational, State, and Local Capital in Brazil* (1979).

velopment is, of course, less desirable from the point of view of national autonomy than development largely controlled by domestic actors, but the point is that the dependent status of the manufacturing sector is not in itself a barrier to growth. Moreover, growth may lead to a strengthening of domestic actors vis-à-vis foreign capital, and thus to a reduction of the level of dependency. Finally, Braun's assertion about the existence of severe restrictions to the access of peripheral exports into central markets is correct basically in relation to commodities that displace inefficient central producers with some political clout. As a generalization, the statement does not hold, as the experience of the new industrial countries of southeast Asia shows.

In the Argentine experience, the correlation between dependency and economic and political development was, as I showed, positive. The linkage with Britain and other consumers of temperate agricultural products allowed the country to develop and, to some extent, diversify its economy and generate the surplus that made possible the growth of liberal institutions. Furthermore, the most important means of production were controlled by the domestic upper class. It was a development tied into dependency networks, and a democracy under the hegemony of an agrarian elite reluctant to share power, but the evolution of other lands of recent settlement indicates that diversification, in the evolutionary path of the staples model, *can* lead to economies with export-oriented agricultural and manufacturing sectors, and to polities in which liberal democracy is institutionalized. Argentina's failure to develop along these lines cannot be the consequence, therefore, of the country's peripheral or dependent status.

The Argentine case is not encompassed either by explanations in terms of the level of social and political development or of characteristics of the preindustrial social structure. This is clear in relation to the level of development as such. Argentina stands out as a deviant case with respect to Seymour Martin Lipset's propositions linking democratic institutions to aspects of modernization, such as the per capita product, and to levels of industrialization, education, and urbanization.[29] Also in this connection, O'Donnell's hypothesis about the affinity, in South America, between "high" modernization and bureaucratic authoritarianism is not

29. Lipset, *Political Man*, chap. 2.

relevant for the explanation of the reversal, but it is plausible for the understanding of its aftermath. O'Donnell's proposition does not postulate that there is such a thing as a necessary relationship between development and authoritarianism, that is, that military regimes are caused by the level of development *as such*. Rather, they are the consequence of development *as it has taken place* in these countries (Argentina and Brazil in the sixties are his primary referent). He argues that industrialization has led to low growth rates on the one hand and to the activation of the popular sector on the other, so that mass praetorianism results. In turn, mass praetorianism triggers authoritarian regimes, by which bourgeois-military-technocratic coalitions endeavor to disactivate the popular sector and to "deepen" import substitution.[30] The proposition, then, refers to the period *after* the Argentine reversal, and it assumes import-substituting industrialization as a precondition. In the Argentine case, mass praetorianism, and hence the affinity for bureaucratic authoritarian regimes, was the result of the turn of the economy inward and of the state downward, both in the forties; but neither autarkic industrialization nor state corporatism, I will argue, were necessary traits of Argentine development.

A dualistic or "conservative modernization" hypothesis seems plausible, for Argentina is a late developer in which a powerful agrarian upper class was in control of the state when industrialization began. A strand of Marxist analysis and Barrington Moore's arguments focus on this factor.[31] Mainstream Argentine Marxists have traditionally classified the road of capitalist development in the country as "Prussian." Fuchs's work is again typical in this connection. He contends that the country's agrarian development is characterized by the interlacing between the capitalist system and semifeudal residuals. These residuals would be the large agrarian units ("latifundia") and tenant farming, which for him are not

30. O'Donnell, *Modernization*.

31. Engels, prefaces to *The Peasant War in Germany*, translated by M. J. Olguin, and *Germany: Revolution and Counter-revolution*, chaps. 1 and 2 and passim, in *German Revolutions*; idem, *The Role of Force in History*, chap. 7; Moore, *Social Origins*. The best discussion of the settlement of the agrarian question in the United States as a precondition for capitalist democracy is Moore, *Social Origins*, chap. 3. The solution of the agrarian question in Australia is discussed in Philip McMichael, *Settlers and the Agrarian Question: Foundations of Capitalism in Colonial Australia* (1984).

capitalist forms.[32] He describes the oligarchy as a "landowning bourgeoisie," which is in part a carrier of precapitalist relations.[33]

David Rock's argument is more elaborate. In his view, Argentina is, like Canada and Australia, and perhaps Ireland, South Korea, Singapore, or even Cuba, a "classical colony": throughout its history, the country was an importer of manufactures and capital, its economic growth stemmed from complementary relationships with other nations, its upper and middle classes resembled the collaborating and *comprador* types, its culture was imitative rather than innovative, and so on.[34] In some respects, this definition is stronger than the usual one of periphery (many "core" nations have high trade concentration rates and derivative cultures), and one could argue about the temporal range within which some of these criteria apply (for instance, Canada, South Korea, and Singapore are today manufacturing exporters rather than importers) and about the characterization of Argentine upper and middle classes (my impression is that they were much more autonomous and stronger than the terms "collaborating" and especially "*comprador*" connote); but I will focus on Rock's explanation of why Argentina evolved differently from Canada or Australia. A first reason is generic: complementary partnerships are a precondition for the progress of societies with these characteristics, and Argentina weakened, in the past decades, its economic links with Europe. But he refers to another cause, a more important one because it focuses specifically on the differences between Argentina and other lands of recent settlement; the contrasting social origins: "Spaniards established in the River Plate region a standard microcosm of their American imperial system . . . [whose] most basic principle was the exploitation of indigenous peoples by a white elite through tribute institutions. Remote as this early colonizing era is . . . it deserves closer attention as the origin of an enduring colonial tradition." The reason is that "tributary institutions prompted the emergence of a simple agropastoral economy but one inherently impeded from diversifying and developing."[35] In refuting the argument that the country's industrialization was ob-

32. Fuchs, *Argentina: Su desarrollo*, p. 523, and *Argentina: Actual estructura*, pp. 180–81.

33. Fuchs, *Argentina: Actual estructura*, p. 297.

34. Rock, *Argentina 1516–1982*, p. xxiv.

35. Ibid., p. xxv.

structed by the lack of raw materials, he compares Argentina with the (northern) United States: "Argentina's path was not determined by resources alone, but by the interaction of its resources and its early colonial institutions. Had those institutions been different, the resources would have been sufficient for the emergence of a small farmers' commonwealth."[36]

Finally, a conservative modernization hypothesis would also explain the nondemocratic political outcome. The survival of a landed upper class is expected to produce, in Moore's words, "modernization from above," which is conducive to authoritarian and fascist regimes.

Let us examine arguments of this type. I agree with Rock's contention that family farming would have allowed for a more egalitarian—and perhaps a more dynamic—pattern of economic and political development in the country, but it is not clear to me that the patterns of land tenure and social organization in the preindustrial period explain the reversal. The reason is that Argentina had no surviving precapitalist ruling class when industrialization began. As I noted above, the self-styled "aristocrats" were agrarian capitalist producers, and so were the tenant farmers. But even if the agrarian upper class was not "feudal," its existence could have still been incompatible with democracy. In this regard, the difference between causes and effects should be clear. The fact that, at the outset of the Depression, the agrarians turned away from democracy does not prove that there was an intrinsic incompatibility between a class of this type and industrial democracy. If this shift, as I concluded above, was a result of the combination of the economic crisis and the lack of institutionalization of liberal institutions because of their novelty, *any* ruling class, agrarian or industrial, typically capitalist or not, would have acted in the same manner.

Of course, it is impossible to prove that the economic and political reversal would not have taken place without the Depression or if liberal institutions were more established. But a hypothesis of this type is more consistent with the evidence than the one propounding an intrinsic incompatibility between the oligarchy and industrialization or democracy, for at least three reasons. First, the half-century prior to the Depression indicates that the existing economic and social organization was consistent with significant industrialization and with expanding liberal democracy. Second,

36. Ibid., p. 378.

as Miguel Murmis and Juan Carlos Portantiero, Carlos Díaz Alejandro, and others have shown,[37] the industrialization drive after the Depression was deliberately pursued by the Conservatives, rather than being an unintended consequence of other policies. And third, in the elections following the war, the majority of the Conservatives supported the anti-Peronist coalition, the goal of which was the reestablishment of liberal democracy and also, it makes sense to assume, a return to a more open industrialization. Of course, the agrarian upper class fostered a type of manufacturing consistent with its economic interests, and it supported liberal institutions as long as other classes and strata were willing to accept its hegemony, but this is, again, standard ruling class behavior, especially in a context of low political institutionalization. The important issue is that the Argentine oligarchs were not, like the German Junkers, the American slaveholders, or the Russian nobles, the carriers of relations of production whose preservation would be threatened by the development of capitalism in the economy and liberalism in the polity.

There is a point in Rock's analysis that can be set apart from the argument based on the survival of preindustrial groups and institutions: his contention that a cause of the Argentine decline was the fact that complementary partnerships are a precondition for the development of "classical colonies." If this means that it was the weakening of the country's integration into the international economy what led eventually to low growth rates and political instability, we are in full agreement. I would argue, though, that such consequences would obtain in any modern society. In any case, the inward turn of the Argentine economy is one of the keys to the explanation of the reversal. I will return to this issue.

Huntingtonian hypotheses have been formulated either in terms of excessive mobilization or of deficient institutionalization of participation.[38] Both factors lead to what Samuel Huntington calls praetorianism, but the causes are different in each case.

As far as mobilization is concerned, the sudden growth of the electorate after the reform of 1912 has been discussed often, but it is not obvious that this is a causal factor in the breakdown of liberal democracy. Atilio Borón has related political instability to the intensity of electoral mobilization, but Oscar Cornblitt has noted

37. Díaz Alejandro, *Essays*, chap. 2; and Murmis and Portantiero, *Estudios*, pp. 3–55.

38. See Huntington, *Political Order*, especially pp. 78–92, 192–98.

that, even if there was a sharp increase after the Reform, the electorate had been growing steadily since 1890.[39] However, the problem lies less in numbers than in the impact of mobilization. In my
opinion, an overloading hypothesis is not applicable because the
classes that mobilized prior to the reversal—the middle and working classes—made demands that were moderate in quantity and
quality, and were therefore absorbable in an expanding economy.
Labor demands were mainly economic (involving typical immediate goals), and those made by the middle class were mainly political (participation). Yet both could be met within the existing
social order. As I noted, neither class, with the exception of the
Anarchist fraction of the labor movement, challenged the hegemony of the agrarian elite. Working class demands did overload the
system only *after* the reversal, when Argentina had a highly organized labor movement in a context characterized by a sluggish
economy and the absence of a large labor reserve.

There are two types of argument based on the institutionalization of participation. The first, which I have discussed already, focuses on the degree of legitimacy of liberal democratic norms
among various groups. The different analyses are complementary:
neither the Conservative elite, as Robert Dahl noted, nor the opposition Radicals, as Peter Smith and Anne Potter remarked, had
developed a high level of support for competitive politics.[40] The
absence of a democratic culture would have rendered industrial
democracy unfeasible.

My conclusion above was that there was a process of institutionalization under way and that it was interrupted by the Depression. The stunted institutionalization of democracy, together
with the crisis, determined the coup of 1930, but it was not the
cause of the long-term reversal of economic and political development. I argued that beliefs are not inherent properties of social
groups. The process of legitimation was definitively interrupted
after the Depression and the war because the changes that took
place in the social structure, namely the large-scale development
of noncompetitive manufacturing and, its consequence, the commitment of a large proportion of the active population to that ac-

39. Atilio A. Borón, "El estudio de la movilización política en América
Latina: La movilización en la Argentina y Chile," *Desarrollo económico*
(1972); Oscar Cornblitt, "La opción conservadora en la política
argentina," *Desarrollo económico* (1975).

40. Dahl, *Polyarchy*; pp. 133–36; Smith, *Failure of Democracy*, chap. 6;
and "Breakdown of Democracy"; Potter, "Political Institutions."

tivity. These changes rendered unworkable the formula of liberal democracy under agrarian hegemony. It was the society that had changed, rather than the ideology of Conservatives or Radicals.

The new industrialists and the labor movement's relationship with the agrarian upper class was ambivalent. On the one hand, they needed it, for the imported machinery and intermediate inputs required by a noncompetitive consumer goods industry could only be purchased with the foreign exchange generated by agriculture. On the other hand, these urban classes could not become subordinate to the agrarians, for the reestablishment of oligarchic hegemony would lead to an abandonment of extreme protectionism and, hence, to the dismantling of much of the new industrial sector. Speculation about roads not taken is not very productive. There is, however, a safe hypothesis. If different economic policies had been pursued in the forties and the growth of non-competitive manufacturing had been arrested, there would have been no domestic structural barriers to the re-establishment of the model of economic and political development that existed prior to the Depression.

The second type of argument based on the institutionalization of participation deals with the party system. Torcuato Di Tella and Oscar Cornblitt have noted the peculiarity that postwar Argentina lacks a right-wing or conservative party with a mass base.[41] The interests of economic elites could not be, therefore, articulated through the party system, and the discontinuity between economic and political power would have made liberal democracy unfeasible.

I think that this discontinuity is more a *consequence* than a cause of the failure to establish an industrial democracy in Argentina. There was not such a gap before the electoral reform, and the failure of the attempt, by a segment of the upper class, to form a "modern" Conservative Party that could compete with the Radicals—that is, a party that would be based on an organization and an electoral machine, rather than being a coalition of provincial notables—is explained by the nature of the Radical Party. It did not challenge the oligarchic hegemony, and it could be penetrated by agrarian elites. After the reversal, the social and political equation had changed. Then, there could not be a mass conservative

41. Torcuato S. Di Tella, "La búsqueda de la fórmula politica argentina," *Desarrollo económico* (1972); Oscar Cornblitt, "La opción conservadora."

party, for two reasons. First, after Argentine society was transformed by large-scale import substitution geared toward the internal market, economic elites were split into two segments, the old agrarian oligarchy and forward-linkage industrialists on the one hand, and the new manufacturers on the other. These two segments could not coexist in a single party, for their interests were not similar; they contended for the same surplus. And the "new" sector was initially allied with labor in the Peronist coalition. Second, there was no "available" mass base. After World War II, the two support classes that existed in Argentine society, the urban middle class and the industrial working class, were already "taken" by Radicals and Peronists, respectively. Moreover, the Radical constituency included sectors that depended on import-substituting activities, so that this party could not be converted by the agrarian upper class into its direct representative.

In discussing Di Tella and Cornblitt's argument, Alain Rouquié pointed to a contrary peculiarity in the Argentine political system, the absence of a mass left-wing party.[42] This refers to the period following the reversal, for the Socialist Party was a substantial organization prior to the advent of Peronism. It is not clear whether this is an institutionalization argument of the type discussed above, for its focus is not the correspondence between classes and parties, that is, the issue whether the interests of a specific group are represented through the party system. Rather, the argument refers to the ideology of the party representing that group. Rouquié's statement concerns the working class and Peronism. Unlike the parties representing working class interests in almost all industrial societies, Peronism does not have a socialist ideology. In this respect, Argentina is, like the United States, an exceptional case.

Anyhow, one could not develop an argument for the explanation of the reversal on the basis of this peculiarity, for Peronism has represented what most workers considered to be the working class interest, as the absence of major discontinuities between the leadership and the rank and file, up to the early eighties, indicates. In general, Peronist political or labor organizations have controlled the political participation of their membership, and there have not been many instances of anomic political participation by the working class. Thus, this peculiarity of Argentina does not mean that a large proportion of the population is not represented in the

42. Rouquié, *Pouvoir militaire*, pp. 700–1.

polity, or that organizations purporting to represent that population fail to do so because their ideology and action differ widely from the mentality or aspirations of their constituency. The absence of a mass left-wing party in post-World War II Argentina is, in any case, the consequence of several factors: the changes in the size and composition of the labor force as a consequence of intense industrialization in the thirties and forties, the fact that a considerable segment of the working class was socialized into politics by Peronism, the absence of a large revolutionary intelligentsia, and the tactical blunders made by the leftist parties themselves.

Thus, neither do political inputs (mobilization and institutionalization of participation) seem to be the mechanism of the reversal of Argentine development. The examination of political outputs, more specifically of industrialization and labor policies in the forties, and of their structural consequences will be more helpful.

### The Institutionalization of Ungovernability

The institutionalization of these political outputs provides the most parsimonious explanation of the reversal of development in Argentina. The social structure of the country was transformed by two policies carried out in the postwar period: radical protection for industries oriented to the internal market, and a corporatist strategy toward labor. These policies, in the context of a society characterized by concentration in the ownership of land and the absence of a large labor reserve ultimately produced a sluggish and unstable economy and an illegitimate polity.

The prevailing description of the Argentine social and political reality in the post-Peronist period focuses on the notion of stalemate. As Torcuato Di Tella and Guillermo O'Donnell have depicted the situation,[43] political instability has been the consequence of stalemate among the different social and political forces. Since none of the contenders or coalitions of contenders could accumulate enough power to overcome the other contenders or coalitions and establish hegemony over them, illegitimacy and praetorianism resulted. The relation of forces underlying this conflict has been described by Mario Brodersohn, Marcelo Diamand, Aldo Ferrer, Gilbert Merkx, Guillermo O'Donnell, Lars

---

43. Torcuato S. Di Tella, "Stalemate or coexistence in Argentina," in James Petras and Maurice Zeitlin, eds., *Latin America, Reform or Revolution?* (1968); O'Donnell, *Modernization*.

Schoultz, and Gary Wynia.[44] Two coalitions have opposed each other. On the one hand, agrarian interests and the fraction of the industrial bourgeoisie linked to them, such as international capital and the segment of domestic capital less dependent on protection, make up one coalition. The other coalition has consisted of the bulk of the industrial bourgeoisie, particularly its weaker segment, and the labor movement. Different fractions of the middle classes participated in each alliance.

Besides this major line of cleavage, there were secondary conflicts within each bloc, such as the friction between the agrarians and big industrial capital at different points in time since the sixties onward, as the latter became preponderant; and there was also an intermittent cleavage between labor and the bourgeoisie as a whole. The interrelationship among the groups, in interaction with the political parties representing some of them, was thus very complex, and different alliances, with varying degrees of mobilization among their constituent members, were formed in particular circumstances or in relation to specific issues. The state apparatus and, especially, the armed forces, has intervened in different situations as an arbiter of the conflict or as the political representative of the agrarians or big industry.

In this conflict, success could only be limited in scope and temporary, and it was eventually reversed. Whenever one of the coalitions prevailed and seized control of the government, it carried out policies that protected or advanced the interests of its members. But it could not drastically alter the power position of the opposing bloc. The application of government programs led to economic or political outcomes that triggered the mobilization of the other coalition, which eventually accumulated enough power to block the implementation of policies, force a retreat, or even capture the government. Economic policies, thus, have protected the basic or immediate interests of the two blocs in a sequential pattern, wavering, as Diamand has put it, like a pendulum[45] between

44. Mario Brodersohn, "Conflicto entre los objetivos de política económica de corto plazo de la economía argentina" (1977); Marcelo Diamand, *Doctrinas económicas, desarrollo e independencia* (1973); and "El péndulo argentino: Empate político o fracasos económicos?" (1976); Aldo Ferrer, *Crisis y alternativas*; Gilbert W. Merkx, "Sectoral Clashes and Political Change: The Argentine Experience," *Latin American Research Review* (1969); Guillermo A. O'Donnell, "Estado y alianzas en la Argentina, 1956–1976," *Desarrollo económico* (1977); Schoultz, *Populist Challenge*, pp. 85–95; Wynia, *Argentina*.

45. Diamand, *Doctrinas económicas*, and "El péndulo."

two poles: conservative—or, in the Argentine vocabulary, "liberal"—policies, such as incentives to agriculture, lower tariffs, wage controls, and reduction of government spending; and "populist" policies, like lower prices for agrarian commodities, higher tariffs and other incentives for manufacturing, higher wages, and increased government spending.

The range of oscillation of this pendulum was determined by the power of the social forces. Until the late seventies, whenever the interests of one of the opposing coalitions have been affected beyond a certain point, the pendulum was pushed toward the other pole. The barriers to conservative measures were mainly political; the mobilization of the labor movement, segments of the middle classes, and the sector of the bourgeoisie that was hurt by these policies raised the specter of popular revolt. In this situation, the big bourgeoisie and the oligarchy yielded power. The obstacles to populist strategies, on the other hand, were mainly economic; their implementation led to declines in agrarian output and crises in the balance of payments. When that happened, labor and the less competitive segments of the industrial bourgeoisie were paralyzed by the inefficacy of their program, and a segment of the middle class usually swang to the right, thus becoming a support for the reinstatement of conservative policies, often as a consequence of military intervention and the establishment of an authoritarian regime.[46]

What caused this stalemate? The above description of Argentine political dynamics suggests an institutionalization model, and two causes. This state of affairs is the consequence of the structural linkages of the two policies I mentioned above: radical protectionism for industries oriented to the internal market, and a corporatist strategy toward the working class. These two policies, as we have seen already, were followed by the Peronist regime in the postwar period. Their effects on the social structure were similar and cumulative: economic growth and legitimacy in the short run, a sluggish economy and political illegitimacy in the long run.

After the war, Argentina renounced the model of industrialization based on integration into the world economy. Instead, autarkic policies adopted as a response to the Depression and the war, were intensified when the world economy was reorganized. In the two decades following the war, industrial policy focused on quantitative trade restrictions and direct prohibitions against im-

46. Ferrer, *Crisis y alternativas*, O'Donnell, "Estado y alianzas."

porting consumer goods already produced locally, rather than re-
lying mainly on tariffs and exchange controls, the weaker instruments stressed in the thirties. The outcome was described by
Carlos Díaz Alejandro, Richard Mallon, and Juan Sorrouille, and
others.[47] What occurred was the formation of a large noncompetitive manufacturing sector, whose existence was made possible
only by the automatic and unlimited protection granted to existing and new industries without regard to current or prospective
competitiveness.

Thus, the internationally efficient agrarian sector coexists with
a manufacturing sector that is tied to a captive market, and operates behind effective protection barriers, which are among the
highest in the world. At the end of the fifties, the average rate of
effective protection was estimated at 151 percent. This rate was
higher than those of Brazil and Chile, and eight times that of
France. As a result of these policies, the prices of Argentine manufactured goods were much higher than those of the United States
and Western Europe.[48] This situation has been aptly characterized
as a new form of dualism by Mallon and Sorrouille.[49] As in the old
form, though, the connections between the sectors are more important than the differences; the survival of manufacturing depends on the surplus generated by agriculture. This follows, as we
have seen in Chapter 3, from a difference between Argentine industrialization and that of lands of recent settlement (and a similarity with the Latin American pattern): the concentration on the
manufacturing of consumer goods. Manufacturers can only import machinery and other necessary inputs with the foreign exchange generated by agriculture. This is the root of the stalemate
described above; the conflict between the two sectors is coupled
with a unilateral dependency of manufacturing on agriculture. In
this situation, the oligarchy and its allies have retained a great deal
of power, in spite of the fact that the majority of the country's capital and nonservice labor force have been committed to manufacturing.[50]

47. Díaz Alejandro, *Essays;* Mallon and Sorrouille, *Economic
Policymaking;* see also Adalbert Krieger Vasena and Javier Pazos, *Latin
America: A Broader World Role* (1973).

48. See Santiago Macario, "Protectionism and Industrialization in
Latin America," *Economic Bulletin for Latin America* (1964); Díaz
Alejandro, *Essays,* pp. 255–76; Julio Berlinski and Daniel M.
Schydlowsky, "Incentives for Industrialization in Argentina" (1977).

49. Mallon and Sorrouille, *Economic Policymaking,* p. 159.

50. Some sectors of the Argentine Left stress the underlying unity

The economic consequences of hothouse capitalism are well known: high rates of growth until the captive market is saturated, and sluggishness thereafter. The latter occurs because the size of the internal market limits the possibility of "deepening" the industrialization process, and the large-scale export of manufacturing goods is not possible without subsidies. The stagnation of Argentina was not the result of protection as such—protection is widely practiced everywhere, but of the intensity and the range of protection. In Argentina, the non-competitive sector is both highly protected and very large, to the extent that it probably encompasses most of the non-service labor force. This is why this sector absorbs a major share of the agrarian surplus, thus hindering efficient investment. Neither a highly protected but small nor a large but moderately protected manufacturing sector would have had such a crippling effect.

The political consequences of radical protectionism have also varied with time. In the short run, the expansion of employment and income produced a satisfied working class, which consented to the control of the labor movement by the state. In the long run, the working class generated by this type of industrialization became the foremost delegitimating force. This was so because large scale industrialization, in an economy averse to the adoption of technological innovation and in a society without a large labor reserve, generated a highly mobilized and organized labor movement. The demands made by labor and by the other social forces, in a very unstable economy, are likely to lead at times to situations that contenders perceive as a zero-sum game. This is not necessarily due to actual stagnation, but to the existence of a large gap between the size of the surplus and the combined demands made by the different strata. This situation can only lead to illegitimacy and political instability.

The integration of the working class into the political system through a corporatist strategy, in the sense in which I am using the term, that is, as a strategy presupposing both participation and control by the state,[51] had similar political effects—a positive relationship with legitimacy in the short run and a negative one in the long run. It also had similar economic long-term effects; it contributed to the low and unstable rate of growth. These consequences follow from what I called above the contradiction of cor-

among the different economic elites. For an articulate argument along these lines, see Peña, *La clase dirigente*, pp. 7–53.

51. See Chapter 3 above, and Waisman, *Modernization*, pp. 20–23.

poratism; the utilization of the working class as a political base by Perón required the constitution of a powerful labor movement, albeit under state control. But redistribution was a precondition for the stability of the corporatist arrangement. When radical protectionism led to an economic slowdown, and the regime collapsed, this labor movement became an autonomous political force, one much more powerful than it would have been *without* organization from above.

It is the ability of the labor movement to protect its interests that has prevented so far the resolution of the stalemate through the hegemony of the big bourgeoisie and the agrarian elite. Such an outcome would eliminate the "new dualism." The most vulnerable sectors of the bourgeoisie would have been incapable, by themselves, to prevent a result of this type. Labor mobilization allowed these sectors to have a "free ride" by conjuring up the specter of revolt in case their noncompetitive industries were dismantled. The working class was the central actor in the struggle against "liberal" attempts to restructure the Argentine economy in the late sixties and in the late seventies.

Thus, the Argentine crisis is the long-term result of the Peronist policies that, on the one hand, allocated economic and human resources in an inefficient manner and, on the other, increased the level of mobilization and organization of the labor movement. The first process led to a segmented integration into the international economy, a consequence of which, as noted above, is the fact that the world economy became a brake on development. This was so because the surplus generated by the export sector was used to support and expand noncompetitive manufacturing. The second process led to the formation of an ungovernable polity, in which military rule became the response to the structural transformations generated by this new type of relationship with the international economy.

In the post-Peronist period, there were significant changes in the relation of forces. The wave of foreign investment in the sixties increased the weight of big industry, and the agrarian elite was no longer the leader of the conservative coalition. This class, however, retained its veto power because of its key role as the supplier of the foreign exchange that made import-substituting manufactures possible. Furthermore, the softening of protection in the late seventies, through the overvaluation of the currency and the lowering of tariffs, weakened the less competitive manufacturers and the labor movement as a whole. The pendulum swang wider, but it is not yet clear whether the equilibrium was broken.

The package of radical protectionism and corporatism would have had other consequences in a society with different structural characteristics. Two of the peculiarities of Argentina vis-à-vis the lands of recent settlement and the Latin American pattern are important in this connection: the high concentration of landowner-ship and the absence of a large labor reserve. Lands of recent settlement have the latter trait and not the former, while typical Latin American societies have the former and not the latter. Argentina combined both. It is because of these structural constraints that stalemate and ungovernability ensued.

In the first place, had the Argentine pattern of land tenure been like that of the lands of recent settlement at the time of their industrialization, agrarian interests would have been weaker. A class of farmers would have had a more limited ability to protect its interests than was the case with a small and well organized agrarian elite, which controlled the state until the war and is still considered an aristocracy. Radical protectionism would have led to a sluggish and unstable economy anyway, but the agrarian sector would not have been hegemonic. In a situation of this type, with other things being equal, the populist alliance would prevail over the farmers and the less vulnerable sector of the bourgeoisie. There would be no stalemate as was the case in Argentina, and protectionist interests would control economic policy in a continued manner. The problem is, of course, that the populist economic formula is nonviable in the long run. With or without an agrarian upper class, the large-scale development of noncompetitive manufacturing would lead to a massive misallocation of capital and labor, and eventually to stagnation. If this process of hothouse industrialization was coupled with the development of a powerful labor movement by a corporatist state, the consequence would be, as in Argentina, the dissolution of the corporatist pact and the fall of legitimacy. But, in the absence of agrarian-industrial stalemate, there would be no need for an intermittent coalition between inefficient industrialists and the unions, as in Argentina, and an intense conflict between them would ensue. Since lands of recent settlement lack a large labor reserve, such a situation could lead to high levels of social and political polarization.

Second, in the typical Latin American situation, the existence of a large labor reserve prevents the conversion of the labor movement into an independent political force. If the working class is in-

corporated into the political system under state control, the availability of a surplus for redistribution would still be a prerequisite
for the stability of corporatism,[52] but the absence of such a surplus
would not automatically trigger a high level of polarization. The
conversion of the working class into an independent political actor is, of course, a complex process, many of whose determinants
are exogenous to the economic and social structure. (For instance,
the contents of preindustrial culture, the availability of a revolutionary intelligentsia, or the toleration of dissent by the state.)
However, the presence or absence of a large labor reserve is a central factor in this process. In the absence of a corporatist relationship with the state, control of the labor supply would be the main
source of economic power for the working class, and such control
is very weak wherever there is a large labor reserve. This is what
the cases of Mexico, Brazil, Peru, Colombia, and other countries
with a peasantry and large urban informal sectors indicate. It is
only in Argentina (and, to a lesser extent, in Uruguay, where there
was until recently relatively less manufacturing, and Chile, where
the labor reserve is substantially larger), that the labor movement
has had a considerable degree of market control.

Therefore, had Argentina been a typical Latin American society,
the working class would not be a central power contender. Other
things being equal, this would facilitate the control of the state by
the agrarians and their industrial allies, and, thus, the opening up
of the economy. Once the noncompetitive sector is dismantled, a
cohesive ruling class would face no structural obstacles to hegemonic rule.

Thus, the outcomes would have been different had the radical
protectionism/corporatism package been applied in a society in
which one of the two structural conditions, land concentration
and lack of a large labor reserve, were not present.

It is important to understand the options available to the Argentine elites in the postwar period. The alternative to blanket protectionism would have been the development of some export
manufactures, a policy compatible with selective protection, in a
few cases for welfare or defense considerations but more generally
on the basis of the "infant industry" argument, and the alternative
to corporatism would have been a resumption of the inclusionary
strategies toward the labor movement followed prior to the

52. Ibid., pp. 26–27, 38–42, 58–67.

Depression. This other road would have produced different long-term economic and political outcomes.

Whether selective protection would have led to the formation of an internationally competitive manufacturing sector is an open question, but an industrialization of this type would have been free of most of the self-limiting traits inherent to manufacturing tied to a captive market. With a reasonable mix of protected and nonprotected industries, there would have been a greater likelihood that some competitive industries develop. In any case, since only some activities would be intensely protected at a time, the volume of resources extracted from agriculture for the support of manufacturing could have been more limited. If this was the case, the domestic determinants of periodic foreign exchange crises and thus sharp economic fluctuations would disappear, and the intersectoral conflict would be lessened. The political consequences of a situation of this type are also clear. Since noncompetitive activities would lack a mass base, the Argentine polity would resemble that of other industrial societies. Whether the more unified capitalist class that would develop could become hegemonic and establish a legitimate liberal democracy is also an open question, for this would also depend on processes in the noneconomic areas of the society—efficacy of the state and its ideological apparatuses, existence of counterideologies, and so on. But at least two obstacles to liberal democracy that exist in contemporary Argentina would not be present: the intense cleavage within the capitalist class, and the relative autonomy of the state that such cleavage induces.

In the context of an industrialization policy of limited protectionism, an inclusionary elite strategy toward the labor movement would have removed another component of the stalemate, the fact that the unions are a central and relatively autonomous power contender. There are four reasons for this. First, without the powerful push given to it by the corporatist apparatus, the labor movement would have been weaker. If it had not been a transmission belt for the state, it could not turn later into an organizational weapon. Second, the industrial working class would probably be smaller than has been the case with automatic protectionism. Third, labor would be less likely to expand its power through a coalition with a sector of the capitalist class, since the noncompetitive bourgeoisie would not be a major and differentiated political actor. Finally, the more stable economic course and the higher growth rates would reduce the incentives for the large-scale political mobilization of labor. A lower level of social conflict would remove another of the factors facilitating the emergence of the Bonapartist state in contemporary Argentina.

Of course, an inclusionary strategy toward the working class would have facilitated a legitimate liberal democracy only in the absence of radical protectionism. As the case of pre-Pinochet Chile shows, the combination of an inclusionary strategy with high protectionism has explosive consequences. On the one hand, economic policy creates the conditions for labor discontent; on the other, by renouncing the corporatist strategy, the state gives up the possibility of controlling that discontent through organizational mechanisms. The Chilean elite applied a package of this type from the Depression onward. High protectionism led to stagnation, which facilitated the mobilization of the lower classes and the establishment of the Allende government in the early seventies. This was a truly revolutionary situation, whose outcome was the breakdown of liberal institutions and the establishment of an authoritarian state that has attempted to reshape the social structure by opening up the economy. The outcome was massive unemployment and the intensification of the preexisting legitimacy crisis.

Therefore, the institutionalization of extreme protectionism and of a corporatist strategy toward the labor movement was the immediate cause of the reversal of Argentine development. The identification of this mechanism is the first step for the understanding of the Argentine riddle, but it is not in itself an explanation. From the discussion above I conclude that it was in the realm of political outputs, rather than in that of political inputs, or in the economic structures, or in the value system, that the reversal began. Policy changes set in motion the process that eventually transformed the country's economic and political institutions. But this in itself calls for an explanation, for these two policies represented a departure from the past.

The institutionalization argument is then a specification of the problem. The issue is to understand why these policies were adopted. Policymaking is seldom, of course, a neutral process by which government and interest groups evaluate, on the basis of the norm of objectivity, the potential costs and benefits of different alternatives in relation to a shared definition of the general interest. Rather, it is usually a highly biased process, by which government and organizations representing particular groups, within the limits determined by their knowledge and by economic, political, and cultural constraints, make choices based on their perceived interests, and deploy the resources under their control in order to protect or advance these interests. To understand Argentina's change of developmental tracks, we must untangle the main actors' cognitive frameworks, perceived interests, and relative power; their coalitions and conflicts; and the constraints within which they operated at the time of the reversal, that is, between the Depression and the early postwar period.

# 5 Why the State Became Autonomous in the Forties

Even though they illuminate different aspects of the process, standard explanations of the institutionalization of the new industrial and labor policies in the postwar period are not satisfactory to the sociologist.

As a first approximation, it makes sense to impute these policies to ideological and psychological factors. Thus, radical protectionism and state corporatism are obviously linked to nationalist and fascist ideologies. They are also consistent with traditional Catholic doctrines, whose relationship is manifest with corporatism and indirect with autarkic industrialization (there are two links: the affinity between an organicist conception of society and the idea of economic self-sufficiency, and the shunning of commerce and finance). At a more structural level, radical protectionism can be related to the intellectual influence, in the thirties and forties, of advocates of manufacturing, both in the academic and professional world and in the state bureaucracy. The obvious intellectual figure is the prolific economist Alejandro E. Bunge, publisher of the *Revista de economía argentina*, and his associates, who in the forties were grouped at the Bunge Institute for Economic and Social Research. And one cannot fail to note that Raúl Prebisch, the head of the Central Bank before the coup of 1943, would become, at the end of the forties, the leader of CEPAL (in English, ECLA), the Economic Commission for Latin America of the United Nations, and the chief ideologist of import substitution. Also, in relation to radical protectionism, Carlos Díaz Alejandro has propounded a psychological interpretation: this policy would have been a delayed response to the Depression.

As for the control of labor by the state, it had been championed by important members of the bureaucratic and political elites, such as José Figuerola, a former functionary of the Primo de Rivera regime in Spain, who was an official at the Labor Department, and

Manuel A. Fresco, a Conservative governor of the Province of Buenos Aires, who attempted to set up corporatist mechanisms there in the late thirties. Finally, the shift to corporatism has been interpreted by Rodolfo Puiggrós, Roberto Carri, and others as an alliance between the labor movement and a sector of the state that shifted its ideological orientation to popular nationalism.[1]

I do not deny the influence of doctrines and of advocates of the new policies, but ideas or intellectual influences do not just transmute themselves into policies (especiallly when, as in the case of right-wing nationalism and Catholic corporatism at the time of the reversal, these ideas were not the dominant ones). Interpretations of the type listed above do not address two questions, which are important to the sociologist. The first is the question of power, both within the society and in the international system. What were the objective circumstances allowing for the implementation of the new industrial and labor policies? Government policy had, for the previous three generations, corresponded to the dominant class interest. Were the new policies consistent with such interest? Further, to what extent were these policies a consequence of external constraints? The second question, not addressed either by such interpretations as the ones I mentioned above, is the specific contents of the new policies. Radical protectionism was not espoused by the most articulate advocates of manufacturing, and it is not the only possible industrial policy that could be considered a response to the traumatic experience of the Depression. Limited, contingent protection, for instance, would be another such policy. Likewise, the characterization of Perón and his faction as popular nationalist is purely descriptive. Why was *this* specific variety of antiliberal ideology selected by a sector of the state?

In this chapter, I argue that extreme import substitution and a corporatist labor policy were not in the interest of the dominant classes, were not demanded by them, and were not determined ex-

1. See Alejandro E. Bunge, *Una nueva Argentina* (1940); and the *Revista de economía Argentina*. Examples of literature on the topic are Pedro J. Cristiá et al., *Argentina en la post guerra* (1946); and Solano Peña Guzmán, *La autarquía en la economía argentina* (1942); for autarky in fascist thought, see Ferruccio Lantini et al., *L'autarchia economica della nazione* (1939); see also Díaz Alejandro, *Essays*, pp. 106–38; José Figuerola, *La colaboración social en Hispanoamérica* (1943); Manuel A. Fresco, *Cómo encaré la política obrera durante mi gobierno* (1940); Rodolfo Puiggrós, *El peronismo: Sus causas* (1969), chaps. 1–4; and Roberto Carri, *Sindicatos y poder en la Argentina* (1967), chaps. 1–2.

ogenously. Thus, they were an instance of state autonomy. However, even if these policies were not the direct or necessary effect of external constraints, these constraints still played a role in the process leading to their formation. Further, I show that the watershed in the development of the autonomy of the state was not the coup of 1930, but the one of 1943. The first of these coups paved the way for military and limited democracy regimes, which were instruments of the agrarian upper class. However, it was in 1943 that a significant breach between the policies of the state and the interests of the economic elites became manifest. Also, I discuss the causes of autonomization on the basis of different hypotheses extracted from the theory of the state. Finally, I conclude that state autonomy made the new industrial and labor policies possible, but it did not determine by itself the specific contents of these policies.

## The Shift in Industrial and Labor Policies

In 1930, precisely when the cycle of positive interaction between Argentina and the international economy came to an end, the first nondemocratic regime since the organization of the country was established. This was a "state of exception" in Poulantzas's sense, but not all states of exception represent a break between the state and the ruling classes. In fact, the coup of 1930 was a restoration of oligarchical rule. Later, the Roca-Runciman pact showed that the protection of the agrarian interest was the paramount goal of the state in the thirties. There is no question that the army, which seized power in 1930 and inaugurated a period of military and limited democracy regimes, was substituting for an oligarchy whose ability for hegemony was collapsing. The policies engineered by Federico Pinedo, Raúl Prebisch, and the other technocrats who administered the economy in the thirties, were not in contradiction with the interests of the agrarian elite. Industrialization was deliberately promoted by the oligarchy,[2] but these policies increased the fragmentation of the ruling classes. This, together with the external constraints to be discussed in this chapter, made it possible for a sector of the armed forces to seize power in 1943 and to for-

2. Díaz Alejandro, *Essays*, pp. 104–5; Murmis and Portantiero, *Estudios*, pp. 3–48; Javier Villanueva, "Aspectos de la estrategia de industrialización argentina," in Di Tella and Halperin Donghi, eds., *Los fragmentos del poder*, pp. 329–30; and Villanueva, "Economic Development," in Falcoff and Dolkart, eds., *Prologue*, p. 65.

mulate policies that were definitely at variance with the objective and subjective interests of the dominant sectors. This process can be seen in the evolution of both industrial policy and state-labor relations before and after the coup.

The industrialization policy pursued before the coup of 1943 was based on the distinction between "natural" and "artificial" manufactures. The criterion used for this classification was the utilization of domestic raw materials.[3] The terminology foretells the expected fate of the industries developed as a consequence of the Depression and the war once the international economy was reorganized. The "artificial" ones would be phased out. The underlying assumption was that, labor costs being similar or lower than those of industrial countries, the use of local inputs (many of which were produced by Argentina with a comparative advantage) maximized the chances of eventual competitiveness. The Pinedo Plan, submitted to the Congress in 1940, proposed a strategy of developing the industrial sector as a "minor wheel" of the Argentine economy. The focus would be on "natural" manufactures, and the underlying goal was exporting to the U.S. market.[4]

Protection, as intended by the agrarian upper class controlling the state prior to the coup of 1943, would be limited and contingent on eventual competitiveness. This position was expounded very clearly in 1942 by Agriculture Minister Daniel Amadeo y Videla, whose jurisdiction included industrial development (this is in itself an indicator of the role of manufacturing for the Conservative administration). He categorized three types of manufactures being promoted at that time: defense industries, permanent, and transient industries. The distinction between the latter two

3. Villanueva, "Aspectos," pp. 339–50; and "Economic Development," pp. 72–79; Jorge, *Industria y concentración*, pp. 67, 131–32.

4. Argentine, Republic, Ministerio de Hacienda de la Nación, *El plan de reactivación económica ante el Honorable Senado* (1940). The plan was approved, with significant modifications, by the Conservative-controlled Senate, but it was not discussed by the Chamber of Deputies, where the opposition was in the majority. The Radicals refused to consider any bill submitted by the Executive. On the contents of the plan and the reaction to it by different social and political forces, see Juan J. Llach, "El plan Pinedo de 1940, su significado histórico y los orígenes de la economía política del peronismo," *Desarrollo económico* (1984); Weil, *Argentine Riddle*, pp. 164–70; Murmis and Portantiero, *Estudios*, pp. 33–42; and Villanueva, "Economic Development," pp. 78–79. For an overview of the Argentine economic structure in the early forties, see José C. Moure García, *La realidad económica y política argentina en el curso de la segunda guerra mundial, 1939–1945* (1982).

was based on the availability of raw materials. The goal was "the absolute processing of all the products of our soil . . . and the manufacturing of . . . agrarian goods we do not yet produce. . . ."[5] As for transient industries, their purpose was to ". . . compensate for supply deficiencies in anti-economical conditions," and they had to be developed with eventual reconversion in mind: "When no longer necessary, [such industries] must be devoted to other goals."[6] He was totally opposed to autarky, even at the continental scale: "Economic autarkies, even when designed on a plane as large as that of a continent, fatally resolve themselves in anti-economic production, and consequently in sterile efforts, grave damage to the standard of living of the population, and infinite risks."[7]

This was not the only position within the economic and political elite. The *Sociedad Rural Argentina* (SRA, Argentine Rural Society), which stood for the landed oligarchy, did not oppose an industrialization subordinate to agriculture, but it was nevertheless wary of the consequences that wartime protection of manufacturing could have on international trade in the postwar period.[8] Other groups, having different perspectives and different goals, supported industrial policies that would converge into radical protectionism. Javier Villanueva has studied the different proposals in the early forties. Thus, the Central Bank advocated the local production of imports, with foreign inputs and capital, which was a policy similar to postwar import substitution.[9] The army, whose main spokesman was the then Col. Manuel Savio, the General Director of *Fabricaciones Militares* (defense industries), was concerned about heavy industry. Savio did not advocate autarky, but his moderate program for development of a steel industry under state control fit into the radical protectionist policies implemented later.[10] The *Unión Industrial Argentina* (UIA, Argentine Industrial Union), which represented established manufacturers, was split between the supporters of "natural" industry and the ad-

5. Daniel Amadeo y Videla, *El desarrollo industrial y la economía de guerra* (1942), pp. 30–32.

6. Ibid., p. 32.

7. Ibid., pp. 28–30.

8. Murmis and Portantiero, *Estudios*, p. 38.

9. Villanueva, "Aspectos," pp. 343, 399, and "Economic Development," pp. 78–79.

10. See Manuel N. Savio, *Política de la producción metalúrgica argentina* (1942).

vocates of protecting what existed, regardless of the source of its inputs.

The segment of the political elite that seized control of the state after the military coup of 1943 was also divided among those different positions, but the distinction between "natural" or "permanent" and "artificial" or "transient" industries was gradually abandoned, and the group proposing radical protectionism eventually prevailed. The Armour Report of 1944, commissioned by a trade organization set up by the government and committed to the limited protection option, classified industries into advantageous, intermediate, and disadvantageous, on the basis of their ability to process local inputs and their export potential.[11] That same year the Central Bank still categorized manufactures developed since the beginning of the war into "permanent" and "artificial" ones.[12]

Nevertheless, the radical protectionist position emerged victorious. Also in 1944, Lt. Col. Mariano Abarca, the General Director of Industries in the Ministry of Agriculture, proposed, as the only solution to avoid "a catastrophe at the end of the war," to protect three types of industry: "(1) Industries that depend on domestic raw materials and an internal market, or that interest defense; (2) industries that depend on domestic raw materials and that, having satisfied the internal market, can export elaborate products; and (3) industries that produce essential goods, but that require, in part or totally, foreign raw materials."[13] This list covers "natural" industries plus all kinds of industries for which there is domestic demand, except those considered nonessential. A decree of "promotion and defense of industry" granted protection to the types (1) and (3) in that list.[14]

An important agency of the new regime was the *Consejo Nacional de Postguerra* (National Postwar Council), established in 1944 under the leadership of the then Vice-President Perón. The council, which consisted of cabinet members and high civil ser-

11. Armour Research Foundation, *Technological and Economic Survey*; and Corporación para la Promoción del Intercambio, *La estructura económica y el desarrollo industrial de la República Argentina* (1944).

12. Banco Central de la República Argentina, *Memoria anual 1944* (1945).

13. Mariano Abarca, *La industrialización de la Argentina* (1944), p. 35.

14. Argentine Republic, Vicepresidencia de la Nación Argentina, Consejo Nacional de Postguerra, *Ordenamiento económico-social* (1945), p. 68.

vants and which later integrated leading businessmen to its advisory committees, had a sweeping mandate: "To propose the coordination, planning, and execution in relation to all questions of an economic and social character."[15] Some of its proposals were cautious. Thus, in a general analysis of the Argentine economy and society, the council proposed "three basic orientations" for the postwar period: "(a) To support those activities that are already consolidated; (b) to suppress those which, at the end of the war, . . . yield before a superior competition from abroad; and (c) to replace the latter with new industries that have reasonable prospects (*arraigo*)."[16] However, as Villanueva notes, the council's emphasis on the promotion of activities that would maximize employment and wages meant the support of all existing industry and an exclusive focus on the internal market.[17] And some of its papers implied radical autarky, as far as industry was concerned.[18]

When Perón became President in 1946, the unconditional defense of all existing industry became the official policy. As he would argue later in front of an audience of manufacturers, "no market can replace the internal market. Regardless of how big, how beautiful they may be, because (other markets) are always aleatory, never safe. . . . If something is left over, we will sell it somewhere, but the Argentine people come first." And, in reminiscing about the wartime debates, he referred to the need, at that point, to prevent foreign competition from putting an end to the industrial progress accomplished during the war: "Anti-economical, everybody said [with reference to the new industries], but I prefer the anti-economical that we produce to the economical coming from outside. I always thought that way."[19] This was the policy that would lead to the inefficient allocation of capital and human resources, and ultimately to economic decline.

The change, of course, was much more drastic in the pattern of

15. Decree number 23, 847/44, in Consejo Nacional de Postguerra, *Ordenamiento*, p. 78.

16. Ibid., pp. 40–41.

17. Villanueva, "Aspectos," p. 350.

18. The policies advocated by the National Postwar Council are discussed in Chapter 6.

19. Discurso del Exmo. Sr. Presidente de la Nación, in Confederación General de la Industria, *Congreso General de la Industria* (1953), pp. xxiv–xxv. On the policy instruments used by the Peronist government, see Oscar Altimir et al., "Los instrumentos de promoción industrial en la postguerra," *Desarrollo económico* (1966–67).

relations between state and labor. There had been experiences of government intervention in the conflict between unions and employers. In the late thirties, as Ricardo Gaudio and Jorge Pilone have shown, the Department of Labor had begun to regulate collective bargaining and to mediate in industrial disputes,[20] and Governor Fresco had introduced his corporatist schemes in the province of Buenos Aires. But it was only after the coup of 1943 that an inclusionary or state corporatist apparatus for the incorporation of labor as a *political* force began to develop. Perón and his faction discarded classical authoritarian exclusion and liberal-democratic inclusion, the two elite strategies toward labor tried before in Argentina, and proposed, to the elites as well as to the working class, a synthesis of both, that is, incorporation into the political system under the control of the state. In that arrangement, the labor movement would get economic and political benefits, such as better wages and protective legislation, and a high level of political participation, albeit a dependent one, in exchange for serving as a power base. The only condition asked from the workers willing to enter into that deal was the repudiation of left-wing ideologies ("communism"), and the guarantee ("the reinsurance") offered to the ruling classes, disturbed by the unprecedented level of labor participation this arrangement would produce, was the promise to use exclusion as an alternative if the deal failed and labor became radicalized.[21]

Thus, while the military regime repressed the Communists and other groups on the Left and the unions controlled by them, Perón, the new secretary of labor, rewarded the unions and leaders willing to cooperate, regardless, in most cases, of their ideological history, with favorable wage settlements and protective legislation. Eventually, he "organized" labor (as he would put it) by fostering cooperating unions, the existing ones as well as the new organizations formed by the regime, and by setting up a system in which unions had to be recognized by the state. The outcome was a mass labor movement, which served as a power base for the secretary of labor.[22]

20. Ricardo Gaudio and Jorge Pilone, "El desarrollo de la negociación colectiva durante la etapa de modernización industrial en la Argentina, 1935–1943," *Desarrollo económico* (1983), and "Estado y relaciones laborales en el período previo al surgimiento del peronismo, 1935–1943," *Desarrollo económico* (1984).

21. See Waisman, *Modernization*, pp. 61–62.

22. See Germani, "El surgimento del peronismo," Halperín Donghi,

"We are neither state syndicalists, nor corporatists, nor any of these strange things," Perón disclaimed in 1944 before an audience of transportation workers; "we are just men who want unified and well-led trade unions, for inorganic masses are always the most dangerous ones for the state and for themselves."[23] "In the past," he argued, "the state kept its distance from the working class. It did not regulate social activities, as it was its duty."[24] But the nature of such regulation was explained very clearly to a group of obstetricians: "Thus we aspire to regulate in an absolute manner the activities of all the persons working within the boundaries of the country. For, should some professions, trades, unions, or any activity escape our control, it is likely that the harmony we aspire to, for the good of all the inhabitants, may not be realized in an integral manner."[25]

The blueprint was not fulfilled, of course, because of the intrinsic contradiction of corporatism: workers exchanged independence for economic benefits. The corporatist façade hid a continuous renegotiation of the terms in which support was given.[26] Since radical protectionism fostered the quantitative growth of the working class at the same time as corporatist incorporation strengthened its organization, the power of labor and its potential as a threat also increased over time. The "reinsurance" had to be used: the military regimes that attempted to rule Argentina for most of the three decades following the overthrow of Perón. This in itself indicates the failure of the attempt at corporatist inclusion.

"Algunas observaciones sobre Germani," and Kenworthy, "Interpretaciones ortodoxas y revisionistas," in Mora y Araujo and Llorente; eds., *El voto peronista*; Felix Luna, *El 45: Crónica de un año decisivo* (1975); Hiroschi Matsushita, *Movimiento obrero argentino, 1930–1945: Sus proyecciones en la historia del peronismo* (1983).

23. Juan Perón, *El pueblo ya sabe de qué se trata: Discursos* (1946), p. 8.

24. Juan Perón, *El pueblo quiere saber de qué se trata* (1944), p. 30.

25. Ibid., p. 138.

26. See Louise M. Doyon, "Conflictos obreros bajo el régimen peronista (1946–1955)," *Desarrollo económico* (1977); "El movimiento sindical bajo el peronismo," *Desarrollo económico* (1975); and "Organised Labour and Perón: A Study of the Conflictual Dynamics of the Peronist Movement" (1978); Walter Little, "La organización obrera y el estado peronista," *Desarrollo económico* (1979); and Ricardo Sidicaro, "Consideraciones sociológicas sobre las relaciones entre el peronismo y la clase obrera en la Argentina," *Boletín de estudios latinoamericanos y del Caribe* (1981).

### Ruling Class Interests and External Determinants

The institutionalization of the two policies whose joint effects transformed the structure of Argentine society, radical protectionism to manufacturing and a corporatist strategy toward labor, poses a problem for the theory of the state. This is so for the two reasons noted above: these policies were not in the interests of the central segments of the dominant classes, and they were not imposed on Argentina by inescapable external constraints. Rather, they were the product of autonomous state action. Since, prior to the reversal, state policies had been geared to the protection of the basic interests of the upper classes, the problem is the understanding of the factors leading to such a separation between the state and the dominant social forces.

The new policies were institutionalized during the Peronist regime of 1946–55 through the expansion and strengthening of their social base: the import-substituting bourgeoisie and the working class. The persistence of radical protectionism and of corporatism *under* Perón was a function of the nature of populism and of the relation of forces between the regime and the opposition.

First, the central goal of the Peronist coalition and the necessary condition for its survival was the transfer of surplus to manufacturing, in order to maintain full employment. Considerations of efficiency or competitiveness had little relevance. As I explained already, working-class support of the corporatist arrangement was not primarily an instance of blind submission to traditional authority, charisma, or bureaucratic controls. Some of these aspects may have been present as secondary factors, but the espousal of Peronism among workers was essentially a pragmatic exchange of active support for distributive policies. Second, the power differential between this coalition and the opposition was very narrow; Perón was elected with the 52 percent of the vote in a two-way race.[27] Furthermore, the opposition controlled wealth (that of the agrarian upper class and the big industrialists) and organizational resources (the anti-Peronist parties on the Center and Left). It also had a ready mass base, the large and mostly anti-Peronist middle classes in Buenos Aires and other cities of the core region. In this situation, it is clear that Perón could not afford alienating any segment of the Peronist coalition, not even temporarily. It is in a social context of this type that radical protectionism and corporatism were institutionalized.

27. See the figures in Cantón, *Elecciones y partidos*, p. 272.

The fate of these policies *after* Perón was overthrown needs no explanation either. Their persistence in the decades following the forties is easily explained by the relation of forces. But in 1943, at the time of the military coup from which Peronism sprang, or in 1946, at the outset of Perón's constitutional government, neither policy was in the interest of the central segments of the dominant classes: the agrarian elite, the manufacturers linked to it, and foreign capital. Radical protectionism and corporatism were in fact against the interests of these groups, the agrarian upper class in particular.

It is important to understand that this was not one of those frequent situations in which groups that are weak and do not control major resources can extract favorable policies from the government even when these policies are not in the interest of larger and more powerful groups, because the former are sharply defined constituencies, are highly organized and politically well connected, and pursue their vital interests, while the latter are diffuse or disorganized, or fail to mobilize because their central interests are not at stake. In this case, the new industrial and labor policies were initiated from above, and they were not a concession to the demands and mobilization for these policies in civil society. The main beneficiaries of radical protectionism were the small and new manufacturers, who were a diffuse and disorganized group, without substantial economic, social, or political power. Labor was organized and had a considerable potential for mobilization, but it was not demanding state corporatism. Against the groups in the state espousing these policies, on the other hand, were the agrarian upper class and the big industrial bourgeoisie, that is, specific interest groups, which controlled major economic resources, were highly organized and strongly connected to the political system, and were negatively affected in their central interests by the shift to radical protection and corporatism.

The landed oligarchy would have to finance noncompetitive industry through the appropriation by the state of a considerable share of the foreign exchange generated by agrarian exports. Most of the "older" industrial bourgeoisie, on the other hand, could manage with protection for "natural" industries, as it had done in the past. For both segments, finally, corporatism was a major threat to their power, for it entailed not only a strong state controlling the society, but also a setting in which the economic interests of the lower classes would loom much larger than in the liberal inclusionary and authoritarian exclusionary arrangements with which they were familiar and which, from the point of view of the dominant class interest, had demonstrated their efficacy in different periods of modern Argentine history.

Nor were these policies the necessary consequence of external constraint. This is obvious with regard to the corporatist apparatus, but the thesis is arguable in relation to radical protection to manufacturing; the proposition that the partial closure of the Argentine economy in the postwar period was inevitable seems, at first sight, plausible. Nevertheless, my conclusion in this regard is also negative.

As far as corporatism is concerned, it is impossible to identify any external economic or political constraint of which this arrangement would be a direct consequence. It can be argued, of course, that the beginning of corporatist policies, after the coup of 1943, could have been part of a strategy of anticipatory adjustment to a postwar world ruled by Germany. This reorientation seems, with hindsight, irrational (the coup took place after Stalingrad), but it was not just a case of perception distorted by ideology or the result of unshakable confidence in the ability of the German armed forces (whose missions had trained the Argentine army for several decades).[28] It is necessary to recall the extreme uncertainty felt by the elites at the time and the formidable impact of the sweeping German triumphs, in the first half of the war, against first-rate military powers on the Western and Eastern fronts. Some time had to elapse before the new developments could modify the impressions produced by these facts. An example of the confusion that prevailed in that period is a statement made by José María Cantilo, the pro-Allied foreign minister of the pro-Allied Ortiz administration, in mid-1940. After Germany had refused to pay compensation for the sinking of an Argentine freighter, the Argentine ambassador to Berlin had made the (under the circumstances) unusual assertion that victorious Germany would find opportunities "of an economic and political nature" in Argentina. Cantilo, in the same vein, argued that the country, while committed to "Pan-Americanism," was constrained to take into account the implications of a Europe organized by totalitarian Germany.[29] Even

28. See Frederick M. Nunn, *Yesterday's Soldiers: European Military Professionalism in South America* (1983); and George Pope Atkins and Larry V. Thompson, "German Military Influence in Argentina, 1921–1940," *Journal of Latin American Studies* (1972).

29. R. A. Humphreys, *Latin America and the Second World War*, vol. 1 (1981), pp. 61–62.

at the end of 1942, General José María Sarobe, one of the top officers in the army, who was known as a liberal, argued in a public lecture that Argentina should prepare itself for a postwar world of autarkic continents, including a Europe ruled by the "new order," that is by Nazi Germany.[30] These statements reveal how measured and contingent was the support for the Allied cause even among leading members of the "liberal" faction of the state bureaucracy, then in control of the government. This helps understand the apparently more unrealistic behaviors and expectations among pro-Axis groups. In any case, even if the espousal of corporatism by the latter reflected a strategy of accommodation with the anticipated victors, this was not, still, an externally induced response, or the effect of ineluctable constraints. Not only that: corporatism was one of the ingredients of the image of Argentina as a "fascist" country in the postwar period, and this, together with traditional Argentine opposition to U.S. hegemony in South America, determined the anti-Argentine economic policy of the Truman Administration.

As for the partial closure of the Argentine economy, it is tempting to argue that, since other Latin American countries also shifted to more or less radical types of import-substituting industrialization in the postwar years, such an inward turn must have been the necessary or inevitable consequence of the disarray in the international economy at that time. I have strong reservations about the validity of this standard dependency argument in general, but I do not see, in any case, how it can apply to Argentina. As a country whose previous development had approached the open spaces rather than the typical underdevelopment model, Argentina had options that may not have been available in countries closer to the Latin American modal pattern. It had the basic economic and social infrastructure that may have allowed for either open industrialization or, perhaps more reasonably, an industrial policy based on selective, contingent, and temporary protection.

Let us recall that the defining characteristics of the land of recent settlement are a high land-labor ratio and a population shortage. The fact that the export sector was labor-extensive agriculture operated by the domestic elite rather then an enclave economy had two consequences that are relevant for industrialization policies in the forties: since the central means of production were locally owned, a local capitalist class developed; and a large share of

30. José Maria Sarobe, *Política económica argentina* (1942), pp. 16–17.

the surplus, together with foreign capital, was invested in the development of a substantial sector of forward-linkage manufacturing. And the fact that, during the externally-led growth period, Argentine society had a labor shortage and as a consequence most of the population consisted of free immigrants from Europe implied that the society was not structurally heterogeneous but thoroughly capitalist, that the economy operated on the basis of relatively high wages, that there was substantial social mobility, and that, in order to retain and socialize the immigrants, a mass educational system developed. Thus, the country had domestic capital, forward-linkage manufacturing, strong ties to Europe that were not only economic but also social and cultural, and not restricted to the elite but spread throughout the society, and a mobile and relatively educated labor force. Overall, Argentina was still more developed, economically and socially, than most southern European nations. In Latin America, only Uruguay replicated this pattern of evolution, but Uruguay is a much smaller country, and these resources were present at a more reduced scale. But, in any case, Brazil, a more typical Latin American country, had also developed a very substantial manufacturing sector (which was the urban component of the "modern" pole in a structurally heterogeneous society), but I do not see either why the dislocation of the international economy would have forced this country to partially close its economy. In summary: the proposition does not look, in general, plausible to me, but it is most implausible when used to explain Argentine autarkic industrialization.

But the argument has been advanced that the anti-Argentine policy of the United States, together with the paralysis of the European economies in the late forties, created an environment in which the partial closure of the Argentine economy was inevitable, or at least a reasonable response. Jorge Fodor has made a case along these lines. At the end of the war, Argentina could sell beef and grain, and the terms of trade were very favorable to her, but Europe could not pay, and trade was hindered further by currency inconvertibility. The only possible large importer, the United States, would not buy. As a consequence, while parts of Europe faced major food shortages, grain was burned in Argentina as railroad fuel.[31]

31. Jorge Fodor, "Perón's Policies for Agricultural Exports, 1946–1948: Dogmatism or Commonsense?" in David Rock, ed., *Argentina in the Twentieth Century* (1975), pp. 135–61.

This situation was aggravated by the American boycott. During the war, as a response to the Argentine refusal to enter the conflict, the United States banned exports not only of arms, but also, at different periods and in the context of high-pressure negotiations, of fuel, basic raw materials, vehicles, and other critical items. It also blocked the assets of Argentine banks and pressured Britain and other countries in Europe and Latin America to restrict trade with Argentina.[32] Until the end of the forties, Argentina was still treated in U.S. trade policy as an enemy nation. Carlos Escudé has shown how comprehensive was this policy. The Truman administration prevented European nations to import Argentine foodstuffs with Marshall Plan funds (a restriction not applied, of course, to other exporters such as Canada and Australia), practiced a partial fuel embargo (oil and coal were indispensable imports for Argentina), attempted to restrict trade between Argentina and Britain and other countries, opposed Argentine participation in international trade conferences, tried to block the development of the Argentine merchant marine, and so on.[33] Since this discrimination coincided with the declaration of inconvertibility of the pound by Britain, the Argentine financial situation became very difficult.

In this context, autarky may have seemed a reasonable policy to Perón and his advisers, but still it was not the only option. Selective protection, limited in time and with a view to long-term competitiveness, was even then a reasonable alternative. At any rate, it is important to understand two things: first, American antagonism was provoked by the Argentine short-sighted foreign policy itself, and second, these constraints disappeared very soon, at the

32. See Ciria, *Partidos y poder*, pp. 132–39; Alberto Conil Paz and Gustavo Ferrari, *Política exterior*, pp. 65–161; Díaz Araujo, *La conspiración*, passim; Carlos Escudé, *Gran Bretaña*, pp. 23–162; Michael J. Francis, *The Limits of Hegemony: United States Relations with Argentina and Chile during World War II* (1977), pp. 190–240; Gary Frank, *Struggle for Hegemony in South America: Argentina, Brazil, and the United States during the Second World War* (1979), passim; Humphreys, *Latin America*, vol. 2 pp. 146–202; C. A. Macdonald, "The Politics of Intervention: The United States and Argentina, 1941–1946," *Journal of Latin American Studies* (1980); Moure García, *La Realidad*, chaps. 3–4; Potash, *Army and Politics, 1928–1945*, pp. 141–237; Mario Rapoport, *Gran Bretaña, Estados Unidos y las clases dirigentes argentinas, 1940–1945* (1980), pp. 239–92.

33. Escudé, *Gran Bretaña*, pp. 91–330. But Escudé does not argue that these external constraints caused the partial closure of the Argentine economy. He is aware of the choices available to the country.

end of the forties, as the European economies regained their dynamism and the American trade war came to an end. But at that time it was Argentina that had less to offer on the world markets. Exportable surpluses of agrarian commodities had been reduced considerably. As a consequence of Perón's economic policy, domestic consumption rose, due to the improvement in the standard of living of the working class, and output declined, because of the lower prices the government purchasing boards paid to the producers. As for manufacturing, it was, thanks to the regime of blanket protection, totally geared to the lucrative and safe domestic market. When Perón was overthrown in 1955, the autarkic option had already been institutionalized.

In conclusion, both corporatism and radical protectionism were implemented in an environment in which they made sense or appeared reasonable to government officials or some other groups either as an adjustment to expected events (in the case of corporatism) or as a response to a hostile or insolvent world (in the case of radical protectionism). However, these policies were not the necessary consequence of external constraints.

If the new policies were determined neither by the interests of the economic elite nor by foreign factors, then their institutionalization was an instance of the autonomy of the state.

### The Autonomy of the State: "Eastern" Society and Vertical Cleavage Hypotheses

The lack of correspondence between dominant class interests and government policy in the period of institutionalization of radical protectionism and corporatism cannot be encompassed by any of the models generated by theories of the state for "normal" times.

All these theories,[34] be they determinist or functionalist, liberal or Marxist, predict that, except in special situations, there will be congruence between government policies and the balance of interests in civil society. Congruence does not imply the automatic translation of ruling class demands into state policy: the concept encompasses a continuum, ranging from the rare instance of con-

34. For general discussions, see Robert R. Alford and Roger Friedland, *Powers of Theory: Capitalism, the State, and Democracy* (1985); Bertrand Badie and Pierre Birnbaum, *The Sociology of the State* (1983); Martin Carnoy, *The State and Political Theory* (1984); Bob Jessop, *Theories of the State* (1983); Eric Nordlinger, *On the Autonomy of the Democratic State* (1981); Stepan, *State and Society*, chap. 1.

sistent overlap between policies and manifest dominant class interests to the situation in which policies protect some fundamental upper class interests, but in which these policies are in contradiction with the short-term interests of some or even all its segments.

Both pluralist theory and the conventional type of Marxist theory of the state [35] are determinist. They view the state as an effect of the social structure. In these theories, the elite or dominant class interests at stake are primarily the "subjective" ones. The underlying assumption is that elites or dominant classes are very likely to be conscious of their objective interests, so that subjective and objective interests overlap. Pluralist theories view state policy as the result of the balance of power in the society, while "instrumentalism," as the classical definitions by Engels and Lenin came to be known, considers the state as an apparatus at the service of the ruling class. The "executive committee" metaphor in the *Manifesto*, however, is complex. The executive committee of an organization is not just the agent of the membership of that organization. The leadership is expected to have the "longer view," that is, to embody the "objective" interests of its followers. Sometimes this implies a gulf and even a contradiction between the members' subjective interests and what the leadership considers to be their "objective" ones. A formulation of this type, therefore, fits more the functionalist than the determinist category.

Functionalist theories of the state, be they Parsonian or Marxist, do not make any assumptions about the long-term rationality or class consciousness of those who control the economy. Since these theories focus on the interaction between the state and the other subsystems of society and emphasize the study of latent consequences, they expect correspondence between state policies and the objective interests of the elites or dominant classes. In the Parsonian version, the state is expected to accomplish this primarily by enhancing the goal-attainment capability of the system, while in the case of Poulantzas' "structuralist" Marxism, the focus of state activity is integration. (By the way, this type of Marxism, which is "unconscious" of its functionalist logic, provides a more adequate tool for the functional analysis of state activity than does the Parsonian framework.)

It is clear that none of these theories is an adequate representation of the relationship between state and society in Argentina at

35. Poulantzas, *Political Power*, chap. 2. See also idem, "The Problem of the Capitalist State," *New Left Review* (1969).

the time of the reversal. The institutionalization of the new industrial and labor policies in the forties is a case in which the policies of the state differed from both the subjective and the objective interests of those who controlled the economy.

Theories of the state recognize a series of exceptional situations in which the state is expected to be independent (or, in the hallowed but less precise formulation, "relatively autonomous") of the upper classes. There are, it seems to me, four of these exceptional situations.

The first instance is autonomy by default; it corresponds to the type of society in which the social groups or organizations outside the state are weak or, in the extreme case, nonexistent. This case encompasses Antonio Gramsci's "Eastern" model of society. As is well known, he contrasted "Western" societies, which have strong interest groups and other social organizations that are independent of state control with the "Eastern" ones, in which strong states preside over weak civil societies.[36] Examples would be the "oriental" agrarian empires, many revolutionary regimes, and most contemporary socialist societies.

Exogenously determined autonomy is a second case. Following Otto Hintze, contemporary authors such as Samuel Finer, Theda Skocpol, and Ellen Trimberger have noted that the activities of a state are determined in part by opportunities and constraints derived from the interaction, both military and nonmilitary, with other states.[37] In some circumstances, such as military competition, these external factors may be central determinants of state behavior, and, thus, policies may be at variance with the domestic balance of forces.

The remaining two cases correspond to the classical Marxist theory of Bonapartism.[38] The focus is on domestic determinants

36. See Antonio Gramsci, *Selections from the Prison Notebooks* (1971), p. 238.

37. Samuel E. Finer, "State and Nation-Building in Europe: The Role of the Military," in Charles Tilly, ed., *The Formation of National States in Western Europe* (1975); Otto Hintze, "Military Organization and the Organization of the State," in Felix Gilbert, ed., *The Historical Essays of Otto Hintze* (1975); Skocpol, *States*, pp. 28–31; Ellen K. Trimberger, *Revolution from Above* (1978), pp. 70–74.

38. See Karl Marx, *The Eighteenth Brumaire of Louis Bonaparte*, in Marx and Engels, *Works*; Engels, *German Revolutions*, and *Role of Force*. See also Dietrich Rueschemeyer and Peter B. Evans, "The State and Economic Transformation: Toward an Analysis of the Conditions Underlying Effective Intervention," in Peter B. Evans, Dietrich

and, more specifically, on a condition of equilibrium or stalemate among social forces. In a situation of this type, the state is expected to become a relatively autonomous arbiter. The first variety of stalemate is a horizontal cleavage at the superordinate level: a fragmentation of the upper classes, typically between a traditional agrarian aristocracy and a more modern industrial bourgeoisie. The classical case is Bismarckian Germany as analyzed by Engels.[39] A.F.K. Organski's concept of syncratism[40] is also a description of this situation. Finally, the fourth exceptional condition is the stalemate based on a vertical cleavage, one between superordinate and subordinate classes. Analyses of the genesis of right-wing dictatorships, ranging from August Thailheimer's and Trotsky's characterization of fascism as a special variety of Bonapartism to O'Donnell's discussion of the role of threat in the emergence of bureaucratic authoritarian regimes, commonly focus on hypotheses of this type.[41]

Argentina in the period of the reversal does not fit the first nor the fourth of these special situations. This is obvious with respect to the first case, that in which social groups or organizations outside the state are weak or nonexistent. It is true that the state apparatus, particularly the armed forces, strengthened considerably after the Depression: as Robert Potash shows, one of the basic changes in the structure of the state since 1930 has been the growth in size and complexity of the armed forces along with the overall expansion of the state apparatus and the increase of its regulatory power over the economy and the society. In the thirties and forties, the military augmented their forces (the army doubled its officer corps and tripled its personnel), and created a network of arsenals and defense industries.[42] The relationship between state and society had changed in the period of the reversal, but Argen-

Rueschemeyer, and Theda Skocpol, eds., *Bringing the State Back In* (1985), pp. 63–65.

39. Engels, *German Revolutions*, and *Role of Force*.

40. A.F.K. Organski, *The Stages of Political Development* (1968).

41. See August Thailheimer, "Sul fascismo," in Renzo De Felice, ed., *Il Fascismo: Le interpretazioni dei contemporanei e degli storici* (1970), pp. 272 ff.; and Leon Trotsky, "Bonapartism and Fascism," in *Writings of Leon Trotsky (1934–35)* (1971), pp. 51–57; O'Donnell, *Modernization*, and "Reflections on the Patterns of Change in the Bureaucratic Authoritarian Regime," *Latin American Research Review* (1978).

42. Potash, *Army and Politics, 1928–1945* (1969), p. 283; Marta Panaia and Ricardo Lesser, "Las estrategias militares frente al proceso de industrialización (1943–1947)," in Marta Panaia et al., eds., *Estudios sobre los orígenes del peronismo*, vol. 2 (1973).

tina was far from being a weak society. The country had a differentiated social structure, a complex institutional system most of whose spheres were still independent from, or weakly controlled by, the state, and strong interest groups. This does not fit the image of an "Eastern" society in Gramsci's sense of the term.

Likewise, a vertical equilibrium hypothesis does not correspond to Argentine society in the forties. This hypothesis would entail an actual stalemate between an autonomous subordinate class, in the Argentine case the working class, and the superordinate one. A situation of this type, which obtained at times in post-Peronist Argentina, did not exist in the period between the Depression and the end of the war (or, for that matter, at any previous time in Argentine history).

In this period, the labor movement was in a state of transition, due to two processes: the assimilation and Argentinization of the older, predominantly immigrant, working class, and the formation of a new working class as a consequence of rapid industrialization in the thirties and forties.

Much of the foreign-born labor movement of the pre-World War I period, which was concentrated on railroads, food-related industries, and general services such as construction, and was under socialist and anarchist influence, had disappeared after the Depression as a consequence of biological replacement and of upward mobility. It was being replaced by a new cohort of first-generation Argentines or assimilated immigrants, who were more interested in specific economic and professional demands and in integration into the new society than in diffuse ideological involvements. In addition, that older working class benefited from the economic expansion in the first decade of the century, and also from the mobility opportunities created by import substitution. A substantial proportion of the immigrant blue collar workers climbed to the middle class. As the immigrant working class shrank, manufacturing expanded and new industries developed (textiles, metals, and others). Most of the new labor originated in the interior and was of Creole ethnicity. There was a cultural cleavage between the two groups, in terms of the overall ethnic culture as well as of the culture of the working class.

The degree of mobilization of the labor movement was affected by these changes in the composition of the working class as well as by the modifications in the political environment.[43]

43. For histories of the labor movement in that period, see Samuel L. Baily, *Labor, Nationalism, and Politics in Argentina* (1967); Rubens

The older labor movement, in spite of its political fragmentation between socialist and anarchist wings, had developed at times
intense levels of mobilization. In the first decade of the century
and in the recession following World War I, there were massive
strikes, demonstrations, and violent repression. In the twenties,
however, the confrontation between labor and the state decreased.
A correlate of the assimilation and nationalization of labor noted
above was the waning of the traditional type of anarchist influence, and the emergence of the more "economicist" and pragmatic
syndicalist wing. At the same time, the ties between the Socialist
party and the unions it influenced would become looser. The other
important change took place in the political environment. As the
proportion of Argentines in the working class grew, the delayed effects of the Electoral Reform Law were felt, and labor was being
gradually enfranchised. The Radical governments, in spite of isolated instances of repression in the first Yrigoyen administration
(1916–1922), provided, with their clientelistic style of politics, an
environment conducive to the political integration of labor. Even
though the radicals were not specifically pro-union, they tended to
side with labor when political gains could be attained by doing so,
as Rock has shown.[44]

In the thirties, labor militance was at first inhibited by the new
cultural cleavages in the labor movement and by the establishment of nondemocratic regimes, which persecuted the radical
Left. Toward the middle of the decade, however, there were significant changes. The small Communist Party began to make inroads
among workers in many industries. The party gained control of
important unions, and some major strikes took place under its
leadership. Nevertheless, mobilization was limited in volume and
intensity, there was little penetration by radical ideologies, and
antistatus quo parties were small. The Communist Party was nu-

Iscaro, *Origen y desarrollo del movimiento sindical argentino* (1958);
Alfredo López, *Historia del movimiento social y la clase obrera
argentina* (n.d.); Sebastián Marotta, *El movimiento sindical argentino,
vol. 3, Período 1920–1935* (1970); Matsushita, *Movimiento obrero;*
Jacinto Oddone, *Gremialismo proletario argentino* (1949); Rubén
Rotondaro, *Realidad y cambio en el sindicalismo* (1971); and David
Tamarin, *The Argentine Labor Movement, 1930–1945* (1985). See also
Isidoro Cheresky, "Sindicatos y fuerzas políticas en la Argentina pre-
peronista," *Boletín de estudios latinoamericanos y del Caribe* (1981);
Doyon, "Organized Labour"; Germani, "El surgimiento"; Halperín
Donghi, "Algunas observaciones", Murmis and Portantiero, *Estudios;*
and José Peter, *Crónicas proletarias* (1968).

44. Rock, *Politics in Argentina.*

merically weak, and the Socialist Party, strong only in the capital, was ideologically moderate. In summary, this was not an instance of intense and sustained mass mobilization, or of an actual vertical cleavage in which superordinate and subordinate classes contended for hegemony.

Thus, neither the "Eastern" model nor the vertical cleavage hypothesis fit the Argentine case in this period. My conclusion is that the autonomization of the state at the time of the reversal was produced by the two other determinants discussed above: constraints derived from international factors, and the fragmentation of the dominant classes.

### The Autonomy of the State: The External Constraint Factor

The breakdown of the international economy in 1930 was the main determinant of the collapse of the hegemony of the agrarian upper class. With the Depression, the correlation between the rule of that class and the welfare of Argentine society began to vanish.

At that point, the agrarian elite was restored to power; the crisis was such that those who controlled the economy could not tolerate not being also in control of the state. From then on, nonelite groups became gradually aware that the nexus binding their interests with those of the elite was broken. After 1930, what was good for the landed upper class was not necessarily good for Argentine society. The belief that agrarian interests could no longer be entrusted with the direction of economic and social life became widespread.

Thus, legitimacy declined, albeit slowly, and from 1930 to 1943 the agrarian elite could only control the state on the basis of coercion and fraud. This transgression of constitutional norms served the elite to protect its economic interests, but at the expense of its legitimacy. Agrarian hegemony was eroded further by changes that altered drastically Argentina's position in the international system. These changes were caused by two processes that began before the Depression: import substitution, which not only transformed the country's economic and social structure but also modified the terms of its economic interactions with the outside world, and the large-scale inflow of American capital, whose presence affected the preexisting relationship between Argentina and Britain.

Import substitution had three main long-term effects on Argentina's international economic position. First, it enhanced, albeit inefficiently, the country's autonomy. Argentina became gradually self-sufficient not only in food and other agrarian inputs, but also in a wide range of manufactured consumer goods. Second, the country's import needs changed. It is true that, with the diversification of manufacturing, Argentina was able to lessen the impact of contractive processes in the world economy, but it was still dependent on the importation of machinery and other industrial inputs. Third, with the commitment of a large proportion of the labor force to manufacturing, domestic consumption of exportables eventually increased. The stage was thus set for the stagnation of exports and balance-of-payment difficulties.

The inflow of American investment in the interwar period is the second process that changed Argentina's social structure and international position. This inflow deepened Anglo-American rivalry, for it enhanced the ability of the United States to advance its economic and political interests in Argentina.

At the economic level, the Argentine relationship with the two core countries was of a different nature. Most British capital was concentrated in the export sector—railroads, meat-packing, and so on—and the Argentine and the British economies were complementary. A major share of the new American investment, on the other hand, was in manufacturing activities geared to the domestic market. As for trade, Argentine and American agrarian exports competed, but Argentina was a consumer of American manufactures. A triangular relationship developed. Argentina exported to Britain and other European markets, but the United States became the most important source of its imports.

This pattern was hampered by the bilateralization of trade that followed the Depression. Bilateralization forced Argentina to reduce its imports from the United States precisely at the time in which the substitution process would have benefitted from an intensification of these imports, for the United States was a key supplier of machinery and other manufacturing inputs. British and American economic interests in Argentina were therefore in contradiction. Britain needed Argentina as a steady supplier of food, but this Argentine role was of no direct relevance to the United States. In addition, import-substituting industrialization was not in the long-term British interest, for it decreased the complementarity between the two economies. But import substitution in Argentina was in the long-term American interest, for partial industrialization expanded the opportunities for American trade and investment.

At the political level as well, the two core countries competed. The United States aimed at extricating Argentina from informal membership in the British Empire and at including the country in the orbit of the evolving "Pan-American" system, a network of treaties and agreements with which the United States was consolidating its sphere of influence in the continent.

These changes in the position of the country in the international economy were taking place at the same time as the Depression and the war presented major challenges to the Argentine state. We have already seen how it responded to the Depression. It was quite successful at the economic level, by adjusting to the fall in exports through bilateral trade agreements, import substitution, and increased government control of the economy; and quite deficient at the political level, by putting an end to the seventy years of expanding liberalism and inaugurating the period known as the "infamous decade."

World War II brought about a question of a different order. The issue now was not how to adapt to external processes, but how to deal with direct external pressures requiring the country's response. In the perception of the economic and political elites, the potential cost at stake was not just impoverishment, but also national survival, or at least the survival of the upper classes; some groups also saw in the war, and on the basis of diametrically opposed international alignments, opportunities for the improvement of the economic or the political positions of the country.

Documents from the period convey the acute anxiety experienced by the economic and political elites. In 1944, Mariano Abarca, the National Director of Industries, exhorted an audience of manufacturers to conduct the necessary studies in order to avoid a catastrophe at the end of the war, so that the dominant class could maintain its position as such.[45] Some segments of the elite expected the resumption in the postwar period of the linkages tying Argentina to Europe before the Depression. Carlos Saavedra Lamas, a leading statesman and a liberal, asserted pompously in 1942: "We should look from afar the light of the fire, we must stand erect . . . over our rich, fertile, ample soil, convinced that the human masses of Europe will have to come to us, in search of their

45. Abarca, *La industrialización*, p. 35.

nourishment. . . ."[46] But other sectors saw also an opportunity to enhance national economic and political autonomy, thanks to industrialization: "As an agrarian country, with an homogeneous and simple economy," wrote Sarobe, "we have been tributaries of the powers with perfected and complex economies . . . ; throughout our political existence we have been absorbed by this economic regime of a colonial type. . . . Countries producing raw materials, like ours, must conquer some economic autonomy, if they aspire to preserve their political independence. . . ."[47] Abarca went farther and asserted that only industrial nations could be independent: ". . . either one supports the colonial economy or that of a state power . . . ; [only] those countries that are capable of working what nature has placed at their reach are worthy of preserving their independence. . . ."[48]

Argentina's neutrality in the war, supported by the stronger segments of the state bureaucracy and the upper classes, fitted the goals of different groups and international forces. This policy suited the agrarian elite and it was not inconsistent with British interests, for it ensured the stability of the Argentine-British trade: 40 percent of British meat imports indispensable for the war effort still originated in Argentina.[49] Neutrality was also the most favorable policy that Germany and the pro-Axis groups in the state apparatus, mostly in the army, could expect. Thus, as Alberto Ciria notes, British and German interests were parallel as far as Argentina was concerned: "England needed supplies, Germany sought to infiltrate Latin America. Argentine neutrality seemed to favor both purposes."[50]

Britain, while not actively encouraging Argentine neutrality, as Humphreys has shown,[51] did not contest this policy, and this fueled the American suspicion of Anglo-Argentine connivance. Britain even resisted American appeals to join in the intense and at times obsessive anti-Argentine campaign undertaken by the Roosevelt administration after Pearl Harbor, a crusade predicated on the principle that Argentina was the headquarters of fascism in

46. Carlos Saavedra Lamas, "Palabras de presentación," in Amadeo y Videla, El desarrollo industrial, p. 15.

47. Sarobe, Política económica argentina, pp. 29, 51.

48. Abarca, La industrialización, p. 27.

49. David Kelly, The Ruling Few (1952), p. 289.

50. Ciria, Partidos y poder, p. 105.

51. Humphreys, Latin America, vol. 2, pp. 139–42.

the Western hemisphere.[52] In the end, the need for cooperation between the Allies was stronger then their competition for economic and political influence in Argentina, and the British government supported the American strategy of intimidation in order to force Argentina to fall into line. As diplomatic documents show, however, such support was measured.[53] Finally, neutrality was advocated by the Argentine nationalists. This segment of the intelligentsia and the officer corps defined Argentina as a British dependency, and saw no gain for the country in joining the war on the side of its informal metropolis; moreover, they thought, an Axis victory would destroy the forces responsible for Argentina's colonial status.

In any case, neutrality seemed to many groups the safest policy for a peripheral nation, especially in the early stages of the war, when the Axis prevailed. This prudence was not attenuated by the explicit admission made by the American government that it lacked the capabilty to defend the Southern Cone in the event of a German attack. And the American offensive against Argentina predictably strengthened the determination of the neutralist forces.

Interventionist sentiment, on the other hand, was strong among the liberal and left-wing segments of the middle classes, and also in a sector of the upper classes. Some agrarian and industrial groups realized that the pre-Depression complementary relationship with Britain was unlikely to be reestablished in the postwar period, and they expected the United States to become the pivot of Argentine trade and her key supplier of capital.

Pinedo was the spokesman of these groups: "The belief that a shattered and starving Europe could offer great prospects to countries like ours is fallacious," he said in 1942, "for it is impossible to foresee from where will the old continent extract, in the short term, means of payment to acquire the goods it urgently needs."[54] More specifically, it was unlikely that Britain could resume its role as Argentina's best customer: "The catastrophic reduction of her purchasing power, which . . . was the consequence of her overseas investments now lost, of its financial services now disorgan-

52. See Francis, *Limits of Hegemony*; Frank, *Struggle for Hegemony*; Macdonald, "The Politics of Intervention."

53. See Kelly, *The Ruling Few*, pp. 287–319, and Rapoport, *Gran Bretaña*, pp. 72–238.

54. Federico Pinedo, *Argentina en la vorágine* (1943), p. 73.

ized, of its magnificent merchant marine now worse than deci-
mated, is in itself enough to dissipate the illusions of prosperity
held by the most optimistic Argentines. Will England be able to
continue buying? Will she be able to pay, with the labor of her
metropolitan population?"[55] In any case, Britain was likely to
strengthen her ties to the dominions, the empire, and the United
States. The solution for Argentina was to turn to the United
States, ". . . that immense nation, which until recently appeared
to be so far from ours, and so foreign to our future fate. . . ."[56] That
linkage would be hard to establish as far as trade was concerned,
for Argentina and the United States competed with each other on
the agrarian markets. But Argentina could export manufactured
goods and also beef to the United States if protectionist pressures
by American farmers were overcome.[57] Argentina's "genuine" industries could orient part of their output to American markets.
With this objective, policy studies such as the Armour report, referred to above, were conducted.

A strong pro-Allied stance was also supported by segments of
the established manufacturing class represented in the UIA. Without supporting necessarily the massive reconversion project advocated by Pinedo and others, these manufacturers realized that
the United States was the only source of the machinery and equipment their firms needed. American imports were closed to them
due to the boycott, but were available to Brazil and other Latin
American countries.[58] For one result of the conflict with the
United States and the consequent economic and political isolation
of the country in the region was the re-kindling of the economic
and military rivalry with Brazil and, to a much lesser extent, with
Chile. Brazil did enter the war and benefited from large-scale
American aid. In particular, the Argentine military and civilian
nationalists regarded with anxiety the rupture of the traditional
equilibrium between the two competitors for regional hegemony,
as Brazil developed its basic industries, and modernized its armed
forces thanks to the considerable inflow of American arms, which
were denied to Argentina and were unavailable from other
sources.

55. Ibid.
56. Ibid., p. 46.
57. Weil, *Argentine Riddle*, pp. 195–221.
58. Rapoport, *Gran Bretaña*, p. 41.

### The Autonomy of the State:
### The Elite Fragmentation Factor

Some of the cleavages that split the economic elite at the time of the reversal were based on divisions that had developed prior to the Depression, while others emerged as a consequence of changes associated with the Depression and the war. The conflicts between agriculture and industry and, within the agrarian elite, between breeders and fatteners, were determined by the basic characteristics of the Argentine export economy, but they intensified after the breakdown of the international division of labor. On the other hand, the opposition between the new manufacturers and the other segments of the possessing classes, and the domestic frictions derived from the Anglo-American rivalry, reflected the new traits of the Argentine social structure.

The relationship between agriculture and industry before the Depression was, as we have seen, nonantagonistic. Manufacturing, much of which was a forward linkage of agriculture, adapted itself to the country's position in the international division of labor; the manufacturers' organization, the UIA, basically consented to the subaltern nature of industry in the national economy.

This acceptance of the hegemony of the agrarian upper class did not preclude, of course, secondary conflicts over tariffs and other aspects of economic policy. The interests of the two groups became more divergent after the economic crisis hit the country. The basic alliance was maintained, however. But as manufacturing expanded, cleavages became more salient. The Roca-Runciman Pact, through which the oligarchy secured a share of the British market, facilitated also the entry of British manufactured goods, and thus disprotected sectors of domestic industry.[59] Import policy was another issue. Manufacturers needed desperately to import machinery and other inputs. This requirement intensified over time, as industry grew and foreign goods became less available as a consequence of the war. Pro-agrarian administrations were sensitive to this need, but their main concern was the export of primary goods. As noted above, this concern led to a weakening of the trade relationship with the United States, as a consequence of bilateralism in the thirties and of the neutrality policy during the war.

A cleavage within the agrarian sector pitted the breeders against

59. Conil Paz and Ferrari, *Política exterior*, pp. 16–34.

the fatteners, who were the dominant fraction of the cattlemen and who were allied with the foreign packing houses.[60] The conflict also had regional overtones, for breeders predominated in the richer Pampean areas, especially in the west of Buenos Aires province, while the fattening grounds were located in the east and south of Buenos Aires and in the other littoral provinces.[61] This was a contest over the distribution of the gains of the export trade, in which the cattle buyers (fatteners and packers) had a stronger market position than the sellers (the breeders). Fatteners were also more powerful politically, for they controlled the SRA, whose influence on government policy up to the early forties was paramount. As a consequence of the economic turmoil in the thirties, breeders formed an alternative organization for the defense of their interests, the *Confederación de Asociaciones Rurales de Buenos Aires y la Pampa* (CARBAP). The two associations diverged not only in their economic interests, but also in their political ideologies, the SRA being more "liberal" and CARBAP more "nationalist."

The cleavage between the new and old manufacturers is obvious. The two fractions of the industrial bourgeoisie shared some basic needs, such as tariffs, foreign inputs, and government credit, but their economic and political positions were so different that the divergent interests were much more salient than the common ones. The new industrialists were much more likely than the old bourgeoisie to produce goods that were imported prior to the Depression and the war, and thus were more vulnerable to foreign competition when the international economy was re-organized. Moreover, they were much weaker politically. New manufacturers had much smaller firms than their older counterparts, and were much less likely to be tied with the landed elite or with foreign capital. Most of them were new arrivals to the capitalist class. They had moved upwardly, from the skilled working class, or laterally, from the merchant strata of the middle class. Also, most were immigrants, and many were newcomers to the country. An important number were Jews.[62] Neither the UIA nor the upper or middle class political parties (Conservatives, Radicals) repre-

60. Peter H. Smith, *Politics and Beef in Argentina* (1969), pp. 32–56.

61. Ibid., pp. 35–37.

62. Cornblitt, "Inmigrantes y empresarios"; Jorge, *Industria y concentración*, pp. 34, 151–52.

sented the interests of this new group, although, as I noted, a segment of the UIA supported protection for all kinds of industries.

Finally, the changing relation of power between Britain and the United States affected the Argentine ruling classes. With American investment in manufacturing, the sector of the economy under direct external control grew and became more heterogeneous, even though the strategically central means of production (Pampean land, cattle) as well as most of manufacturing remained in domestic hands. The most important impact of the Anglo-American rivalry was indirect: it created constraints, mostly in relation to short-term issues, such as Argentina's participation in the war, and opportunities, mostly in relation to the country's long-term development (whether to seek, after the war, a return to the preexisting position in the world economy; or to try something different, a link-up with the United States as a segment of the elite wished, or autarky as a diffuse military and civilian nationalist group wanted).

In conclusion, the dominant class was fragmented along several lines of cleavage. These divisions interacted with the external constraints that had caused the decline of the hegemony of the agrarian elite since the Depression. Not only had the economic elite ceased to be accepted by the rest of the society as the governing class, but its own divisions rendered it incapable of ruling effectively. It is at this point that the military intervened and established a regime that was more independent of the upper classes than the previous ones.

### The Resolution of the Crisis

In determining the autonomy of the state, external factors operated mostly as constraints to which the country needed to adjust, while the fragmentation of the economic and political elite provided the opportunity for the relaxation of ties between the state apparatus and the major social forces. This configuration is clear in relation to the military coup of 1943, which started the period of institutionalization of the new industrial and labor policies.

The event that triggered the coup was a presidential succession in which a pro-Allied Conservative politician was expected to come to power through what would probably be another fraudulent election. Neutralists were also urged by the possibility that the electoral process might serve as the catalyst for the formation of a pro-Allied Center-Left coalition, the Argentine version of the

Popular Front. They feared that the growth of antifascist mobilization would tip the scales toward intervention in the war. There were two factions among the military who took power: the neutralists and a pro-Allied group. This cleavage was parallel to the division of the economic elite into the traditional pro-British faction and the "modern," pro-American, one.[63] Paradoxically, the pro-German and other neutralists in the armed forces coincided with the pro-British agrarians in their refusal to enter the war, while the pro-Allied officers and the pro-American sector of the bourgeoisie supported mild and negotiated forms of interventionism. The economic elite was incapacitated by its divisions and could not face the dangers emanating from the international scene. This provided an opportunity for the military takeover, but the armed state managers did not prove to be more efficacious or lucid than their civilian counterparts. The refusal to join the Allies, even when the complete defeat of the Axis was an absolute certainty, is an extreme instance of their lack of realism. "[Argentina]," said Churchill with a bit of sarcasm in August of 1944, "has chosen to dally with the evil, and not only with the evil, but with the losing side. . . ."[64] The military were as fragmented as the upper classes, and future developments would show that they were notoriously less capable of evaluating international trends and of formulating realistic policies for the reintegration of Argentina into the international economy.

The coup was a response to the American pressures and to the changes in the regional balance of power that had been caused by American intervention. The British ambassador, in a dispatch to the Foreign Office soon after the takeover, characterized the new regime as nationalist, and described its objectives as follows: in foreign policy, the attainment of better relationships with the United States, in order to be able to buy military equipment and thus reestablish the balance of power with Brazil (and presumably to maintain superiority over Chile), and in domestic policy, the

63. Ciria, *Partidos y poder*, pp. 110–47; Díaz Araujo, *La conspiración*, pp. 11–201; Halperín Donghi, *Argentina*, chap. 1; Marvin Goldwert, *Democracy, Militarism, and Nationalism in Argentina, 1930–1966* (1972), chap. 4; Potash, *Army and Politics, 1928–1945*, pp. 182–200; Rapoport, *Gran Bretaña*, passim; Rouquié, *Pouvoir militaire*, pp. 275–317.

64. *The Times* (London), August 3, 1944, quoted in Humphreys, *Latin America*, vol. 2, p. 183.

fight against corruption.[65] The aims vis-à-vis the United States were more complex than that, and weapons procurement was only the most manifest of these aims. The different factions agreed on this, but their other foreign policy objectives diverged. The goal of improving relations with the United States can only be imputed to the pro-Allied faction of the military. Bonifacio Del Carril has argued that the leaders of the armed forces wanted to control the negotiations with the United States with regard to the conditions and circumstances in which Argentina would enter the war.[66] But the leadership also included the more nationalist oriented neutralist faction, whose influence on the new regime would grow rapidly. These officers' international concerns focused on resisting American hegemony, developing instead the Argentine sphere of influence in the region, and positioning the country favorably for a possible Axis victory.

Several authors have tried to downplay this faction's right-wing authoritarian and fascist orientations,[67] but these are evident, even if diffusely, in the documents of the secret organization that guided the group, the GOU (*Grupo Obra de Unificación*, Unification Work Group), recently published in an authoritative edition. Perón, one of the faction's most important leaders, was most likely the author of the programmatic documents, written before the seizure of power. In these documents, the GOU asserted as its central goals the officers' "material and spiritual unity," and the defense of the army against its enemies.[68] In a telling image, it saw the country as the victim of apparently diverse but in fact unified "hidden forces, controlled from abroad."[69] The roster was the standard one for the extreme Right: international banks, Communism, Jews, Free-masonry. . . .[70] All worked in a synchronized manner, in order to attain two goals: in the short run, plunging Argentina into the war; in the long one, assuring the country's exploitation in the postwar period.[71] In the coming national elec-

65. Document cited by Rapoport, *Gran Bretaña*, p. 166.

66. Bonifacio Del Carril, *Crónica interna de la Revolución Libertadora* (1959), p. 26.

67. See Díaz Araujo, *La conspiración*; Rogelio García Lupo, *La rebelión de los generales* (1963).

68. Robert A. Potash, ed., *Perón y el G.O.U.: Los documentos de una logia secreta* (1984), p. 25.

69. Ibid., p. 207.

70. Ibid., pp. 101, 103, 109, 173, 202.

71. Ibid., p. 208.

tions, which the coup would block, these hidden forces planned to operate, in a two-pronged strategy, through both the fraudulent Conservative candidate and the projected Popular Front.[72] The most direct threat was the American offensive, which also affected Argentine relations with South America: "[The United States] pressures our country and forces the neighboring ones, which follow it in its war policy, to do the same," this in spite of the fact that Argentine neutrality, since the country kept supplying Britain, "affects the interests of the plutocracies [sic] only spiritually"; other Latin American nations, however, "realize the danger of extraordinary growth of Argentine influence should the Axis win the war."[73] In such a critical situation, power was in the hands of a despised and corrupt elite; "a leading class without . . . prestige with politicians [who are] verifiably criminal. . . ."[74] The only possible solution laid in the demise of this incapacitated ruling class, an end to liberal politics, and the erection of a corporatist dictatorship.[75]

The concern about the upgrading of Brazilian military and strategic capabilities as a consequence of American aid was paramount. Not only had the United States supplied to Brazil large amounts of military equipment through the lend-lease program, but it had also contributed to develop that country's steel and rubber industries and to improve its ports and airports.[76] That this collaboration was in exchange for Brazil's resolute participation in the war does not seem to have been registered by Argentine nationalists, who only perceived the consequence, the disruption of the regional military balance.[77]

After the coup, the supply of arms would be, for the Argentine side, the central issue in the relationship with the United States. This was, however, an impossible bargain, for the new regime was still reluctant to enter the war. The primacy of the regional balance of power as a determinant of Argentine policy is evident in two desperate gambles by Buenos Aires that weakened Argentine-

72. Ibid., pp. 198–99.

73. Ibid., p. 192.

74. Ibid., p. 203.

75. Ibid., p. 202.

76. See John W. F. Dulles, *Vargas of Brazil* (1967), pp. 203–27; Frank, *Struggle for Hegemony.*

77. See Ciria, *Partidos y poder*, p. 81; Conil Paz and Ferrari, *Política exterior*, pp. 19–22; Díaz Araujo, *La conspiración*, p. 58; Rapoport, *Gran Bretaña*, p. 60; Weil, *Argentine Riddle*, pp. 29–30.

American relations to a critical point: the organization of a coup and the establishment of a client government in Bolivia, and the attempt to buy arms from Nazi Germany. Both actions were un- covered by Allied intelligence, and it was under the threat of sanc- tions that Argentina finally broke diplomatic ties with the Axis in early 1944.[78] But the country still refused to go to war, and rela- tions deteriorated even further. The American ambassador was withdrawn, and later his British colleague followed suit, after American insistence on a reluctant Foreign Office. Also, Argen- tine gold reserves in the United States were frozen, and American trade with Argentina was restricted. Eventually, the country de- clared war, but this was a purely symbolic act. Hostilities were about to finish, and Argentine forces did not enter combat or even participate in support activities. Perhaps it was embarrassment, rather than sorrow, what laid behind that most unusual act for a triumphant government, the banning of victory demonstrations at the fall of Berlin. . . .

### Conclusion

The overall conclusion is that the autonomy of the state was made possible by the combination of external constraints and the frag- mentation of the established elite. These structural factors, how- ever, did not determine the *contents* of state autonomy, the direc- tion of state policies. These factors made radical protectionism and corporatism possible, but did not determine them specifically. If the new industrial and labor policies were not, as we have seen, in the dominant class interest, nor were they determined by exter- nal forces, the question becomes: why were they selected?

Two hypotheses must be rejected. The first is that these policies were the most likely ones that an autonomous state would follow. The second is that radical protectionism and corporatism were a function of the military's professional concerns.

First, it seems attractive to argue that both radical protection- ism and corporatism were logical or even necessary outcomes of an autonomous state, for these policies expand the control of the society by the state, a goal it seems reasonable to impute to state

78. See Conil Paz and Ferrari, *Política exterior*, pp. 123–61; Francis, *Limits of Hegemony*, pp. 201–29; Frank, *Struggle for Hegemony*, pp. 45–78; Humphreys, *Latin America*, vol. 2, passim; Potash, *Army and Politics, 1928–1945*, pp. 201–37; and Rapoport, *Gran Bretaña*, pp. 156– 238, 259–78.

managers (as a special case of the general proposition according to which leaders of organizations endeavor to control the environment in which their organizations operate). The problem, again, is that a hypothesis of this type is too general, for there are many ways in which an autonomous state may expand its control over its society. Radical protection in the economy and corporatism in the polity were one of several possible policy packages that could have enhanced state power.

Second, since the military was the leading force in the autonomous state apparatus, it could be thought that its industrial and labor policy would reflect the military's professional concerns. Two of these would be paramount: the improvement of the country's defense capabilities, and the preservation of order. The trouble with an argument of this type is that neither radical protection for manufacturing nor a corporatist relationship between labor and the state are the only policies that could fit these broad interests.

The argument that a concern with defense in the Argentine context at that time would have necessarily impelled the military to pursue radical protectionism is not correct. A concern with defense would have entailed an interest in further industrialization, but there were several possible industrialization policies, as influential officers such as Savio understood well. In addition, radical protectionism for existing manufactures was not very consistent with this defense goal. Radical protectionism led to partial autonomy in relation to consumer goods, but by itself it failed to develop efficient manufactures such as heavy industry, machinery and equipment, and vehicles; that is, the types that provide external economies to military and strategic production. The selective protection of some of these strategically important manufactures, even at the cost of dismantling noncompetitive consumer goods industries, would have been more effective from a defense point of view and perhaps more efficient for the economy as a whole.

As for the preservation of order, there is no reason to assume that absolute protection to manufacturing and a corporatist relationship between labor and the state had necessarily to be perceived by the military as the only or the best mean for the achievement of that goal. In the past, an economy integrated into the international division of labor and liberal political institutions had produced a legitimate social order. Why think, then, that only the policy package of radical protection and corporatism could lead to such an outcome in the future? The practice of state corporatism, in particular, was an unknown quantity.

State autonomy in itself does not predict, then, the direction of the policies. It tells us the how, not the why. In order to understand why "relatively autonomous" state managers resorted to radical protection for manufacturing and attempted to incorporate the working class on the basis of corporatist controls, it is necessary to go beyond the fact that the state was separate from the dominant classes. The question becomes: what were the interests defended by this "relatively autonomous" state elite? Further, why were these interests defined in such a way that radical protection and corporatism came to be understood as means to their defense? What was the relationship between the interests so defined and the interests of the upper classes?

# 6 The Primacy of Politics: The Question of Revolution in the Forties

This chapter focuses on the election of 1946, which marked the formal end to the military regime established in 1943 and the beginning of the Peronist period, or, in other words, the crucial point in the institutionalization of the new industrial and labor policies. The chapter examines three issues: Perón's arguments in defense of radical import substitution and corporatism, the response among economic and political elites, and the realism of the danger of revolution, whose existence was asserted by Perón and apparently believed by his elite supports (the military, the church hierarchy, and some Conservatives).

I will show that Perón justified his policies on the basis of this danger. In his view, not only corporatism but also autarkic industrialization was an antidote to communism. Further, I will try to understand the extent to which opposition to and support for Perón among segments of the economic and political elite were based on material or ideological interests. I conclude that state elites supporting Perón were moved basically by ideological interests, while those opposing him (the economic elite) had a clearer view of their material interests. Finally, I will examine the objective basis for the fear of revolution and argue that such fear was unfounded; the military, the bishops, and the Conservatives supporting Perón were guided by an inordinate fear of communism.

## Political Entrepreneurship and the Rhetorical Uses of Economic Policy: Protection as an Antidote to Revolution

To understand the selection of the radical protectionism/corporatism package by the segment of the political elite in power after the coup of 1943 and especially after Perón's access to power in 1946, it is necessary to reconstruct the image this segment of the elite had of the "social question" in Argentina. If most of the leadership of the Army and the Catholic church, and considerable segments of Conservative and other politicians aligned themselves behind Perón at such a critical juncture, it is reasonable to assume that, in addition to other possible reasons for such support, they accepted his diagnosis of the Argentine situation and agreed with his prescriptions.

In this section I discuss Perón's justification for radical protectionism and corporatism. His grounds for espousing corporatism are obvious and well known, but the argument connecting radical import substitution and the communist threat deserves analysis. In discussing the functions of industrialization, Perón contended that a manufacturing sector developed on the basis of blanket protection would help prevent a revolution. I will show that this was a central part of his argument.

The thesis appears in the speeches he made from the end of 1943, when he was the secretary of labor, to the beginning of 1946, when he was elected president. Several authors, myself included, have analyzed different aspects of these speeches,[1] but the connection between radical protection and communism has not been dealt with in detail.

In a sense, all these were campaign speeches addressed to specific audiences, most of which were working-class. He discussed bread and butter issues and also major political and economic matters. He had a message for everyone. Thus, he reassured industrial workers that his goal would be a more just distribution of wealth, and he promised rural workers that land would be a production good, rather than a rent good. In order to win the favor of retail merchants, Perón even told them they were the "proletarians of commerce" and, thus, the good guys,[2] and he assured capitalists that he was a resolute defender of the interests of capital. . . .[3]

The advantage of analyzing these speeches is clear: mentalities, including the mentality of elites, are diffuse, but political messages emitted by strategic communicators may uncover some of their components. These messages may not reveal the "true" ideology of the sender but, since they were successful in persuading some of their recipients, they expose areas of *their recipients'* mentality. Perón's inner beliefs are irrelevant for my argument. It should be clear that I am not making any assumptions regarding

1. Ciria, *Perón;* Little, "La organización obrera"; Puiggrós, *El peronismo: Sus causas;* Schoultz, *Populist Challenge,* chap. 2; Waisman, *Modernization,* chap. 4; etc.

2. Juan Perón, *El pueblo quiere saber,* p. 147.

3. Ibid., p. 165.

these beliefs. Perón may have been either sincere or cynical, and probably he was both to some extent. Like other pragmatic politicians, he had an ideology, a quite articulate one in his case, but he also aimed at attaining the support of a constituency, the working class first and the larger population later, and he probably said what was practical or efficient in order to reach his objective. But the fact that the message was accepted by most of the working class and some non–working-class groups indicates that there was some correspondence between the contents of the messages and the recipients' own perceptions or anxieties. Moreover, Perón's prescriptions were vehemently rejected by other groups, and this rejection reveals some aspects of these groups' mentalities as well. With a chemical metaphor, Perón could be viewed as a catalyst, whose actions forced different groups to react, and to bare themselves in the process. Or else one could use a gambling image, and characterize him as a player who compelled the other players to show their cards. I will focus on some of the recipients of the message, rather than on the sender. My purpose is to infer, on the basis of their reaction to Perón, how upper classes and state elites defined their interests, and the relative weight they gave to material and ideological interests.

If Perón's messages to the two most important social classes, the workers and the capitalists, are compared, differences are obvious. To the workers, he talked about social justice; to the capitalists, he advocated anticommunism. But these are different emphases, different variants of the same underlying conceptual framework and not ad hoc messages designed to please diverse audiences. Like the fascists in the interwar period and the third-world nationalists in the postwar period, he saw himself as an anticapitalist and an anticommunist at the same time. These oppositions were, however, of a different nature. His rejection of communism seems to be absolute, but his opposition to capitalism is not, for he distinguished between two types of capitalism. In a typical formulation, these types were called "despotic" and "humane." The latter was presumably the type of capitalism that reconciles itself with "social justice" for the working class. And also like the fascists and the third-world nationalists, he proposed, as the means for social reform, an expansion of the control of the society by the state, a process designed to save capitalism by "humanizing" it and thus to prevent a communist revolution.

He was, however, an eclectic, and his diagnosis and remedies were predicated on what may be called his "Marxism in reverse."

To his chagrin, he seems to have conceded the validity of some of the basic tenets of Marxist political ideology, a recognition that, with a similar negative perspective, can also be discerned in facist doctrines.

In a typical formulation of his discourse to the workers, Perón described his objectives as the dignification of labor and the humanization of capital:

> This change of course could not be attained without . . . *dignifying labor*, [by] giving workers their worth, and the standing they deserve in social life, [and by] providing them the economic means they need in order to enjoy the gratifications enjoyed by other social groups. . . . It is also necessary to *humanize capital.* Capital has been unjust, because it has provoked economic slavery, and it has forced workers to defend themselves to the death, so that their children would not starve.[4]

In an address to retail merchants, he characterized capitalism thus: "In our concept, capitalism is a force of accumulation (*aglomeración*). [It is] cold, international, without a fatherland and without a heart. It is . . . the spuriousness of money. It is also the monopolization (*acaparamiento*) of wealth. . . ."[5]

Perón advised workers to organize, in order to improve their power position vis-à-vis the capitalists: "You must strive day after day to have a stronger and more unified union"—he told municipal workers, in a language drawn from the traditional left-wing labor tradition—"Workers have, when facing the economic and political powers, one defense: their unity. It is the only thing which makes them strong and capable of defending their own rights."[6] The similarity with the Left ends here. The organization he envisioned would be "nonpolitical" and controlled by the state, as would be the capitalists' associations. He said this explicitly in his speech at the stock exchange:

> And the State has the obligation to defend an association as much as the other [that is, trade unions and capitalists' organizations], because it suits the State to have organic forces it can control and lead, rather than inorganic forces that escape its leadership and its

4. Juan Perón, *El pueblo ya sabe*, p. 13.
5. Idem, *El pueblo quiere saber*, p. 189.
6. Idem, *El pueblo ya sabe*, p. 69.

control. For this reason, we have sponsored . . . the union
movement, but [it is] the true workers' unions
(*sindicalismo gremial*). We do not want unions divided
into political fractions, for what is dangerous is,
precisely, the political unions.[7]

The purpose of state intervention would be to suppress social
conflict by regulating labor relations. In the corporatist tradition,
he thought that only this could ensure a "just" distribution of
wealth: "We think that, from now on, political power will be organized in such a way that the state will . . . prevent a conflict between the forces of capital and labor, by ensuring the harmony that
must govern their relationship, and . . . with the goal of securing a
respectable life to the workers, and an equitable profit for the capitalists."[8]

Perón's discourse to the capitalists focused on the communist
threat, which, he said, only his proposed policies could dispel: "I
ask you, gentlemen, to reflect, to think in whose hands the Argentine working masses were [before the coup of 1943], and what
would have been these masses' future. In a large proportion [these
masses] were in the hands of communists, who were not even Argentines, but imported, supported, and financed from abroad."[9]
Rooting out these elements, as well as any other extremists, was
the Secretariat of Labor's task.[10] In controlling the threat, the organization of labor under state control and the regulation of social
conflict by the state would provide the insurance, and the coercive
apparatus would be the reinsurance:

> In order to prevent the masses who have received the
> necessary and logical [amount of] social justice from
> going beyond that level in their claims, the first remedy
> would be the organization of these masses. . . . This
> would be the insurance . . . still the State would organize
> the reinsurance, which is the authority necessary to
> keep people in their places . . . because the State has the
> instrument that, if necessary, would make things fit (*en
> quicio*) through force.[11]

7. Idem, *El pueblo quiere saber*, p. 161.

8. Idem, *El pueblo ya sabe*, p. 46.

9. Idem, *El pueblo quiere saber*, p. 159.

10. Ibid., pp. 50–51.

11. Ibid., p. 165. I have also discussed this aspect in my *Modernization*,
p. 62.

Perón's belief in the existence of a revolutionary threat followed from his Marxism in reverse. He seems to have accepted the validity of two central Marxist propositions. The first is that the working class is an intrinsically revolutionary force, and that the central process of our epoch is the coming to power of the working class. The second proposition is that the radicalization of the working class is a function of at least three environmental factors: the experience of economic deprivation, the experience of class conflict, and political indoctrination "from without."

The first proposition can be inferred from this lecture to metalworkers:

> The world, in the past two centuries, underwent two major evolutionary stages, . . . mankind has lived for a century under the influence of the French revolution. Our institutions were born in that revolution, and our culture is its product. . . . But in 1914 the cycle . . . of the French revolution comes to a close, and that of the Russian revolution opens. . . . How can it but project a century of influence in the development and evolution of the future world? . . . The rule of the popular masses—whose center of gravity are the workers—has been producing in different countries the disappearance of many institutions belonging to the epoch of the French revolution. Thus, in the political realm, Russia suppressed political parties completely. By different means, Germany and Italy produced the same phenomenon. . . .[12]

Thus, fascist regimes were, in accordance with their own definition as revolutionary movements, considered by him as another variant of this process of seizure of power by the "popular masses," as were "evolutionary" developments he also refers to, such as the labor government in postwar Britain, the New Deal in the United States and even the organization of labor in Mexico.

His view about the economic, social, and political determinants of working class mobilization was clearly stated in the stock exchange speech. In reference to the situation in the postwar period, he argued:

> The postwar period will inevitably bring mass agitation, due to natural causes: [the] expected (*lógica*) paralysis,

12. Perón, *El pueblo ya sabe*, pp. 175–76.

unemployment, etc, which [will] . . . produce gradual impoverishment. These will be the natural causes of mass agitation, but in addition . . . there will also be artificial causes, such as ideological penetration . . . abundant funds for agitation [and] . . . a resurgence of [the now] dormant communism, which pulsates like an endemic disease within the masses. . . .[13]

In addition to economic deprivation and ideological indoctrination, he considered the experience of injustice to be also a determinant of working class radicalization. In reviewing his activity as secretary of labor, he asked rhetorically: "Is not this [policies aimed at greater welfare for the workers] the most efficacious means to remove or sweep away definitively the Red Revolution, which appears wherever it finds ferments in which it can germinate and multiply?"[14] In his view, "without it [social welfare], fortune is a true mirage, which can be broken at any moment. Wealth without social stability can be powerful, but it will always be fragile. . . ."[15]

Perón saw the Argentine working class as especially susceptible to these environmental causes of radicalization, and he feared that the situation of Argentina in the postwar period would be conducive to revolutionary developments. The susceptibility of the working class, especially before the 1943 coup, arose from what he considered a low level of "organization," which meant a not very high rate of unionization (in absolute terms, probably) and, especially, the fact that the labor movement was independent of the state. This situation and the absence of "social justice" rendered the working class a dangerous class: "The working masses that have not been organized present a dangerous picture, for the most dangerous mass is, without any doubt, the inorganic one. . . . These inorganic masses, abandoned, lacking a general culture, lacking a political culture, were a culture medium for these foreign professional agitators. . . ."[16]

He predicted a stark scenario for the postwar years: "We have not suffered during the war," he told an audience of glassworkers, "but we will suffer during the postwar period, with all the phe-

13. Idem, *El pueblo quiere saber*, p. 164.
14. Idem, *El pueblo ya sabe*, p. 38.
15. Ibid., pp. 157–58.
16. Idem, *El pueblo quiere saber*, pp. 158–59.

nomena that will reverberate in our economy, the state of our society, and the state of our polity."[17] "The postwar period can bring about problems that only those with privileged imagination can foresee in all their intensity," he said to a group of tramway workers. "These conflicts, which sometimes lead to civil wars, represent an extraordinary destruction of values. . . ."[18] The specter of civil war appears also in his discourse to the capitalists. He argued that the resolution of the Argentine ideological conflict would not take place in the country, but in the European battlefields. The outcome of the war could have profound political consequences in Argentina, ranging from widespread agitation to a civil war.[19] We know already the reason for his pessimism: the postwar period would mean "paralysis and unemployment" and a resumption of communist agitation.[20]

It is in order to avert the social explosions which may ensue from such a situation that Perón proposed his plan: elites must give something, in order not to lose everything. He said apocalyptically in reference to the worst possible scenario: "All the Argentines will have something to lose [but] this loss will be directly proportional to what everyone possesses: he who has a great deal will lose everything, and he who has nothing, will lose nothing."[21] As a preventative remedy, industry must be preserved and developed, in order to give jobs to the lower classes and improve their standard of living. When discussing the promotion of manufacturing, he still referred to the distinction between natural and artificial industries: "Industries can resist well any dangers when they are naturally developed and grounded. The ones which are *protected* for just reasons will also resist with the help of the state. The *occasional* or *fictitious* ones could die or disappear without a grave risk of perturbation for the economy as a whole."[22]

However, the central argument for protection was the creation of jobs and, in general, welfare considerations. And only autarky could ensure full employment.

In a revealing statement, Perón said: "Protection to industry is

17. Idem, *El pueblo ya sabe*, p. 113.

18. Idem, *El pueblo quiere saber*, p. 111.

19. Ibid., p. 162.

20. See above for the argument, and Chapter 6 below for an evaluation of these prospects.

21. Perón, *El pueblo quiere saber*, p. 163.

22. Idem, *El pueblo ya sabe*, p. 24.

justified only when it flows back to the masses who work and make sacrifices."[23] He was referring to the sugar industry, one of the most extreme cases of protected inefficiency in the Argentine economy. And, if mass unemployment was to be avoided in the postwar period, production should be geared exclusively to the internal market. A report on employment and unemployment, produced by the National Postwar Council (headed by Perón) described a gloomy scenario for the postwar years, unless manufacturing expanded as much as possible. In the council's view, neither agriculture nor tertiary activities could absorb the unemployment that the resumption of imported manufactures and the new contingents added yearly to the labor force would produce. "In its simplest terms," said the report, "the problem of full employment boils down to achieving that internal consumption that could absorb the totality of the labor power of the active population,"[24] that is, autarky.

Avoidance of revolution was not, of course, the only reason offered by Perón in 1943–46 to justify blanket protection. Industry was also necessary for national sovereignty: "Either the country has an industrial future," he said to an audience of manufacturers, "or we will have to submit to being a semicolonial country."[25] And there were, no doubt, considerations of national defense, which the painful situation during the war rendered urgent: "National defense requires a powerful . . . industry, and not of any type, but a heavy industry."[26] Military needs were a significant component of his industrialist mystique, but events would show it was a secondary one. In line with the concern for the maximization of employment, the emphasis was put on "light," labor-intensive manufactures.

Years later, Perón still credited the expansion of industry in the postwar period for avoiding a major social explosion: "A few days ago, the United Nations, through . . . ECLA, has established that the only solution for those semideveloped countries lies in industrialization, the only means whereby these peoples will be able to reach the indispensable standard of living, in order not to be

23. Ibid., p. 54.

24. Argentine Republic, Vicepresidencia de la Nación, Consejo Nacional de Postguerra, *Ocupación y desocupación en la Argentina* (1945), p. 19 (pages are unnumbered). I discuss this report in detail below.

25. Perón, *El pueblo ya sabe*, p. 44.

26. Idem, *El pueblo quiere saber*, p. 82.

dragged down to dissociation and communism"—he said in 1953, ". . . We said the same ten years ago, [and] for the past ten years . . . we have been carrying it out in the Argentine Republic."[27]

By that time, he should have known better. The failures of radical import substitution were then obvious. In the early fifties, the external constraints that may have contributed seven years before to make a partial closure of the economy appear as a reasonable option had disappeared. Neither the European inability to import, pointed out by Fodor,[28] nor the American boycott, discussed by Escudé,[29] were then factors in the equation. As for communism, its expansion had stopped at the Elbe and southeast Asia, an expansion that owed more to Red Army victories and to the unforeseen consequences of Western colonialism than to proletarian revolt.

### Responses by Upper Classes and State Elites: Instrumental versus Ideological Interests

I will now examine the reception of Perón's argument among economic and state elites. My focus will be the interests that guided the responses made by different segments of these elites. In particular, I will look into the relative weight of instrumental and ideological interests. This is important for assessing whether "ideology matters" and in which way. This issue has been rekindled in sociology since the spread of structuralism, a theory that denies an independent causal role for ideology, which is considered a conduit for structural effects,[30] and of empirical analyses such as Theda Skocpol's, who argues that ideology is not necessary for the prediction of the outcomes of revolutionary processes.[31] Here I conclude that the choices made by economic elites were determined by their economic interests, but in the responses of antiliberal groups of the political elite (the military, the church hierarchy, some Conservatives) ideological factors were prevalent.

Perón's diagnosis and proposed solutions received a mixed response among established elites. They were supported by the political and ideological elites in control of the state or close to it: the

27. Confederación General de la Industria, *Congreso general*, p. xxiv.

28. Fodor, "Perón's Policies."

29. Escudé, *Gran Bretaña*.

30. See especially Louis Althusser and Etienne Balibar, *Reading Capital* (1970).

31. Theda Skocpol, *States*.

leadership of the army and the church, a segment of the Conservative Party, and groups linked to these organizations. They were
opposed by the economic elites, both agrarian and industrial (the
large landowners, represented by the SRA, and the big industrialists, represented by the UIA), by a majority segment of the Conservatives, and by other groups linked to these organizations. The
opposition parties, the Radicals and the Left, were also, of course,
against, and allied themselves with the economic elites in an electoral front, the *Union Democrática* (Democratic Union), led by
the Radicals. External forces were also present. The United States,
for the first time in Argentine history, intervened openly in a domestic conflict. The American government mobilized against Perón through the "antifascist" activities of Ambassador Spruille
Braden and the *Blue Book*, published by the State Department in
order to expose Perón's German connections.

Even though the armed forces were divided, the state apparatus
under their control provided Perón with what Potash has called "a
guaranteed election,"[32] which was, however, fair in terms of its organization and of the counting of the votes. The bishops forbade
Catholics to vote for some of the educational and religious planks
of the Democratic Union and some of its constituent parties, and
some members of the hierarchy and lower-rank clerics publicly
supported Perón.[33] On the other side, the Democratic Union was
resolutely backed by the Rural Society and the Industrial Union,
the latter in a most militant manner.[34] The Conservative Party, finally, was split. Many of its leaders and organizations promoted
the cause of the Democratic Union, in spite of the traditional antagonism between Conservatives and Radicals, but some leaders
and the party apparatus in important districts (including areas of
the key provinces of Buenos Aires and Córdoba) opted for Peronism.[35]

32. Robert A. Potash, *The Army and Politics in Argentina, 1945–1962:
Perón to Frondizi* (1980), p. 15. See also Rouquié, *Pouvoir militaire*, p.
384.

33. See Ciria, *Partidos y poder*, pp. 238–48; Hugo Gambini, *El
peronismo y la iglesia* (1971); John J. Kennedy, *Catholicism,
Nationalism, and Democracy in Argentina* (1958), pp. 204–8; Félix
Luna, *El 45*, pp. 407–10; Alejandro Magnet, *Nuestros vecinos argentinos*
(1956), pp. 181–85.

34. See Dardo Cúneo, *Comportamiento y crisis de la clase empresaria*
(1967), pp. 153–58, 174–78; Halperín Donghi, *Argentina*, p. 53; Félix
Luna, *El 45*.

35. See Ignacio Llorente, "Alianzas políticas en el surgimiento del

Why this cleavage between the economic and political segments of the established elites? The different interests of the leaders of the five most important organizations of these elites—the SRA, the UIA, the armed forces, the Conservatives, and the church—provide an answer.

If Perón's plan was to be carried out, economic elites had to "give, in order not to lose everything," not only a share of their wealth, but also a share, and a very considerable one, of their power.

As we know already, the agrarian upper class would have to finance industrialization. Also, it was concerned about potential retaliation against the high tariffs that a closed industrialization program would require. The "big" or established industrialists grouped in the UIA, many of whom had links with the agrarian upper class and with foreign capital, had immediate reasons not to be enthusiastic about the plan. Perón's performance as secretary of labor led them to believe that "social justice" would be attained at their own expense. Perón's spectacular measures—major wage increases, compulsory thirteenth-month bonuses, social security, and other protective legislation—were partially or totally financed by employers. Moreover, it is reasonable to assume that autarky was not the industrial policy needed by either the "natural" industries, to use the terminology that was popular at the time, or those linked to foreign capital, that is, the sectors in control of the UIA. Perón, then, was offering a very costly remedy most of them did not need.

Perón's plan entailed more than the "socialization" of a share of the surplus previously appropriated by the agrarian and industrial upper classes. It also implied a more permanent redistribution of political power. Economic elites were called upon to contribute to the institutionalization of this "independent" state, which they viewed more as an instrument of an individual, Perón, than as a neutral machinery regulating social conflict. Why would they prefer placing their fate into the hands of an individual they did not trust to the traditional elite linkages with the Conservatives and the moderate wing of the Radicals? Economic elites will not only surrender, but also actively seek a Bonapartist savior only in one situation: when they panic, as a consequence of a credible threat from below. And Argentine agrarian and industrial capitalists

peronismo: El caso de la Provincia de Buenos Aires"; and Luis A. J. González Esteves, "Las elecciones de 1946 en la provincia de Córdoba," in Mora y Araujo and Llorente, eds., *El voto peronista.*

were very skeptical of Perón's assertions in this regard. They were concerned about workers' mobilization, including the apparently spontaneous Peronist rally of October 17, 1945 (which took place when it became known that the army faction opposed to Perón had forced him to resign his government posts and placed him under custody; as a consequence of the rally, Perón was freed, and the relation of forces within the army changed in his favor). But capitalists viewed Perón as a cause of the problem, rather than as the solution to it. "As they cannot say we are making politics"—a disappointed Perón would grumble"—they say that we are demagogues, that we are awakening the lowest passions in the masses. To require that labor be compensated, that it be organized, that rest be established, that social security laws be adopted, that labor laws be complied with; all this, those accusing me say, is to awaken passions."[36] In sum, economic elites viewed his appeal to them as extortion. In their eyes, Perón, like the mafia, first created the danger and then demanded protection money in order to keep the danger under control.

The support by the military, the church, and a sector of the Conservative party can be attributed to two factors: what, following Jimmy Carter, can be called an "inordinate fear of communism," and organizational interests.

The military, the army in particular, and the church hierarchy were especially susceptible to the anticommunist appeal. Even though both organizations included liberal and pro-Allied individuals, they contained the most important clusters of antiliberal and antirevolutionary ideologies in Argentine society. With respect to the military, Tulio Halperín Donghi has characterized anticommunism as the most stable element in their vision of the world,[37] and Alain Rouquié has wondered about the curious phenomenon of their anticommunism without communists.[38] As for the church, much of it was still influenced, in varying degrees, by the traditionalist doctrines that questioned popular sovereignty and defined both communism and liberalism as "errors," the latter being the most perverse. In addition, the church hierarchy was still mobilized by its fervent support of the Franco side in the Spanish civil war, and leading Catholic intellectuals and publica-

36. Perón, *El pueblo ya sabe*, p. 142.
37. Halperín Donghi, *Argentina*, p. 29.
38. Rouquié, *Pouvoir militaire*, p. 11.

tions, while criticizing central elements of fascist doctrine, had viewed the Mussolini regime with sympathy.[39]

Both the army and the church had been influenced, in the thirties and forties, by the right-wing "nationalist" and integralist intelligentsia. This group, while a secondary strand in the country's cultural establishment, had developed a considerable infrastructure: nationalist intellectuals formed cultural and political associations, taught courses for adults, published magazines and newspapers.[40] Yet, they never attained direct influence for long periods. One of their number, Jordán B. Genta, was the ideological mentor of the GOU and was popular in right-wing military circles; and the GOU issued to its members a reading list that included nondoctrinaire nationalist publications. However, the assertion by Marcelo Sánchez Sorondo, later a leading nationalist, that there is no proof that the coup was the product of their proselytism, seems to be correct.[41] After the coup, right-wing intellectuals colonized the new regime, especially in the areas of education and culture, but they never retained important positions in central policy areas for long, and the most doctrinaire ones were eventually displaced by the pragmatic Perón.

Their effects were indirect. They did influence groups within the army and the church, whose hierarchical structure, antiliberal values, and rationalist (as opposed to pragmatic) approach to politics generated a strong affinity with authoritarian ideologies. Members of both organizations tended, for reasons of professional specialization, to be more susceptible to different ideological themes. For instance, the right-wing military, due to their concern with national defense and the balance of power between Argentina and its neighbors, were more sensitive to nationalism and industrialization, whereas the integralist clerics, whose outlook was more internationalist and whose sphere was the belief system, were more concerned with opposing leftist—and liberal—ideas in the political and cultural realms. But both right-wing officers and

39. Ciria, *Partidos y poder*, pp. 234–37; Kennedy, *Catholicism*, pp. 171–80.

40. See Navarro Gerassi, *Los nacionalistas*; Zulueta Alvarez, *El nacionalismo argentino*.

41. Marcelo Sánchez Sorondo, *La Revolución que anunciamos* (1945), p. 16. See Jordán B. Genta's lectures to the military, "La formación de la inteligencia éticopolítica del militar argentino" and "La función militar en la existencia de la libertad," in his *Acerca de la libertad de enseñar y de la enseñanza de la libertad* (1976), pp. 35–78. The G.O.U. reading list is in Potash, ed., *Perón*, p. 115.

churchmen saw their organizations as the central components of an organically conceived ideal nation whose interests these organizations had the privilege to define and interpret. They tended to view their relationship with the concrete nation in a paternalistic manner, as a relationship between vanguard and followers.

Nationalists, integrists, and their followers differed from the fascist model in that their rejection of political modernity was total. They not only opposed communism and liberalism, but mass politics as well. Their organicism was authoritarian, rather than mobilizational. Therefore, the "fascist" label, so often pinned on this fundamentalist right wing, is inappropriate. This is important, for the mistrust of political participation, even of the heteronomous type, is one of the keys to understanding the subsequent relationship between the rightists and the Peronist regime.

Since support for Perón was also consistent with the organizational or instrumental interests of the military and the church, the issue of the relative weight of these interests and of the fear of communism can be raised. The issue is, more specifically, whether ideology was just an intervening variable, a rationalization, or even a conscious camouflage, of these material interests. In my view, instrumental interests were significant, but they were not the chief determinant. The reason is that the instrumental interests of the military and the church could have also been protected if the anti-Peronist coalition, the Democratic Union, had won. This point is not self-evident, so it requires clarification.

Let us see first how these instrumental interests were served by opting for the Peronist ticket in the 1946 election. For the military, a Peronist government would have at least two advantages. First, it would be a continuation of the current military regime. This insured that neither the right-wing authoritarian domestic policies of that regime nor its pro-Axis neutrality would be subject to review. This, in turn, minimized the possibility that individual careers would suffer. This important point was emphasized by Halperín Donghi.[42] Second, Perón's nationalist ideology and support for radical import substitution made it likely that his government would be sympathetic to the military's armament needs, and that he would foster industries necessary for national defense. The Democratic Union, on the other hand, advocated political liberalism, and the free-trade interests (the agrarian and the big industrialists, domestic and foreign) were aligned with it. Should it suc-

42. Halperín-Donghi, *Argentina*, p. 43.

ceed, the revision of the past would be more likely and, it was reasonable to assume, economic policies would be less sensitive to military preferences.

As far as the church was concerned, its support for Peronism could be linked to three specific issues: religious education in public schools, divorce (or, strictly, permission for legally separated individuals to remarry), and, more broadly, the relationship between church and state. The military regime, driven by its integralist ideology, had broken the long tradition of secular public education and introduced optional religious education in public schools. Perón promised to uphold this policy, while the Democratic Union would support a return to "lay" education. Moreover, there was a long-standing policy of the church banning Catholics from voting for or belonging to parties that advocated divorce or the total separation between church and state.[43] The parties in question—Socialists, Communists, Progressive Democrats— formed part of the Democratic Union.

Finally, the Conservative Party machines that supported Peronism in parts of Buenos Aires and Córdoba, but mostly in less developed rural areas, would have also been guided by their instrumental interests. Given the deep-seated hostility between the Conservative and Radical parties, these organizations were simply protecting themselves and the safety of their members, as a Conservative politician remarked, when supporting their enemies' opponent.[44]

The issue is: could it have been possible for the military, the church, and these Conservatives to protect their instrumental interests under the administration of a victorious Democratic Union? My conclusion is positive. Since the Conservatives were fragmented, and their main impact was pro–Democratic Union, I will focus on the military and the church. I think that these organizations could have perceived the liberal-democratic option as a less complete but more legitimate and, thus, in the long run, more effective mechanism for the protection of their material interests. The reason lies in the political and ideological context of the time (1946). The Axis was defeated (with the Franco regime as a lone and beleaguered marginal remnant), the Soviet Union was still the strategic ally of Britain and the United States (and communists and liberal democrats still collaborated in several European gov-

43. Ciria, *Partidos y poder*, pp. 238–39; Kennedy, *Catholicism*, p. 184.
44. González Esteves, "Las elecciones"; Llorente, "Alianzas políticas."

ernments), and the United States now faced no major obstacles for the pursuit of its long-standing project of incorporating Argentina into its sphere of influence (as its ill-managed attempt to support the Democratic Union indicated).[45] In that international environment, betting for the antiliberal alternative represented by Perón was not an instance of pragmatic behavior for organizations such as the military or the church. Their basic interests could have been redefined and made consistent with the liberal democratic regime.

The military could have rediscovered their profound "democratic" calling and jumped into the liberal bandwagon where they would have been welcomed by the forgiving and relieved centrists and leftists. (This is more or less what eventually happened, when the armed forces overthrew Perón almost ten years later.) This about-face would not have been totally cynical; after all, there had been an important pro-Allied segment within the military. Many neutralist officers were not antiliberal, and it was far from certain that the support for Perón as such was very high. Political use could have been made of two facts: the palace coup against Perón the previous year, and the well known division about his candidacy. By Potash's count, only about one-third of the active-duty generals in early 1946 were known as pro-Peronists.[46] Besides, the anti-Peronist sentiment in the navy was notorious. The turnaround could have been presented as a spontaneous development rather than as a change forced by a political defeat. In this situation, the revision of the past and the injury to individual careers could be held to a minimum (perhaps, as happened after the reestablishment of democracy in the early eighties, only to a handful of the officers, most by then retired, who had top posts during the dictatorship).

Moreover, the military would have been in an excellent position to equip themselves. In fact, in their own experience, it was the conflict with the United States that had prevented a regular flow of arms. The Brazilian example had showed that good relations with the Allies was a precondition for obtaining weapons and strategic supplies of different kinds. (They could not foresee, of course,

45. On American attempts to influence the elections, see Ciria, *Partidos y poder*, pp. 139–46; Luna, *El 45*, pp. 344–84; Potash, *Army and Politics, 1945–1962*, pp. 35–69; Puiggros, *El peronismo*, pp. 143–52. See also the "blue book": United States, Department of State, *Consultation among the American Republics with Respect to the Argentine Situation* (1946).

46. Potash, *Army and Politics, 1945–1962*, pp. 8–10.

that shortly thereafter the Cold War would facilitate their procurement plans anyway.) It was even conceivable that the military could use their bargaining power and the memories of the blockade to persuade the civilian authorities that some defense manufactures and the emerging steel industry were necessary and should be preserved.

An about-face of this type would have been more difficult in the case of the church. Unlike the military, it had a firm official doctrine that was still very skeptical of liberal institutions. However, the church had the experience of two generations under liberal democracy (prior to 1930) during which it had successfully blocked all the attempts to upset the settlement of the religious question reached in the nineteenth century. This settlement, some of whose clauses are in force still today, provided for a limited establishment of the Catholic church (and it is for this reason that I call the church hierarchy at that time a state elite). According to this settlement, the state supported the church, a formula that included economic support, and participated in the appointment of bishops by nominating candidates and formally appointing them when designated by the pope; in addition, the president and vice-president were required to be Catholic and to give a Christian oath, divorce was not allowed, and religious schools were authorized and subsidized by the state. On the other hand, religious marriages lacked legal validity, and public schools and church were separate.[47] The most important issue in church-state relations after that settlement was the divorce question. The church had foiled several efforts by liberals and leftists to legalize remarriage for separated persons.[48]

In the past, then, the status of the church had been secure. Not opposing the Democratic Union in 1946 would have meant a loss only in one area, religious education in public schools, but pragmatic church leaders should have realized that the legitimacy of such policy was very low for two reasons: secular public education was one of the core issues in the liberal tradition of the country, and religious education was one of the most controversial domestic policies adopted by an unconstitutional regime actively opposed by most of the economic elites, the political parties, and the intelligentsia. The extent of its nonviability in the long run would be demonstrated by the fact that the policy was changed by Perón

47. See Kennedy, *Catholicism*, pp. 11–28, 186–204.
48. See Ciria, *Partidos y poder*, pp. 220–28.

himself when, nine years later, he sought a popular issue to divert attention from economic difficulties and to fight back at sectors of the middle class close to the church. As for the future, there were no reasons to think that a Radical administration established after a victory of the Democratic Union would have a confrontational policy with the church or be more "intractable" than previous Radical governments (and, in fact, the vice-presidential candidate was known to be sympathetic to the existing relationship between church and state). A reasonable conclusion is that the endorsement of Perón was the product of an unrealistic fear of the Left: Communists and Socialists were highly visible but in fact secondary forces in the Democratic Union, and their influence on very controversial matters such as the religious question would be limited by the reluctance among Radicals and Conservatives to trigger a polarizing conflict about issues that did not require immediate solutions and whose consequences were uncertain.

This brings us back to the relationship between ideological and instrumental goals. The support for Perón by these state elites was not just a "structural" factor, the necessary consequence of the elites' organizational goals. Instrumental interests do not exist in a vacuum. Except for extreme situations in which the survival of the organization is at stake, short-term or instrumental interests are compatible with alternative long-term or ideological conceptions. In this case, the support for Perón was not "necessary": instrumental interests were guided, or defined, in terms of the ideological ones. The segments of the elite supporting Perón were betting on the development of a new type of social and political legitimacy based on a movement combining a right-wing ideology (strong state, corporatism as a mechanism for the regulation of conflict, and opposition to pluralism and the other liberal tenets) with populist appeals (distributionism in the economy and mobilized participation in the polity). Before their eyes, the long-sought miracle of such a formula attaining popular support seemed to be realized.

They should have known better, though. On the basis of the cognitive equipment at their disposal and of observation of the current international scene, they should have realized that such a project was nonviable at the time and place. The ideal of autarky was associated with fascism, and conventional economic wisdom maintained that radical, absolute import substitution in a relatively small economy would lead to stagnation. Moreover, the least literate political observer should have understood that a corporatist populist regime was the least congenial one with the international political and ideological developments of the early postwar period. Ideological considerations, then, were not a rationalization of instrumental interests. It was the opposite, for the option for Peronism in the name of instrumental interests was a rationalization of ideology, of the inordinate fear of communism among these groups.

The contrast with the economic elites is instructive. Agrarians and big industrialists, as well as the sectors of the Conservative Party closest to them, shared the profound distaste for "communism" and had not been exempt from anxiety about that danger. They appeared as committed democrats in the mid-forties, but they had not objected to the severe repression against the Left in the thirties, and some of them were quickly forgetting their past approval of fascism. (Luis Colombo, the new-born democrat at the helm of the bellicose UIA, was one of their number.) Their economic interests dictated support for the Allies during the war, but assisting an alliance that included the Soviet Union was hard to stomach for some of their leaders. Robustiano Patrón Costas, a politician who was defined by the British ambassador as the representative of "the Conservative oligarchy of Anglophile landowners and pro-American financiers" and whose candidacy for the presidency was the pretext for the military coup of 1943, disclosed to the British diplomat Evelyn Baring, also in 1943, his concern about the communist threat and its implications for the postwar period (and also, as fitted his own pro-British interests, his deep worry about American penetration.)[49]

More generally, these were the groups that had supported enthusiastically the overthrow of the last constitutional administration in 1930 and the regimes of limited democracy during the "infamous decade" thereafter. The authenticity of their political liberalism was, at best, dubious. But their strong anticommunism did not lead economic elites to give much consideration to Perón's prescriptions. They not only mobilized with the liberal democratic center and the Left during the wartime "resistance" and the anti-Peronist crusade, but in some cases they were pragmatic enough to establish privileged relationships with the Communist Party. Both the pro-British and the pro-American sectors of the economic elites understood in the postwar period that their instrumental interests prescribed a reintegration into the world

49. Rapoport, *Gran Bretaña*, p. 148.

economy and that a return to liberal democracy was the best political formula for the reestablishment of the hegemony they lost in 1930. They betted for the liberal type of legitimacy, with the expectation that, as had been the case prior to the Depression, the efficient and the popular would be correlated again in the future. If this were to be the case, dominant classes would again rule legitimately.

The policies of the Peronist regime confirmed the apprehensions of the economic elite. Manufacturing expanded under radical import substitution policies and was financed through the expropriation by the state of a large share of the earnings obtained by the agrarian exporters. Moreover, landowners' interests were hurt by the freezing of land rents and the extension of tenancy contracts. The agrarians reacted by restricting their output. Toward the end of the forties, the economy slowed down, and this forced the government to improve agrarian earnings in order to expand exports. By then, however, the pendular mechanism was already in existence, and such a policy was contrary to the interests of the labor movement, which was the central base of support for the regime. This set limits to the reorientation of economic policy, for the government could not allow a significant deterioration in the standard of living of the working class.[50]

The big industrialists did benefit from the captive market created for them by import substitution, but the main beneficiary at the superordinate level was the new segment of the bourgeoisie, the small and medium-size manufacturers who grew in the thirties and forties and who thrived with government support and in a strategic alliance with the labor movement, for most of it would have disappeared with any industrial policy other than radical protectionism.[51] Both fractions of the bourgeoisie had to accept the

50. See Díaz Alejandro, *Essays,* pp. 106–26; Di Tella and Zymelman, *Las etapas,* pp. 91–120; José A. Martínez de Hoz, "Agricultura y ganadería," in *Argentina, 1930–1960* (1961); Wynia, *Argentina,* pp. 43–77.

51. Kenworthy has argued that no group among the industrialists participated in the Peronist coalition from its beginning. See Eldon Kenworthy, "Did the 'New Industrialists' Play a Significant Role in the Formation of Perón's Coalition, 1943–1946?" in Alberto Ciria et al., eds., *New Perspectives on Modern Argentina* (1972). There is no doubt, however, about the industrialist-labor alliance once the regime was in power. For the political alignments of different manufacturing associations in 1946, see Judith Teichman, "Interest Conflict and Entrepreneurial Support for Perón," *Latin American Research Review* (1981). For the alignments in the thirties and early forties, see Javier

major increase in real wages that took place in the late forties and that was the main quid-pro-quo for the workers' acceptance of a labor movement subordinate to the government and for their militant support of the Peronist regime. With the emergence of stagnating tendencies, the struggle for the distribution of the surplus surfaced. In the early fifties, the economy already presented the traits that would characterize it for the following generation: low growth rates, inflation, and unability to break the impasse through the diversification of exports.

At the political level, the economic elite was not only excluded from power, but even subject to repression. As Gary Wynia notes, the economic elite and its representatives were totally excluded from regulatory boards and from policy making in general.[52] The SRA was not repressed, but the UIA, as a punishment for its militant anti-Peronist stand prior to the election, was "intervened" and ceased to exist. In its place, the government promoted the formation of an organization encompassing the old big industrialists and the new small and medium size bourgeoisie, the *Confederación General Económica* (General Economic Confederation). The net effect was that the big manufacturers lost their corporate organization.

At a more global level, Peronist policies were against the interests of the old economic elites, for these policies were not conducive to the reintegration of Argentina into the international economy. The first reason is that, with the expansion of the domestic consumption of grains and beef and the antiagrarian price policies, exports were lower than they would be otherwise. This in turn reduced the potential imports of manufacturing inputs. Secondly, the nationalist policies of Peronism did not contribute to the inflow of foreign capital, with which much of the old bourgeoisie was closely linked. (The government changed its policy toward foreign investment in the fifties, but this was too late to affect the views of the economic elite.) Third, the Peronist regime was regarded by the United States and other countries as the successor to the pro-Axis military dictatorship and treated accordingly until the late forties, as noted above.

The issue can be raised of why a regime antagonistic to the economic elites lasted for almost a decade. Did these elites mobilize

Lindenboim, "El empresariado industrial argentino y sus organizaciones gremiales entre 1930 y 1946," *Desarrollo económico* (1976).

52. Wynia, *Argentina*, pp. 79–80.

all the resources at their disposal in the opposition to Peronism? If they did not, it would be possible to entertain the hypothesis that they eventually accepted Perón's diagnosis and remedy and decided to concede their short-term economic interests and political power in exchange for long-term security, that is, a working class vaccinated against communism and controlled by Perón. The answer is negative. They put up with Perón because they had no option. They collaborated with the opposition as much as it was reasonable, that is, with the caution that could be expected from large property owners in a context in which their social and political legitimacy was low and in which they were confronting an autonomous state, whose main base of support was their potential social antagonist, the working class.[53]

In the beginning of the regime, the relation of forces was unfavorable to economic elites. The fact that the post-1943 state was relatively autonomous meant not only that the government was not accountable to them, but also that the central coercive apparatus, the military, was no longer their instrument. In addition, the government could count on a mobilized power base, the labor movement, for which the economic elite did not have a counterpart. Its potential support against the regime was the middle class, but it took time until this heterogeneous class was available as a power base for destabilization. Eventually, the middle class mobilized as a consequence of four factors: the status panic caused by the dramatic rise in the standard of living and social status of the working class, the stagflation of the fifties (which intensified social conflict, and thus provided another cause for status panic), the increasingly repressive nature of the regime, as a consequence of that conflict; and, among religious groups, the struggle with the church, to which I refer below.

In the beginning, the armed forces, the church, and nationalist intellectual circles were staunch supporters of the regime. Their expectations were satisfied, for the Peronist formula denied a mass base to the Left. As the size of the working class increased, its organization expanded, and the powerful unions appeared to be firmly controlled by the government. Since the welfare of the working class improved sharply, and the Left was practically eliminated from the labor movement, the counterrevolutionary project seemed to have succeeded. But state elites slowly came to the realization of two painful facts: first, what I have called the con-

53. See Cúneo, *Comportamiento*, pp. 158–65.

tradiction of corporatism and, second, that Perón's project was not only different from theirs, but also that the two projects (Perón's and the counterrevolutionary one) could eventually collide. As a consequence, the elites' organizational interests could be affected.

We know already why a corporatist strategy for the control of labor was nonviable in conjunction with an economic policy of radical import substitution and in the context of a society without a large labor reserve. For those fearing working class mobilization, Peronist policies had in fact magnified the danger. Counterrevolutionaries also became aware that the economic elites had been right in their assessment of Perón as a political entrepreneur who created a threat and later demanded "protection payments" to keep it under control. They realized that Perón's latent plan, behind the fear of revolution theme, was to create a new power base that would be under his command, that this plan would imply a long-term alteration of the economy and society, and that the new structure would have a lower level of legitimacy than the one that existed prior to the Depression.

Since Perón had now his power base, his dependence on the elite supports that were crucial for his access to power gradually diminished. And conflict with these elites occurred for three reasons. As described above, the first was the disenchantment felt by the leaders of the army and the church. The second was that the leaders and members of these organizations were linked by social origin and interaction networks to sectors hostile to Perón and, in particular, to the progressively more militant middle class. The last reason was Perón's often unpredictable behavior.

Thus, when stagflation developed and labor discontent rose, Perón sought to divert attention by unleashing a conflict with the church, whose gradual distancing from the regime had become apparent. Paradoxically, it was this government, so warmly endorsed by the integralist Catholics, that launched the most frontal attack on the immediate interests of their institution in Argentine history, an offensive that ranged from the abolition of religious education in public schools and the legalization of remarriage for divorced individuals to the proposal of a constitutional reform that would totally separate church and state, and that would culminate in the burning of churches "by communist agitators," the expulsion of leading church dignitaries, and the excommunication of Perón.[54] The offensive was in retaliation for the shift by the church

54. See Gambini, *El peronismo*; Ludovico Garcia de Loydi, *La Iglesia*

to a mild opposition, and its consequence was the intensification of this opposition among middle-class Catholics, who were galvanized by the attack.

Relations between the regime and the military were, for most of the Peronist period, good but distant. Perón showered them with equipment and economic benefits, but perceived them as an organization beyond his control, and thus as a limit to his power. In fact, they were a veto force: on several important issues, he tailored his decisions to expected military reactions. On the side of the armed forces, they were uncomfortable at attempts to politicize them or to bring them under government control. Strains developed in the fifties, as stagflation set in, as labor unrest began, and as the middle class mobilized against the regime. After several conspiratorial attempts, the military moved in opposition to the government when signs appeared of an assault against their central organizational interest, the maintenance of the monopoly of force: when the first serious coup against the regime took place, arms were distributed to small groups of workers, and, thereafter, there was talk about forming workers' militias.[55]

Perón, then, ended up attacking the material interests of the organizations that were his elite supports and, in pursuing the expansion of his power, he changed the social structure of the country in a way that cannot be considered but detrimental to the ideological interests defended by the leaders of these organizations.

The autonomy of the state progressed a step further: after the coup of 1943, the state had become independent of economic elites; under Perón, the government became autonomous with respect to central components of the coercive and cultural apparatuses of the state, the military and the church. This forced a regrouping of the economic elite and the state against the government. In the name of "freedom," Perón was overthrown by a coalition of agrarians and big industrialists, the armed forces and the church, with a support base in the mobilized middle class; that is, a coalition similar to the one that brought the Franco regime to

*frente al peronismo* (1956); Julio Godio, *La caída de Perón* (1973); Joseph Page, *Perón: A Biography* (1983), pp. 296–305; Arthur P. Whitaker, *Argentine Upheaval: Perón's Fall and the New Regime* (1956).

55. See Godio, *La caída de Perón*, pp. 37, 183–86; Page, *Perón*, p. 318; Rubén Rotondaro, *Realidad*, p. 232; Rouquié, *Pouvoir militaire*, pp. 420, 428.

power. A fitting end for a regime with a semifascist ideology and the typical social base of socialist movements. . . .

The coup of 1955 could not be, however, a restoration of the regime existing prior to 1943 or prior to 1930, because Peronism had already reshaped Argentina.[56] The hegemony of the old economic elites could not be reestablished for two reasons. First, the economic interests of these elites were inconsistent with those of the new classes generated by radical import substitution: the new small and medium bourgeoisie, oriented toward the domestic market, and the much larger and now powerfully organized working class. Estimates of the growth of manufacturing output from 1943 to 1955, based on different definitions, are 45 percent and 79 percent.[57] The manufacturing labor force increased by 45 percent from 1940–44 to 1955, when it became 25 percent of the total labor force.[58] A large share of these workers were part of the new import-substituting industries: in 1954, 41 percent of the manufacturing workers were employed by firms founded after 1940.[59] As for the size of the labor movement, the number of union members grew by about 600 percent from 1945 to 1951. The social weight of the small and medium bourgeoisie can be inferred from the fact that, also in 1954, 52 percent of the industrial workers were employed by firms with up to 100 workers.[60] The noncompetitive industry could have been dismantled in the immediate postwar period at a moderate social and political cost, but such reconversion would be extremely difficult at the end of the regime, when a large proportion of the economic and human resources of the society were committed to it and when its producers were major political forces.

Second, one of the initial causes of the autonomization of the military from the economic elites was still present, and another cause of state autonomy had developed. The factor still present

56. I am alluding here to the title of a collection of essays that present quite a favorable view of this reshaping: Turner and Miguens, eds., *Juan Perón.*

57. Estimates made by the Central Bank and the CONADE (Consejo Nacional de Desarrollo), reproduced in Díaz Alejandro, *Essays,* pp. 443 and 446.

58. Estimates made by ECLA and CONADE, reproduced in Díaz Alejandro, *Essays,* pp. 428–29.

59. Argentine Republic, Dirección Nacional de Estadística y Censos, *Censo industrial, 1939* (1939), and *Censo industrial, 1954* (1960).

60. Ibid.

was the fragmentation of the dominant classes. The new factor was the appearance of vertical cleavage: the existence of a militant and well-organized labor movement, which could not be easily placed again under state control, was not conducive to the reassertion of the power of the old economic elite over autonomous armed forces.

### How Realistic Was the Fear of Revolution?

The communist threat is the most common tool in the ideological stockpile of the Right. Regardless of whether his assessment of the communist danger had any empirical validity, there is no question that using the argument was very productive for Perón. It helped him gain the support of the strategic state elites, without whom he would not have won a close race. But the divergent response of the upper classes and the state elites raises the issue of false consciousness. The rejection of the argument by the former and its acceptance by the latter were both categoric and passionate. Either the upper classes negated the reality of the dangers they faced, or the state elites had a paranoid mind-set.

I have already shown that the military coup of 1943 was not caused by an *existing* vertical cleavage; that is, the separation of the state from economic elites was not made possible by the fact that there was an "equilibrium," to use the traditional formula, between the dominant classes and an actually autonomous working class, threatening the power of the dominant class. The inexistence of manifest vertical cleavage is enough to disconfirm one of the classical hypotheses about the autonomy of the state. Perón's argument, however, did not refer to an actuality, but to a future danger. I will now assess the realism of that forecast.[61]

Let us recapitulate the situation in 1943. The majority of the labor movement was controlled by moderate Socialists and Syndicalists. The Communists had become in the late thirties a significant force and led some major strikes, but they were a small organization and controlled a minority segment of the labor movement. The expansion of their influence in the thirties and early forties was hindered mainly by three factors: police repression, of which Communists were the central target, the strength of the So-

---

61. Torcuato S. Di Tella refers to the fear felt by the Argentine elites in his *Sociología*, pp. 291–98. He considers the issue within a general analysis of the causes of military intervention in Latin America, and does not deal in particular with the realism of that fear.

cialist and Syndicalist traditions, and the cultural cleavage separating the "old" working class, which had trade union experience and was socialized into the left-wing ideologies, and the "new" one, of Creole origin, which had little or no exposure to union activities and little or no understanding of radical doctrines.

The evaluation of the likely dynamics of the labor movement and the Left if the strategy proposed by Perón (radical protection for existing manufactures and the institutionalization of the new corporatist linkages established between labor and the state since 1943) had not been applied can be disaggregated into four issues: first, the extent of labor militancy in the period prior to 1943; second, whether there was a growth trend in Communist influence; third, whether there were signs of radicalization in the non-Communist majority of the labor movement; and fourth and foremost, the plausibility of Perón's estimate of mass unemployment if the noncompetitive industries had been dismantled in the postwar period.

First, there is no question that, in the late thirties and early forties, the labor movement grew in size and strength. From 1936 to 1940, the number of unionized workers grew by 28 percent (however, it declined by 7 percent in 1941). Only one third of these were industrial workers, and unions in manufacturing had less members than unions in transportation: in 1941, there were once and a half as many workers in the railroad unions as in all of manufacturing.[62] The largest federation, the CGT (*Confederación General del Trabajo*, General Confederation of Labor), had over 330,000 members in 1941, and it was led by Socialists, Communists, and Syndicalists. The latter also controlled a much smaller federation, the USA (*Unión Sindical Argentina*, Argentine Syndical Union), and several independent unions. In 1943, prior to the coup, the CGT split into two organizations of about similar size: the CGT 1, which was more independent of political parties, and the CGT 2, led by Socialists and with a strong Communist minority.

There was a sharp increase in strike activity in the second half of the thirties. The data are available only for Buenos Aires, but this city contained in 1935 almost half the industrial employment in the country. These data show that the average number of strikers in the second half of the decade was almost 50 percent higher than in the first half. The peak was in the years 1935–37, which

62. Murmis and Portantiero, *Estudios*, pp. 77–81; Tamarin, *Argentine Labor*, p. 150.

had on the average three times as many strikers as the remainder of the decade (1931–34 and 1938–40).[63] The most important instances of mobilization were the great construction strikes of 1935–36 and 1937, led by the Communists, which elicited solidarity strikes and clashes in the streets.[64] The year 1942, just before the coup, also had significant strike activity; the most important case was a metalworkers' strike, also led by the Communists.

These facts have to be viewed in perspective. The number of unionized workers and of strikers grew, but so did the size of the working class, due to import-substituting industrialization. If, as we have seen, in the second half of the decade the number of unionized workers grew by a fifth and the number of strikers in the capital by almost a half, these processes took place in a working class whose size was increasing rapidly. From 1930–34 to 1940–44, the active population in manufacturing in the whole country grew by 35 percent, and the rate of growth in manufacturing, mining, construction, transport and utilities was 28 percent.[65] Overall, about 30 percent of the manufacturing workers and 10 percent of the wage earners were unionized at the end of the thirties.[66] In analyzing the strikes, it is important to keep in mind that conflict was concentrated in a few very militant unions, which tended to be led by the Communists. This is clear in the four years of highest strike activity in the 1930–43 period: the peak years of 1935–37 and 1942. In 1935–37, construction workers represented 55 percent of all the strikers in the city of Buenos Aires, and in 1942 metalworkers were 63 percent of all the strikers.[67]

In relative terms, labor mobilization in the period was significant but moderate. In no way did it resemble the major waves of general strikes, mass demonstrations, and even large-scale riots or plant seizures that took place in Argentina at the end of World War

63. Computed on the basis of data provided in: Argentine Republic, Departamento Nacional del Trabajo, *Estadística de huelgas* (1940); and Departamento Nacional del Trabajo, Dirección de Estadística Social, *Investigaciones sociales 1943–1945* (1946).

64. See Celia Durruty, *Clase obrera y peronismo* (1969), pp. 49–112; Iscaro, *Origen*, pp. 152–58; Rotondaro, *Realidad*, p. 134.

65. Computed on the basis of data in: United Nations, *El desarrollo económico*, p. 400.

66. Baily, *Labor*, p. 70.

67. Computed on the basis of data in: Argentine Republic, Departamento Nacional del Trabajo, *Estadística*; Departamento Nacional del Trabajo, División de Estadística, *Investigaciones sociales 1942* (1943).

I or at some points in the sixties (or, to compare with classical instances of major labor mobilization, in Italy at the end of World War I and in France in the thirties). Overall, it must be remembered, the Socialist and Syndicalist leaders that controlled the majority of the labor movement were anticapitalist in ideology, but moderate and reformist in behavior.

The strongest force in the labor movement, the Socialist Party, had won the elections in the city of Buenos Aires in 1942, but its influence was limited. In the presidential elections of 1937, it got only 2.5 percent of the national vote. It performed better in congressional elections, but the percentages were 9 percent in 1936, 5 percent in 1938, 8 percent in 1940, and 9 percent in 1942.[68] Incidentally, these figures are reliable: the Conservative government practiced "patriotic fraud" in that period, but elections were fair in the city of Buenos Aires, where Socialist strength was concentrated. It is true that a large proportion of the working class was foreign and did not vote, but immigration had been restricted after the Depression, and the proportion of foreigners in the population was dropping sharply. In spite of this, the Socialist vote was not growing very significantly.

The most important issue, however, is the constitutional and parliamentary orientation of the party. Thanks to the banning of the Radicals and later to their abstention and to fraudulent practices against them, the Socialists had a strong representation in the Congress, where they behaved as the loyal opposition to the ruling Conservatives, whose commitment to democratic norms was notoriously restrained.

In conclusion, before the coup of 1943, working-class mobilization was substantial but not very intense. It was after Perón became secretary of labor, in late 1943, that unionization increased sharply (in 1945 the number of unionized workers was 20 percent higher than in 1941) and that large scale labor political activity took place, mostly in support of Perón. The most dramatic instance, which shocked the opposition to the regime as well as Perón's opponents within it, was the mass demonstration of October 17, 1945, which was followed by a general strike the next day. These mass actions were the most important ones since the Tragic Week of 1919. The difference, however, was that this time the mobilization was not just a protest, but a part of a power struggle

68. Data in Cantón, *Elecciones y partidos* (1973), p. 120. Percentages have been rounded.

within the government. In fact, the demonstration was made possible by the cooperation of the federal police, which was controlled by Perón's faction and which, in any case, had the capability to prevent the rally, as it had successfully done with previous protests. That day foes and friends of labor alike realized that the working class had been incorporated into the political system and that the issue from then on was whether it would be a power base for a sector of the elite or an autonomous actor.

The second issue under analysis is the extent to which the Communist influence was growing or could be expected to grow.

The construction workers' union, the FONC (*Federación Obrera Nacional de la Construcción*, Construction Workers National Federation) was the second largest in the country and larger than any manufacturing union. In 1939, the FONC had more dues-paying members than all the manufacturing unions combined.[69] In addition to the FONC, the Communists controlled labor organizations in some traditional activities such as meatpacking, which was of strategic importance for the Argentine economy, and the wood industry. More significantly in terms of trends, they had also organized some of the expanding industries in the import-substituting areas of manufacturing, such as metals and textiles. The party had developed a group of very capable labor leaders, such as Pedro Chiaranti, Guido Fioravanti, Rubén Iscaro, and José Peter. The political leadership was of uneven sophistication, but toward the end of the period the main leader was Victorio Codovilla, an experienced Comintern official, who, as the delegate of the Comintern before the Spanish Communist Party (in fact, this party's controller or overseer), has played a very important role in the Civil War.

Most ominously from the point of view of those possessed by anticommunism was, as we know, the fact that a Popular Front had been in gestation since the second half of the thirties. The electoral coalition of the antifascist parties and the labor movement was being seriously discussed, and major unity rallies took place, with Radical, Socialist, Progressive Democrat, and Communist participation (such as the ones on May Day, 1936, and in August of 1941, which was accompanied by a general strike). There were large May Day demonstrations, whose graphic and choral revolutionary rituals were watched with horror by army of-

---

69. Data in Matsushita, *Movimiento obrero*, pp. 161–62.

ficers on intelligence assignment.[70] The front was definitely taking shape with a view to the elections the coup finally prevented. In that election, centrist and leftist parties would support the Radical presidential candidate, even in the knowledge that the Conservatives would probably rig the results, as they had been doing since 1930. (Eventually, this coalition was formed, and it became the Democratic Union.) In the atmosphere of the period, the Communists had gained, for the first time in their history, legitimacy among mainstream parties. Like in other countries in which the antifascist movement was in the opposition, the ideological differences between the Communists and other parties subsided, as the situation turned more critical, as the Communists became ardent supporters of liberal democracy, and as a relatively closed subculture emerged among activists from the different parties.

In perspective, however, the ghost of communism appears to be much less powerful than those haunted by it believed it to be. Except for the FONC, the party's roots in the labor movement were very shallow. The Communist-controlled textile union, the UOT (*Unión Obrera Textil*, Textile Workers Union, of Entre Ríos street), had only 4,516 dues-paying members in 1942, and the metalworkers union, the SOIM (*Sindicato Obrero de la Industria Metalúrgica*, Metal Industry Workers Union), had 1,540.[71] These figures corresponded to only 5 and 2 percent of the total number of workers in each of these industries. The party itself was a small organization, with only a few thousand activists, and the growth of its influence in the early forties was due more to its participation as a liberal-democratic organization in the antifascist "resistance," whose social base was mostly middle-class and whose very development, paradoxically, was a reaction to the pro-Axis policies of the state, than to its functioning as a revolutionary agent in the labor movement.[72]

70. Gen. José E. Sosa Molina, recorded testimony, archive of the Argentine Center of I.L.A.R.I., in Fayt, ed., *La naturaleza del peronismo*, p. 92.

71. Percentages based on data in Matsushita, *Movimiento obrero*, p. 285.

72. It is difficult to estimate the direct influence of the Communist Party on the basis of the electoral results of 1946, for the Communist vote cannot be satisfactorily disaggregated from the total obtained by the Democratic Union. The party supported the Radical presidential ticket, but it presented slates of congressional candidates. However, the Communists formed coalition slates with the Progressive Democrats and with Independents in the city of Buenos Aires, and with the

I have already mentioned the obstacles to the growth of party influence in the labor movement. The most important one was the inability to reach the "new" working class, the migrants of the interior for whom concepts such as surplus value or fascism were not precisely household words. The difficulties faced by organizers of European origin attempting to overcome cultural differences were overwhelming, as was widely documented and as Communist leaders explain in their memoirs.[73] This was compounded by a second factor, police repression, which was quite strong during most of the period. Finally, the non-Communist labor movement was far from being a political and ideological vacuum: Socialists and Syndicalists, who were strongly established, fought the Communist advance with tenacity. They counterattacked within the organizations, through the labor press, and by forming parallel unions to those controlled by the Communists. Moreover, the ideological changes that were taking place among these non-Communist workers were not conducive to the spread of the party's influence, as will be seen below.

These were the main barriers the party faced, but in addition there was an internal factor, the wide gyrations of overall party strategy, as a consequence of changes in Soviet policy. This factor was common to all Communist parties, but its consequences were more serious in Argentina, due to the large proportion of workers of recent migrant origin. It must have been very hard to explain, especially to these workers, the shifts in the thirties and early forties. In this period, the party line swung from the left-wing extremism of the "third period" of the Comintern, when Socialists

Progressive Democrats in Santa Fe, and it is not possible to control for coattail effects. These effects were very strong in Santa Fe, the Progressive Democrats' central base, but they also existed in the city of Buenos Aires, where the Communist Party had its strongest organization, because the coalition slate included prestigious non-Communist candidates. This slate got 12.45 percent. There is no way to estimate the Communist share, but it may have been half of the total: in the Constitutional Assembly elections of 1948, the party got 5.45 percent of the vote in the city of Buenos Aires. In the province of Buenos Aires, the largest electoral district in the country and the one that includes the industrial areas around the city of Buenos Aires, the party got 2.95 percent. In the rest of the country, its share was 1.21 percent. The data are taken from Darío Cantón, *Materiales para el estudio de las sociología política en la Argentina* (1968). See also Partido Comunista, *Esbozo de historia del Partido Communista de la Argentina* (1947), p. 126n.

73. See Peter, *Crónicas proletarias*, pp. 27–28; Juan José Real, *Treinta años de historia argentina* (1962), p. 60.

were branded "social fascists," to the moderation and liberalism of the Popular Front period; and then from the abstract pacifism during the Hitler-Stalin pact (which in Argentina meant a support for neutrality), to passionate antifascism once the Soviet Union was attacked (and the subsequent campaign for Argentine participation in the war).

These changes affected not only the relation with other parties, but also concrete union activity. Indeed, in many cases they harmed the party. Thus, during the period of the Hitler-Stalin pact, the different international positions caused strain between Communists and Socialists. This was the cause of the division of the AOT, the textile workers union, and of an intense conflict in the UF (*Unión Ferroviaria*, Railroad Union), the railroad workers union, the largest in the country. In both unions, the Communists, while officially supporting neutrality, concentrated their antagonism on imperialist firms, which happened to be from Allied countries. Predictably, their line changed after the Soviet entry into the war. The party focused its strike offensive on the construction industry not only because of objective grievances and of its own strength, but also because there were many German-owned firms (the Construction Chamber was labeled as "Nazi"), and it strove to contain strikes in the meat-packing industry, where there were British-owned firms whose output was in part exported to Britain.[74]

Finally in relation to Communist strength, there is the matter of whether there were grounds to expect a substantial growth of the party's influence if the nascent Popular Front had materialized and come to power. There is no question that such an eventuality would have been beneficial to the party, for it would have removed one of the external obstacles it faced—harsh police repression. Moreover, the party would have increased its respectability. It is doubtful, however, that this would have given it access to policy making or allowed it to fulfill any part of its program (such as expropriation of large landholdings). Given its composition and liberal democratic leadership, an Argentine Popular Front in power would have been more similar to the moderate Chilean front that came to power in the late thirties than to the more radical and polarizing Spanish one. Neither the Radicals nor the other non-Communist parties in such a front would be inclined to launch an at-

74. Matsushita, *Movimiento obrero*, pp. 232, 284; Puiggros, *El peronismo*, pp. 37–40; Tamarin, *Argentine Labor*, pp. 153–57.

tack on the upper classes, something the latter understood well in 1946.

In my opinion, then, there were no prospects for a significant growth in the size or influence of the Communist Party at the time of the 1943 coup. Such a possibility became even less likely after the coup. The CGT 2 was dissolved, powerful organizations such as the railroad workers' union were intervened, Communist-led unions were dismantled through intervention and the formation of parallel organizations, many labor leaders were jailed, and the party was driven underground for much of the period. The Communists thrived, nevertheless, as an effective engine of the political opposition and of the interventionist and pro-Allied movement, and it was in this capacity that the party played a salient role in the formation of the Democratic Union.

This tactical success, however, was the counterpart of the most important strategic mistake in its history, a blunder that eventually condemned the party to being no more than a small community of friends of the Soviet Union. This mistake was the characterization of Peronism as the Argentine variant of fascism, and the total opposition to it as a consequence. Total opposition entailed an alliance with the big capitalists and most Conservatives against the majority of organized labor. The Communists' evaluation was carried out at the level of ideology (and from this point of view, the assessment was substantially correct) rather than at the level of the social structure, as their own theory called for.[75] Since the social base of Peronism was labor and its opponents were the big capitalists and the middle class, the institutions and policies the regime would by necessity differ from those of fascism, even though, of course, no one could predict the direction to which Peronism would move once in power. It was a genuine leap in the dark. In any case, opposing a reform movement ardently supported by the majority of the working class was in fact a return to the "sectarianism" of the "third period," this time in the name of freedom and hand-in-hand with the "class enemy." Perón used this alignment very skillfully and discredited the party for a generation. It was only after the election that the party discovered the more effective

---

75. For Communist evaluations of Peronism written in the forties, see Victorio Codovilla, *Batir al nazi-peronismo, para abrir una era de libertad y progreso* (1945); and Partido Comunista, *Esbozo de historia*, pp. 92–108; for later Communist analyses, see Eugenio Moreno, *El fenómeno social del peronismo* (1966); and Fernando Nadra, *Perón hoy y ayer, 1971–1943* (1972).

but at that point futile strategy of "accompanying the working class in its experience with bourgeois reformism."

Unlike Rodolfo Puiggros, Jorge Abelardo Ramos, and others,[76] I think that the eclipse of the Communist Party owed more to the external constraints discussed above—repression, heterogeneity of the working class, and effective competition—than to its own strategic blunders. The reason is that the effects of the two types of factor were different: external constraints limited first and then practically eliminated the influence of the party in the labor movement, while the inexpedient political line complicated the links between the party militants and their expected constituency—the rank and file of the working class. Had the external constraints been absent, the party would have developed a substantial following, which the strategic miscalculation would have isolated into a self-contained political subculture, like the one of the French and other European parties during the Cold War.

The third main issue under consideration is the extent to which there were signs of radicalization in the majority, the non-Communist segment of the labor movement. The only indication in this regard was the emergence of a revolutionary Marxist left in the Socialist Party, which attained considerable strength in that organization (27 percent of the votes in the party congress of 1934). Toward the end of the decade this group formed the small *Partido Socialista Obrero* (Workers' Socialist Party), many of whose members eventually entered the Communist Party. Its influence on the labor movement was concentrated on the Printers' Union (*Federación Gráfica Bonaerense*, Buenos Aires Printers' Federation), a traditionally politicized organization made up of skilled workers (3,000 dues-paying members in 1938).[77]

But the dominant trend was precisely in the opposite direction, toward pragmatic and even nationalist orientations. Without abandoning their basically anticapitalist position, many Socialist and Syndicalist activists were shifting from traditional ideological stands to the search for agreements with the government and management in order to secure the short-term goals of their unions. At the same time, workers were developing what Hiroschi Matsushita calls a "national consciousness," whose characteris-

76. Puiggros, *El peronismo*; Jorge A. Ramos, *El Partido Comunista en la política argentina* (1962).

77. See Matsushita, *Movimiento obrero*, pp. 105, 111–12, 116–18, 173, 202. See also Tamarin, *Argentine Labor*, p. 149.

tics were patriotism and an emphasis on the anti-imperialist theme.[78] This ideological reorientation was taking place in the late thirties and early forties among the Socialists active in the CGT and the Syndicalists of the USA. One can only speculate about the possible causes of that shift: the change in the composition of the working class during the period (including the fact that a large proportion of the foreign-born workers had lived in Argentina most of their adult lives), the tradition in the Socialist Party of noninterference in union activities (the party held the view that political and union domains should be kept separate), the experience of the labor movement itself, especially during the Radical Party administrations (when the government sided many times with the workers in union disputes), and the diffusion of different varieties of nationalism in Argentine culture following the shock produced by the Depression.

In any case, these tendencies were slowly transforming the political outlook of the labor movement. Among the unionists less linked to the Socialist Party, there were discussions about forming a Labor Party along the lines of the British model. The affinity between this sector and a political entrepreneur in search of a power base, such as Perón, was obvious. Eventually, these unionists provided the core of labor support for Perón. In conclusion, the counterpart of the limited spread of communism in the late thirties and early forties was the growth of more powerful reformist tendencies. The labor movement was becoming more polarized, but it was definitely not moving toward the left.

The last aspect in the evaluation of Perón's diagnosis is the likelihood of mass unemployment in the postwar period in case protection for the less competitive industries would have been lifted. This is a key point in his argument for a corporatist state and for autarkic industrialization.

My view in this regard can be summarized in two propositions. First, there was not a threat of mass unemployment and, second, Perón was aware of this. He was, therefore, deliberately raising the issue in order to obtain the support of the economic elites, the military, and other groups which would be concerned by a menace of this type. This view is based on the analysis of the two documents that Javier Villanueva considers representative of opposing stands within the government in 1945: the report prepared by the Central

---

78. Ibid., pp. 240–42, 297–98; see also Murmis and Portantiero, *Estudios*, pp. 83, 93; Tamarin, *Argentine Labor*, pp. 60–64, 100–02.

Bank on the possible effects of the resumption of imports on domestic industrial activities, and the report issued by the National Postwar Council on employment and unemployment. Since this council was presided by Perón and its secretary general was José Figuerola, his foremost adviser on social matters, it is reasonable to assume that the report reflected Perón's views and that he knew its contents. The Central Bank predicted a rate of unemployment in manufacturing, if imports were resumed after the war, of 5 percent, while the National Postwar Council forecast a rate of direct unemployment of 9 percent in manufacturing, and multiplier effects that would produce a total of 180,000 unemployed in the industrial and nonindustrial urban population.[79] Let us look at the basis for these estimates.

The council[80] classified sectors of industry according to their vulnerability to the resumption of imports. The criteria were source of inputs (domestic/foreign), competition with foreign goods (in the domestic or in the foreign markets), and elasticity of demand. I have arranged employment data in Table 6.1, which shows the percentages of the working class and of the active population in each of these sectors.

The paper estimated the direct and indirect rates of unemployment that could follow the resumption of imports. In terms of direct effects it considered groups 3, 5, and 6 to be the the most vulnerable and estimated the percentages of jobs that would be lost as follows: in sector 3, 70 percent of the jobs added during the war, in sector 5, 30 percent of the increase, and in sector 6, 70 percent of the total labor force. This yields the figure of 70,000 unemployed or 9 percent of the working class. As for multiplier effects, sector 2 would be affected, as would be other areas of urban nonindustrial employment (construction, transportation, commerce). The report estimated that, since these nonindustrial activities absorbed as much labor as manufacturing, the likely loss would be similar to the one in manufacturing, that is, another 70,000 jobs. (This second figure included, however, the reduction of sector 2, so that the decline of employment in nonmanufacturing urban activities was expected to be lower than in manufacturing). Finally, the report added the total cohort joining the active population the fol-

79. Villanueva, "Aspectos," p. 348.

80. Argentine Republic, Vicepresidencia de la Nación, Consejo Nacional de Postguerra, *Ocupación*.

*Table 6.1.*
*Industrial Employment in Manufacturing According to Its Vulnerability to the Resumption of Imports, Argentina, 1944.*

| Sector | Growth Rate (%), 1939–44 | Industrial Working Class (%), 1944 | Active Population (%), 1943 |
|---|---|---|---|
| 1. Domestic inputs/ Domestic Market, inelastic demand | 23 | 27 | 4 |
| 2. Domestic Inputs/ Domestic Market, elastic demand | 19 | 34 | 5 |
| 3. Import-substituting | 39 | 21 | 3 |
| 4. Foreign inputs | 1 | 7 | 1 |
| 5. Export market, prewar | 18 | 5 | 1 |
| 6. Export market, New | a | 6 | 1 |
| Total | | (806,300) | (5,061,000) |

*Source*: Computed on the basis of data in Vicepresidencia de la Nación, Consejo Nacional de Postguerra, *Ocupación y desocupación en la Argentina* (Buenos Aires, 1945).

*Note*: Data refer to blue-collar workers only. They exclude employers, the members of their families, managerial personnel, and white-collar employees. The excluded categories made up one fifth of manufacturing employment.

ᵃ This sector did not exist in 1939. Employment in 1944 was 46,000 (industrial workers only).

lowing year (40,000), and this is how the figure of 180,000 was reached.

The council deduced policy recommendations from the study. Since employment in agriculture was not expected to grow, it proposed the expansion of industry producing for the internal market and public works or direct government investment in manufacturing as emergency devices if necessary.

This analysis suggests several comments. First, even if one accepts these estimates, the resulting rate of unemployment would be relatively low. 180,000 unemployed represented less than 4 percent of the active population. This was lower than the 263,835 unemployed and the 5 percent rate that Argentina had, according to the council, in 1932, at the bottom of the Depression.[81] Second,

81. Ibid., p. 7.

the estimates of likely unemployment for sectors 3 and 6 seem reasonable (even though, as we will see, the one for sector 3 is probably excessive), but it is not obvious that there would be a decline in sector 5, the export industries (mostly food), which were competitive before the war. Third, sector 4 could also be expected to expand if international trade was resumed. Fourth, the addition of the whole contingent of newcomers into the labor force to the labor reserve army seems totally arbitrary. Fifth, the recommendations are a non sequitur. From the data, it does not follow that autarkic industrialization is the most reasonable option. In fact, the distinction underlying the report, a totally open economy versus autarky, functions as an ideological device masking an intermediate alternative—limited, contingent protection linked with government financing in order to improve the efficiency of sectors 2, 5, and 6.

The report from the Central Bank, which was issued before the one from the Postwar Council and is quoted in it, clarifies some of these issues further.[82] Its main argument was that the competitive sector was larger than usually assumed, and it included not only the activities in group 1 of Table 6.1, but also important segments of the other groups. This competitive sector was formed by three types of manufacturing: activities such as construction materials or printing, which must be located near their sources of inputs or their markets; relatively efficient industries that could compete favorably on domestic or foreign markets (food processing, chemicals); and the competitive segments of other industries. The first two categories encompassed 60 percent of the working class, an estimate of the viable sector close to that made by the council (groups 1 and 2 in Table 6.1).

The report stated that other activities were in an exposed situation, but their degree of vulnerability was very variable. The industrial expansion that took place since the beginning of the war was mostly based on pre-existing industries, which were viable even if at lower output levels. The truly new manufacturing activities encompassed only 16,000 workers, 2 percent of the working class and 8 percent of the total number of workers added to the manufacturing sector since 1939, but even in this group some activities were already competitive.

82. Banco Central de la República Argentina, Departamento de Investigaciones Económicas, *Informe preliminar sobre los efectos que tendría en las actividades industriales internas la libre reanudación de las importaciones* [1945].

The report examined with some detail the "exposed" industries (those in group 3 in Table 6.1), such as textiles, paper, machinery, auto parts, and found a variety of levels of vulnerability. This contrasts with the council's blanket estimate that 70 percent of the jobs added to groups 3 and 6 would be lost. That estimate seems to have been an assumption based on an impressionistic evaluation, while the Central Bank report examined the market situation for the most important of these industries. Thus, in the textile industry, the largest in manufacturing after foodstuffs, only one product line, cotton, was vulnerable, while the others—wool, stockings, and silk—were safe. So was most of the machinery production industry; its nonviable segment employed only 27 percent of the workers. Even in the steel industry, so dear to the economic nationalists, 10 percent of the output was produced in relatively efficient conditions, and the overall competitive position of the industry could be raised if melting and rolling operations were centralized and the government provided protection for a few years.

It was on the basis of this analysis that the bank calculated the maximum rate of direct unemployment as a consequence of the resumption of imports at 5 percent of the manufacturing jobs. The report acknowledged that there would also be indirect effects, but it did not provide an estimate of their intensity. On the basis of the criteria used by the council (according to which the rate of indirect unemployment was similar to the one of direct unemployment), it is reasonable to estimate a total rate of 10 percent of the working class and related urban strata, or 2 percent of the active population. This would have been a manageable rate, especially if some of the "safe" industries were expanding as the noncompetitive ones were contracting. In any case, it makes sense to conclude that the prediction of mass unemployment and social chaos was unwarranted. Even if one accepts the worst scenario, the Postwar Council estimates, the resulting rate would have been what is today considered a "low" level of unemployment in industrial economies.

Nevertheless, the feasibility of industrial reconversion does not depend upon abstract efficiency or welfare considerations. Society as a whole may benefit with reconversion, but some groups stand to lose, and they can usually mobilize economic and political resources. And, to use the language that invariably surfaces whenever an issue of this type is discussed, governments, even authoritarian ones, are notoriously disinclined to economic policies aimed at breaking eggs, regardless of how succulent the resulting omelette may be.

However, the phasing out of the nonviable manufacturing sector would have been entirely feasible in postwar Argentina. There are three reasons for this. The first is economic. If the absolute numbers involved are taken into account (about 40,000 "direct" unemployed and 40,000 "indirect" ones) and one recalls that most industrial establishments were located in a small geographical area, it is clear that effective public works or government-sponsored reconversion programs would have been practicable, in terms of both the scale of the investment and the organizational capability required.

The second reason is political. The forces accepting reconversion would have been much stronger than those opposing it. The phasing out of nonviable industries would have been supported by the agrarians, most big manufacturers (especially if a policy of selective protection was formulated as the alternative to autarky), and assuming a minimum level of efficiency in the leadership of the government and the non-Peronist parties, by most of the middle classes. As for the losing groups, we know already that the owners of nonviable industries tended to be small and relatively new manufacturers, and that many were immigrants with little or no ties to the elites, interest groups, and political parties. Finally, it is not obvious that labor opposition would have been total: protectionist sentiment had increased in the working class in the thirties and early forties, but the Socialists' traditional free trade position could still be supported by a significant constituency.[83] Besides, such programs were not foreign to labor demands. For example, when the Depression hit, in 1930, the CGT had asked the government to undertake a road-building program in order to absorb unemployment.[84]

83. This is what Juan B. Justo, the founder of the Socialist Party and its main leader before the Depression, had to say about the subject at the time of World War I: "It is the inept entrepreneurs, the entrepreneurs anxious to establish their monopoly, the entrepreneurs eager for profits reaped off from their own people, who always hoist the flag of tariff protection, and endeavor to impose it as the nation's flag. . . . Protectionism is an enormous lie, which sometimes can conciliate the interests of business and labor in certain sectors of industry, but always at the expense of the whole population of the country." See Justo, "La falacia proteccionista," *La Vanguardia* (Buenos Aires), May 8, 1916, reprinted in his *Internacionalismo y patria* (1925), pp. 282–84.

84. Matsushita, *Movimiento obrero*, p. 81.

The third reason is psychological. All groups in Argentine society had shared for several years an intense anxiety about the postwar period. There was a collective preparedness for substantial adjustments in the economy and the society, which was reinforced by the knowledge of the extremely difficult conditions in European nations, still the direct reference societies for a considerable proportion of the Argentines. This awareness could have been translated into support for a program of industrial recoversion whose costs, in any case, would be borne by a small proportion of the population.

The panic was unrealistic, but the fact remains that a sector of the state elite seems to have accepted Perón's definition of the situation and the solutions he proposed. The next chapter discusses hypotheses about the sources of this inordinate fear of communism.

# 7 Social Integration and the Inordinate Fear of Communism

Thus, Perón's discourse to the elites focused on the danger of revolution and on a set of proposed courses of action to face this danger, which was, essentially, the package of new industrial and labor policies. As we have seen, his interpretation of Argentine reality in the forties was based on the acceptance of "Marxism in reverse." The fact that he, a smart political entrepreneur, chose to focus on this theme, indicates that he knew that the inordinate fear of communism was, in a manifest or a latent form, a central component of the political culture of at least some sectors of the elites. Why this fear?

I mentioned two contributing factors of an ideological nature: they were the influence of nationalist and integrist intellectuals and, in relation to the military and the church, the institutional values or doctrines of these organizations. These contributing factors, however, were not in themselves the source of the inordinate fear of communism.

With regard to right-wing nationalist and integrist ideologies, the fact that anticommunism and the ideal of the corporatist state were central themes of these ideologies implies that their supporters were predisposed to accept Perón's interpretation of Argentine reality. But to assume that prior exposure to and partial acceptance of these ideologies caused elite support for Peronism would be begging the issue. These ideologies became influential in the thirties and early forties: why was it so? A regress from the ideology of Peronism to the ideology of integral nationalism would not explain why some sectors became susceptible *to both*. The question would remain unanswered.

As for institutional values or doctrines, it is reasonable to think that the structure of military organizations and the type of socialization that prevailed in them predisposed officers to authoritar-

ian and Manichaean views of the world. Also, the Argentine
church was at that time still dominated by the traditionalist conception of society and politics, which rejected both liberalism and
socialism on religious grounds. Its opposition to communism, as
in the case of the military, was vehement.

However, neither the army nor the church in Argentina were
homogeneous. Within each, there was a variety of political and
ideological circles, and both organizations included liberal and
pro-Allied groups. Also, the political behavior of the military and
religious hierarchies varied from country to country, in spite of
the fact that their institutional values and doctrines were not very
different, especially in the Hispanic world. The contrast with
Chile is instructive here. Although Chile did have a much larger
and more articulate Left than Argentina (the Popular Front was
formed in that country, and it did come to power), its military had
in substance a constitutionalist outlook, and the church had accepted liberal democratic institutions and did not view the Left in
the apocalyptic terms that inspired its Argentine counterpart.[1]
Worldwide, the political behavior of the military and of the Catholic church prior to the Vatican Council has been extremely variable. In the thirties, the church rallied to the Franco side in Spain,
but the Catholic Center party was initially in opposition to Hitler in Germany. In the decades following the war, the military
were antiliberal in Argentina and Spain, constitutionalist in Colombia and Venezuela, leftist in Peru and Portugal, and so on.

In conclusion, the spread of nationalist and integralist ideologies and the institutional values or doctrines were conducive to
the support for Perón's interpretation, but they were not in themselves the central causes. In order to advance the analysis, it is necessary to move from the realm of ideas to the realm of experience.
Ideology and values do not just come from without, as both Vol-
taire and Lenin thought, to individuals who are the oversocialized
actors of conventional sociology. Ideology, when effective, that is,
when accepted sincerely, is always "true," since its acceptance
necessarily implies a correspondence between the ideology and
the facts as experienced by the carriers of the ideology.

Perón's argument must have corresponded to the common
sense of the segments of the political elite that supported him.
But, as Clifford Geertz writes, "Common sense is not what the
mind cleared of cant spontaneously apprehends; it is what the

1. See Brian H. Smith, *The Church and Politics in Chile* (1982), chap. 3.

mind filled with presuppositions . . . concludes."[2] Since the fear of revolution was unrealistic, the problem is to understand the underlying presuppositions, that is, what aspects of these elites' experience made Perón's Marxism in reverse a "reasonable" framework for the interpretation of reality. Moreover, when the ideology, as in this case, is based on false premises, it can only be accepted by individuals whose knowledge of the facts is distorted.

What was, then, the tie between Perón's discourse to the elites and the common sense of these segments of the elite who supported him? Why was their understanding of reality so distorted that it corresponded with that discourse?

### The Cognitive Dimension of Elite Strategies

Elite strategies toward the working class during the process of industrialization have, like any other type of action, a cognitive dimension. This cognitive dimension involves an assessment by elites of the likely behavior of the working class under different institutional arrangements. Elite rationality is a function of the accuracy of these expectations.

This cognitive process is, of course, influenced by formal ideologies and by the instrumental interests of different segments of the elite, but it is always grounded in the political experience of the elite with the lower classes. This experience can be of two types: local or transferred. The first type can be either direct or vicarious, and the second type is always vicarious.

Local experience is the past experience the elite of the country in question had with "its" lower classes. The "past" could be recent or remote. Also, the elite, whose experience is recalled by a contemporary elite, could be the same elite in the past or its predecessors in previous stages of development. Likewise, the lower classes involved could be the ones existing in the present or other subordinate classes, which were central in previous historical stages. For instance, an industrial bourgeoisie in the twentieth century may be influenced by images of the lower classes developed by the bourgeoisie of the same country a century before, or even by the landed aristocracy two centuries before. These images would be based, of course, on different types of lower class: an emergent proletariat in the nineteenth century, or a peasantry in

2. Clifford Geertz, "Common Sense as a Cultural System," in his *Local Knowledge* (1983), p. 84.

the eighteenth. Nevertheless, the images may still affect the perception of the contemporary working class. On the basis of that past experience, elites generate rather stable images of their lower classes as either "loyal" or "dangerous."

The second type, transferred experience, involves international demonstration effects. The experiences foreign elites had with their own lower classes is transposed to another country. The basis for this transfer is a postulated similarity or equivalence between the situations faced by elites in different societies.

After the crisis connected with the participation of the working class in the political system arose, past experience and international examples, as interpreted by national elites, have affected their strategies toward labor. Structural factors, such as the relative power of agrarian and industrial upper classes, determined the instrumental interests of elites. Moreover, prevailing elite ideologies allowed elites to justify these interests and to link them to political doctrines and institutional arrangements. In addition, environmental factors such as the availability of a surplus for redistribution or the existence of an effective apparatus of coercion became constraints and opportunities for the actualization of different elite strategies. However, past experience and international demonstration effects were key elements in the collective action of elites. These images from the national past and from abroad were the "evidence," the social knowledge in whose light instrumental and ideological interests and environmental constraints and opportunities were defined and evaluated.

In the Argentine case at the time of the reversal, the segments of the elites that accepted Perón's "Marxism in reverse" were influenced by an image of the working class as dangerous and by international demonstration effects consistent with the interpretation offered by Perón. The image of the working class had been developed in previous generations by the nativists and by segments of the upper classes reacting to labor mobilization. Paradoxically, this image became salient after the Depression in state elites such as the army and the church hierarchies, most of whose members did not originate in the economic elite. The international demonstration effects affecting the expectations of these segments of the elite originated primarily in Latin Europe (mainly in Spain and Italy). The causes of the prevalence of this image and these demonstration effects lie ultimately, as we will see, in the peculiarities of Argentine society and in the place occupied by Argentina in the international system.

### Threats from Below:
### The Image of a Dangerous Working Class

These stable definitions of the working class as either acquiescent or rebellious influence elite behavior during the process of incorporation of the working class into the political system. For instance, I have pointed out elsewhere that, in the second half of the nineteenth century, different images of the working class prevailed among the groups controlling the state in England and Germany. While in England different sectors of the political elite agreed on evaluating the mobilized working class as essentially loyal to the existing social order and thus "includable," in Germany the leaders of the state defined the working class as intrinsically antagonistic, and thus considered that its inclusion could only lead to chaos.[3]

Be it because the working class is mobilized and demands participation or because it is "out there" and available as a power base, those groups controlling the state face the dilemma of inclusion versus exclusion. The range of choice available to elites varies empirically, according to the degree of mobilization of the working class, but elite strategies always imply major changes with respect to the past, and, thus, they always are "leaps in the dark," for the active or passive presence of labor will always impact upon the nature of politics. In confronting the issue, elites project into the future their own and others' past experience on the political action of the working class or of lower classes in general.

Therefore, in the examples mentioned above, different elite responses in England and Germany were affected by the current political action of the working class. While the labor movement was mobilized in England at the time of the extension of suffrage, it was not guided by anticapitalist and antiregime political doctrines. In contrast, the working class in Germany at the time of Bismarck was led by the largest and best organized Socialist Party in the world.

But elite strategies were also affected by the past history of the lower classes in the two societies. That the stability of nineteenth-century England and the revolutionary processes in mid-nineteenth-century Germany influenced elite strategies is more or less obvious, but it also makes sense to conjecture that the political action of the peasantry in these societies in precapitalist times was another factor, for agrarian vertical cleavage had been much more

3. See Waisman, *Modernization*, chap. 4.

important in Germany than in England. These more remote experiences belonged to other elites of other state apparatuses in other modes of production in the same territories, but they could be transposed to the present, because the industrial working classes, whose incorporation was currently at issue, were in a structural position analogous to that of the previous subordinate classes. Thus, even a double identification could be involved in an evocation of this type: that of working classes with previous subordinate classes and that of current elites with the ones in the previous period.

I think that, in Argentina at the time of the reversal, the definition of the working class as dangerous by the segments of the political elite that agreed with Perón's interpretation was possible only because the current political action of the labor movement was interpreted in the light of other instances of lower-class mobilization. Some of these instances were foreign, as we will see when discussing demonstration effects, but others were domestic. These were recalled from the recent as well as from the distant past. Without a hypothesis of this type, it is not possible to understand why the limited mobilization of the working class at the time could be successfully adduced by Perón and others as evidence in support of their catastrophic forecast for the postwar period; why the electoral success of the moderate Socialist Party in the capital in 1942, or why the formation of a Popular Front under Radical Party leadership would cause panic among the military, the clergy, and a segment of the Conservatives.

Thus, it makes sense to infer that elites supporting Perón were interpreting these current events against the background of labor and left-wing mobilization in the previous generation, the intense political action in the beginning of the century and, especially, the traumatic episode at the end of World War I, which became known as the Tragic Week. But the background I refer to is these groups' distorted "common sense" understanding of the past, not the facts as they happened but the myths about these facts that became established in the consciousness of the antiliberal Right.

The protagonist of the events in question had been a very different working class than the one the elite faced in the forties. As we know, the working class in the first two decades of the century was made up predominately of European immigrants, many of them recent arrivals. It is useful to recall some figures here. In 1895, the proportion of foreigners in the industrial sector of the economy was 81 percent in the capital, the manufacturing center of the

country, and 55 percent and 56 percent in two other core provinces, Buenos Aires and Santa Fé. In 1914, just before the Tragic
Week, the proportions were 73 percent, 58 percent, and 57 percent,
respectively. The native proportion included, of course, the children of the immigrants, many of whom were still highly integrated in the immigrant subcultures. The situation, however,
changed in the forties. The percentage of the foreign born in the
industrial sector of the economy, in the country as a whole,
dropped from 53 percent in 1914 to 26 percent in 1947.[4]

In the early years of the century, prior to World War I, the elite
viewed with alarm the intense mobilization of the labor movement, which pursued its economic demands and reacted to political exclusion and police repression with boycotts and strikes, including several general strikes; with demonstrations, some of
which turned violent; and with political activity, both legal and
extralegal. The latter included terrorism, which was carried out by
the then significant anarchist faction.

The labor movement was organized into unions and workers'
associations, labor federations, and political organizations, such
as the Socialist Party and the anarchist movement. These two political groups were small, consisting of a few thousand activists
each, but their influence was strong, both at the direct organizational level and through their press. The level of participation was
high for the times. Hobart Spalding estimates that, in 1912, 20 to
30 percent of the working class belonged or had belonged to a
union, a workers' association, or a labor political organization.[5]

A few facts will give an idea of the degree of mobilization prior
to World War I. Data on strikes in the capital beginning in 1906
show very intense strike activity in 1906–7 and significant waves
in 1910–11 and 1913. The number of strikers in 1907 was twice as
large as in 1936, the peak year of the 1930–45 period, and more
than three times larger than in 1935, the next higher year.[6] In assessing these figures, it should be remembered that the working
class in the capital was much smaller in 1907 than in the nineteen

4. Data from population censuses of 1895, 1914, and 1947.

5. Hobart Spalding, ed., *La clase trabajadora argentina (documentos
para su historia, 1890–1912)* (1970), p. 51.

6. Data from the *Boletín del Departamento Nacional del Trabajo*, no.
26 (1914) in Spalding, ed., *La clase trabajadora*, p. 88, and from
Departamento Nacional del Trabajo, *Estadística de huelgas* (1940), in
Durruty, *Clase obrera*, (1969), p. 116. See also Rotondaro, *Realidad y
cambio*, p. 98.

thirties. Also in international terms, strike activity was high in Argentina. According to the Labor Department, 32 percent of the industrial workers had struck in 1907. This percentage was much higher than the ones for workers in other countries in the same year: 3 percent in Germany, 1.5 percent in England, 4 percent in France, 5 percent in Canada, 7 percent in Austria, and 13 percent in Italy.[7] With varying degree of success, general strikes were also frequent. Over ten such strikes were declared between 1900 and 1914, and four of them (in 1902, 1903, 1909, and 1910) halted industrial activity in the capital and other urban areas. These strikes and the May Day rallies were often accompanied by demonstrations, and they faced repression by the police and, occasionally, by vigilante groups.[8]

At the political level, the Socialist Party was an organizing force, an agent of ideological socialization of the working class, and the representative of labor interests in Congress. As an opposition party, it faced the same constraints as the Radicals—the fraudulent electoral practices of the ruling Conservatives. In addition to this, the party had a predominantly foreign constituency, the members of which could not participate in elections. In spite of these restrictions, the party elected deputies since 1904. Its parliamentary delegation fought effectively for legislation of interest to labor, and, in general, it functioned as a responsible opposition to the regime.[9]

As for the anarchists, they spurned electoral activity and parliamentary opposition, but they were efficient labor organizers and propagandists of their ideology. They were also involved in direct action. Anarchists encouraged mass violence in strikes and demonstrations, and they carried out bombings and assassination attempts. The most important of these were the ones against three

7. *Boletín del Departamento Nacional del Trabajo*, no. 5 (1908), in José Panettieri, *Los trabajadores* (1967), p. 143 n.

8. See Baily, *Labor*, chap. 1; Julio Godio, *Historia del movimiento obrero argentino: Inmigrantes, asalariados y lucha de clases, 1880–1910* (1973); Iscaro, *Origen*, chap. 5; López, *Historia*, chaps. 20–27; Sebastián Marotta, *El movimiento sindical argentino* (1961), vol. 2; Oddone, *Gremialismo*, chaps. 16–36; Panettieri, *Los trabajadores*, chaps. 6–7; Rotondaro, *Realidad*, chap. 2; Spalding, ed., *La clase trabajadora*.

9. See Oddone, *Gremialismo*, and *Historia del socialismo argentino* (1983); Nicolás Repetto, *Mi paso por la política (de Roca a Yrigoyen)* (1957); José Vazeilles, *Los socialistas* (1967); Richard J. Walter, *The Socialist Party of Argentina, 1890–1930* (1977).

presidents and a chief of police. The latter was successful, and it triggered a wave of repression.[10]

Elite strategies toward the labor movement were rather rational. The elite realized that labor radicalism was a common occurrence in the early stages of industrialization and that violent activities were not the behavioral counterpart of an articulate anti–status quo ideology. Rank and file workers supported Socialists and anarchists because they represented their economic interests. However, the workers' had very strong mobility orientations. Individual mobility was a reachable goal in the expanding economy and flexible society of Argentina, whose contrasts with the homelands left behind loomed large in their minds. Further, the emotional impact of the anarchist violence did not preclude the realization among the elite that the Socialists were an excellent vehicle for the incorporation of the working class into the political system, not only because of their reformism, but also because of their foreign and nonvoting social base, which prevented the party from winning elections. The Socialists were, then, less threatening to the elite than the liberal-democratic Radicals, for the latter did not reject the revolutionary option against the Conservatives and, if included, could win elections, which did eventually happen after the Electoral Reform of 1912.

Consequently, the strategy of the elite toward the labor movement was inclusionary, with a secondary exclusionary aspect. As in most other countries at the time of the irruption of the working class into the political scene, elite responses were of the carrot-and-stick type, but the repressive aspect was limited in time and intensity, and its strongest instances occurred as a response to anarchist direct action.

The range of repressive measures covers the familiar spectrum. Police were used against strikers and demonstrators, "patriotic" vigilante squads and right-wing terrorist groups attacked unionists sporadically, some organizations and publications were banned, and activists were jailed at times. Antiworker legislation was also passed. For instance, the state of siege, which suspended some constitutional rights, was imposed in 1902 and several times thereafter. Also, the Law of Residence (1902) authorized the government to deport foreigners considered a threat to national secu-

10. On anarchism, see Diego Abad de Santillán, *El movimiento anarquista en la Argentina* (1930), and *La FORA: Ideología y trayectoria* (1971); Iaacov Oved, *El anarquismo y el movimiento obrero en Argentina* (1978).

rity and public order. The Law of Social Defense (1910) established harsh penalties for persons who committed acts of violence or defended such acts.

Finally, as could be predicted, strikes and violence elicited negative images of the labor activists, of the anarchists in particular, among government officials, Conservatives, and industrialists. Their theme was that violence was not caused by the situation of the working class, but was introduced by foreign agitators. "The Argentine Republic," said President José Figueroa Alcorta in his 1910 annual address to the Congress, "receives from the old nations the individual who is seized by the affronts generated by his harsh situation there, and thus sectarianism and other social ills are transplanted here. [These] have no reasons and no propitious environment among us."[11] A police report in 1909 had used a more acerbic language. According to it, violence was generated by "anonymous" and largely foreign individuals, "debris rejected by other countries, who take refuge in our bosom but constitute an exotic factor, not assimilable to our sociability."[12] Industrialists were, of course, alarmed as well. In 1904, the year of its founding, the UIA complained, in a letter to the minister of the interior, about "the professional agitators, who nowadays abound in the republic. [They are] an eminently nefarious foreign element, whose influence is very efficacious because of the almost absolute freedom of action it enjoys."[13]

Exclusionary policies were, however, limited. Activists were jailed (by the thousands in 1910), but they were generally treated according to the law. Except for the occasional activities of vigilante groups and the more frequent lack of control of police behavior, the labor movement and the Left were not subject in this period to the systematic terrorist violence from above that Argentines would experience two generations later. Penalties were harsh, but limited in intensity and application. Only terrorists were given long prison terms, and only several hundred foreigners were deported under the terms of the Law of Residence.

11. Quoted in Jorge N. Solomonoff, *Ideologías del movimiento obrero y conflicto social: De la Organización Nacional hasta la Primera Guerra Mundial* (1971) p. 236.

12. Quoted in Panettieri, *Los trabajadores*, p. 145.

13. Petition from the Unión Industrial to the minister of the interior, requesting the government to guarantee industrialists and their workers freedom to work, December 1, 1904, in Spalding, ed., *La clase trabajadora*, p. 573.

Restrictions on the unions, the Socialist Party, and the leftist press were again temporary and were usually applied in accordance with preexisting rules.

In contrast to post-Depression Argentina, basic rights of speech and organization were usually respected (except often for the Anarchists), the unions were independent of the state, and the Socialist Party was allowed to function legally. Several pieces of protective legislation were passed by the Conservative-controlled Congress, and important officials and members of the elite attempted to face the "social question" through reform. The most important of these attempts was the project of the Labor Code presented to the Congress in 1904 by one of the most articulate Conservatives, Interior Minister Joaquín V. González.[14] This reformist approach can be synthesized in three propositions. First, labor mobilization is an inevitable characteristic of modern industrial society. Second, threats to the social order can be averted with preemptive reform. And third, the focus of this reform should be the protection of the legitimate economic interests of the working class and the institutionalization of industrial conflict. President Julio A. Roca, the leading figure of the Conservative elite at the turn of the century, argued in relation to the bill on the Labor Code: "A long experience has indicated to the governments the most effective way to ward off violent crises: it consists in anticipating inevitable events, and in offering more advantageous alternatives." [The bill aims at] "improving the conditions of the working class and of industrialists, by offering them conciliation mechanisms," so that industrial peace could be an incentive to immigration. He went on to say that foreign experience showed that the better the situation of the workers vis-à-vis the businessmen, the greater the output and the development of the country.[15]

Not all the groups in the political elite were so enlightened. The Labor Code bill, which explicitly recognized the legitimacy of unions and set up mechanisms for the management of labor conflicts, died in committee. But these principles were more or less shared. All the presidents in the period made statements consistent with the propositions stated above. Legislative reform ac-

14. Joaquin V. González, *Obras completas* (1935), vol. 6, pp. 311–578. See also Panettieri, *Los trabajadores*, pp. 149–54; and Solomonoff, *Ideologías*, chap. 6.

15. Julio A. Roca, "Mensaje del Presidente de la República Julio A. Roca al abrir las sesiones del Congreso argentino," in H. Mabragaña, ed., *Los mensajes* (1910), vol. 6, pp. 75–76.

tually implemented was scanty, but the inclusionary nature of elite policies was less a matter of action than a matter of omission: the legitimacy of workers' economic grievances was by and large recognized, there was no systematic repression of the nonviolent types of labor organization and action, and repressive legislation was usually applied in a measured manner.

There is no doubt that, in relative terms, inclusion was the dominant aspect of the elite strategy in the period. This statement is based on two comparisons: longitudinal and international. First, the contrast between elite strategies in the early twentieth century and in later stages of Argentine history is obvious. For most of the post–1930 period, elites applied exclusionary or cooptive strategies, both of which aimed at the control of labor by the state. Second, if the strategies of the Argentine elite vis-à-vis labor prior to World War I are compared with those of other elites at similar stages of development, Argentina is closer to the paradigmatic cases of inclusion (Britain or the United States) than to those of exclusion (Germany or the extreme case of Russia). The limited nature of this inclusionary policy, however, must be remembered: the working class was foreign, it did not vote, nor could its party become an effective contender for power. If the liberal democratic regime is defined in terms of participation and toleration of dissent,[16] it is clear that the inclusion the Argentine elite was willing to grant the working class implied basically the second of these dimensions or, at most, participation in the sense of ability to make demands, never in the sense of actual sharing of power. The Argentine elite was thus in a different situation than other elites implementing inclusionary strategies. Until the working class became Argentine, the possibility of losing control of the state through elections was not at stake.

Nevertheless, there was a choice, and the Argentine elite chose the inclusionary road when it would have been possible, in terms of the relation of forces, to follow a policy of systematic exclusion. This interpretation of the elite strategy as inclusionary, with the limitations noted above, differs from the conventional view held by most Argentine writers on the labor movement, who consider the issue in absolute rather than in relative terms, and tend to emphasize the secondary repressive or exclusionary component in government and elite policy.[17]

16. Dahl, *Polyarchy*.

17. See, for instance, Godio, *Historia*; Iscaro, *Origen*; Marotta, *El movimiento sindical*; Oddone, *Gremialismo*.

These strategies of the Argentine political elite in the period under discussion were quite efficient from the point of view of the protection of long-term ruling-class interests. They were, no doubt, more conducive to the preservation of legitimacy than the systematic exclusion or the cooptive attempts that would prevail in later periods. Why such lucidity? An inclusionary strategy was facilitated by characteristics of the working class and by traits of the social environment in which the agrarian upper class and its Conservative Party operated. On the side of the workers, I have already mentioned the factors conducive to inclusion. They sought individual mobility rather than radical political change, they did not vote, and their party was moderate. On the side of the elites, three factors are, I think, central: the fact that, until World War I, Argentina was an expanding economy, which meant that a surplus was available for redistribution, so that the contest for the surplus would not be a zero-sum game; the mobility opportunities offered by what was still a new society, in which the economic and educational mobility of the immigrants was not hampered by very stiff status barriers; and the foreign nature of the industrial bourgeoisie. This latter fact allowed the Conservative political elite, whose primary ties were with the agrarian sector, to look beyond the immediate economic interests of the industrial employers.

The antiliberal Right that became prominent after the Depression was influenced by the memories of labor mobilization prior to World War I. Among these elite groups, only the Conservative sectors, some right-wing intellectuals, and the minority of the military officers who were of nonimmigrant origin may have inherited this fear of the labor movement from their families. The majority of the officers and priests, who were of immigrant origin, acquired these images from less immediate sources. Ironically, their own ancestors may have been among the strikers and militants one or two generations before. . . .

Some right-wing spokesmen, especially those of old Argentine background, still resorted in the thirties to the nativist language of the previous generation to articulate the more contemporary themes of the rejection of liberal democracy and the fear of communism. In this view, the inclusionary strategy toward labor followed by the elite before the Depression had to have catastrophic consequences, because immigration and the revolutionary danger were inextricably linked. Senator Matías G. Sánchez Sorondo, a leading antiliberal Conservative, said, when presenting a bill for the repression of communism, that that day was an important one in the parliamentary history of the country, for it signaled the beginning of a "realistic stage." "The country, like a great lord, opened its gates to all those who stepped aboard," he explained, "without asking them . . . who they were, or what they were after." As long as "healthiness prevailed," the country was seized by a romantic state of consciousness, the "love for the foreigner." Thus, Argentina received "mingled in the alluvion . . . everything Europe wished to send . . . or to expel, including the professional agitator, the anarchist, syndicalist or communist, [who was] rotten, irremissibly rotten, an inoculator of his own virus and a powerful agent of social infection."[18]

Another senator, Benjamin Villafañe, a nativist of the extreme Right, was in total agreement. In *La hora oscura* (1935), a book whose cover has the telling subtitle "if you have anything to lose, read this book," he wrote: "[In the beginning of this century] makes its appearance on the national scene this extremism that, under the names of socialism, communism, etcetera, only means a war of foreign conquest, a struggle for the destruction of the old national soul. . . ."[19] This was a continuing danger, for political radicalism and the foreign population were, in his view, inseparable. He claimed that there were hundreds of thousands of "terrorists" in the country, and that almost all were foreign;[20] in Buenos Aires, most were Italian, Spanish, and especially Russian anarchists and communists, "a phalanx of fanatics who came from different parts of the world with the deliberate purpose of disputing what is ours."[21] And he quoted approvingly what appears to be a description of Jews as "a crowd of barbarians who . . . could rise tomorrow like a sinister horde. . . ."[22]

But Mgr. Gustavo J. Franceschi, the publisher of *Criterio*, the most important Catholic magazine, and a leading church intellectual in his own right, realized, perhaps because he was more sophisticated than reactionary politicians like Sánchez Sorondo or Villafañe, and perhaps also because he was of immigrant background, that the "social question" was not the product of immi-

18. Matías G. Sánchez Sorondo, *Represión del comunismo: Informe y réplica* (1937), pp. 15–16.

19. Benjamín Villafañe, *Hora obscura* (1935), p. 20.

20. Ibid., p. 67.

21. Ibid., p. 96.

22. Ibid., p. 72.

gration as such. (Both he and the magazine would later heed the lessons of history and become liberal-democratic.) Franceschi argued that the revolutionary danger was inherent in the situation of the lower classes in a liberal capitalist society. Writing in 1936, he criticized what he called the "anti" approach for, he said, "it arises from an almost puerile view of the social crisis, in its universality as well as in its peculiarities in each nation; from the belief that [the crisis] is the invention of a few perverted minds, [who have no] roots in reality. . . ." And he went on recollecting how, thirty years before, the slates of "Red" candidates had been greeted with laughter ("Zacagnini, typesetter; Dagnino, photographer. . . ."). "It was said [by the elites, one assumes] that socialism was an import, . . . that it could not thrive in this bounteous soil where everyone can attain well-being and freedom," he reminisced. "Not even the events of 1908, nor those that bloodied Buenos Aires in 1910 opened people's eyes. . . ."[23]

The events that were definitely evoked by the state elites supporting Perón in the forties were those in their own lifetime, especially the one that took place at the end of World War I, the Tragic Week. This was the most important strike and working-class revolt in Argentine history, and its significance was magnified in the right-wing myth, which interpreted the Tragic Week as the local repercussion of the Russian revolution.

At the end of World War I, both the labor movement and the government had different leadership than in the prewar period I discussed above. In the labor movement, the Syndicalists had become a very important force. In alliance with the Socialists, they controlled the larger union federation, and the other was led by the Anarchists. The government had changed hands as a consequence of the Electoral Reform, and the Radicals, based on the native middle classes, were now in power. There was a natural affinity between the new ruling party, an electoral machine in the process of consolidation and in control of the patronage resources provided by the state apparatus, and the Syndicalist leaders, whose apolitical principles did not preclude negotiations with the government.[24]

World War I produced a dislocation in the international economy. Argentine exports fell and the inflow of foreign capital and

23. Gustavo J. Franceschi, "Comunista o católico?" *Criterio* (1936), p. 414.

24. See David Rock, *Politics in Argentina*, pp. 117–56.

imported manufacturers dropped. There was a fast recovery in the postwar years (in 1918–20 growth rates were very high, and the value of exports was higher than in 1914), but the recessive effects in manufacturing lasted until the end of the decade: in 1915–19, real wages were 22 percent lower than in 1914.[25] In order to understand the psychological impact of the recession among industrial workers, it is necessary to recall that the immigrants' central orientation was mobility and that the Argentine economy had expanded continuously since the beginning of the century.[26]

The consequence was the most intense strike wave in pre-Peronist Argentina. From 1917 to 1921 there were more strikers in the capital than in any year between 1907 and 1946, when Perón was elected. The peak year was 1919, the year of the Tragic Week. According to these statistics, there were 1.8 times more strikers that year than in the previous peak of 1907, and 3.6 times more than in 1936, the year of the construction strike I have discussed already.[27] But the significance of these events lies in the characteristics of the labor mobilization and of its repression, more than in the sheer numbers of strikers.

The spark was a strike at the Vasena metalworks, one of the largest factories in the country (2,500 workers). Strikers were harassed and attacked by the police, whose hostility to the labor movement was not tempered by the coming to power of the Radicals. The Anarchists reacted violently to repression, the police fired on a workers' funeral procession, and riots exploded all over the city. The strike spread throughout the city and country (and even to the neighbouring Uruguay) and lasted for a week. Anarchist groups attacked police stations and clashed with the police and upper class vigilante groups. Repression was harsh. Hundreds of workers were killed, thousands were arrested, leftist buildings and newspapers were sacked, and the vigilante bands provoked disturbances of different types, including attacks on "Russian" (actually Jewish) immigrant neighborhoods.[28]

The government was paralyzed. President Yrigoyen mediated

25. Díaz Alejandro, *Essays*, p. 24.

26. Di Tella and Zymelman, *Las etapas del desarrollo*, p. 24.

27. See data from the Departamento Nacional del Trabajo in Rotondaro, *Realidad*, p. 98.

28. See Julio Godio, *La semana trágica de enero de 1919* (1972); Marotta, *El movimiento sindical*, chap. 16; David Rock, "Lucha civil en la Argentina, la semana trágica de enero de 1919," *Desarrollo económico* (1972), and ibid., *Politics in Argentina*, chap. 7.

the original conflict at Vasena, where a settlement favorable to the workers was reached, and negotiated with the Syndicalists an end to the strike in exchange for the release of the prisoners. But the police were not curbed, and the upper class terrorists (the Defenders of Order, later the Patriotic League) were not only tolerated, but even granted semiofficial status. More ominously, the government did not react when troops occupied the city, at the initiative of the garrison commander, who was a Radical sympathizer. The Conservative opposition blamed the government for the turmoil, alleging that it took place because of the lack of adequate precautions. The "sportsmen" of the Patriotic League (as a Conservative politician described them[29]) were enthusiastically supported by all segments of the established elite: agrarians and industrialists, foreign capitalists, Conservatives, and right-wing Radicals, the military and some churchmen. . . .

The myth that the disturbances were the local reverberation of the Russian revolution and, also, the direct product of communist intervention became firmly established among mainstream segments of the elite. The police duly uncovered the "Maximalist" conspirators (a total fabrication), and apocalyptic language became commonplace. "The objective of communism was to spread throughout the entire world, thus securing the domination it had just established over Russia. Our fatherland was one of the first coveted victims. This is the true origin of the Tragic Week of January 1919," said Mgr. Miguel De Andrea, who was considered a liberal churchman (in 1945, he would be the only bishop not signing the pastoral letter opposing Perón's adversaries).[30] In 1943, Villafañe recalled, in a book that was at the top of the reading list the GOU distributed to its members, ". . . the 'Tragic Week' of January 1919, in which the city endured days similar to those of anarchy in Russia when Lenin got to power, or to those in Spain during the recent revolution."[31] (In an instance of characteristic paranoia, he blamed the Radicals themselves for the events.) Carlos Ibarguren, a leading nationalist, in his memoirs published in the fifties, still referred to "the germs of agitation, cultivated here, as all over the world, after the war's end, by the Russian revolution, whose So-

29. Godio, *La semana trágica*, p. 151.
30. Quoted in Godio, *La semana trágica*, p. 180.
31. Benjamín Villafañe, *La tragedia argentina* (1943), p. 69. See Potash, ed., *Perón*, p. 115.

viet agents availed themselves, for their propaganda, of the peoples whose environment was most favorable. . . ."[32]

However, paranoia was not universal at the time of the events. Government legislators, some Conservatives, and establishment newspapers like *La Prensa* clung to the traditional, and more realistic, interpretations. For them, violence was the consequence of agitation by foreign activists. But they still recognized that most immigrants were innocent, that workers' demands were legitimate, that the solution to the social question laid in legislative reform, and so on. The truth is that, of course, there was no communist intervention. The local Communist Party, just founded, was a small group without any significance, and, in fact, it supported the moderate Syndicalists rather than the violence-prone Anarchists. Furthermore, the Russian communists had by then much more pressing concerns than the promotion of disturbances at the other end of the earth. Workers' discontent was profound, but its causes were bread-and-butter issues. Violence was produced by the counterpoint between an uncontrolled police and the Anarchists, whose initiatives were quite irrational (such as the insistence on attacking police stations), and almost all casualties were on the demonstrators' side.

Conspiratorial theories notwithstanding, the fear of the elite at the time was understandable. Disturbances erupted spontaneously, and the strike continued for a while even after the Syndicalist leaders reached a settlement. The Anarchists, in a performance that would be their swan song in Argentine politics, believed their hallowed social revolution had begun and behaved accordingly. On the other side, the Radical administration was clearly ineffective.

The action of the army and what may have been a relative independence of the police indicate clearly that the Radicals controlled the government, but the state apparatus was still the instrument of the traditional upper classes. And the emergence of the Patriotic League shows that the upper classes were ready, if necessary, to take direct control of repression. The reluctance of the government even to separate the "legitimate" apparatus of coercion from the unofficial one is an obvious demonstration of the organic nature of the latter. Had the disturbances continued for much longer or intensified, the economic elite would have done away with the Radicals, which they eventually did do at the

32. Carlos Ibarguren, *La historia que he vivido* (1955), p. 341.

time of the Depression, when the need to face another emergency, this time of an economic nature, drove them to take the helm of the state in their own hands.

The elites and the government responded similarly to the other major disturbance in the Yrigoyen administration, the strikes in Patagonia in 1920–21. There the strikers were mostly rural laborers, primarily creole immigrants from Chile, but the leadership was urban and European. In this case, repression was in the hands of an apparently autonomous army with which local landowners cooperated enthusiastically. Without any regard for legal norms, hundreds were shot in cold blood. Again, in this case, the attitude of the Yrigoyen administration was at best equivocal.[33] In any case, these events demonstrated the determination of the elite to respond disproportionately to minor outbursts of spontaneous violence. Unlike the Tragic Week, the massacre in Patagonia was buried with its victims, and neither official history nor right-wing rhetoric developed a lasting myth about it. This was so because the level of threat was much lower than in the Tragic Week, for these events occurred in the outer periphery of the country and had no repercussions elsewhere or, perhaps, because repression was so excessive that no legend could be fashioned to justify it. In any case, these disturbances occupied only a minor place in the collective memory of the society, most of the elite included, a generation later.

There are clear parallels between the situation that generated the Tragic Week and the one that apprehensive elites in the mid-forties could expect for the postwar years. In the first place, both postwar periods produced, internationally, major advances of the Left. Moreover, if conspiratorial theories were outlandish in 1919, they seemed more respectable in 1945, when the Comintern was perceived by objective observers as an efficient apparatus, under the control of a nation that would emerge from the war as a superpower. Secondly, there were no reasons to expect a priori that the consequences of this new postwar period for the Argentine economy would be less intense than those of the previous one. In fact, whatever adverse effects occurred would be broader, given the much larger size of the working class after a decade of import substitution.

33. The best account is Osvaldo Bayer, *Los vengadores de la Patagonia trágica* (1972–74). For a summary, see also his *La Patagonia rebelde* (1980).

The flaw with a forecast of this type is, of course, that the working class and the labor movement were very different in the forties, as I have shown. The Anarchists had disappeared, and their radical equivalent, the Communists, were not only weaker than the Anarchists had been, but also had no insurrectionary line. Moreover, foreigners were now a minority of the working class, and few of them were the recent arrivals to whom alien mentality and anomic orientations were commonly attributed.

However, there was another segment, of higher visibility than in 1919, whose political behavior was uncertain: the Creole migrants from the interior, who were at least one third of the working class in 1946.[34]

The European core of Argentine society was suddenly confronted with the other side of the country, the Latin American interior. It felt invaded by the *cabecitas negras* (little blackheads), as the darker mestizos from the interior began to be derogatorily called. Their irruption elicited images and strategies couched in the language of mass society theory. The opposition between "civilization and barbariousness," still a central theme of Argentine culture, became incarnate. The migrants were perceived, by the Left and the Right alike, as unsocialized beings, closer to nature than to culture. The Communist Party referred to their "instinctual rebelliousness," and an anti-Peronist politician later called Perón's working-class supporters—whom anti-Peronists identified with the internal migrants—as a "zoological alluvion. . . ."[35]

But both the Left and the Right understood very well the potential of this combination of biological energy and cultural marginality. They conceptualized the migrants' mind as a tabula rasa and realized that whoever wrote his ideology on it would harness the floating energy. The Left failed to do so, for the reasons I discussed in Chapter 6, but the fear of the radicalization of these masses was a central component in Perón's discourse to the elites. When he argued that the unorganized or undirected masses were the dangerous ones and that the Communists were effective organizers, he was making a classical mass theory argument: these unincorporated masses were "available" as a power base, and the issue

34. See estimates in Kenworthy, "Interpretaciones ortodoxas," in Mora y Araujo and Llorente, eds., *El voto peronista*, p. 203.

35. Partido Comunista, *Esbozo de historia*, pp. 121–22. The remark was made by Ernesto Sammartino, a Radical congressman.

was who would take control of them, the Marxist Left or the new, populist Right that he represented.

The implicit argument was that neither the liberal center, the Radicals, nor the liberal Left, the Socialists, could articulate a discourse consistent with the mentality of these masses. Since the Conservatives were totally discredited, only the new Right could prevent a Communist success. This could have been a purely instrumental argument on Perón's part, but it worked because it fitted the state elites' "common sense" presuppositions. The mass society interpretation of the social base of Peronism became established among the anti-Peronist opposition at the time and also in academic analyses for the following generation. The standard conclusion among anti-Peronists in the forties was that Perón's "social demagogery" could only be successful because of the "backwardness" of the new migrants,[36] and Gino Germani's argument that these migrants were the central base of Peronism went unchallenged until the late sixties, when scholars began to rediscover the crucial role played by the "old" labor movement in the emergence of the new movement.[37]

This concern about the danger posed by an apparently unattached or free-floating mass may have been associated, in spite of the nativist rhetoric of much of the Right, with even more remote memories than those of the early-century Anarchists and of the Tragic Week: those of the civil wars of the first half of the nineteenth century, which were fought among rival armies of peasants and rural laborers, led by provincial chieftains. For urban Argentines a century after the events, and especially for those of recent immigrant origin, these conflicts appeared as irrational outbursts, in which the issues separating the parties were often obscure, and in which ideologies appeared to be weakly related to material interests.

In any case, we know that the memory of that turbulent period was present in the minds of those who controlled the state before

36. The Communist interpretation above is representative of the Unión Democrática.

37. For Gino Germani's interpretation see his *Política y sociedad*, chap. 9. See also his partial revision in his "El surgimiento," in Mora y Araujo and Llorente, eds., *El voto peronista*. For revisionist analyses, see Murmis and Portantiero, *Estudios*, and the following articles: Peter H. Smith, "La base social del peronismo," and "Las elecciones de 1946 y las inferencias ecológicas," Kenworthy, "Interpretaciones ortodoxas," and Halperín Donghi, "Algunas observaciones," in Mora y Araujo and Llorente, eds., *El voto peronista*.

the Depression. Well after the organization of the national state, the transformation of Argentina into a large-scale agrarian producer, and the reception of millions of immigrants, leading figures of the Conservative elite still considered national unity as a fragile achievement, threatened by an intrinsically ungovernable society. General Roca, the most influential Conservative politician, wrote as late as 1914, that is, at the apogee of Argentine economic and political development and only a generation before the election of Perón, that "[all those who ruled] . . . constantly endeavored, in a continuous struggle, to defend these two essential things, always in danger: the authority principle and national unity, against the latent forces . . . of rebellion, of anarchy, of dissolution. For it is not a good thing to harbor illusions about the solidity of our organization, or of national unity. . . . Anarchy is not a plant that disappears in the space of half a century, or a century, in badly cemented societies such as ours."[38] This concern may have endured, in an implicit form, in sectors of the state apparatus such as the army, whose institutional ideology represented the military as the original and continuing creator of the nation itself, through the construction of a mythical link between the existing regular army and the mostly nonprofessional armies of the wars of independence, and the much more realistic conception of the draft army as a central agency for the constitution of the nation, through the socialization of rural native and immigrant youths into the values of the national community.

Thus, it makes sense to think that the sectors of the political elite supporting Perón felt besieged by a working class whose two components, the "old" European and the "new" Creole, appeared as dangerous because of the persistence of images from the past, in which true instances of militancy and even rebelliousness were magnified by myth. Why were not these images operative among the upper classes, who portrayed Perón as the cause of, rather than as the remedy for, social agitation? Because they faced an actual, more immediate threat: Perón's justification for his policies in terms of the long-run or fundamental upper-class interests appeared to the economic elites as just a cynical pretext by a political entrepreneur interested in building his own power at their expense. This immediate threat cancelled the effects of the fear of the lower classes. On the side of Perón and his supporters, on the other hand, this behavior of the upper classes appeared as false

38. Quoted in Botana, *El orden conservador*, p. 337.

consciousness. The antiliberal officers and clerics, politicians and intellectuals, not linked directly to the means of production, were in a position to take what they believed to be the longer view and analyze the future in the light of the past. Since their judgment was less clouded by economic interests, they could recall the memories of rebelliousness and anarchy, and they could predict a cataclysm for the postwar period, unless the upper classes regained their class consciousness and, as Perón advised, gave 30 percent in time rather than losing everything a posteriori.[39]

### Models from Without:
### The Logic of International Demonstration Effects

The role of international demonstration effects in the process of development has been explored by many authors. These effects are implicit in the work of Marx, and they have been discussed, albeit nonsystematically, by Barrington Moore and scholars linked to the Marxist tradition.[40] But it is in the work of Thorstein Veblen and Reinhard Bendix that international demonstration effects appear as major variables that explain important characteristics of the development process. Veblen focused on the borrowing of technology and forms of economic organization, mostly between England and Germany,[41] while Bendix dealt with the cross-national diffusion of broad cultural and institutional patterns, mainly among countries in early modern Europe.[42] The discussion here will be more specific. I will concentrate on the role of demonstration effects in elite strategies toward the labor movement.

These effects have been both positive and negative, that is, models to be copied and errors or failures to be avoided. Interpretation is the critical process, for it affects both the cognitive dimension—whether the foreign experience is relevant to local conditions, and therefore applicable—and the evaluative one—whether the example is correctly assessed as "positive" or "negative." The accuracy of interpretations varies. The soundness of the local interpretations of foreign examples is one of the key criteria for the assessment of the degree of consistency between elite goals

39. Perón, *El pueblo quiere saber*, p. 165.

40. Moore, *Social Origins*.

41. Thorstein Veblen, *Imperial Germany and the Industrial Revolution* (1915).

42. Reinhard Bendix, *Kings or People?* (1978).

and the consequences of policy, that is, of the rationality of elite strategies.

In the international system, demonstration effects related to elite strategies circulate in all directions: between central countries, from center to periphery, between peripheral countries, and from periphery to center.

In industrializing Europe, elite strategies toward labor were affected by positive and negative demonstration effects going back to a preindustrial upheaval such as the French revolution, whose diffusive and reactive impacts, the spread of liberal-democratic movements on the one hand and the constitution of the Holy Alliance on the other, would be repeated over and over. In the case of England, Moore has argued that the neutralization of the revolutionary threat on the continent, that is, the defeat of revolutionary France and the Napoleonic regime, was a precondition for nineteenth-century political reform, which included the inclusionary strategy toward labor.[43]

A generation later, it was the Commune which had a dual impact of the same type than the one of the French revolution. I have discussed elsewhere the demonstration effects of the Commune on Bismarckian Germany. It rekindled the Socialists' millenarian expectations, and it also contributed to Bismarck's fears that the legalization of the Socialists would lead to chaos and tyranny.[44] The German experience itself, under Bismarck, was also a model for other countries. A strategy of limited exclusion kept the working class insulated, but the Socialists eventually became the largest political party. This outcome was not lost to the contending forces in other European countries, such as Russia, which industrialized later and whose social forces were influenced by the German model. For the Russian autocratic elite, German bureaucratic absolutism had been the ideal since the time of Nicholas I, and German developments confirmed its preference for the total exclusion of labor. At the same time, for the Russian revolutionaries at the turn of the century, the German Socialists were the standard of evaluation, something clear in Lenin's early works on organization and tactics.

Demonstration effects from center to periphery are plain, for the political development of the periphery is to a large extent derivative. It is a process of borrowing and adaptation to local conditions

43. Moore, *Social Origins*, p. 31.
44. Waisman, *Modernization*, pp. 51–52.

and to local elite interests of the ideologies and institutional forms born in the core. Ensuing differences express more the structural diversity between center and periphery and the bias in the local interpretation of foreign examples than the originality of ideologies and institutions in the periphery.

In the specific case of the incorporation of the working class, elites in late industrializing countries could "shop around" and select foreign models on the basis of their expected or presumed consistency with the elites' own instrumental interests and ideology, the forms of political action of their lower classes, and the environmental conditions in which their political systems operated. If we take, for example, the Latin American elites at the turn of the century, Europe was for them a museum of elite strategies toward labor. The English experience with accommodation showed them how a liberal democracy could manage the "social question" by expanding citizenship to the lower classes. At the same time, the example of France since 1848 revealed the dangers inherent in industrial democracy, and the German case showed that authoritarianism could not prevent the growth of a Socialist Party. After World War I, the challenge was the assimilation of the complex experiences of communism and fascism which, as we will see, were not very well understood for a long time.

Effects in the opposite direction, from periphery to center, are less significant, and they circulate mostly among the Left. Sometimes these effects are marginal, such as the formation of "Maoist" parties in Europe and the United States in the sixties, but others can have a profound impact. For example, the Chilean experience under Allende affected the strategy of Communist and Socialist parties in Latin Europe in the seventies and eighties. The strategy of "historical compromise" of the Italian Communists and the moderation of the Socialist Left in France under Mitterand and in Spain under González reflected this influence.

Demonstration effects also circulate from country to country in the periphery. In Latin America, the Cuban Revolution produced not only its direct aftereffects (feeble and mostly failed guerrilla movements in some countries), but also the spread of authoritarian dictatorships in the sixties. The establishment of military regimes based on the so-called "national security doctrine" in Brazil in 1964 and Argentina in 1966 was not determined mainly by the mobilization of the lower classes and the low degree of legitimacy of political institutions. These factors of course existed, but the fear of revolution experienced by economic elites, the armed forces, and, in the case of Brazil, a segment of the middle classes, was not realistic. It was fueled by the demonstration effect of the Cuban revolution. In the early seventies, the experience of Chile under Allende had similar consequences on Uruguay and Argentina. The radicalism of the repressive regimes established in these countries in 1973 and 1976, respectively, was not produced only by the intense labor mobilization and urban terrorism that existed prior to the coups. The cumulative impacts of the Cuban revolution and of the Allende government also contributed to the apocalyptic ideology of these regimes. The Chilean experience, in particular, provided the evidence for the remarkable proposition, adduced by these southern cone regimes and also by the Pinochet dictatorship in Chile, that democracy is, inevitably, the prologue to communism.

The mechanism involved in these demonstration effects is identification, through empathy, between a local established elite (or a revolutionary counterelite, in the case of the radical Left) and a foreign one, whose experience in its own environment is assumed to have experimental value, that is, to lead to similar results if replicated in the local environment. The underlying assumption is a high degree of fit between the interests and ideologies of the elites, the nature of the society, and the issues faced in both settings. Since this fit is variable, so is the degree of realism of the identification and, thus, the replicability of consequences. But the less realistic the identification, the more likely it is that the behavior of the elite that reacts to the demonstration effect, by copying or by avoiding the foreign experience, will have unintended consequences. These are not necessarily negative for the "borrowers": after all, the Asian Communist parties, which began their political histories by declaring themselves the vanguards of nonexistent proletariats, did carry out their revolutions.

The problem is that the demonstration effect involves abstracting an outcome from the structural context that produced it, usually through a process of overdetermination (in the Althusserian sense), and predicting that the same outcome will be replicated in a different structural context, where the factors producing or inhibiting the outcome in the original setting may or may not be present in the same manner or at all.

In situations of this type, counterproductive consequences occur often, as discovered by Latin American counterrevolutionaries and revolutionaries who were influenced by the demonstration effect of the Cuban revolution in the sixties and seventies. The former, as we have seen, established "national security" authoritarian regimes in Brazil and Argentina in the sixties, antirevolutionary regimes that were not the response to actual revolutionary threats. They forcefully demobilized the working class and leftist sectors of the middle classes. At least in Argentina, these policies backfired: forced exclusion led to the formation, in the early seventies, of a mass radical movement, which ranged from guerrilla groups to mass organizations with a middle-class and labor base. The revolutionary threat that did not exist at the inception of the regime was clearly present at its conclusion, when mass mobilization forced the military to step down, and the stage was set for the wave of terrorism from below and of massive terrorism from above, which rocked the country in the late seventies. On the other side of the political spectrum, most of the guerrilla movements that spread throughout Latin America in the sixties were predicated on the "focus" model that had been successful in Cuba. They failed, and even Che Guevara, the theorist of the new military-political strategy, was a victim of the untransferability of the Cuban experience to Bolivia, a country with a very different social structure, political system, and culture.

International demonstration effects do not circulate randomly in the international system. If established, their impact on similar groups in different societies is variable. Also, effects that were powerful once may extinguish in a brief period. In short, the "lessons of history" are selectively stored and recalled. What are the determinants of the direction and intensity of these effects? At least three factors are obvious: the strength of cultural networks between countries, the degree of similarity, as interpreted by the recipient group, between the situations faced by the groups in the sending and recipient countries, and the perceived efficacy of the different examples or models.

In the first place, demonstration effects circulate through cultural channels; the greater the degree of interaction between cultures, the more likely the demonstration effects. Thus, the Russian revolution "shook the world," but its direct effects were stronger on the societies that were culturally and geographically close to Russia (such as Poland or Germany). The Cuban revolution affected elites throughout Latin America, in spite of the obvious differences among social structures, levels of development, culture, and political institutions. Second, the "lessons from history" are more likely to be received and reinterpreted by groups that believe they are in a similar situation than their counterparts in the "reference society." For example, the Brazilian elite felt more threatened than the Mexican one by the Cuban revolution (in Mexico, the myth that a revolution took place already in the beginning of the century is very well established), while the Iranian revolution had, in the Islamic world, a greater impact on the traditional Saudi monarchy than on the modern secular Turkish elite. Third, the strength of positive and negative models depends on their perceived efficacy. Soviet-style communism has been respected and feared by its enemies since its establishment, while anarchism became little more than an intellectual curiosity. Likewise, very few anticommunists are haunted by the ghost of Trotskyism. In the interwar period, classical fascism was regarded by friends and foes alike as a workable social order—see the sympathy it evoked among many nationalists in the third world—while nowadays it is the patrimony of small fringe groups and elderly nostalgics.

Let us go back to Argentina at the time of the reversal. Until the Depression, political elites were influenced, as regards the "social question," by the liberal models of Britain and the United States. Since they perceived themselves as the rulers of a new and expanding society, their expectation was that the "social question" could be managed, as in the liberal-democratic models, by an inclusionary strategy, which would shift to exclusion whenever labor turned violent. The Hispanic world, both in Europe and in Latin America, was a negative model for most of the elite. It epitomized economic and political backwardness. Some segments of the society were open to other foreign experiences, but these did not contradict the confidence placed by the elite in the liberal model. Thus, the army was trained by German missions, but the Prussian military tradition emphasized professionalism. In fact, when the military became involved in politics, training in Germany was not a predictor of authoritarian or pro-Axis sympathies.[45] For the mass of immigrants, Italy and Spain were, of course, the reference societies, but most of these immigrants shared with the Argentine elite the perception of the new country as more open and, therefore, preferable as a habitat to the homeland left behind.

This consensus on positive and negative reference societies broke down after the Depression, when the model of society based on economic and political liberalism lost its effectiveness. The erosion, however, began before, at the end of World War I, when

45. Potash, *Army and Politics, 1945–1962,* pp. 51–52, 117–25, 170–74.

the international division of labor experienced its most important jolt since the depression of the 1870's. Both the Russian revolution and the fascist reaction affected segments of the Argentine elite. The revolution was a threat, and fascism and kindred antiliberal movements and regimes on the right (Action Française, the Primo de Rivera dictatorship in Spain) seemed to offer a response, which some groups in Argentina found intriguing, and in some cases worthy of applause. But, up to the Depression, the liberal model was still dominant in the elite.

In the thirties, confidence in liberalism was shaken, and nonliberal solutions became more respectable. At the same time, Argentine society, its elite included, received the powerful demonstration effect of the Spanish civil war. The antiliberal new Right, composed of nationalist intellectuals, integrist Catholics, and authoritarian Conservatives became an important segment of the state apparatus and the political elite. At the time of World War II, then, while most of the Right still clung to the discredited liberal model, others were trying to draw lessons from what they perceived as the failure of liberalism, from the rise of fascism and related movements, and from the war in Spain, the event that seemed to epitomize the dangers of liberalism and communism.

Fascism and the Spanish civil war weighed so much on Argentine society, probably much more than on any other non-European country, because of the obvious personal and cultural linkages. There were large Italian and Spanish emigrant communities in other countries, but in Argentina the majority of the population was of recent Italian and Spanish origin. Moreover, cultural ties with Spain and, to a lesser extent, with Italy, were very strong, in spite of the orientation of the elite toward French and English culture and political models. Throughout the West, the Italian and Spanish developments were interpreted as paradigmatic cases, having worldwide significance, by most groups in the political spectrum (Argentina was not an exception in this regard), but the segments of the political elite that supported Perón in the mid-forties interpreted fascism and the Spanish civil war in a specific manner. This interpretation focused almost exclusively on an issue: the incorporation of the working class into the political system. Simplifying, the chaotic end of the Spanish Republic was understood by them as representing the logical and necessary evolution of democracy, while the fascist regime appeared as a workable and just remedy to such a catastrophe. Gradually, a large segment of the political spectrum, even beyond the new Right, came to accept two propositions: that liberalism, in its economic but especially in its political sense, was no longer viable as a form of social organization; and that there were only two viable and efficacious alternatives to it, communism and fascism. Both were antiliberal, for their effect was the control of the society by the state. For an anticommunist, fascism was the only possible choice.

Thus, Spain and Italy were interpreted as two efficacious, generalizable, demonstration cases, one negative and the other positive. In the minds of these groups, then, the Latin European lands, which prior to World War I had supplied most of the current population, continued being the source of vital inputs. They were now real life laboratories, in which the alternative futures Argentina faced could be observed and compared. These were, of course, inadequate interpretations, for the war in Spain was not the necessary product of democratization, but the consequence of specific characteristics of Spanish society, and fascism was very far from being an effective remedy to the "social question." Moreover, neither the diagnosis nor the solution corresponded to the problems and peculiarities of Argentine society.

As we will see, the attractiveness of the fascist model to the new Right was based on its apparent completeness as a response to the revolutionary threat: on the one hand, the corporatist structure seemed to provide an equitable solution to the "social question"; on the other, the strong monistic state was the best possible instrument for facing the communist advance. Moreover, fascism was not a utopia like the nineteenth-century corporatist schemes: it worked, and in a country like Italy, with a Latin-Catholic-Mediterranean population and culture. Seen from the Argentine periphery, the Mussolini regime could be defined as a success by the Argentine extreme Right. Not only did it control effectively the communist menace that brought it to power, but it also tried to extricate Italy, a "proletarian nation," from the control by the capitalist metropolises. Fascism was interpreted, then, as both an economic and political alternative to the decaying liberal institutions.

These themes were prominent in the works of the right-wing nationalist intellectuals. One of the most systematic presentations of fascism was Carlos Ibarguren's La inquietud de esta hora (The anxiety of this hour), published in 1934. The crisis of liberalism was his point of departure. He argued that the bankruptcy of the capitalist economy and of the polity based on the personal and universal suffrage led to a transformation in the conception of the state. From being a static entity, the guardian of freedom and order, lives, and property, the state became the "upholding, regulating, and animating axis of the whole society."[46] Ibarguren pointed out that dictatorship was the usual response to the chaos brought about by capitalism and liberal democracy, but that "this situation could not stabilize and become definitive. Dictatorship is [just] an exceptional state of emergency."[47] The solution was a new system, "based not on individualism, but on the group, the collectivity, the corporation. The era of functional democracy dawns."[48] The moving forces behind this transformation were two: the Russian revolution on the one hand and the "Italian and German" ones on the other. Both developed a strong state and created an order in which social interests prevailed over individual ones, but communism and fascism were very different. While the former established the dictatorship of one class, the proletariat, the latter "seeks social equilibrium in order to prevent the class struggle,"[49] through the creation of "a productive and solidary, that is social, labor system: that of the corporations."[50] Also, communism was materialist and antireligious, while fascism, according to Mussolini, "believes in sanctity and heroism"; it also considered religion "one of the most profound manifestations of the spirit," and upheld national traditions.[51] The attractiveness of fascism, then, derived from its alleged efficacy to control social conflict in a society with private property of the means of production, and from its compatibility with religious and national institutions and doctrines.

Besides these rational reasons, the fascination with fascism rested, as one could expect, on emotional factors. Mario Amadeo, another articulate nationalist who was a young man in the thirties, wrote in his memoirs: "The decline of the value 'freedom' vis-à-vis the value 'authority' was determined by universal trends and, above all, by the crisis of the legal institutions charged with preserving freedom. . . . [It] was . . . impossible to prohibit that generation from sympathizing with those who proclaimed the

46. Carlos Ibarguren, *La inquietud de esta hora* (1934), pp. 35–36.
47. Ibid., p. 57.
48. Ibid., p. 59.
49. Ibid., p. 61.
50. Ibid., pp. 63–64.
51. Ibid., p. 64.

strengthening of weakened authority. To this, one must add the 'clothing,' the rhetoric of fascism . . ." and, as unlikely as this seems from our standpoint, the personality of Mussolini, "who embodied the defense of the order broken down by the anarchy of the postwar period."[52]

These were nationalists, an influential but still secondary strand in the cultural and political world. But very similar analyses were made, even if in a more qualified manner, by a group in control of much larger resources, and much closer to the state, the right-wing Catholics.[53] Franceschi was one of the most articulate of these in the political sphere. Like the nationalists and the conservatives of the antiliberal Right, he opposed liberal democracy, and was a passionate anticommunist. However, he strictly adhered to the traditional social doctrine of the church. Unlike the nationalists, therefore, he approved fascism in a qualified and partial manner, for he objected to the totalitarian organization of the state and, in the case of the nazi ideology, to racism. Unlike the old Right conservatives, he was opposed to liberal democracy on principle rather than on practical grounds, and he was a propounder of corporatist social reform.

In opposition to the purely reactionary Right, he argued that a coercive response to the communist advance was not enough. "In order to avoid a catastrophe like the one in Spain," he wrote, the first duty was "not to attach ourselves blindly to a past regime, already dead. . . . Undoubtedly, no regime, not even the most authoritarian, is able to maintain the individualist capitalist regime that the nineteenth century knew. All the parties that attempted this have failed. . . ."[54] The fascist and corporatist regimes showed that this was the case: "The examples of Hitler, Mussolini, Oliveira Salazar are invoked many times," he argued. "These men, independently of the value of their doctrines, do not satisfy themselves with an 'anti' approach. Their economic and social reforms are so audacious and profound that our good Conservatives would be horrified if they learned about them."[55]

*Totalitarismo, liberalismo, catolicismo (Totalitariansim, lib-*

52. Mario Amadeo, *Ayer, hoy, mañana* (1956) pp. 113–14.

53. On Franceschi and the right-wing clergy, see Ciria, *Partidos y poder*, chap. 6; and Kennedy, *Catholicism*, chap. 6.

54. Gustavo J. Franceschi, "Las barbas del vecino," *Criterio* (1936), p. 248.

55. Franceschi, "Comunista o católico?" p. 414.

*eralism, Catholicism)*, published in 1940, is a good summary of Franceschi's political views at that time. In this book, he argued that, beyond the crisis of liberal democracy, liberalism and Catholicism were irreconcilable in general; that social conflict between workers and employers was inherent in liberal democracy, and that the only solution consistent with Catholic doctrine was a corporatist state. A Catholic cannot support liberal democracy, he wrote, for "liberalism is essentially a proclamation of autonomy, an exaltation of the individual," the logical consequences of which were "complete religious freedom, the treatment of all cults and beliefs as equal and, above all, the absolute freedom of thought and of speech,"[56] "[freedom] of association extended to whatever group one can imagine, [freedom] to preach . . . the right of the people to remove from . . . its leaders and rulers, even by revolutionary means, the authority invested in them," and so on.[57] Totalitarianism was equally pernicious, for it postulated the citizens' total subordination to, and dependence on, the state.[58] However, Franceschi distinguished between "true" totalitarianism, to which his opposition was total (although he argued that a Catholic, if a citizen of such a totalitarian regime, must serve it loyally and contribute to its defense,[59] and "pragmatic" totalitarianism, such as Mussolini's, who, Franceschi claimed, "attends to the facts rather than to the doctrines, and adapts the latter to the former according to the requirements of the moment."[60] The alternative to both liberalism and totalitarianism was a corporatist state, in the tradition of "social" Catholicism, whose doctrine predated fascist theories and regimes.[61] Only such a state, democratic but not liberal, could be an effective barrier to communism while avoiding the objectionable aspects of "true" totalitarianism.

The demonstration effect of fascist and corporatist regimes was not confined to these intellectual circles attached to antiliberal ideologies. It reached groups in the mainstream of the Conservative Party and the state bureaucracy, even if it never captured the minds of the dominant faction of the party, the purely reactionary

56. Gustavo J. Franceschi, *Totalitarismo, liberalismo, catolicismo* (1940), pp. 30–31.

57. Ibid., p. 35.

58. Ibid., p. 13.

59. Ibid., p. 24.

60. Ibid., p. 22.

61. Ibid., pp. 48, 54.

Right, willing to dispose of the trappings of liberal democracy but not ready to undertake a corporatist revolution. The first president after the coup of 1930, José Félix Uriburu, and his minister of the interior (in charge of political matters), Matías Sánchez Sorondo, whom we already know, were avowed admirers of fascism, the Primo de Rivera regime, and Action Française. Uriburu discussed openly his plans for the reorganization of the political system on the basis of corporatism. This faction was, however, weaker than the "liberal" one, which supported the formula of limited democracy I have discussed already, and Uriburu had to surrender the presidency in 1932.

*El estado equitativo (The equitable state)*, published in 1932 by Lugones, who was an apologist of the military regime, is a programmatic statement of the purposes of the defeated faction. In the familiar manner, Lugones started out with the crisis of liberalism: "The whole world suffers a crisis in which we participate, and which consists of . . . the conflict of a system at its end: liberalism. . . ."[62] This created a specially difficult situation for a country like Argentina, with a large foreign population that could be mobilized by subversive ideas: "the peoples with an immigrant makeup, like ours, are . . . the most susceptible to anarchy."[63]

Liberal democracy was inappropriate in a context of this type, where "the foreigners, who live in a permanent status of subversion and who despise the country, are many, even in the Congress, where they represent, however, the Argentine people; and not a few of them educate their children in such animosity."[64] More specifically, liberal democracy led to socialism: " 'Leftism,' as the socialist tendency in which liberalism degenerates calls itself, is here a foreign phenomenon, and it satisfies mostly the working-class mass in the cities, which is to a large extent foreign as well."[65] In liberal democracy, representation is based on "the gross population figure," and thus big cities are preponderant. This produced, in Argentina, the two consequences: "laborism" (*obrerismo*) and the "fatal foreignness of legislation and of legislators." This happened in spite of the fact that the country was "an agrarian republic."[66] That is, the ruling class was agrarian, but liberal

62. Leopoldo Lugones, *El estado equitativo* (1932), p. 5.
63. Ibid., p. 75.
64. Ibid., p. 55.
65. Ibid., p. 11.
66. Ibid., p. 70.

democracy caused the preponderance of urban classes, so that a discontinuity between economic and political power arose.

Ideology aside, this is a good diagnosis of the Argentine crisis at the time. The remedy proposed by Lugones was the corporatist state. He argued that, in a society with such a low level of integration, "we need a stronger authority, that is, one proportionate to the weakness of the social body."[67] This entailed the transformation of the state, from an organization based on equality to one based on equity.[68] This is what he called a "reactionary" task,[69] the constitution of the new state "as an entity that represents production and labor organized . . . into responsible guilds (*gremios*), in which representation would correspond only to the natives, and in which agrarian interests would be preponderant." Only when "there will not be within the state anything superior to the state itself," the government "will be able to impose equity."[70] The fascist echoes are obvious in the book. It included the standard anti-Semitic images (". . . international banking [is] a Hebrew organization, and international socialism a veritable Jewish sect"[71]) as well as typical aesthetic invocations ("the coming times are times of rude austerity, of virile humility, of noble danger"[72]).

Even though this profascist faction was defeated, its members and sympathizers continued operating as an important wing of the Conservatives throughout the thirties. Sánchez Sorondo was a prominent senator and Manuel Fresco was in 1936–40 the governor of the Province of Buenos Aires, the largest and most important in the country.

Senator Sánchez Sorondo supported fascism on pragmatic grounds. In the debate of the anticommunist bill, he described the superiority of fascism over communism, like Ibarguren had done, on the basis of its compatibility with national institutions and traditions. "Communism," he said, "is a danger for the existence of the nationalities as such. . . . Fascism, on the other hand, is respectful of our social organization." He went on by saying that one might argue about fascist institutions and doctrines, but ". . . no one could deny that they stand over the very foundations of our

67. Ibid., p. 75.
68. Ibid., p. 16.
69. Ibid., p. 12.
70. Ibid., pp. 38–39.
71. Ibid., p. 31.
72. Ibid., p. 17.

civilization. Communism seeks to destroy [these foundations], fascism wants to confirm them. . . . fascism erects its state over religion, family, private property; while communism wants to raze them."[73]

Governor Fresco, Sánchez Sorondo's fellow Conservative, was more aware of the revolutionary claims of fascism. His administration is justly notorious for its practice of electoral fraud and of administrative corruption, but it also attempted to develop, for the first time in Argentina, a corporatist machinery for the control of labor by the state.[74] In fact, its analysis of the "social question" was essentially similar to the Peronist formulation a few years later. On the one hand, the Fresco administration repressed the radical Left in a severe manner and carried out policies such as the establishment of religious education in public schools, which had an antiliberal meaning. On the other hand, Fresco and his faction realized that exclusion was not an effective mechanism for the control of the working class, and they set up a system of labor representation in which unions would be granted recognition by the state and would be required to submit their demands to compulsory arbitration, also by the state.

These norms were formulated in the Organic Labor Act of 1937. In presenting the bill to the provincial Senate, Roberto J. Noble, the government minister, explicitly linked the proposed arrangements with fascism. Invoking the Russian example, he argued that the "social question" could not be solved through repression. He emphasized the solid anticommunist and antiliberal credentials of the Fresco administration by reminding the legislators that "the government that presents this bill . . . is the same one that has promulgated the decree of repression of communism, and it is the same that has the pride and the honor of having established religious education in the Province of Buenos Aires." But he also raised the crucial issue that distinguished the new Right from the old authoritarian one: "However . . . we do not have the right to think that in the year of 1937, and in the Argentine Republic, it is

73. Sánchez Sorondo, *Represión del comunismo*, pp. 17–18.

74. On the Fresco administration, see Ronald H. Dolkart, "Manuel A. Fresco, Governor of the Province of Buenos Aires 1936–1940: A Study of the Argentine Right and Its Response to Economic and Social Change" (1969); and Richard J. Walter, *The Province of Buenos Aires and Argentine Politics, 1912–1943* (1985). On Fresco's labor policies, see his *Cómo encaré la política obrera.*

possible to uphold czarist criteria, and solve social problems with the whip, or in an improvised manner (*a ponchazos*)!"[75]

The social question should be faced with corporatist controls, but the state should be ready to use exclusionary policies if these controls fail: ". . . the parties [to the industrial conflict] . . . must try to reach an agreement under the tutelage of the state and, should one of these parties escape the legal procedure in order to adopt, by its free will, attitudes of force that harm the collective interests, the government will use all its political power to return the matter to the legal course."[76] This is, almost literally, the language Perón would use seven years later.

In the debate, Noble argued, in response to a Socialist senator, that fascist and socialist economic and social policies were essentially similar, and he castigated Socialists for betraying their own doctrine and shifting to the most disastrous one of liberalism. He claimed, resorting to the authority of Antonio Labriola, that "fascism constitutes, in the contemporary epoch, the broadest and most categoric fulfillment of the economic program of socialism." The difference between the two doctrines lay in "a different . . . interpretation of the concepts of life and of individual and political freedom." Unlike other rightists, whose support for fascism was pragmatic and restrained, Noble was a passionate admirer of the Italian regime: "Fascism . . . proclaims, together with its concept of dangerous and heroic life and of the imperial destiny of cultures, its new concept of freedom: individual freedom within order, collective freedom based on discipline and hierarchy, totalitarian and authoritarian democracy."[77]

The argument that liberalism was no longer effective and that fascist and socialist forms of state intervention in the society were, in spite of their differences, similar or equivalent alternatives to it was commonplace in mainstream and even center-left political discourse. A left-wing liberal democrat such as Lisandro de la Torre, the leader of the Progressive Democratic Party, who stood on the opposite side of the political spectrum from Noble or Fresco, stated the issue on the basis of a similar framework. In the

75. Roberto J. Noble, "La nueva ley orgánica del trabajo" (discurso pronunciado en el Senado por el Ministro de Gobierno), in Argentine Republic, Provincia de Buenos Aires, Departamento del Trabajo, *Política obrera y legislación del trabajo del gobierno de Buenos Aires* (1937), p. 27.

76. Ibid., p. 23.

77. Ibid., pp. 24–25.

same year of 1937, in a polemic with Franceschi, he also argued that liberal capitalism was doomed: "The current situation in the world is the most critical one since the barbarian invasions. There is a state of decomposition and uncertainty which cannot last. I understand that many reject the communist regime, but they cannot deny the need to quit this other regime. It may be called bourgeois, capitalist, imperialist or whatever, [but] it is the cause of the situation of bankruptcy, tax spoliation, and imminent war, which prevails in all the big nations."[78] De la Torre was mildly sympathetic to the Soviet Union and resolutely opposed to fascism, which he described as a militaristic regime that ignored popular sovereignty and rested on the exaltation of national pride. Nevertheless, he considered that fascist and communist policies had substantial similarities. "Fascism," he said, "has adjusted its policies to the procedures followed by Lenin in Russia. . . . Mussolini pretends to be the discoverer of the recipes prepared by Lenin, which he has incorporated into Italian cuisine."[79] And, more strongly, ". . . Fascism is another form of communism."[80]

There is no question, finally, that Perón was influenced by fascism. The influence was both direct and indirect. It is obvious that his ideas, and even the language with which he expressed them, and some of the rhetorical arguments he used, can be traced to those of the nationalists, integrist Catholics, and Fresco-style Conservatives I have discussed in this chapter. By his own account, he had read fascist works and *Mein Kampf*.[81] Perón had also direct exposure to fascist regimes. He was sent to Italy by the army in 1939, to observe the military, and also the regime there. In his two-year stay, he was attached to several units, attended a service school, and assisted the Argentine military attaché.[82] Fascinated by the regime, and by the figure of Mussolini, he tried to penetrate the "social phenomenon" that was incubating in Italy and Germany, and was particularly interested in corporative forms of participation.[83] Perón was present at one of Mussolini's most dra-

78. Lisandro De la Torre, "La cuestión social y los cristianos sociales," in his *Intermedio filosófico* (1961), p. 53.

79. Ibid., p. 45.

80. Ibid., p. 46.

81. Recorded statement, in Torcuato Luca de Tena, Luis Calvo, and Esteban Peicovich, *Yo, Juan Perón* (1976), p. 28.

82. See Page, *Perón*, pp. 35–36.

83. Recorded statement, in Luca de Tena et al., *Yo, Juan Perón*, pp. 28–29.

matic speeches, the declaration of war, and even decades afterward he recalled the emotion that seized him when he met the fascist leader.[84] Finally, Perón took courses in fascist political economy at Turin University. By his own account, it was these courses that enlightened him about the labor question.[85]

Even a generation later, when he was in exile and presented himself as a moderate mainstream politician, willing to play by the democratic rules, Perón emphasized the direct lineage between his doctrine, movement, and regime, and the fascist ones. He argued that fascism represented a "third position" between capitalism and communism, a system based on true popular representation and in which the state was the instrument of an organized community;[86] all formulas he normally used to describe Peronism.

The whole Argentine society was rocked by the Spanish civil war. Unlike Western Europe and the United States, this war became a traumatic experience not only for the intelligentsia and the Left, but also for large sectors of the middle and working classes.

The memoirs from the period convey the intense and generalized nature of this impact. José Luis de Imaz, a sociologist born in a middle-class Spanish and Catholic family, describes well the climate in a milieu belonging neither to the elite nor to the intelligentsia:

> No other Argentine generation arrived at intelligence within the frame of so many events alien to its direct lived experience, and I say direct because we did not endure that civil war in Buenos Aires, even though it also 'occurred' in Buenos Aires. Those who were born just four or five years before me were awakened with the echoes of Abyssinia. Their parents 'already' were for or against Italy, for or against Mussolini. . . . I learned to read with the civil war because together with my schoolbooks I spelled the large headlines of the afternoon papers—for us *La Razón*, for others *Crítica* [a pro-Franco and a pro-loyalist newspaper, C.H.W.]—

84. Ibid., p. 27.

85. Interviews with Esteban Peicovich, in his *Hola Perón* (1965), p. 39; and with Felix Luna, in Luna, *El 45*, pp. 58–59.

86. Interview with Felix Luna, in Luna, *El 45*, p. 58; and recorded statement, in Luca de Tena et al., *Yo, Juan Perón*, p. 29.

which during these years only gave us the names of towns and places in Spain.[87]

Juan José Real, a former Communist who fought for the republic, was right when he wrote that the civil war "produced in Argentina, more than in any other part of the continent, a profound commotion: it affected all the sectors of society, and all the political groups."[88] Helvio Botana, whose family owned *Crítica*, the largest circulation newspaper, concurred: "In all the republic, we were invaded by a polemical belligerence. . . . The 'do not get involved' disappeared. Argentina vibrated, and cherished passionately an event that was ours."[89] The reason for this strong effect beyond the politicized public and the intelligentsia is clear. Mark Falcoff has estimated that, in 1936, 15 percent of the Argentine population consisted of Spanish citizens.[90] The strength of cultural ties can be indicated by the fact that Argentina was the largest foreign market for books published in Spain.[91] Cultural connections were intense, especially in literature and art, in spite of the fact that the Argentine elite had traditionally looked down upon Spanish culture.

The whole society quickly mobilized in support of either of the two sides, and large groups of people who were previously apolitical or apathetic plunged into politics with passion. The war was a watershed in the lives of many individuals from all the social classes, whatever their ethnicity. The theme recurs in published memoirs and in statements by the people who lived through the period. As in many other countries, support for the republic was a mass movement. It was based on leftist and center parties (Socialists, Communists, Radicals, Progressive Democrats), trade unions, student federations, and ad hoc organizations, some of which had large memberships. Loyalist agitation was continuous and massive, and large scale fundraising took place. According to the Communist Party, Argentina ranked second in the world in

87. José Luis de Imaz, *Promediados los cuarenta* (1977), pp. 19–20.

88. Real, *Treinta años*, p. 52.

89. Helvio I. Botana, *Memorias: Tras los dientes del perro* (1977), p. 183.

90. Mark Falcoff, "Argentina," in Mark Falcoff and Frederick B. Pike, eds., *The Spanish Civil War, 1936–1939: American Hemispheric Perspectives* (1982), p. 291.

91. Ibid., pp. 292–93.

terms of financial support for the Republican government.[92] Finally, hundreds of Argentines fought in the International Brigades.[93]

On the other side, supporting the insurgents, were the nationalists, the church, and most Conservatives, especially those of the new Right. "During the Civil War I felt intimate solidarity with the national forces," Mario Amadeo, a nationalist who presented himself as a moderate statesman, wrote in the fifties, "because I understood that the question then at issue was not a purely domestic one, but it was the option between the highest religious and cultural values of the West and Marxist barbarousness."[94] Franceschi stated the issue in mystical terms, in a polemic with Jacques Maritain: "I understand very well that in this war there are only two opposing forces: one, truly demonic, that synthesizes everything that is abhorrence of Christ; and another that . . . serves God and will allow souls to raise to Him."[95] He was, no doubt, affected by the anticlerical disturbances in republican areas, but his advocacy of the Franco side led him even to countenance its avowed totalitarian goals: "I think that Spain's fundamental Catholicism will eliminate almost automatically what is anti-Catholic in totalitarianism, as a robust body eliminates venom."[96] Antiliberal Conservatives such as Senator Sánchez Sorondo and Governor Fresco were also militant supporters of the rebels. Mainstream Conservatives varied in their views toward Franco, but in general they were not sympathetic to the republic, as could be expected.

In the evaluation of the Spanish Republic, old and new Right coincided. Obsessed by the image of their own working class as dangerous, they interpreted the Spanish experience as an ideal model of democratization and its aftermath. It showed how an inclusionary elite strategy, whereby the lower classes were incorporated into the political system as an independent force, produced the victory of the Popular Front. As Senator Villafañe put it, "democracy, understood as the rule by half the nation plus one, fatally

92. Partido Comunista, *Esbozo*, p. 85.

93. See Falcoff, "Argentina," pp. 316–20.

94. Amadeo, *Ayer, hoy, mañana*, pp. 34–35.

95. Franceschi, in Jacques Maritain and Gustavo J. Franceschi, "Posiciones," *Criterio* (1937), p. 352.

96. Gustavo J. Franceschi, *El movimiento español y el criterio católico* (1937), p. 18.

leads to suicidal wars like the one in Spain, or to disasters like the one in France."[97] The government of the Popular Front was described by an Argentine diplomat in Spain as one "powerless to impose authority ... dominated not only by workers' associations, but also by roving bands of common criminals."[98] This provoked the civil war, which was considered by the conservative newspaper *La Prensa* as "the unexpected result of the preaching of class struggle."[99] The aftermath, as described by right-wing appraisals after the end of the war, would be one million dead (the official figure repeated over and over by the victors) and massive destruction of property. In the interpretation, this sequence of stages was considered necessary, flowing from an original cause that was the revolutionary nature of the working class.

However, the majority of the Conservatives and the new Right differed in terms of the practical consequences they extracted from the Spanish negative example. While the former remained satisfied with the limited exclusion of the working class, the latter were prompted to introduce changes in the society in order to prevent a process like the one that had taken place in Spain. Such was the purpose of the GOU, according to its basic document, most likely written by Perón. This document argued that the politicization of the army was necessary to avert danger to the state and the army itself. It claimed that preemptive action by the military would have avoided communism in Russia and the civil war in Spain. In these two countries, apoliticism rendered the military blind to the red danger. In Argentina, communist propaganda was attempting to subvert the army: "A situation similar to that in Spain is being prepared for us. An intense reaction and a constant concern about this question are imperative."[100]

Finally, the Spanish example was continuously adduced by Perón in order to justify his prognosis for the postwar period. He stated that he had spent six months in Spain after the war and that he was shocked by what he had seen. He argued that it was this traumatic experience, together with his observation of Europe (that is, Italy), which prompted him to enter politics, in order to ward off a similar catastrophe in Argentina.[101] In his speech at the

97. Villafañe, *La tragedia argentina*, p. 190.

98. Falcoff, "Argentina," p. 310.

99. Ibid., p. 328.

100. Potash, ed., *Perón*, p. 40. See also pp. 57, 58, 199, 205.

101. Perón, in an interview with Luna, in Luna, *El 45*, pp. 59–60.

stock exchange, he told businessmen that the central problem Argentina faced was the avoidance of a social explosion in the postwar years, like the one Spain had known. He argued that a social cataclysm would lead to the loss of all assets, as in Spain.[102] Perón even claimed that there were stronger causes for a revolution in Argentina in the postwar period than in Spain in the thirties. The argument revolved around exploitation: he contended that average wages were lower and profits higher in Argentina than in Spain.[103] (I do not know about profits, but he was most likely mistaken in relation to wages.) The specter of the civil war lingered in Perón's mind for a long period. Even after he was overthrown in 1955, his standard justification for having resigned and left the country without fighting was that he wanted above all to spare Argentina a civil war like that in Spain.[104]

In conclusion, the sectors of the elite that were sensitive to the Spanish and Italian demonstration effects were interpreting these examples incorrectly. Both the Spanish civil war and Italian fascism were phenomena specific to their societies, produced by local overdetermination processes, rather than necessary stages of historical development. Moreover, these cases were inaccurately understood by the Argentine borrowers. Democratization does not lead necessarily to chaos and revolution, and corporatism is neither more efficacious than liberalism, nor equivalent to communism.

Further, Argentine society was roughly at the same level of development as Italy or Spain, and the population and culture were very similar, but neither the Spanish nor the Italian examples could be replicated in Argentina. The fear that democracy could lead to civil war as in Spain was unfounded, for two reasons. First, polarization was much lower in Argentina in the thirties and forties than in Spain at the time of the republic. Both the radical Left and the antiliberal Right were much weaker in Argentina than in Spain. Second, liberal-democratic institutions and culture were probably more legitimate in Argentina at that time than in Spain when the republic was established. Argentines had experienced and been socialized into a democratic political culture to a larger extent than Spaniards.

The expectation that fascist-style corporatist institutions could

102. Perón, *El pueblo quiere saber*, p. 163.
103. Ibid., p. 164.
104. Perón, in an interview with Luna, in Luna, *El 45*, p. 59.

be easily transferred was also unrealistic, for the Argentine and Italian political systems were very different. Argentina lacked all the sociological ingredients of Italian fascism. It did not have a radicalized working class that would pose a real threat to the social order, nor frightened economic elites ready to accept the embrace of a political entrepreneur who would protect them from that threat, nor a social base provided by middle classes also frightened by the advance of the Left. Argentina had a moderately mobilized but not revolutionary working class, economic elites who were not afraid and who wavered between restrictive and open liberal-democratic formulas, and a middle class that was mostly liberal-democratic as well. . . . As a result, the antiliberal mass movement had to be labor based, and the product, Peronism, was as different from fascism as a constitutional monarchy is from an absolute one. The trappings of fascism were there in the ideology, in the relationship between the leader and the masses, and in the "movement" type of organization, but the substance gradually became a very different one, that of a union-based labor party.

### The Argentine Paradox

I conclude with a paradox: the reversal of Argentine economic and political development was caused, to a large extent, by the very "modernity" of the society, by the fact that it was a "new country" type of peripheral nation rather than an "underdeveloped" one.

This chapter showed that, at a time of very high uncertainty about the evolution of the international system and about the place of Argentina in that system, a sector of the state elite panicked because of its distorted image of the working class and of its strong sensitivity to demonstration effects originating in Latin Europe. It is important to note that both this distorted image and the sensitivity to these demonstration effects were produced by the "new country" character of Argentina.

We have seen that the image of a dangerous working class was caused by the low level of national integration of the country at the time of the reversal, especially by the large proportion of foreigners and migrants from the periphery in the working class, and by the significant level of labor mobilization. Further, I showed that the direction of the demonstration effects was determined by the strong social and cultural networks linking Argentina and Latin Europe, the perceived efficacy of the Italian and Spanish models (positive and negative, respectively) in relation to the "social question," and the perceived transferability of these foreign experiences to local conditions. This panicky sector of the elite discerned the impending danger in the Spanish case and a reasonable solution in the Italian one. A local adaptation of fascism, like the one proposed by Perón and, before him, by Lugones or Fresco, seemed the best response to the menace of a revolutionary upheaval in the postwar period. This response was the control of the society by a double-faced state, which could, on the one hand, guarantee justice to the workers by satisfying their legitimate demands and, on the other, repress communism. This was not just a centralizing response to high uncertainty; it was a kind of centralization that, its supporters expected, could evolve into a new type of legitimacy.

This twisted image of the working class and the susceptibility to demonstration effects among the segments of the elite accepting Perón's diagnosis and proposed solutions were strongly influenced by the factors that made Argentina "modern" and different from the standard Latin American pattern: the high land-labor ratio and the labor shortage at the time of large-scale incorporation into the world economy. These two factors account for the foreign nature of a large proportion of the working class and for the mobilization of labor. Since there was a high land-labor ratio, there was no large peasant population, and, since there was a labor shortage, labor had to be imported, at first from Europe and later from the internal periphery. The immigrants carried with them two traits conducive to mobilization: some cultural affinity with Latin European variants of socialism and anarchism, and very strong mobility orientations. But the host country provided a crucial structural determinant of mobilization. Since there was no large labor reserve army, labor's market power was relatively high. This factor was still operative in the late thirties and early forties, when Creoles from the interior joined the working class.

It was the relatively weak national integration at the lower levels of the class structure, in a context of high uncertainty, that caused a sector of the political elite to be receptive to the demonstration effects from the countries from which the majority of the Argentine population and a large proportion of the working class had originated. And these foreign experiences were interpreted in terms of the integration question: the Spanish case as an extreme instance of a society with low integration, the Italian one as a mechanism for the reconstruction of the national community.

It was this distorted political knowledge that induced a sector of the state elite to accept Perón's two key policies, the granting of extreme protection to manufacturing and the attempt to develop a corporatist relationship between state and labor. As we have seen, these were the policies that transformed the Argentine economy and polity and led to decades of stagnation and illegitimacy.

# 8 The Disadvantages of Modernity

Not ideas, but material and ideal interests, directly govern men's conduct. Yet very frequently the "world images" that have been created by "ideas" have, like switchmen, determined the tracks along which action has been pushed by the dynamic of interest.

Max Weber, "The Social Psychology of the World Religions"

## A Recapitulation: The Argentine Question Reconsidered

This book examined what can be called the Argentine question. It tried to understand why Argentina failed to become an industrial democracy.

My central theme was that Argentina was not an underdeveloped country prior to the Depression, but that it was converted into one as a consequence of social and political processes in the postwar years. As I put it, the country switched developmental tracks: from being a "new country" type of peripheral society, it turned into an "underdeveloped" one. I argued that this reversal was the unintended consequence of industrial and labor policies institutionalized in the forties. A central justification for these policies was the need to thwart a revolutionary mobilization in the postwar period. I also contended that there was no danger of revolution, that the apprehension held by a segment of the state elite was the product of distorted political knowledge, and that these policies had the consequences they did because of specific characteristics of the Argentine social structure.

I want to make it clear that I am not tracing the reversal of Argentine development to the ideas and actions of an individual, Juan Perón. He played a salient role in the period of the reversal, but he did so as the leader or representative of a segment of the state elite, which was the strategic actor in the processes leading to the economic and political decline of Argentina. Nor am I propounding a bivariate argument of the type "the fear of revolution was the cause of the change of developmental tracks." This fear was an important justification for the support by a segment of the state elite for industrial autarky and state corporatism, but it was not the only justification (radical protectionism, in particular, was

*253*

also advocated on the grounds of economic independence and national defense); it was itself caused by structural factors, and its effects were mediated by structural processes. My argument combines internal structural factors (the land-labor ratio and the labor supply), the changing position of Argentina in the international system (as a consequence of Depression and war), political processes (the autonomy of the state), and ideological-cognitive ones (the fear of revolution by a sector of the state elite at a crucial juncture in Argentine development). A recapitulation of the contents of the previous chapters will be useful at this point.

Chapter 1 showed that the question I am asking is not trivial, for both empirical and theoretical reasons. First, the economic and political development of the country was curvilinear: high levels of economic and social development and an expanding liberal democracy up to the Depression, followed by economic sluggishness and political instability ever since. More specifically, the reversal of Argentine development began as industry expanded and diversified. This relationship focused the question to a consideration of why Argentina has not been able to link liberal democracy with an industrial society. Second, Argentina also poses a question for social theory, for its development is paradoxical in relation to the classical versions of both Marxism and functionalism.

Chapter 2 established why Argentina is a deviant case in terms of development theory. It showed that Adam Smith, Tocqueville, Marx and Engels, Turner, and the staple theorists distinguished between two types of peripheral society: the "new country" and the "underdeveloped" case. The first, characterized by a high land-labor ratio and the absence of a large labor reserve, was expected to develop along the lines of efficient capitalism, social egalitarianism, and liberal democracy. The second type of society, defined by a low land-labor ratio and a large labor reserve, would be prone to economic backwardness, and to becoming both an inegalitarian society and a nondemocratic state. The Argentine question was redefined thus: why did Argentina, which had the structural characteristics of a new country and which had a pattern of evolution that conformed to the course predicted by development theory for that type of society up to the Depression and the war, switch developmental tracks thereafter and begin to resemble the "underdevelopment" case?

Chapter 3 reviewed the basic traits of Argentine society against the "new country" and Latin American mirrors. Images of Argentina reflected its development. From the large-scale incorporation of the country into the international economy to the Depression, domestic and foreign observers conceptualized Argentina as a land of recent settlement, while, since the war, the prevailing image has been that of an underdeveloped and dependent country. The structure of the society was that of a "new country" both in terms of the land-labor ratio and of the constitution of the population mainly on the basis of European immigration, especially from Italy and Spain. However, Argentina departed from the "new country" type in two respects: it had greater concentration of land-ownership, and most of its immigrants originated in countries other than the original metropolis.

During the period of ascent, Argentina was an informal member of the British empire, and the agrarian elite was the hegemonic class. There was significant industrialization, but it was subordinate to agriculture. In this period, there existed a considerable degree of pluralism and participation was expanded to the middle classes. The working class remained excluded because most immigrants did not become Argentine citizens.

Constitutional rule was interrupted at the onset of the Depression. The coup of 1930 started a period of military rule and limited democracy, which lasted until 1943, when another coup established a right-wing nationalist regime with corporatist overtones. Perón's constitutional administration of 1946–55 was the successor of that regime. From the overthrow of Perón to the present time, the Argentine polity has been highly unstable; it has been a succession of illegitimate military regimes and weak constitutional administrations. Economic development since the Depression has been focused on industry; through import substitution, the manufacturing sector grew and diversified from the thirties onward. In the thirties, however, protection to industry was provisional and contingent; with Peronism, it became definitive and absolute. The economy grew in the first postwar years and became sluggish from the fifties onward. Internationally, Argentina slipped. In 1929, its per capita product was slightly lower than that of France, and in 1982 it was slightly higher than that of Brazil.

Chapter 4 examined the adequacy of different hypotheses to the explanation of Argentina's curvilinear pattern of economic and political development. It concluded that this reversal cannot be satisfactorily explained by cultural factors, by dependency as such, by the country's degree or type of development, by political mobilization, or by characteristics of the party system. The Argentine decline was produced by the institutionalization of the two policies applied in the post-war period: radical or absolute protection to manufactures oriented to the internal market, and the development of an inclusionary corporatist relationship between labor and the state. The first of these policies led in a short time to large-scale industrialization, and thus to the maldistribution of capital and human resources on a large scale. Most industries produced consumer goods, and they required imported machinery and other inputs. Since these industries could not export, their import needs had to be met with the foreign exchange obtained by agriculture. Thus, Argentina developed a self-limiting economic system, in which a large share of the surplus generated by the competitive sector was allocated to the noncompetitive one. The second policy expanded and strengthened the labor movement. When stagnating tendencies set in, the tie between state and labor broke down, and the conflict over the distribution of the surplus led to illegitimacy and political instability. The issue was thus redefined further: the understanding of the Argentine reversal depends on an understanding of the origin of these two policies.

Chapter 5 focused on this question. It concluded that the new industrial and labor policies were an instance of the autonomy of the state, for autarky and inclusionary corporatism were not in the interest of the upper classes nor were they the effect of exogenous determinants. The fact that radical protectionism, in particular, was the pattern in Latin America does not mean that this industrial policy was preordained, especially in the case of Argentina, which as a land of recent settlement had developed an economic and social infrastructure that could have permitted either open industrialization or a policy of selective protection.

The autonomy of the state was a consequence of the economic and political processes associated with the Depression and the war. The link, however, was not direct. The Depression triggered the period of military and limited democracy governments (1930–43), but these regimes did represent the interests of the agrarian upper class. This class began to lose its hegemony, but it still controlled the state apparatus through a "regime of exception." The decline of oligarchic hegemony was a precondition for the autonomy of the state, but not a cause in itself. State autonomy began with the coup of 1943, after which the new industrial and labor policies were applied.

The problem became, then, to ascertain the determinants of the autonomy of the state in the early forties. I discarded two hypotheses, weakness of the civil society and vertical cleavage, and accepted two others, external constraints and elite fragmentation. The coup was triggered by the need to face competing British and American pressures in relation to Argentine participation in the war and military competition with Brazil. Domestically, the take-over by the armed forces was made possible by the fragmentation that developed in the elite along economic and political lines, as a consequence of the economic and social changes produced by the Depression and of the international alignments of different factions. But neither external constraints nor elite fragmentation explain the contents of the policies applied by the autonomous state; that is, why these specific policies, radical protectionism and state corporatism, were selected. In order to understand this issue, it was necessary to probe the "subjective" domain; how the groups in control of the state formulated their goals, why these industrial and labor policies were considered adequate means for the attainment of these goals, and what was the relationship between the interests so defined and the interests of established economic elites.

Chapter 6 dealt with this problem. It examined the choices made by the different segments of the established elite at a crucial juncture: the election of 1946, in which Perón was supported by the military, the clergy, and the new Right, and opposed by the upper classes, agrarian and industrial, and most Conservatives. The sector supporting Perón was obsessed with the fear of revolution. As for Perón himself, he focused on that fear in his discourse to the elites. It should be clear that I am not assuming that Perón himself was so obsessed: he might have used the conventional anticommunist argument just because it was expedient. What I am asserting is that the acceptance of his assessment by a sector of the elites shows that *they* had a siege mentality. In particular, Perón contended that the postwar years would produce mass unemployment and that this would increase the danger of revolution. On the basis of the analysis of his speeches in 1944–46, I showed that Perón presented not only inclusionary corporatism but also radical protectionism as an antidote to revolution. Agrarian and industrial upper classes rejected his program because it was incompatible with their economic interests. As for the revolutionary danger, they understood very well that Perón was more a cause of, than a remedy for, labor agitation. The segments of the state elite supporting Perón, on the other hand, were guided by ideological considerations—their inordinate fear of communism—for their instrumental or organizational interests could have been compatible with the alternative choice, that is, the support for the liberal and proagrarian coalition opposing Perón.

I concluded that such fear of revolution was unrealistic. Not only was there no *actual* vertical cleavage between a revolutionary labor movement and the ruling classes and the state, but the forecast that such a cleavage was in the making and would emerge after the war was not reasonable. I showed that the extent of labor mobilization prior to the coup of 1943 was substantial but not threatening to the social order; that the Communist Party, the only important revolutionary organization, was small, and its influence was limited by environmental factors (repression, cultural cleavages in the working class) and by internal ones (the party's own line); that there were no signs of radicalization in the non-communist majority of the labor movement; and that the fear of mass unemployment in the postwar period was unfounded.

Finally, Chapter 7 examined the cognitive infrastructure of the fear of revolution. I argued that the sectors of the elite accepting Perón's diagnosis and prescriptions defined their ideological interests on the basis of distorted political knowledge. First, they had a deformed image of the working class, which they represented as intrinsically dangerous. The inaccurate evaluation of the current labor movement was the product of the recall of past experiences the Argentine elite had with the working class, which were also perceived in a distorted manner. These experiences were the intense mobilization in the beginning of the century and the "Tragic Week," in the first postwar period. As a result of these memories, the image of the working class as an intrinsically threatening force was established in the collective memory of the Right. Secondly, they were influenced by the demonstration effects of Italian fascism and the Spanish civil war. These effects were facilitated by the social and cultural networks between Argentina and Latin Europe, the perceived efficacy of these examples, and their perceived appropriateness to the Argentine situation. The Spanish civil war was interpreted as a model of what could happen in Argentina after the war, and the fascist regime as an enlightened and legitimizing response to labor agitation. Of course, the perception of these foreign experiences was also distorted, and their relevance to the Argentine situation was unwarranted.

Also, I argued that the fact that Argentina was a "new country" rather than an "underdeveloped" type of peripheral society was, paradoxically, a determinant of this distortion of political knowledge. More specifically, the high land-labor ratio and the labor shortage at the time of large-scale integration into the international economy contributed to both the image of the dangerous working class and the sensitivity to demonstration effects from Latin Europe. The ratio and the shortage determined the foreign origin of much of the working class and its level of mobilization. The latter was a consequence of two factors: the immigrants' strong mobility orientations and relative sensitivity to left-wing ideologies, and the absence of a large labor reserve army in Argentina. In turn, foreign origin and mobilization determined the crystallization of the image of the dangerous working class.

This image was activated at a time of very high uncertainty by a sector of the state elite. Its panic, then, was produced by a structural factor, the low level of national integration, especially at the lower levels of the class structure, and a contextual one, high uncertainty as a consequence of the Depression and the war. This sector of the elite, possessed by an unrealistic fear of revolution, was sensitive to the demonstration effects emanating from the region of the world where most Argentines had originated and which seemed to spell out the consequences of low integration (Spain) and the solution to the problem (Italy). Thus, these foreign experiences were interpreted by these elite groups in terms of what they saw as the Argentine problem, that is, a question of integration.

The fateful option for the new industrial and labor policies at a critical juncture of Argentine development led to the transformation of the social structure, and thus to stagnation and illegitimacy. When a large proportion of the economic and human resources of the society were committed to noncompetitive forms of manufacturing, the economy turned sluggish and unstable, and the state corporatist mechanisms broke down. As a consequence of what I called the contradiction of corporatism, the labor movement was larger and more powerful than what would have been the case without the inclusionary corporatist attempt. Since its opponent in the contest for the distribution of the surplus was a weak industrial bourgeoisie, producing for a captive market and dependent on the state for financing, tariff protection, and the control of labor, the stage was set for political instability and the progressive delegitimation of the social order.

Thus, external and domestic factors and economic as well as political and ideological-cognitive ones interacted in producing the Argentine reversal. The Depression and the war per se did not cause the reversal, but they produced the autonomy of the state and were the contextual factors that caused the sector of the elite in control of the state to panic. The autonomy of the state did not cause the reversal either, but the independence of the state from the dominant class was a precondition for the institutionalization of policies (radical protectionism and state corporatism) that were against the interests of the dominant class. The inordinate fear of revolution in a sector of the elite was the product of distorted cognitive processes, which in turn were produced by the high uncertainty derived from the Depression and the war and by the "new country" traits of Argentina. These traits—the high land-labor ratio and the shortage of labor—were not, of course, the cause of the reversal, but they contributed strongly to the low level of national integration, to the mobilization of the labor movement and, thus, to the image of the dangerous lower class, and also to the direction of the demonstration effects to which the sector of the elite in control of the state was sensitive.

I argued in Chapter 4 that, had Argentina been a "typical" Latin American country like Brazil or Mexico, that is, one with a substantial peasantry and a large urban informal sector, the long-term consequences of the industrial and labor policies practiced in the forties would have been different. Other things being equal, autarkic economic policies would have produced low growth rates in any case, but inclusionary corporatism would not have led to the conversion of labor into a powerful autonomous actor when stagnating tendencies appeared, for the existence of a large labor reserve would have hindered mobilization and the control of the labor supply by the unions. As a consequence, the structural stalemate characteristic of Argentina in the post-Peronist period would not have developed.

Most likely, however, changes in the international position of the country as a consequence of the Depression and the war would have also led to the autonomization of the state. An indication that a process of this sort was under way in many Latin American countries can be seen in the number of military coups after the Depression. According to Claudio Véliz, seventeen governments were overthrown in the region in 1929–32.[1] (One of the exceptions was Mexico, where the state was already relatively independent of the dominant class.) Also in the thirties, the diversification processes that led to elite fragmentation and that facilitated state autonomy took place in several Latin American countries as a re-

1. Véliz, *Centralist Tradition*, p. 279.

sponse to the Depression. Nevertheless, had Argentina been an "underdeveloped" type of peripheral society, it is not obvious that the policies followed by the autonomous state would have been the same. In much of Latin America, blanket protectionism for manufacturing was practiced after the war, but the other component of the Peronist package, the political incorporation of labor through state corporatist mechanisms, was less so. In full-fledged form, it evolved mainly in Mexico and Brazil at that time, but its development and consequences there were very different from those in Argentina. Since what I called the paradox of corporatism did not occur in these countries, the state there strengthened vis-à-vis civil society. The control of labor by the state on the basis of corporatist mechanisms did succeed; that is, this control persisted over time, even when stagnating tendencies appeared. More than five decades after the beginning of the Depression, such mechanisms are still functioning in Mexico, and only in the last decade did they begin to crumble in Brazil.

There are other aspects of the social structure of typical Latin American societies that affected elite strategies toward labor in the postwar years. In the standard Latin American situation, labor was weaker not only because of the existence of a large labor reserve. Also, the working classes in these countries were smaller and often concentrated in enclaves; and they were mostly native, which meant that strong mobility orientations were probably less prevalent among them than among European immigrants, and that their susceptibility to socialist and anarchist appeals was relatively lower as well (Chile is an exception to this latter point: due to peculiarities of this country's development, a strong Left appeared early in the labor movement).

The existence in most of these counties of smaller, native, and less mobilized working classes had two consequences that are relevant for the "question of revolution." First, local elites were less likely to feel besieged by an intrinsically dangerous working class. The Vargas regime in Brazil was intensely anticommunist, but it did not panic about its lower classes. In Chile, the only Latin American country with a large and well established Communist Party in the thirties and forties, a Popular Front was not only formed but it came to power without triggering a military coup.

Second, due to this image of the working class and to the absence of large immigrant populations from Latin Europe, elite sensitivity to demonstration effects from that origin was not as strong as in Argentina. The Spanish civil war, of course, had a powerful impact throughout the continent,[2] but its reception as a vicarious experience and an object lesson to elites was strongest in Argentina. Brazil was another Latin American country in which fascist and corporatist formulas became influential among sectors of the state elite in the thirties, even though state managers were pragmatic enough to shed these ideas in the forties and to jump into the Allied bandwagon. In any case, the demonstration effect was based on the same mechanism at work in Argentina: Brazil also had a substantial Portuguese population, in absolute terms, and close cultural ties with Portugal.

Thus, most countries with a "typical" Latin American social structure have been as incapable as Argentina of becoming industrial democracies, but the causes are different than in the Argentine case. These countries suffer from the variegated ills of underdevelopment (lack of a diversified resource base, overpopulation, structural heterogeneity, high levels of dependency on single export markets, and so on), while Argentina is a case of reversal from a "new country" situation.

The argument can be summarized as follows:

1. Argentina was not an underdeveloped country in the period of externally-led growth; its social structure resembled the "new country" type rather than the modal Latin American pattern. The two most important characteristics of the "new country" are a high land-labor ratio and a shortage of labor. As a consequence of these traits, labor had to be imported, and there was no large labor reserve army.
2. The reversal of economic and political development and the consequent "Latinoamericanization" of Argentina was the result of processes that took place between the Depression and the postwar period.
3. The changes in the international system in that period did not determine directly the reversal of Argentine development. However, they contributed indirectly, for these changes caused the autonomization of the state from the dominant class. The Depression led to the decline of the hegemony of the agrarian upper class, and to the economic and political fragmentation of the upper class in general. This fragmentation, and the external pressures derived from the war, produced the autonomy of the state. The coup of 1943 marks the beginning of this autonomy.

2. Falcoff and Pike, *The Spanish Civil War.*

4. In the context of high uncertainty during the war, the elite split. At the end of the war, the majority of the upper classes (agrarians and big industrialists, and their political representatives, the Conservative Party and a segment of the Radicals) supported policies conducive to the reintegration of Argentina into the international system on the basis of a relatively open economy (complementary to either Britain or the United States) and a liberal political system. A sector of the political elite (the military, the church, and the antiliberal Right) opted for the policies proposed by Perón: radical protectionism for industries oriented to the internal market and inclusionary corporatism. The first group was primarily guided by its economic interests, and the second by its ideological concerns. The ideology of this second group stressed economic nationalism and was not particularly sympathetic to liberal democracy, but its focus was an inordinate fear of communism. In his discourse to the elites, Perón presented autarky as the best antidote to revolution.

5. The fear of revolution felt by this second group was unrealistic. The extent of working-class mobilization and of communist influence in the labor movement at the time were significant but limited, and there were no prospects for their substantial growth. Finally, fear about potential mass unemployment after the war was unwarranted.

6. Distorted political knowledge contributed to this inordinate fear of revolution. The antiliberal sector of the elite defined the working class as intrinsically dangerous, and was sensitive to the demonstration effects of fascism and the Spanish civil war. These foreign experiences were interpreted in a biased manner and inaccurately transferred to the Argentine context. The image of a dangerous working class developed in the beginning of the century and after World War I, and it was vicariously recalled in the forties. The demonstration effects from Latin Europe were facilitated by social and cultural linkages, the perceived efficacy of these models, and the sentiment that the elites in Italy and Spain had faced threats similar to the one confronting their Argentine counterparts.

7. This distorted image of the working class and these inappropriate demonstration effects were consequences of uncertainty and of the fact that Argentina was a "new country" rather than an "underdeveloped" one. The structural characteristics of the "new country" situation, a high land-labor ratio and a shortage of labor, determined the low level of national integration, the

relative mobilization of the labor movement, and the direction of the demonstration effects.

8. As a consequence of this fateful choice by a sector of the political elite, the autonomous state in the forties institutionalized radical protectionism for existing manufactures and state corporatism. The Argentine economy turned inward and the state downward, and these processes transformed the social structure, and led to stagnation and illegitimacy. Neither of these policies was determined by the balance of domestic economic interests nor by external constraints. With respect to industrialization, in particular, the economic and social resources accumulated by a "new country" type of peripheral nation like Argentina would have allowed for the development of a more open manufacturing sector. Large-scale autarkic industrialization had two effects: it increased the size of the working class, and it ultimately led to low growth rates from the fifties onward. Inclusionary corporatism produced an increase in the size and organizational complexity of the union movement. When the massive misallocation of capital and labor led to low growth rates, the union movement became an autonomous political force and, in the context of a society without a large labor reserve, a very powerful one. After the inclusionary corporatist interlude, labor was a more powerful contender than would have been the case had this system not been attempted. Thus, a policy designed to control labor had precisely the opposite effects. I called this paradox the contradiction of corporatism. The interaction between this labor movement and the weak bourgeoisie created by hothouse capitalism in a context of stagnation led to political instability.

9. Had Argentina been a typical Latin American society rather than a "new country," the long-term structural consequences of autarkic industrialization and inclusionary corporatism would have been partially different. Stagnation would have resulted, but the "paradox of corporatism" would not have occurred, due to the existence of a large labor reserve army in these societies.

### Theoretical Implications

The Argentine case has direct implications for the theory of development, the theory of the state, and the theory of social movements.

In relation to development theory, I pointed out already that the pattern of Argentine development challenges the adequacy of the deterministic evolutionary frameworks such as the classical versions of the Marxist and functionalist theories. Classical Marxism does not encompass a society in which the capitalist mode of production was exclusive, in which there was no intense class polarization and which was prone to economic stagnation and nonliberal forms of the state. As for conventional functionalism, it does not account for a case in which differentiation (economic diversification) led to lower adaptation to the environment (a perverse relationship with the international economy). Deterministic or historicist frameworks must be revised in order to account for cases of stagnation, shift of developmental tracks, or retrogression, such as Argentina's. The distinction between new countries and typical situations of underdevelopment proved useful, but it is still too general, as shown by the fact that other lands of recent settlement "made it" as industrial democracies while Argentina did not.

The Argentine case shows how the developmental path followed by a society is determined by a complex constellation of external and internal processes, and of economic, political, and cognitive-ideological ones. The reversal could not have been explained on the basis of hypotheses extracted *directly* from the Latin American dependency theory nor from its American kindred development, the world-system approach associated with the work of Wallerstein. These approaches tend to privilege external processes over internal ones and economic factors over "superstructural" ones. The Argentine slippage is an instance in which domestic processes were not just a transmission belt for the world economic structure and in which the state and ideological and cognitive factors were not just epiphenomena. As we have seen, the breakdown of the international order with the Depression triggered a series of domestic processes that led to the reversal, but the reversal itself was not caused directly by external factors. The other lands of recent settlement did not slip, in spite of the fact that their social structures were similar to Argentina's, and their location in the world economy was comparable. And my analysis makes it clear that the reversal of Argentine development cannot be understood without taking into consideration the autonomy of the state and the cognitive dimension of elite strategies.

The thesis that Argentina's change of developmental tracks, from the "new country" to the "underdeveloped" types, was caused by the institutionalization of choices made by a segment of the state elite at a critical juncture in the country's development suggests three research problems for development theory. First, it is necessary to construct a typology of more specific kinds of peripheral societies (and of core societies as well: the distinction between center and periphery is too abstract), and to describe more systematically the structural "tracks" that crystallize at different stages of development of the world economy. Second, development is a discontinuous process (an instance of punctuated equilibrium, in Stephen Krasner's formula),[3] but we lack a theory of the transition points, that is, of the crossroads where acceleration, stagnation, retrogression, and change of developmental paths may take place. The Argentine case indicates that these are points where major changes in the world economy interact with domestic processes and overdetermination, in the Althusserian sense, occurs. Comparative analysis would permit a systematic typology of these critical junctures and of their possible consequences for the development process. Third, that we should link micro- and macroanalysis is a trivial desideratum, but the Argentine case suggests a potentially fruitful empirical focus for such a task: the analysis of the relationship between elite choices and changes in the social structure at the transition points described above. The issues in this relationship would be three: the structural and cultural determinants of the repertoire of policy options considered efficacious or at least acceptable by different segments of the elites—including, of course, the counter-elites that may exist; the social and political process of selection from that repertoire; and the institutionalization of policies, that is, the mechanism by which these policies affect the social structure, and may produce different developmental outcomes.

The Argentine case also has implications for the theory of the state. We have seen that conventional analyses, which view the state as a transmission belt for infrastructural or interest group influences, cannot accommodate the Argentine reversal, which was the consequence of policies inconsistent with the dominant class interests. The relationship the military and other sectors of the state bureaucracy had with the economic elites was different from what established approaches would predict: the state was neither the organ of the ruling class in the Engelsian or Leninist formula, nor the guardian and brain of the structure in the Poulantzian frame-

3. Stephen D. Krasner, "Approaches to the State: Alternative Conceptions and Historical Dynamics," *Comparative Politics* (1984).

work. In connection with the latter, it is interesting to note that the Argentine state in the forties did not aim at organizing the ruling class and disorganizing the working class, as the theory would expect, but it did exactly the opposite. My analysis is more consistent with contemporary formulations that define the state as an actor that molds social and political processes rather than with these traditional approaches.[4]

The Argentine state in the forties was not only "relatively autonomous" but also capable of antagonizing the upper classes systematically. It was not a revolutionary state but a profoundly counterrevolutionary one. Perón and the segments of the state supporting him believed they were preventing communism, that is, protecting the long-term interests of a dominant class whose judgment was blinded by short-term interests and ideological concerns. This indicates an area where conceptual development is needed: state autonomy is still a vague concept. Different degrees or types should be distinguished. The Argentine case is an instance of spurious Bonapartism. The managers of the autonomous state acted as if they were playing the Bonapartist role, which is to protect the long-term interest of a dominant class that cannot protect these interests by itself. However, the Argentine upper class did not welcome such protection, which it likened with the unwanted services of the mafia. This role of the state was similar to the one in fascist experiences, where policies designed to prevent revolution were also, in the long run, counterproductive from the point of view of the ruling class (even though in the Italian and German cases ruling classes were not as reluctant to be "saved from communism" as in the Argentine one). In the words of Evans et al., this was an instance of the case in which the state delivers "collective disasters" rather than "collective goods."[5] This type of state autonomy should be distinguished from the strictly Bonapartist form, in which the state does protect the ruling classes, and from the revolutionary state and even some socialist parliamentary regimes, which deliberately oppose the ruling class.

Finally, the Argentine case has implications for the analysis of social movements. We have seen that the policies leading to the reversal were the response to an unrealistic fear of communism.

4. See the essays in Evans et al., *Bringing the State Back In*.

5. Peter B. Evans, Dietrich Rueschemeyer, and Theda Skocpol, "On the Road Toward a More Adequate Understanding of the State," in Evans et al., eds., *Bringing the State Back In*, p. 364.

The ghost of revolution was a mirror on which sectors of the elite projected their anxiety, but it was nevertheless the central character of the play. Just for this reason, I will examine this question in a more detailed manner.

I have already shown that there was no danger of revolution in the forties and that the fear that such a danger would arise after the war was unfounded. Now I will address the issue from a different perspective: why was there not a revolutionary threat?

It is useful to start by looking at the factors that caused apprehension in sectors of the state elite. This will show the missing ingredients. In the first place, there were the current external and internal structural changes. The international system, on which the prosperity of the country depended, had collapsed, and no one knew whether it would be reconstituted, on what basis, and whether it would have room for Argentina. Internally, the traditional ruling class, the agrarian elite, had lost its hegemony, and the agrarian and industrial bourgeoisie and the political elites were fragmented. Second, there was the fear of mass unemployment in the postwar period. The conclusion that factors of this type may cause a revolution resembles the orthodox Marxist analysis, a resemblance that does not occur by chance, given the "Marxism in reverse" practiced by these segments of the Argentine Right.

But their own "Marxism in reverse" should have pointed to the missing element. Had these counterrevolutionaries followed Marxism more systematically, they would have asked themselves whether a "revolutionary situation," that is, a situation in which a revolution is likely, was in the making. Lenin, a competent practitioner in this field, has conceptualized the issue in a way that can be useful for revolutionaries and counterrevolutionaries alike. The West in the interwar period was flooded with books and periodicals expounding Lenin's views on the subject. Also, the focus of the doctrinal work of the Comintern, particularly during the "third period," was precisely the codification and explication of these views. It is indeed strange that neither Perón nor the other counterrevolutionaries asked the question in these more specific terms.

In Lenin's definition, a revolutionary situation is characterized by three factors, two "objective" and one "subjective": a crisis in the ruling class and the state, a severe decline in the standard of living of the working class, and revolutionary mobilization.[6]

6. V. I. Lenin, "The collapse of the Second International," in his

The first "objective" factor was present in Argentina in the forties, but its intensity was only moderate. Legitimacy was low and the ruling class was divided, but the state apparatus was in place and without any threat of collapsing. Even if one accepts the questionable forecast about the postwar years, the conclusion is that, at most, the two "objective" factors were present, and the "subjective" one, revolutionary mobilization, was missing. Had a revolutionary movement been present, the "objective" conditions themselves could have become more conducive to a revolutionary outcome (for instance, the legitimacy of the state would have dropped further).

This "subjective" factor is not an automatic product of structural conditions, but a separate social process, something that the elite analysts failed to understand. More specifically, this missing element would have required two components: first and foremost, a larger and more articulate stratum of revolutionary activists, and, second, a mass base prone to be mobilized by them. The first of these components originates mostly in the revolutionary intelligentsia, and the mass base they would try to mobilize is the working class. Elite analysts did not realize that there was no large revolutionary intelligentsia, and that, in any case, it would not have been easy for such a revolutionary intelligentsia to mobilize a mass base.

Is it necessary to have specifically revolutionary organizations? For a revolutionary outcome, yes. The great historical revolutions show that there is no revolution without a revolutionary movement. Objective factors, including the division of the ruling class and the weakening of the state are, of course, central determinants, but without a revolutionary movement or, more specifically, one or more revolutionary organizations, those activists mobilizing the lower classes will not push the ensuing conflict toward a revolutionary direction. State authority may weaken or even collapse as a consequence of external processes, as in Russia in 1917, or of internal ones, as in Cuba in 1959, but the weakening or collapse of rule may lead to outcomes other than a social revolution. Anarchy in Lebanon in the eighties or Peronism in Argentina in the forties are instances of these nonrevolutionary outcomes. In Argentina, Perón and his faction in the army and

*Selected Works in Twelve Volumes* (1936?), vol. 5, p. 174. Leon Trotsky and Charles Tilly define a revolutionary situation at a more conjunctural level, in terms of dual power, or multiple sovereignty. See Trotsky, *Russian Revolution*, vol. 1, chap. 11, and Charles Tilly, *From Mobilization to Revolution* (1978), chap. 7.

elsewhere were the political entrepreneurs mobilizing the working class, and they socialized it into a nationalist and corporatist ideology. Had the Communists or other leftists been as powerful as the frightened antiliberal Right thought they were, the Argentine economic and political crisis would have produced something closer to what Lenin called a revolutionary situation.

Is it necessary to have a "prone" mass base? Contemporary approaches, such as resource mobilization theory, are right in emphasizing the central role of activists and political entrepreneurs in the generation of social movements, but the assumption they frequently make, that, provided there are activists at work, a mass base can *always* be mobilized, is far from obvious. The orientations and ideology of these masses *do matter*. Skillful movement entrepreneurs may induce people to reinterpret their situation and needs on the basis of the doctrine or ideology provided by these entrepreneurs, but the goal will be achieved only if there is some minimum congruence between the values and orientations of these people and the entrepreneurs' discourse. As I noted in Chapters 6 and 7, when discussing Perón's attempt to convince the elites, such discourse, to be effective, must be congruent with the recipients' common sense, which is not a repository of practical knowledge and sound judgment but a system of socially determined presuppositions. My impression about Argentina in the first half of the century is that an articulation of this type between a revolutionary intelligentsia and the working class would have required a change in workers' orientations, that is, a complex process of resocialization.

The Argentine new Right believed that there was a mass base prone to be mobilized by revolutionaries. This belief was based on an inadequate causal analysis. The elite analysts in the forties, as well as their predecessors who had been similarly alarmed by the labor movement in the beginning of the century and after the first postwar years, were guided in their assessments by lay and most likely indigenous versions of the Durkheimian approach to social movements, more specifically by what came to be known in social science as the mass society approach.[7] Lugones and Perón, whose analyses I have discussed in detail, were among the most articu-

7. On mass society theory, see the classical statement in William Kornhauser, *The Politics of Mass Society* (1960). Gino Germani has interpreted Peronism and fascism in terms of this theory: see his *Política y sociedad*, chap. 9, and "Fascism and Class," in S. J. Woolf, ed., *The Nature of Fascism* (1969).

late expounders of this type of argument, but it underlies, mostly in a latent form, the reasoning of most antilabor and antiliberal writers and, also, of some liberal ones from the beginning of the century onward. The implicit thesis can be summarized in a proposition: masses with a low level of integration pose a threat to the social order. This presupposes a view of human beings as essentially emotional actors: absence of ties to other individuals, to organizations, or to cultural objects would produce discontent, and this discontent can lead, under certain conditions, to antisystem mobilization.

The subjects of the proposition in the Argentine context were, of course, the workers. In the beginning of the century or at the time of the Tragic Week, it was the European immigrants, who were the majority of the working class, and in the forties it was their diminished numbers plus the migrants from the interior.

There are two problems with the proposition. First, the lack of integration of these immigrants and internal migrants was relative. Second, as is the case with other applications of the mass society theory, the conceptualization of these workers as rational actors, who are guided by their interests, appears to be a better explanation of their actual behavior than the Durkheimian model.[8]

In relation to the degree of integration of immigrants and migrants, it is true that for the first half of the century the society had a low level of cultural integration at the aggregate level, but this does not mean that it was full of anomic individuals. Immigrants and migrants were, especially in the first years after their arrival, relatively isolated from national institutions, politics, and culture. This was especially true for the two-thirds of the immigrants who came from European countries other than Spain. But this does not mean that these individuals were unattached; they were strongly integrated into their communities. Again, this was especially so among immigrants, who developed complex associational networks that anchored the first generation in ethnic subcultures. In addition, the ratio of immigrants to natives in the core area of the country in the first two decades of the century was such that the cultural process at work was a fusion among Italian, Spanish, and other communities, as much as the assimilation of a for-

---

8. See the discussion in Charles Tilly et al., *The Rebellious Century, 1830–1930* (1975), chap. 1; and Edward Shorter and Charles Tilly, *Strikes in France, 1830–1968* (1974), chap. 1.

eign minority into a recipient Argentine culture. As for the migrants from the interior who moved to the core area after the
Depression, many of them formed residential communities, but
worked alongside the old European workers, a process that facilitated the gradual disappearance of the cleavages separating the
two groups.

But the fact remains that immigrants in the beginning of the
century and migrants after the Depression were outside the political system. Neither of these groups, however, was the agent of a
revolutionary outburst. The reason was not only the lack of a
larger or more articulate revolutionary intelligentsia, but also the
fact that the orientations of these groups did not make them prone
to revolutionary mobilization.

The immigrants unionized, struck, and demonstrated, but two
facts about them should be recalled. The first is that their central
orientation was individual mobility, which was made possible by
the expanding Argentine economy. The second is that immigrants
were excluded from political participation, but, unlike their counterparts in the United States, they were not interested in acquiring
Argentine citizenship, not even after fraud and corruption had
been eliminated by the Electoral Reform of 1912. The case of the
migrants from the interior was different. They were integrated
into the political system through corporatist mechanisms by Perón at the point these workers began their process of political mobilization. Peronism was an exercise in preemptive modernization. However, the major obstacles the Left encountered when
trying to penetrate these migrants, the development of "national"
tendencies in the labor movement at the time of the war, and especially the relative smoothness with which Perón's project was
accomplished indicate that this segment of the working class was
more oriented toward bread-and-butter issues or integration into
the existing system than toward rebellion. In any case, it was not
readily "available" for revolutionary mobilization either.

We may turn now to the crucial missing ingredient, a larger and
more articulate revolutionary intelligentsia, from which a more
substantial stratum of revolutionary activists could be recruited.

Argentina had, since the beginning of the century, a large intelligentsia. We have already seen that, early in its development, the
country had a mass educational system and large universities, so
that it produced relatively more professionals than most European
nations. But the politicized segment of that intelligentsia consisted almost in its entirety of Conservatives, Radicals, Socialists,

or Catholics. None of these groups was interested in mobilizing the working class for revolution or in contesting the hegemony of capitalism in the central institutions of the society and building a mass alternative culture. The anarchist movement and its revolutionary successor, the Communist Party, were small organizations with a limited ideological impact on the society, and most Socialists were left-wing liberal democrats. A considerable anti-system culture evolved after the slippage began, but we know that its ideology was nationalist, and mostly right-wing nationalist, that is, counterrevolutionary. It was only in the sixties and seventies that a significant revolutionary intelligentsia developed within the middle class and major institutions of the society such as the universities, the professions, the political parties, and the church.

The question is, then, why was there not a broader revolutionary segment in the intelligentsia at the time of the reversal? Comparative analysis suggests some of the factors that may account for such absence. These factors may also clarify the appearance of a revolutionary intelligentsia a generation later.

No "new country" had a large Marxist political intelligentsia in the period of its industrialization. This generalization includes the United States, where even in the thirties, when communism had a limited appeal, no significant Marxist subculture was institutionalized. In Europe, substantial revolutionary intelligentsias developed in two situations: under authoritarian or absolutist regimes, as in Germany or Russia, or where an institutionalized revolutionary-Jacobin culture already existed, as in France.

These facts suggest three generalizations that apply to Argentina. The first is that no large revolutionary intelligentsia will develop during the period of industrialization in societies having high rates of upward mobility and large educational systems. This was the case in all the "new countries," including Argentina up to the time of the slippage. In order to evaluate the significance of mobility opportunities for political orientations, we must return to two facts I mentioned already. These societies had a large (and, in Argentina, mostly) immigrant population, and immigrants were strongly oriented toward individual mobility. In Argentina, in the first half of the century, it was perfectly possible for a male working class immigrant to attain middle class status, and, whether he did or not, his children had considerable access to a university education and a professional career. Thus, mobility for those who sought it by immigrating and for their children prevented the crystallization of a mass anticapitalist culture.

The two other generalizations refer to the institutions and ideas in the polity. The second one is that a factor contributing to the constitution of a mass revolutionary intelligentsia during the period of industrialization is the existence of a nondemocratic state (authoritarian or absolutist). There is a familiar process of transfer of legitimacy (or illegitimacy) from the political system to the social order. Where the state is nondemocratic, large segments of the middle and lower classes, who seek participation but who are being excluded from it, will end up opposing not only the state that keeps them out, but also the social order this state represents. Czarist Russia is a case in point.

Finally, a third generalization is that the existence of an already institutionalized revolutionary ideology is conducive to the generation of a mass revolutionary intelligentsia during the period of industrialization. Some societies, due to the peculiarities of their previous history, have institutionalized, at the time of industrialization, hegemonic or mass-supported ideologies that embody, in a manifest or latent manner, anti–status quo or revolutionary values. On the basis of these ideologies, large segments of the middle classes or the intelligentsia are likely to interpret the process of industrialization in such a way that they develop an anticapitalist orientation. Republican-Jacobin ideology in France is the example I gave above, but two equivalent delegitimizing belief systems are frequently found in the cultural legacy of late industrializers: left-wing forms of nationalism, and anti–status quo types of religion. The first type is common in third world countries with a recent colonial past, especially those whose independence from the metropolis involved a protracted conflict. Algeria or the former Portuguese colonies are examples of this. The second type refers to religious doctrines that can be interpreted as a moral condemnation of capitalism. Catholicism in Latin America is a case in point: both the traditional hierarchical and corporatist social doctrine of integrism and the leftist and even Marxist theology of liberation, which draws from the moral economy tradition and the communitarian practices of early Christianity, can legitimize their positions with reference to the same basic texts. The Nicaraguan revolution is as much a product of radical Catholicism as of Marxism. Shiite Islam seems to contain a similar potential. Since most ideologies, even idiosyncratic forms of nationalism, are part of international culture, this process of interpretation may be triggered not only by domestic processes but also by demonstration effects carried by the international networks in which local intelligentsias participate.

It follows that a political context not conducive to the generation of a revolutionary intelligentsia is one characterized by a democratic state and the absence of hegemonic or mass-supported institutionalized ideologies with a revolutionary content. This was the political context of the lands of recent settlement and of Argentina prior to the reversal. In Argentina in that period, the policies of the state were partially exclusionary, but this exclusion was of little consequence for the middle class or the intelligentsia. As we have seen, these groups were enfranchised with the Electoral Reform of 1912, and pluralism or toleration of dissent was respected most of the time, except in relation to the violence-prone groups on the extreme Left. The timing of the immigration waves and of the Electoral Reform was such that most first generation Argentines who had reached professional or intellectual positions experienced the political system as open since early in their adult lives, and they found appropriate channels for their integration in the Radical or Socialist parties.

Of course this context changed after the coup of 1930, but the ideological reorientation of part of the intelligentsia is a complex political and cultural process, which involves an effective local adaptation of available international ideologies, the development of appropriate channels for their dissemination, and so on. It took a whole generation for this task to be accomplished.

As for the major institutionalized ideologies, political or religious, none of them had a revolutionary or de-legitimizing content at the time of the reversal. Argentine radicalism was a liberal-democratic ideology, with a focus on political reform, and socialism was moderate, reformist, and parliamentarian. The dominant form of Catholicism was antiliberal and antisocialist. Both socialism and, in a more indirect manner, Catholicism contained the seeds of revolutionary opposition to the social order, but these potentialities had developed little in the case of socialism and would be latent for another generation in the case of Catholicism. The conclusion, then, is that none of these major ideologies institutionalized in the educational system, the media, or other areas of the cultural system had an actual, revolutionary content.

Thus, these three generalizations seem to account for the absence of a large revolutionary intelligentsia up to the time of the reversal. They also fit the appearance of such intelligentsia in the sixties and seventies. A few facts will suffice to show the contrast between the two periods.

As far as the first generalization is concerned, let us remember that stagnating tendencies in the Argentine economy appeared in the fifties. Thus, in the fifties and sixties the university system was still expanding, but, at the same time, mobility opportunities for graduates were decreasing. This generalized situation was conducive to professional frustration, especially among the graduates in the nontraditional fields, such as natural and social sciences, which grew in that period, or in established fields whose market situation was particularly bad. Most individuals caught in this situation lowered their expectations and adapted to local conditions, and a significant proportion emigrated. But a large proportion of students and members of the intelligentsia felt blocked.

As for the second generalization, the political context in the sixties and seventies was conducive to the politicization and radicalization of discontent. These blocked members of the intelligentsia found themselves ruled by military dictatorships or by semiconstitutional regimes that banned Peronism, the party of the working class and the poor. Finally, in relation to the third generalization, the spread of revolutionary ideologies was facilitated by the slow growth of a Marxist and left-wing cultural apparatus and especially by international developments, such as the Cuban revolution and the ideological reorientation of the Catholic church after the Vatican Council.

While these three generalizations apply to the Argentine case and throw some light on the differences between lands of recent settlement and other societies, the general issue of why a few countries have generated large revolutionary intelligentsias at the time of industrialization is still obscure. The delegitimation of the social order among a large segment of the intelligentsia—the "desertion of the intellectuals" in Crane Brinton's classical formula[9]—the transformation of a segment of the anti–status quo members of the intelligentsia into political activists, and the emergence among them of an articulate revolutionary leadership are still exogenous variables in all the theories of revolution. Development generates a modern intelligentsia, but the ideology and political behavior of this stratum cannot be predicted on the basis of structural factors. Only the comparative study of intelligentsias will lead to more specific propositions. It is necessary to have in-

9. Crane Brinton, *The Anatomy of Revolution* (1952), pp. 42–53.

formation on the social origin of the intelligentsia, intellectual networks, the political impact of travel and exile, the organization of academic and professional life, and the complex dynamics of international demonstration effects.

### Epilogue: How the Counterrevolutionary Policies of the Forties Generated the Revolutionary Situation in the Seventies[10]

The die was cast in the forties. The institutionalization of radical protectionism and the establishment and failure of a state corporatist apparatus led to the combination of low growth and political instability, which has characterized the country ever since. These policies carried the seeds of the next turning point in contemporary Argentine history, the political crisis of the seventies.

The question of revolution reappeared in the seventies, but this time it was not just a projection of the anxiety felt by sectors of the elite; it was closer to a genuine revolutionary situation. Not only the "objective" ingredients of such a situation seemed to be present, but the "subjective" ones were developing, for the first time. And, paradoxically, this state of affairs was the long-term consequence of the policies designed a generation earlier to prevent revolution. The Marxists in reverse of the forties ended up producing a shocking instance of the dialectics of history. . . .

The objective factors were the economic and political crises. In both respects, the situation was far worse in the seventies than it had been in the forties. In the first place, in the forties there was a very high level of uncertainty about the economic future of the country, but the economy had reacted well to the Depression and had grown during the war. By the seventies, Argentines had experienced over two decades of sharp economic fluctuations, and the contest for the surplus among fractions of the bourgeoisie and the mobilized working class had produced very high levels of inflation.

Second, the political crisis was more profound than in the for-

10. This section is based on two papers in which I discuss the collapse of the military regime of 1976–83 and the prospects for the institutionalization of democracy. See my "The Transition to Democracy in Argentina: Constraints and Opportunities," *LASA Forum* (1984), and "The Legitimation of Democracy under Adverse Conditions: The Case of Argentina," in Mónica Peralta-Ramos and Carlos H. Waisman, eds., *From Military Rule to Liberal Democracy in Argentina* (forthcoming).

ties. Constitutional rule had broken down in the thirties, and the hegemony of the agrarian upper class was crumbling then, but most contemporaries considered these political changes a temporary deviation from the stable liberal institutions in which they had been socialized. The situation was very different in the seventies. At that time, most Argentines had experienced, for most of their lives, military regimes that departed from liberal democracy, and the legitimacy of liberal institutions in general was very low.

These "objective" components of the revolutionary situation were producing, in the seventies, the "subjective" one as well. We know that a large stratum of revolutionary activists was forming, and that the labor movement was a major, and independent, power contender. There is no doubt that the emergence of these two social forces was the long-term result of the institutionalization of autarkic protectionism and of the failure of state corporatism in a society with the structural characteristics of a "new country."

We saw already that the development of a stratum of revolutionary activists occurred in a context characterized by a stagnating economy, a system of mass higher education, a nondemocratic state, and the growth of radical ideologies. Stagnation and ungovernability were the direct structural consequences of Perón's counterrevolutionary policies in the forties. Mass higher education was a legacy of the "new country" past of Argentina: that system grew as a response to the demands from the mobility-oriented immigrant population and from the large middle class it formed during the decades of economic expansion. The spread of radical ideologies, finally, was affected by international demonstration and diffusion effects, but it was the unsatisfactory economic and political performance of the country that rendered plausible the interpretations derived from these conceptual frameworks. As for the conversion of labor into a powerful and autonomous power contender, we also know that it was the result of the interaction between peculiarities of the Argentine social structure (especially the absence, until the nineteen-seventies, of a large labor reserve), and the failure of the state corporatist attempt of the forties.

In the late sixties and early seventies, under an authoritarian regime pompously called "The Argentine Revolution," the first signs of a revolutionary movement began to appear. A mass Marxist Left emerged within Peronism, mostly among middle-class youth, and several guerrilla groups, with orthodox Marxist and left-wing Peronist ideologies, entered the scene and formed effective military apparatuses and large political surface organizations.

While this was happening among the intelligentsia, the labor movement was also changing. For the first time since the forties, small but significant left-wing and Marxist tendencies appeared. These tendencies developed not only in the geographic and social periphery of the working class (backward regions, white collar or craft unions), but also at its very core, in some large blue-collar unions and major plants.

This still does not mean that a revolution was in the making. The relation of forces was favorable to the status quo. The reasons are three. First, and most important, the state was intact, and its coercive apparatus was effective. Moreover, the state was not floating over a disorganized society. The bourgeoisie was fragmented along many lines of cleavage, but it rallied behind the state, as did a segment of the middle classes, when the danger appeared. Second, the newly developed political intelligentsia committed a major strategic blunder. Instead of focusing on the mobilization of labor and the construction of a mass political organization, it emphasized frontal military opposition to the regime. Eventually, guerrilla groups were crushed by superior military force, and a large proportion of the revolutionary activists were eliminated. Third, in spite of the significant inroads by the Left, the labor movement was still controlled by the militant right-wing Peronist leadership. The Peronist bureaucracy and its political allies were an articulate political elite, made up of a large staff of full-time officials controlling substantial economic resources and a still legitimate ideology, Peronism. Had the revolutionary activists focused on political and organizational work rather than on direct action, they might have enlarged their base, but it is unlikely that the revolutionary Left could have prevailed over the established leadership and taken control of the labor movement. At most, the Left could have developed an important working-class following.

In any case, even if revolutionary activists had gained the support of a large sector of the working class, the most important barrier to a revolution would have still been there. This barrier was the coercive apparatus of the state. The armed forces, the police, and the vast array of security agencies, whose acronyms grace every segment of Argentine society, were unified, and solidly supported by the dominant class, most of the political elite, and a large sector of the middle classes. In these circumstances, the generation of a dual power situation was highly unlikely, even in the face of a large-scale political and military offensive by a mass-based revolutionary Left.

But such an outcome did not develop, because the leftists concentrated on violence rather than on political organization, and the managers of the state were not detached analysts of the relation of forces. In the Argentine tradition by now familiar to us, they panicked and overreacted. The military took power in 1976 and started what they called the "Process of National Reorganization." They responded to selective, private left-wing terrorism with mass state terrorism. Repression was directed not only at the actual revolutionaries, but also at a large proportion of the cultural and political intelligentsia and of political and union activists. As a result of excessive and indiscriminate repression, thousands were killed and imprisoned, including many people not involved in guerrilla groups or their surface organizations.

Underlying this political conflict was the continuing stalemate, which characterized the post-Peronist period, between agrarian and industrial coalitions. The coup replaced Isabel Perón's populist government, whose base of support was the domestic bourgeoisie and the labor movement and whose economic policy favored industrial expansion and higher wages, both at the expense of the agrarian exporters. The government change coincided with a swing of the economic policy pendulum toward the interests of the agrarian bourgeoisie and of other sectors not linked to manufacturing for the domestic market (basically, finance capital). This regime conducted the most systematic attack on the interests of the industrial coalition (noncompetitive manufacturers and their workers) in the post-Peronist period. Through the overvaluation of the currency and the lowering of tariffs, the economic policy of the regime led to massive bankruptcies, the fall of real wages, unemployment and, for the first time in twentieth-century Argentina, the formation of a large informal sector. From 1975 to 1980, the size of the industrial working class decreased by 26 percent.[11] As in previous "liberal" stages, though, the limits to the swing of the pendulum in the anti-industrial direction were political. Even an irrationally repressive dictatorship was afraid of mass discontent. In a familiar pattern, the pendulum reversed its course to some extent in the early eighties, thus showing that the stalemate underlying Argentine economic stagnation was not broken

11. Canitrot, "Teoría y práctica."

and that the limits for a policy oriented toward the reopening of the Argentine economy were political.

The change of economic policy under this military regime was more intense than in previous cases but it still followed the habitual mode, for the sequential satisfaction of the interests of the agrarian and industrial coalitions has been the pattern since the institutionalization of radical protectionism and corporatism by Perón. But the structural context of economic policy has been transformed, and this is why this military regime represented a qualitative change in Argentine economic and political development, the most important turning point since Peronism. This was so because of two policies that led to the intensification of the stagnating tendencies in the country's economy and to the disabling of the remedy used by the state to control the political consequences of the economic crisis.

The policy leading to a permanent aggravation of the structural economic crisis was the accumulation of a massive foreign debt, equal to more than five years of exports. It represents an additional, and very effective, brake on the country's development. The policy that ended up weakening the power of the state to control political conflict was, paradoxically, the use of coercion itself. The reckless use of force in domestic policy and, for the first time in contemporary Argentine history, in foreign policy, led to the delegitimation of the military as a political actor among all social forces, the economic elite included.

The debt has changed the parameters of Argentine economic development. Before, the existence of a large sector of noncompetitive manufacturing, to which a large proportion of the economic and human resources of the society were committed, determined the cyclical balance of payment crises. This was so because, as we have seen, this manufacturing sector required machinery and intermediate inputs, which could only be financed with the surplus generated by agriculture. In such a situation, periodic balance of payment crises were inevitable, either because of the policies of populist regimes, which expanded industry and, at the same time, reduced agrarian prices and thus provoked a reduction of the exportable output, or because of international price fluctuations for grains and beef. In the new situation, the balance of payment crisis becomes a permanent trait, and it will remain so for a long period. In the mid-eighties, the regular service of the debt would require more funds than the income from exports, and even the payment of interest due would take about two-thirds of the export income.

Since dramatic rises in the price of grains and beef are not foreseeable, Argentina will continue its secular decline unless the country undertakes export substitution, that is, the reconversion of industry and the constitution of an internationally competitive manufacturing sector.

This military regime also represented a major departure from past practice in its disposition to use force, both in the domestic and the international arenas. In previous military regimes, repression of the opposition was limited and nonsystematic. Some segments of Peronism or of the extreme Left were often persecuted, and force was used, sometimes in a disproportionate manner, to break up demonstrations or to control violent activities. But the regime that came to power in 1976 embarked upon a policy of systematic repression, not only of the actual guerrillas, but of whole categories of the political spectrum and of the intelligentsia. This strategy was effective in the short run, for guerrilla organizations and their kindred parties were destroyed. But indiscriminate violence undermined considerably the legitimacy of the military in all social classes and political parties, except among groups in the Right. Everybody realized that the armed forces were not just another player, or the arbiter, in the game of mass praetorianism.

However, the most significant blow to the legitimacy of the military was their defeat in the war with Britain in 1982. This willingness to go to war over a minor territorial dispute was also a new phenomenon in Argentine history. Since the military coup of 1976, the regime embarked on a weapons procurement policy that went beyond reasonable requirements for training or defense. An attempt to trigger a conflict with Chile in 1978 over another minor territorial issue was thwarted by international pressure. It became clear at that time that the military had discovered the potential offered by foreign policy to divert attention from the difficult economic situation and to increase the legitimacy of the armed forces by showing their professional efficacy. Probably, they were also trying to redeem, before the society and themselves, their image tarnished by the "dirty war" (as the leaders of the regime had called it) against irregulars and civilians. In the parameters of their mentality, nothing could accomplish this redemption better than a territorial acquisition. So, when popular discontent about the regime's economic policies mounted, the military leadership provoked the Malvinas/Falklands war.

This decision epitomizes the extreme irrationality of the managers of the state. Of course, if the conflict had ended in a manner that could be presented to the domestic public opinion as a success, the legitimizing goal would have been accomplished. But the odds were minimal, considering the differential in military and economic capability between Argentina and Britain and the foreseeable unwillingness of the Argentine population, including the military and the economic and political elites in general, to embark upon something similar to a Vietnam-style protracted war. If an unlikely victory would have restored the legitimacy of the military, a more predictable defeat would totally destroy it. And this is what happened. After the end of the brief war, mass mobilization by the middle and working classes and the heightened conflict among the military themselves forced the regime to restore constitutional rule. These elections, held in 1983, were won by the Radicals, who were correctly perceived by the majority of the population, including many Peronists, to be more resolute opponents of the military than the Peronists. Thus, for the first time since the coup of 1930, a liberal-democratic President, Raúl Alfonsín, has won a competitive election.

Thus ended this military regime, which illustrated more than any other the contradiction pointed out by O'Donnell between the values and goals of the civilian and military bureaucrats in authoritarian regimes.[12] While economic policymakers tried to take advantage of the fear and demoralization produced in the society by massive repression in order to "solve" the structural stalemate by defeating the industrial coalition, their military counterparts were busy amassing a nonpayable debt and plotting the war that would demolish the regime.

There is no doubt that this military dictatorship represented the highest level of autonomy of the state vis-à-vis the economic elites since the overthrow of Perón in 1955. Ever since, no government in Argentina had opposed so intensely the interests of a fraction of the dominant class. The targets of the state, however, were different this time. Under Perón, it had been the agrarians and, to a lesser extent, their allies in big industry. However, in the "Process," it was the inefficient industrialists producing for the internal market, both old and new, big and small, foreign and domestic. But if Perón's policies proved irrational in the long run, for their long-term consequences were the opposite of what he sought, the irra-

12. See Guillermo A. O'Donnell, "Tensions in the Bureaucratic Authoritarian State and the Question of Democracy," in David Collier, ed., *The New Authoritarianism in Latin America* (1979).

tionality of the military regime after 1976 was apparent immediately. It certainly attained its most pressing objective, the physical elimination of the guerrillas and of many other people, but it aggravated the structural crisis of the Argentine economy and wrecked the legitimacy of the "ultima ratio," the coercive apparatus of the state.

What are the prospects for Argentina? The determinants of the economic and political crisis—a large and noncompetitive manufacturing sector and highly mobilized social forces, the labor movement in particular—will continue generating a sluggish economy and social and political conflict. The new factor, the staggering debt, will probably reduce the cyclical fluctuations that have characterized the Argentine economy in the past decades. Since the debt service will consume most gains from possible increases of agrarian export earnings, a protracted period or stagnation or low growth is the most likely prospect for the economy. And since the organizations representing the different social and political forces are strong and well endowed with economic resources and since they have an articulate leadership, the sharp conflict for the distribution of the surplus will continue.

The resumption of long-term economic growth and the construction of a stable capitalist democracy would require the unmaking of the wrong choices made in the forties. This entails the reconversion of the manufacturing sector, so that an important part of it becomes internationally competitive, and the dismantling of the institutional infrastructure of corporatism.

The first of these goals would face major political opposition, for reconversion is against the interest of most capitalists and workers, and also of the managers and employees of the large and inefficient state sector, and of much of the middle class. The current constitutional administration is unlikely to pursue a major transformation whose implementation will antagonize the basic interests of central social forces in the society. Since a large inflow of foreign capital into Argentina is unlikely (the country has no strategic raw materials, and has a medium-size market, a militant working class, a massive debt, and high inflation), the extensive importation of competitive technology via foreign investment is not an option. Reconversion, if it takes place, will be a slow process in which more efficient firms develop alongside the existing ones. At any rate, major changes in this regard will not occur in the near future.

Prospects for the other task, the dismantling of the institutional infrastructure of state corporatism, are somewhat brighter as a consequence of the catastrophic failure of the military regime, and the subsequent isolation of the armed forces. This task would involve changes in the state and in the party system: the subordination to the government of the still semi-autonomous areas of the state apparatus, such as the military and the security forces, and the development of parties that are both strong vis-à-vis interest groups and committed to the democratic rules of the game.

Stable state corporatism has been impossible since the appearance of stagnating tendencies, for unions will accept to be subordinate to the state only in exchange for redistribution of income. Inclusionary corporatism is an impossible game in a stagnated economy, for it cannot lead to stable arrangements. Nevertheless, state corporatism still has its players, the most important of which are the unions and the military. The recurring destabilization mechanism at work in previous constitutional administrations has been as follows: balance of payments difficulties (whose frequency was a product of radical protectionism) forced governments to carry out recessionary policies, which triggered the intense mobilization of labor; the consequence was runaway inflation and high levels of polarization, which in turn caused panic among the bourgeoisie and segments of the middle class, government paralysis, and a coup aimed at reestablishing "order" through the coercive demobilization of labor and other social forces.

The delegitimation of the armed forces would make it possible to deactivate this destabilization mechanism. If the military is placed firmly under civilian control, a key player of the corporatist game would be eliminated. No other segment of the state apparatus could fill the vacuum, and this would open the way for the strengthening of political parties. The absence of the praetorian arbiter would facilitate the subordination of interest groups to political parties, and the learning by the parties of the difficult art of peaceful bargaining. An evolution of this type is a distinct possibility as of this writing, but the obstacles to this course are still massive.

Thus, Argentina is again at a crossroads. The country may head toward the institutionalization of a relatively polarized liberal democracy, or toward another round of ungovernability. This last outcome is not in the interest of any social force or political party, but Argentine history in this century is an exercise in unintended consequences: erroneous perception of external factors, distorted evaluation of domestic processes, policies whose effects were precisely the opposite than their supporters expected. . . . The outcome will hinge on how well the power contenders have assimilated the lessons of the past, particularly the traumatic lessons of the recent military regime. Only when these contenders reach an understanding of their objective environment can confrontation politics turn into politics as the art of the possible.

# Bibliography

Abad de Santillán, Diego. 1930. *El movimiento anarquista en la Argentina*. Buenos Aires: Argonauta.

———. 1971. *La FORA: Ideología y trayectoria*, 2nd ed. Buenos Aires: Proyección.

Abarca, Mariano. 1944. *La industrialización de la Argentina*. Buenos Aires: Unión Industrial Argentina.

Alberdi, Juan B. 1946. *Bases y puntos de partida para la organización política de la República Argentina*. Buenos Aires: Jackson (originally published in 1852).

Alemann, Roberto. 1970. *Curso de política económica argentina*. Buenos Aires: Eudeba.

Alford, Robert R., and Roger Friedland. 1985. *Powers of Theory: Capitalism, the State, and Democracy*. Cambridge: Cambridge University Press.

Althusser, Louis, and Etienne Balibar. 1970. *Reading Capital*. London: NLB.

Altimir, Oscar, Horacio Santamaría, and Juan Sorrouille. 1966–67. "Los instrumentos de promoción industrial en la postguerra." *Desarrollo económico* 6, no. 21: 89–144; 6, no. 22–23: 469–87; 6, no. 24: 709–34; 7, no. 25: 893–918; 7, no. 26: 149–72; 7, no. 27: 361–76.

Amadeo, Mario. 1956. *Ayer, hoy, mañana*, 2nd ed. Buenos Aires: Gure.

Amadeo y Videla, Daniel. 1942. *El desarrollo industrial y la economía de guerra*. Buenos Aires: Unión Industrial Argentina.

Amin, Samir. 1974. *Accumulation on a World Scale: A Critique of the Theory of Underdevelopment*. New York: Monthly Review Press.

Argentine Republic, Comisión Directiva del Censo. 1898. *Segundo*

*Censo de la República Argentina, mayo 10 de 1895.* Buenos Aires: Taller Tipográfico de la Penitenciaría Nacional.

———, Comisión Nacional del Censo. 1916–19. *Tercer Censo Nacional levantado el 1 de junio de 1914.* Buenos Aires: Rosso.

———, Departamento Nacional del Trabajo. 1940. *Estadística de huelgas.* Buenos Aires.

———, ———. Dirección de Estadística Social. 1946. *Investigaciones sociales 1943–1945.* Buenos Aires.

———, ———, División de Estadística. 1943. *Investigaciones sociales 1942.*

———, Dirección General de Fabricaciones Militares. 1946. *Plan siderúrgico argentino.* Buenos Aires: Peuser.

———, Dirección Nacional de Estadística y Censos. 1937–38. *Censo industrial 1934–1935.* Buenos Aires.

———, ———. 1939. *Censo industrial, 1939.* Buenos Aires.

———, ———. 1951. *IV Censo general de la nación.* 1947: *Resultados generales del censo de población.* Buenos Aires.

———, ———. 1960. *Censo industrial, 1954.* Buenos Aires.

———, ———. 1965. *Censo nacional de población, 1960.* Buenos Aires.

———, Ministerio de Agricultura. 1940. *Censo Nacional Agropecuario ley 12, 343, 1937.* Buenos Aires: Kraft.

———, Ministerio de Hacienda. 1934. *El plan de acción económica ante el Congreso Nacional.* Buenos Aires: Talleres Gráficos del Ministerio de Agricultura de la Nación.

———, Ministerio de la Hacienda de la Nación. 1940. *El plan de reactivación económica ante el Honorable Senado.* Buenos Aires.

———, ———. 1947. *Fundamentos que inspiran la actual política económico-financiera del gobierno de la Nación.* Buenos Aires.

———, Provincia de Buenos Aires, Departamento del Trabajo. 1937. *Política obrera y legislación del trabajo del gobierno de Buenos Aires.* La Plata.

———, Vicepresidencia de la Nación, Consejo Nacional de Postguerra. 1945. *Ocupación y desocupación en la Argentina.* Buenos Aires.

———, ———. 1945. *Ordenamiento económico-social.* Buenos Aires: Guillermo Kraft Ltda.

Aricó, José. 1980. *Marx y América Latina.* Lima: Ediciones CEDEP.

Armour Research Foundation. 1943. *Technological and Economic Survey of Argentine Industries*. Chicago: Armour Research Foundation.

Atkins, George Pope, and Larry V. Thompson. 1972. "German Military Influence in Argentina, 1921–1940." *Journal of Latin American Studies* 4, no. 2: 257–74.

Avery, Donald. 1979. *"Dangerous Foreigners": European Immigrant Workers and Labour Radicalism in Canada, 1896–1932*. Toronto: McClelland and Stewart.

Ayarragaray, Lucas. 1912. *Socialismo argentino y legislación obrera*. Buenos Aires: J. Lajouane & Cía.

Azar, Carmen Ll. de. 1977. *Argentina, evolución económica, 1915–1976*. Buenos Aires: Fundación Banco de Boston.

Badie, Bertrand, and Pierre Birnbaum. 1983. *The Sociology of the State*. Chicago: University of Chicago Press.

Bagú, Sergio. 1961. "La estructuración económica en la etapa formativa de la Argentina moderna." *Desarrollo económico* 1, no. 2: 113–28.

Baily, Samuel L. 1967. *Labor, Nationalism, and Politics in Argentina*. New Brunswick: Rutgers University Press.

Baldwin, Robert E. 1956. "Patterns of Development in Newly Settled Regions." *The Manchester School* 24: 161–79.

Banco Central de la República Argentina, Departamento de Investigaciones Económicas. n.d. [1945]. *Informe preliminar sobre los efectos que tendría en las actividades industriales internas la libre reanudación de las importaciones*. Buenos Aires.

———. 1945. *Memoria anual 1944*. Buenos Aires.

Baraguer, Joseph R., ed. 1968. *Why Perón Came to Power; the Background to Peronism in Argentina*. New York: Knopf.

Baran, Paul A. 1957. *The Political Economy of Growth*. New York: Monthly Review Press.

Bayer, Osvaldo. 1972–74. *Los vengadores de la Patagonia trágica*, 4 vols. Buenos Aires: Galerna.

———. 1980. *La Patagonia rebelde*. México: Editorial Nueva Imagen.

Bejarano, Manuel. "Inmigrantes y estructuras tradicionales en Buenos Aires, 1854–1930." In Torcuato S. Di Tella and Tulio Halperin Donghi, eds. *Los fragmentos del poder*.

Bendix, Reinhard. 1978. *Kings or People?* Berkeley and Los Angeles: University of California Press.

Berlinski, Julio. 1978. "La estructura de protección de actividades seleccionadas." Buenos Aires: Instituto Di Tella.

———, and Daniel M. Schydlowsky. 1977. "Incentives for Industrialization in Argentina." Washington, D.C.: International Bank for Reconstruction and Development.

Beyhaut, Gustavo, Roberto Cortés Conde, Haydée Gorostegui, and Susana Torrado. 1965. "Los inmigrantes en el sistema ocupacional argentino." In Torcuato S. Di Tella, Gino Germani, and Jorge Graciarena, eds. *Argentina, sociedad de masas.* Buenos Aires: Eudeba.

Bialer, Seweryn. 1981. "The Harsh Decade: Soviet Policies in the 1980's." *Foreign Affairs* 59, no. 5: 999–1020.

Bialet Massé, Juan. 1968. *El estado de las clases obreras argentinas a comienzos de siglo,* 2nd ed. Córdoba: Universidad Nacional de Córdoba.

Blanksten, George I. 1953. *Perón's Argentina.* Chicago: University of Chicago Press.

Blondel, Jacques. 1972. *Comparing Political Systems.* New York: Praeger.

Boehm, Ernst. 1979. "El desarrollo económico australiano a partir de 1930." In John Fogarty et al., eds. *Argentina y Australia.*

Borón, Atilio, A. 1972. "El estudio de la movilización política en América Latina: La movilización en la Argentina y Chile." *Desarrollo económico* 12, no. 46: 211–43.

Botana, Helvio, I. 1977. *Memorias: Tras los dientes del perro.* Buenos Aires: Peña Lillo.

Botana, Natalio R. 1975. "La reforma política de 1912." In Marcos Giménez Zapiola, ed. *El régimen oligárquico: materiales para el estudio de la realidad Argentina (hasta 1930).*

———. 1977. *El orden conservador.* Buenos Aires: Sudamericana.

———. 1984. *La tradición republicana.* Buenos Aires: Sudamericana.

Brady, Alexander. 1960. *Democracy in the Dominions: A Comparative Study in Institutions,* 3rd ed. Toronto: University of Toronto Press.

Braun, Oscar. 1970. *Desarrollo del capital monopolista en la Argentina.* Buenos Aires: Tiempo Contemporáneo.

———, and Leonard Joy. 1968. "A Model of Economic Stagnation: A Case Study of the Argentine Economy." *Economic Journal* 78, no. 312: 868–87.

Brinton, Crane. 1952. *The Anatomy of Revolution.* New York: Prentice-Hall.

Brodersohn, Mario. 1977. "Conflicto entre los objetivos de política económica de corto plazo de la economía argentina." Buenos Aires: Instituto Di Tella.

————, ed. 1970. *Estrategias de industrialización para la Argentina.* Buenos Aires: Instituto Torcuato Di Tella.

Broner, Julio, and Daniel E. Larriqueta. 1969. *La revolución industrial argentina.* Buenos Aires: Sudamericana.

Brown, Bruce M. 1962. *The Rise of New Zealand Labour: A History of the New Zealand Labour Party from 1916 to 1940.* Wellington, New Zealand: Milburn.

Bunge, Alejandro E. 1928–30. *La economía argentina,* 4 vols. Buenos Aires: Agencia General de Librerías y Publicaciones.

————. 1940. *Una nueva Argentina.* Buenos Aires: G. Kraft.

————. 1943. "Prosperidad argentina y perspectivas." *Revista de economía argentina* 42, no. 300: 221–25.

Cafiero, Antonio. 1961. *Cinco años después . . . de la economía social justicialista al régimen liberal-capitalista.* Buenos Aires: n.p.

Canitrot, Adolfo. 1980. "La disciplina como objetivo de la política económica: Un ensayo sobre el programa económico del gobierno argentino desde 1976." *Desarrollo económico* 19, no. 76: 453–75.

————. 1981. "Teoría y práctica del liberalismo: Política anti-inflacionaria y apertura económica en la Argentina (1976–1981)." *Estudios CEDES* (Buenos Aires) 3, no. 10.

Cantón, Darío. 1968. *Materiales para el estudio de la sociología política en la Argentina,* 2 vols. Buenos Aires: Editorial del Instituto.

————. 1971. *La política de los militares argentinos, 1900–1971.* Buenos Aires: Siglo XXI.

————. 1973. *Elecciones y partidos políticos en la Argentina.* Buenos Aires: Siglo XXI.

————, José L. Moreno, and Alberto Ciria. 1972. *La democracia constitucional y su crisis.* Buenos Aires: Paidós.

Cárcano, Miguel Angel. 1963. *Sáenz Peña: La revolución por los comicios.* Buenos Aires: n.p.

Cárdenas, Eduardo J., and Carlos M. Payá. 1980. *En camino a la democracia política, 1904–1910.* Buenos Aires: La Bastilla.

Cardoso, Fernando H. 1971. *Ideologías de la burguesía industrial en sociedades dependientes (Argentina y Brasil).* México: Siglo XXI.

Cardoso, Fernando H., and Enzo Faletto. 1979. *Dependency and Development in Latin America*. Berkeley and Los Angeles: University of California Press.

Carnoy, Martin. 1984. *The State and Political Theory*. Princeton: Princeton University Press.

Carretero, Andrés M. 1975. *Liberalismo y dependencia*. Buenos Aires: Platero.

Carri, Roberto. 1967. *Sindicatos y poder en la Argentina*. Buenos Aires: Sudestada.

Cavarozzi, Marcelo. 1983. *Autoritarismo y democracia (1955–1983)*. Buenos Aires: Centro Editor de América Latina.

Cheresky, Isidoro. 1981. "Sindicatos y fuerzas políticas en la Argentina pre-peronista." *Boletín de estudios latinoamericanos y del Caribe* (Amsterdam) 31: 5–43.

Ciria, Alberto. 1964. *Partidos y poder en la Argentina moderna (1930–1946)*. Buenos Aires: Jorge Alvarez.

————. 1972. *Perón y el justicialismo*. Buenos Aires: Siglo XXI.

————, et al. 1972. *New Perspectives on Modern Argentina*. Bloomington, Indiana: Latin American Studies Program, Indiana University.

Clark, Colin. 1940. *The Conditions of Economic Progress*. London: Macmillan.

Cochran, Thomas C., and Rubén Reina. 1962. *Entrepreneurship in Argentine Culture*. Philadelphia: University of Pennsylvania Press.

Cochrane, Peter. 1980. *Industrialization and Dependence: Australia's Road to Economic Development*. St. Lucia, Queensland: University of Queensland Press.

Codovilla, Victorio. 1945. *Batir al nazi-peronismo, para abrir una era de libertad y progreso*. Buenos Aires: Anteo.

Collier, David, ed. 1979. *The New Authoritarianism in Latin America*. Princeton: Princeton University Press.

Collier, David, and Ruth Berins Collier. 1977. "Who Does What, To Whom, and How: Toward a Comparative Analysis of Latin American Corporatism." In James M. Malloy, ed. *Authoritarianism and Corporatism in Latin America*.

Comisión Nacional sobre la Desaparición de Personas. 1984. *Nunca más*. Buenos Aires: Eudeba.

Condliffe, John B. 1930. *New Zealand in the Making: A Survey of Economic and Social Development*. London: G. Allen and Unwin.

Confederación General de la Industria. 1953. *Congreso General de la Industria, 18 al 23 de mayo de 1953*. Buenos Aires: Guillermo Kraft Ltda.

Conil Paz, Alberto, and Gustavo Ferrari. 1964. *Política exterior argentina, 1930–1962*. Buenos Aires: Huemul.

Conniff, Michael L., ed. 1982. *Latin American Populism in a Comparative Perspective*. Albuquerque: University of New Mexico Press.

Cornblitt, Oscar. 1969. "Inmigrantes y empresarios en la política argentina." In Torcuato S. Di Tella and Tulio Halperín Donghi, eds. *Los fragmentos del poder*.

————. 1975. "La opción conservadora en la política argentina." *Desarrollo económico* 14, no. 56: 599–639.

Corporación para la Promoción del Intercambio. 1944. *La estructura económica y el desarrollo industrial de la República Argentina*. Buenos Aires: Corporación para la Promoción del Intercambio.

Corradi, Juan E. 1974. "Argentina." In Ronald E. Chilcote and Joel C. Edelstein, eds. *Latin America: The Struggle with Dependency and Beyond*. Cambridge, Mass.: Schenkman.

————. 1985. *The Fitful Republic: Economy, Society, and Politics in Argentina*. Boulder: Westview Press.

Cortés Conde, Roberto. 1979. *El progreso argentino, 1880–1914*. Buenos Aires: Sudamericana.

————, and Ezequiel Gallo. 1973. *La formación de la Argentina moderna*. Buenos Aires: Paidós.

Crawley, Eduardo. 1984. *A House Divided: Argentina 1880–1980*. London: Hurst.

Cristiá, Pedro J., et al. 1946. *Argentina en la post guerra*. Rosario: Editorial Rosario.

Cúneo, Dardo. 1967. *Comportamiento y crisis de la clase empresaria*. Buenos Aires: Pleamar.

————. 1975. "La burguesía industrial oligárquica, 1875–1930." In Marcos Giménez Zapiola, ed. *El régimen oligárquico: Materiales para el estudio de la realidad argentina (hasta 1930)*.

Dahl, Robert A. 1971. *Polyarchy: Participation and Opposition*. New Haven: Yale University Press.

Davis, Stanley M. 1972. "United States vs. Latin America: Business and

Culture." In Stanley M. Davis and Louis W. Goodman, eds. *Workers and Managers in Latin America*. Lexington: Heath.

De la Torre, Lisandro. 1961. "La cuestión social y los cristianos sociales." In his *Intermedio filosófico*. Buenos Aires: Elmer.

De Pablo, Juan Carlos. 1977. *Los economistas y la economía argentina*. Buenos Aires: Macchi.

————. 1984. *Política económica argentina*. Buenos Aires: Macchi.

De Riz, Liliana. 1981. *Retorno y derrumbe: El último gobierno peronista*. México: Folios.

Del Carril, Bonifacio. 1959. *Crónica interna de la Revolución Libertadora*. Buenos Aires: Emecé.

Deutsch, Karl W. 1974. "Imperialism and Neocolonialism." *Papers of the Peace Science Society (International)* 23: 1–25.

Di Tella, Guido. 1979. "Controversias económicas en la Argentina, 1930–1970." In John Fogarty et al., eds. *Argentina y Australia*.

————. 1983. *Perón-Perón, 1973–1976*. Buenos Aires: Sudamericana.

————, and Manuel Zymelman. 1973. *Las etapas del desarrollo económico argentino*. Buenos Aires: Paidós.

Di Tella, Torcuato. 1943. "Problemas de la posguerra: Función económica y destino social de la industria argentina." *Revista de economía argentina* 42, no. 303: 367–79.

Di Tella, Torcuato S. 1968. "Stalemate or coexistence in Argentina." In James Petras and Maurice Zeitlin, eds. *Latin America, Reform or Revolution?* Greenwich: Fawcett Publications.

————. 1969. "Raíces de la controversia educacional argentina." In idem and Tulio Halperín Donghi, eds. *Los fragmentos del poder*. Buenos Aires: Jorge Alvarez.

————. 1972. "La búsqueda de la fórmula política argentina." *Desarrollo económico* 11, no. 42–44: 317–25.

————. 1985. *Sociología de los procesos políticos*. Buenos Aires: Grupo Editor Latinoamericano.

Diamand, Marcelo. 1973. *Doctrinas económicas, desarrollo, e independencia*. Buenos Aires: Paidós.

————. 1976. "El péndulo argentino: Empate político o fracasos económicos?" Buenos Aires: Mimeo.

Díaz Alejandro, Carlos F. 1970. *Essays on the Economic History of the Argentine Republic*. New Haven: Yale University Press.

Díaz Araujo, Enrique. 1971. *La conspiración del 43*. Buenos Aires: La Bastilla.

Diéguez, Héctor L. 1969. "Argentina y Australia: Algunos aspectos de su desarrollo económico comparado." *Desarrollo económico* 8, no. 32: 543–63.

Dolkart, Ronald H. 1969. "Manuel A. Fresco, Governor of the Province of Buenos Aires, 1936–1940: A Study of the Argentine Right and Its Response to Economic and Social Change." Ph.D. diss., UCLA.

Dorfman, Adolfo. 1970. *Historia de la industria argentina*. Buenos Aires: Solar-Hachette.

Doyon, Louise M. 1975. "El movimiento sindical bajo el peronismo." *Desarrollo económico* 15, no. 57: 151–63.

———. 1977. "Conflictos obreros bajo el régimen peronista (1946–1955)." *Desarrollo económico* 17, no. 67: 437–74.

———. 1978. "Organised Labour and Perón: A Study of the Conflictual Dynamics of the Peronist Movement." Ph.D. diss., University of Toronto.

Drosdoff, Daniel. 1972. *El gobierno de las vacas, 1933–1956: Tratado Roca-Runciman*. Buenos Aires: La Bastilla.

Duhalde, Eduardo Luis. 1983. *El estado terrorista argentino*. Buenos Aires: El Caballito.

Dulles, John W. F. 1967. *Vargas of Brazil*. Austin: University of Texas Press.

Durruty, Celia. 1969. *Clase obrera y peronismo*. Córdoba: Pasado y Presente.

Eisenstadt, S. N. 1964. "Social Change, Differentiation, and Evolution." *American Sociological Review* 29, no. 3: 375–86.

———. 1966. *Modernization, Protest, and Change*. Englewood Cliffs: Prentice-Hall.

———. 1978. *Revolution and the Transformation of Societies*. New York: Free Press.

Engels, Friedrich. n.d. *The Housing Question*. New York: International Publishers.

———. 1967. *The German Revolutions*. Chicago: University of Chicago Press.

———. 1968. *The Role of Force in History: A Study of Bismarck's Policy of Blood and Iron*. New York: International Publishers.

Escudé, Carlos. 1983. *Gran Bretaña, Estados Unidos y la declinación argentina, 1942–1949*. Buenos Aires: Editorial de Belgrano.

Evans, Peter B. 1979. *Dependent Development: The Alliance of Multinational, State, and Local Capital in Brazil*. Princeton: Princeton University Press.

Evans, Peter B., Dietrich Rueschemeyer, and Theda Skocpol, eds. 1985. *Bringing the State Back In*. Cambridge: Cambridge University Press.

——, ——, ——. 1985. "On the Road Toward a More Adequate Understanding of the State." In Evans et al., eds. *Bringing the State Back In*.

Fajnzylber, Fernando. 1983. *La industrialización trunca de América Latina*. México: Nueva Imagen.

Falcoff, Mark. 1982. "Argentina." In Mark Falcoff and Frederick B. Pike, eds. *The Spanish Civil War 1936–1939: American Hemispheric Perspectives*. Lincoln: University of Nebraska Press.

Falcoff, Mark, and Ronald H. Dolkart, eds. 1975. *Prologue to Perón: Argentina in Depression and War, 1930–1943*. Berkeley and Los Angeles: University of California Press.

Farrell, Frank. 1981. *International Socialism and Australian Labour: The Left in Australia, 1919–1939*. Sydney: Hale and Iremonger.

Fayt, Carlos S., ed. 1967. *La naturaleza del peronismo*. Buenos Aires: Viracocha.

Felix, David. 1968. "The dilemma of Import Substitution. Argentina." In Gustav F. Papanek, ed. *Development Policy, Theory and Practice*. Cambridge, Mass.: Harvard University Press.

Ferns, H. S. 1960. *Britain and Argentina in the Nineteenth Century*. Oxford: Oxford University Press.

Ferrari, Gustavo, and Ezequiel Gallo, eds. 1980. *La Argentina del ochenta al centenario*. Buenos Aires: Sudamericana.

Ferrer, Aldo. 1963. *La economía argentina*. México: Fondo de Cultura Económica.

——. 1980. *Crisis y alternativas de la política económica argentina*. Buenos Aires: Fondo de Cultura Económica.

——. 1981. *Nacionalismo y orden constitucional*. Buenos Aires: Fondo de Cultura Económica.

Ferrero, Roberto A. 1976. *Del fraude a la soberanía popular, 1938–1946*. Buenos Aires: La Bastilla.

Figuerola, José. 1943. *La colaboración social en Hispanoamérica.* Buenos Aires: Sudamericana.

Fillol, Tomás R. 1961. *Social Factors in Economic Development: The Argentine Case.* Cambridge, Mass.: MIT Press.

Finer, Samuel E. 1975. "State and Nation-Building in Europe: The Role of the Military." In Charles Tilly, ed. *The Formation of National States in Western Europe.* Princeton: Princeton University Press.

Fodor, Jorge. 1975. "Perón's Policies for Agricultural Exports, 1946–1948: Dogmatism or Common Sense?" In David Rock, ed. *Argentina in the Twentieth Century.*

Fodor, Jorge, and Arturo O'Connell. 1973. "La Argentina y la economía atlántica en la primera mitad del siglo veinte." *Desarrollo económico* 13, no. 49: 1–67.

Fogarty, John, Ezequiel Gallo, and Héctor Diéguez, eds. 1979. *Argentina y Australia.* Buenos Aires: Instituto Torcuato Di Tella.

Foxley, Alejandro. 1983. *Latin American Experiments in Neo-Conservative Economics.* Berkeley and Los Angeles: University of California Press.

Franceschi, Gustavo J. 1936a. "Las barbas del vecino." *Criterio* 9, no. 437: 245–48.

———. 1936b. "Comunista o católico?" *Criterio* 9, no. 426: 413–16.

———. 1937. *El movimento español y el criterio católico.* Buenos Aires: Difusión.

———. 1940. *Totalitarismo, liberalismo, catolicismo.* Buenos Aires: Asociación de los Jóvenes de la Acción Católica.

Franceschini, Antonio. 1908. *L'emigrazione Italiana nell' America del Sud: Studi nella espansione coloniale transatlantica.* Rome: Forzani.

Francis, Michael J. 1977. *The Limits of Hegemony: United States Relations with Argentina and Chile during World War II.* Notre Dame: University of Notre Dame Press.

Frank, André G. 1969. *Capitalism and Underdevelopment in Latin America.* New York: Monthly Review Press.

Frank, Gary. 1979. *Struggle for Hegemony in South America: Argentina, Brazil, and the United States during the Second World War.* Miami: Center for Advanced International Studies, University of Miami.

Freels, John W., Jr. 1968. "Industrial Trade Associations in Argentine Politics." Ph.D. diss., University of California, Riverside.

Fresco, Manuel A. 1940. *Cómo encaré la política obrera durante mi gobierno*, 2 vols. La Plata: n.p.

Frondizi, Silvio. 1955. *La realidad Argentina: Ensayo de interpretación sociológica*. Buenos Aires: Praxis.

Fuchs, Jaime. 1965. *Argentina: Su desarrollo capitalista*. Buenos Aires: Cartago.

———. 1981. *Argentina: Actual estructura económico-social*. Buenos Aires: Ediciones Estudio.

Furtado, Celso. 1970a. "Development and Stagnation in Latin America." In Irving Louis Horowitz, ed. *Masses in Latin America*. New York: Oxford University Press.

———. 1970b. *Economic Development of Latin America*. Cambridge, Engl.: Cambridge University Press.

Galasso, Norberto. 1975. *Scalabrini Ortiz*. Buenos Aires: Crisis.

Galletti, Alfredo. 1961. *La realidad argentina en el siglo xx: La política y los partidos*. México: Fondo de Cultura Económica.

Gallo, Ezequiel, and Roberto Cortés Conde. 1972. *Argentina: La república conservadora*. Buenos Aires: Paidós.

Gálvez, Manuel. 1920. *El solar de la raza*. Madrid: Saturnino Calleja.

Gambini, Hugo. 1971a. *El peronismo y la Iglesia*. Buenos Aires: Centro Editor de América Latina.

———. 1971b. *El primer gobierno peronista*. Buenos Aires: Centro Editor de América Latina.

García de Loydi, Ludovico. 1956. *La Iglesia frente al peronismo*. Buenos Aires: CIC.

García Lupo, Rogelio. 1963. *La rebelión de los generales*. Buenos Aires: Jamcana.

García Mata, Rafael, and Emilio Llorens. 1940. *Argentina económica*. Buenos Aires: Compañía Impresora Argentina.

Gastiazoro, Eugenio. 1973. *Argentina hoy: Capitalismo dependiente y estructura de clases*. Buenos Aires: Emele.

———. 1980. *Introducción al análisis económico-social de la historia argentina*. Buenos Aires: Agora.

Gaudio, Ricardo, and Jorge Pilone. 1983. "El desarrollo de la negociación colectiva durante la etapa de modernización industrial en la Argentina, 1935–1943." *Desarrollo económico* 23, no. 90: 255–86.

———, ———. 1984. "Estado y relaciones laborales en el período previo al surgimiento del peronismo, 1935–1943." *Desarrollo económico* 24, no. 94: 235–73.

Geertz, Clifford. 1983. "Common Sense as a Cultural System." In his *Local Knowledge*. New York: Basic Books.

Geller, Lucio. 1975. "El crecimento industrial argentino hasta 1914 y la teoría del bien primario exportable." In Marcos Giménez Zapiola, ed. *El régimen oligárquico: Materiales para el estudio de la realidad argentina (hasta 1930)*.

Genta, Jordán B. 1976. *Acerca de la libertad de enseñar y la enseñanza de la libertad*. Buenos Aires: Dictio.

Germani, Gino. 1955. *Estructura social de la Argentina*. Buenos Aires: Raigal.

———. 1962. *Política y sociedad en una época de transición*. Buenos Aires: Paidós.

———. 1963. "Movilidad social en la Argentina." Appendix to Seymour M. Lipset and Reinhard Bendix. *Movilidad social en la sociedad industrial*. Buenos Aires: Eudeba.

———. 1969. "Fascism and Class." In S. J. Woolf, ed. *The Nature of Fascism*. New York: Vintage.

———. 1980. "El surgimiento del peronismo: El rol de los obreros y de los migrantes internos." In Manuel Mora y Araujo and Ignacio Llorente, eds. *El voto peronista*.

Giberti, Horacio C. E. 1961. *Historia económica de la ganadería argentina*. Buenos Aires: Hachette.

———. 1964. *El desarrollo agrario argentino*. Buenos Aires: Eudeba.

Gil, Enrique. 1947. *Política y economía argentinas, 1944–1946*. Buenos Aires: Librería Perlado.

Gillin, John P. 1965. "Ethos Components in Modern Latin American Culture." In Dwight B. Heath and Richard N. Adams, eds. *Contemporary Cultures and Societies of Latin America*. New York: Random House.

———. 1966. "The Middle Segments and Their Values." In Robert D. Tomasek, ed. *Latin American Politics*. Garden City: Anchor Books.

Giménez Zapiola, Marcos, ed. 1975. *El régimen oligárquico: Materiales para el estudio de la realidad argentina (hasta 1930)*. Buenos Aires: Amorrortu.

Godio, Julio. 1972. *La semana trágica de enero de 1919*. Buenos Aires: Granica.

Godio, Julio. 1973a. *La caída de Perón*. Buenos Aires: Granica.

————. 1973b. *Historia del movimento obrero argentino: Inmigrantes, asalariados, y lucha de clases, 1880–1910*. Buenos Aires: Tiempo Contemporáneo.

Goldwert, Marvin. 1972. *Democracy, Militarism, and Nationalism in Argentina, 1930–1966*. Austin: University of Texas Press.

Gollan, Robin. 1975. *Revolutionaries and Reformists: Communism and the Australian Labour Movement, 1920–1955*. Canberra: Australian National University Press.

Gómez Morales, Alfredo. 1951. *Política económica peronista*. Buenos Aires: Escuela Superior Peronista.

González, Joaquin V. 1936. "El juicio del siglo o cien años de historia argentina." In his *Obras Completas*, vol. 21. Buenos Aires: Universidad Nacional de La Plata.

González Estevez, Luis A. J. 1980. "Las elecciones de 1946 en la provincia de Córdoba." In Manuel Mora y Araujo and Ignacio Llorente, eds. *El voto peronista*.

Goodrich, Carter. 1964–65. "Argentina as a New Country." *Comparative Studies in Society and History* 7: 70–88.

Gori, Gastón. 1964. *Inmigración y colonización en la Argentina*. Buenos Aires: Eudeba.

Gramsci, Antonio. 1971. *Selections from the Prison Notebooks*. New York: International Publishers.

Greenup, Ruth, and Leonard Greenup. 1947. *Revolution before Breakfast (Argentina, 1941–1946)*. Chapel Hill: University of North Carolina Press.

Gregor, A. James. 1974. *The Fascist Persuasion in Radical Politics*. Princeton: Princeton University Press.

Greenwood, Gordon. 1975. *Australia: A Social and Political History*. Sydney: Angus and Robertson.

Güemes, Gontrán de. 1956. *Asi se gestó la dictadura: El G.O.U.*. Buenos Aires: Rex.

Guerrero, Américo R. 1944. *La industria argentina: Su origen, organización y desarrollo*. Buenos Aires: Plantié.

Gustafson, Barry. 1980. *Labour's Path to Political Independence: The Origins and Establishment of the New Zealand Labour Party, 1900–19*. Wellington, New Zealand: Oxford University Press.

Habermas, Jürgen. 1973. *Legitimation Crisis*. Boston: Beacon Press.

Halperín Donghi, Tulio. 1972. *Argentina: La democracia de masas.* Buenos Aires: Paidós.

———. 1980. "Algunas observaciones sobre Germani, el surgimiento del peronismo, y los migrantes internos." In Manuel Mora y Araujo and Ignacio Llorente, eds. *El voto peronista.*

———, ed. 1980. *Proyecto y construcción de una nación (Argentina, 1846–1880).* Caracas: Biblioteca Ayacucho.

Hartz, Louis, ed. 1964. *The Founding of New Societies.* New York: Harcourt, Brace, and World.

Herbin, Ernesto L. 1944. *La industrialización del país y el Banco de Crédito Industrial Argentino.* Buenos Aires: Unión Industrial Argentina.

Hintze, Otto. 1975. "Military Organization and the Organization of the State." In Felix Gilbert, ed. *The Historical Essays of Otto Hintze.* New York: Oxford University Press.

Hirschman, Albert O. 1971. "The Political Economy of Import-Substituting Industrialization in Latin America." In his *A Bias for Hope.* New Haven: Yale University Press.

Hodges, Donald C. 1976. *Argentina, 1943–1976: The National Revolution and Resistance.* Albuquerque: University of New Mexico Press.

Hueyo, Alberto. 1938. *La Argentina en la depresión mundial, 1932–1933; discursos-conferencias.* Buenos Aires: El Ateneo.

Humphreys, R. A. 1981–1982. *Latin America and the Second World War,* 2 vols. London: Athlone.

Huntington, Samuel P. 1968. *Political Order in Changing Societies.* New Haven: Yale University Press.

Ibarguren, Carlos. 1934. *La inquietud de esta hora.* Buenos Aires: La Facultad.

———. 1955. *La historia que he vivido.* Buenos Aires: Peuser.

Ibarguren, Federico. 1969. *Orígenes del nacionalismo argentino, 1927–1937.* Buenos Aires: Celsius.

Imaz, José Luis de. 1970. *Los que mandan (Those Who Rule).* Albany: State University of New York Press.

———. 1977. *Promediados los cuarenta.* Buenos Aires: Sudamericana.

Ingenieros, José. 1910. *La evolución sociológica argentina (de la barbarie al imperialismo).* Buenos Aires: J. Menéndez.

Ingenieros, José. 1979. "Las ideas sociológicas de Sarmiento." In Oscar Terán, ed. *Antiimperialismo y nación*. México: Siglo XXI.

Innis, Harold A. 1933. *Problems of Staple Production in Canada*. Toronto: The Ryerson Press.

———. 1956. *Essays in Canadian Economic History*. Mary Q. Innis, ed. Toronto: University of Toronto Press.

Instituto Alejandro E. Bunge de Investigaciones Económicas y Sociales. 1946. "Bosquejo de una economía argentina para 1955. IIa parte (Continuación). Posibilidades de desarrollo industrial." In *Revista de economía argentina* 45, 335: 143–53.

Irazusta, Julio. 1956. *Perón y la crisis argentina*. Buenos Aires: Unión Republicana.

Irazusta, Rodolfo and Julio. 1933. *La Argentina y el imperialismo británico*. Buenos Aires: Tor.

Iscaro, Rubens. 1958. *Origen y desarrollo del movimiento sindical argentino*. Buenos Aires: Anteo.

Jessop, Bob. 1983. *Theories of the State*. New York: New York University Press.

Jitrik, Noé. 1968. *Muerte y resurrección de Facundo*. Buenos Aires: Centro Editor de América Latina.

Jorge, Eduardo. 1970. *Industria y concentración económica*. Buenos Aires: Siglo XXI.

Josephs, Ray. 1944. *Argentine Diary: The Inside Story of the Coming of Fascism*. New York: Random House.

Justo, Juan B. 1920. *Socialismo*. Buenos Aires: La Vanguardia.

———. 1925. *Internacionalismo y patria*. Buenos Aires: La Vanguardia.

Kealey, Gregory, and Peter Warrian, eds. 1976. *Essays in Canadian Working Class History*. Toronto: McClelland and Stewart.

Kelly, David. 1952. *The Ruling Few*. London: Hollis and Carter.

Kelly, Ruth. 1965. "Foreign Trade of Argentina and Australia, 1930 to 1960 (I)." United Nations. *Economic Bulletin for Latin America* 10, no. 1: 49–70.

Kennedy, John J. 1958. *Catholicism, Nationalism, and Democracy in Argentina*. Notre Dame: University of Notre Dame Press.

Kenworthy, Eldon. 1972. "Did the 'New Industrialists' Play a Significant Role in the Formation of Perón's Coalition, 1943–1946?" In Alberto Ciria et al. *New Perspectives on Modern Argentina*.

————. 1973. "The Function of the Little-known Case in Theory Formation, or What Peronism Wasn't." *Comparative Politics* 6, no. 1: 1–35.

————. 1980. "Interpretaciones ortodoxas y revisionistas del apoyo inicial del peronismo." In Manuel Mora y Araujo and Ignacio Llorente, eds. *El voto peronista.*

Kindleberger, Charles P. 1973. *The World in Depression, 1929–1939.* Berkeley and Los Angeles: University of California Press.

Kirkpatrick, Jeane. 1971. *Leader and Vanguard in Mass Society: A Study of Peronist Argentina.* Cambridge, Mass.: MIT Press.

Klein, Herbert S. 1981. "La inmigración italiana a la Argentina y a los E.E.U.U." *Desarrollo económico* 21, no. 81: 3–27.

Koebel, W. H. 1910. *Argentina: Past and Present.* London: Kegan Paul, Trench, Trübner & Co., Ltd.

Kornhauser, William. 1960. *The Politics of Mass Society.* London: Routledge and Kegan Paul.

Krasner, Stephen D. 1984. "Approaches to the State: Alternative Conceptions and Historical Dynamics." *Comparative Politics* 16, no. 2: 223–46.

Krieger Vasena, Adalbert, and Javier Pazos. 1973. *Latin America: A Broader World Role.* Totowa: Rowman and Littlefield.

Laclau, Ernesto. 1969. "Modos de producción, sistemas económicos y población excedente: Aproximación histórica a los casos argentino y chileno." *Revista latinoamericana de sociología* 5, no. 2: 276–316.

Lambert, Jacques. 1974. *Latin America: Social Structures and Political Institutions.* Berkeley and Los Angeles: University of California Press.

Lantini, Ferruccio, et al. 1939. *L'autarchia economica della nazione.* Rome: Istituto Nazionale de Cultura Fascista.

Lenin, V. I. 1936(?). "The Collapse of the Second International." In his *Selected Works in Twelve Volumes,* vol. 5. London: Martin Lawrence.

Lewis, W. Arthur. 1978. *Growth and Fluctuations, 1870–1913.* London: George Allen and Unwin.

Lindenboim, Javier. 1976. "El empresariado industrial argentino y sus organizaciones gremiales entre 1930 y 1946." *Desarrollo económico* 16, no. 62: 163–201.

Linz, Juan J. 1976. "Some Notes toward a Comparative Study of Fascism in Sociological Historical Perspective." In Walter Lacqueur, ed.,

*Fascism: A Reader's Guide*. Berkeley and Los Angeles: University of California Press.

―――. 1978a. *The Breakdown of Democratic Regimes: Crisis, Breakdown, and Reequilibration*. Baltimore: Johns Hopkins University Press.

――― and Alfred Stepan, eds. 1978b. *The Breakdown of Democratic Regimes: Latin America*. Baltimore: Johns Hopkins University Press.

Lipset, Seymour M. 1963. *Political Man: The Social Bases of Politics*. Garden City: Doubleday.

―――. 1967. "Values, Education, and Entrepreneurship." In idem and Aldo Solari, eds. *Elites in Latin America*. New York: Oxford University Press.

Little, Walter. 1979. "La organización obrera y el estado peronista." *Desarrollo económico* 19, no. 75: 331–76.

Llach, Juan J. 1978. "Estructura ocupacional y dinámica del empleo en la Argentina." *Desarrollo económico* 17, no. 68: 539–93.

―――. 1984. "El Plan Pinedo de 1940, su significado histórico y los orígenes de la economía política del peronismo." *Desarrollo económico* 23, no. 92: 515–58.

Llorens, Emilio. 1943. "La industria y la economía argentina." *Revista de economía argentina* 42, no. 301: 303–5.

―――. 1946. "Perspectivas económicas." *Revista de economía argentina* 45, no. 334: 111–13.

―――. 1947. *La Argentina debe industrializarse*. Buenos Aires: Universidad de Buenos Aires, Facultad de Ciencias Económicas.

Llorens, Emilio, and Eduardo A. Coghlan. 1941. "Materias primas para la industria argentina." *Revista de economía argentina* 40, no. 79: 278–84.

Llorente, Ignacio. 1980. "Alianzas políticas en el surgimiento del peronismo: El caso de la provincia de Buenos Aires." In Manuel Mora y Araujo and Ignacio Llorente, eds. *El voto peronista*.

López, Alfredo. n.d. *Historia del movimiento social y la clase obrera argentina*. Buenos Aires: Programa.

Loyber, Ricardo L. 1942. *Política económica y comercio exterior*. Buenos Aires: El Ateneo.

Luca de Tena, Torcuato, Luis Calvo, and Esteban Peicovich. 1976. *Yo, Juan Perón*. Barcelona: Planeta.

Lugones, Leopoldo. 1932. *El estado equitativo*. Buenos Aires: La Editora Argentina.

Luna, Félix. 1975. *El 45: Crónica de un año decisivo*. Buenos Aires: Sudamericana.

―――. 1984. *Perón y su tiempo, vol.1, La Argentina era una fiesta, 1946–1949*. Buenos Aires: Sudamericana.

Lux-Wurm, Pierre. 1965. *Le peronisme*. Paris: Bibliothèque Constitutionnelle et de Science Politique.

Macario, Santiago. 1964. "Protectionism and Industrialization in Latin America." *Economic Bulletin for Latin America* 9, no. 1: 61–103.

Macdonald, C. A. 1980. "The Politics of Intervention: The United States and Argentina, 1941–1946." *Journal of Latin American Studies* 12, no. 2: 365–96.

MacDougall, John. 1913. *Rural Life in Canada, Its Trends and Tasks*. Toronto: Westminster Co.

McMichael, Philip. 1984. *Settlers and the Agrarian Question: Foundations of Capitalism in Colonial Australia*. Cambridge, Engl.: Cambridge University Press.

Magnet, Alejandro. 1953. *Nuestros vecinos justicialistas*. Santiago de Chile: Editorial del Pacífico.

―――. 1956. *Nuestros vecinos argentinos*. Santiago de Chile: Editorial del Pacífico.

Maizels, Alfred. 1963. *Industrial Growth and World Trade*. Cambridge: Cambridge University Press.

Mallon, Richard D., and Juan V. Sorrouille. 1975. *Economic Policymaking in a Conflict Society: The Argentine Case*. Cambridge, Mass.: Harvard University Press.

Malloy, James M., ed. 1977. *Authoritarianism and Corporatism in Latin America*. Pittsburgh: University of Pittsburgh Press.

Maritain, Jacques, and Gustavo J. Franceschi. 1937. "Posiciones." *Criterio* 10, no. 493: 349–52.

Marotta, Sebastián. 1961. *El movimiento sindical argentino*, vol. 2. Buenos Aires: Ediciones Lacio.

―――. 1970. *El movimiento sindical argentino*, vol. 3, *Periodo 1920–1935*. Buenos Aires: Editorial Calomino.

Marsal, Juan F., ed. 1972. *Argentina conflictiva*. Buenos Aires: Paidós.

Martínez, Carlos J. 1943. *La industria siderúrgica nacional*. Buenos Aires: Unión Industrial Argentina.

Martínez de Hoz, José A. 1961. "Agricultura y ganadería." In *Argentina, 1930–1960*. Buenos Aires: Sur.

Marx, Karl. 1967. *Capital*, vol. 1. New York: International Publishers.

———. 1969. *On Colonialism and Modernization*. Schlomo Avineri, ed. Garden City: Doubleday.

———. 1972. *The Class Struggles in France (1848–1850)*. New York: International Publishers.

———. 1977. *The Eighteenth Brumaire of Louis Bonaparte*. In Karl Marx and Friedrich Engels. *Selected Works*.

——— and Friedrich Engels. 1977. *Selected Works*. New York: International Publishers.

Matienzo, José. 1917. *El gobierno representativo federal en la República Argentina*. Madrid: Editorial América.

Matsushita, Hiroschi. 1983. *Movimiento obrero argentino, 1930–1945: Sus proyecciones en la historia del peronismo*. Buenos Aires: Siglo Veinte.

Mayer, Jorge M. 1963. *Alberdi y su tiempo*. Buenos Aires: Eudeba.

Mayo, Carlos A., et al. 1976. *Diplomacia, política y petróleo en Argentina*. Buenos Aires: Rincón.

McCarthy, John D., and Mayer N. Zald. 1977. "Resource Mobilization and Social Movements: A Partial Theory." *American Journal of Sociology* 82, no. 6: 1212–41.

McClelland, David C. 1967. *The Achieving Society*. New York: The Free Press.

Melo, Leopoldo. 1942. *La postguerra y algunos de los planes sobre el nuevo orden económico*. Buenos Aires: Unión Industrial Argentina.

Merkx, Gilbert W. 1968. "Political and Economic Change in Argentina from 1870 to 1966." Ph.D. diss., Yale University.

———. 1969. "Sectoral Clashes and Political Change: The Argentine Experience." *Latin American Research Review* 4: 89–114.

Moore, Barrington. 1966. *Social Origins of Dictatorship and Democracy*. Boston: Beacon Press.

Mora y Araujo, Manuel, and Ignacio Llorente, eds. 1980. *El voto peronista*. Buenos Aires: Sudamericana.

Moran, Theodore H. 1970. "The 'Development' of Argentina and Australia." *Comparative Politics* 3, no. 1: 71–92.

Moreno, Eugenio. 1966. *El fenómeno social del peronismo.* Buenos Aires: Documentos.

Morse, Richard M. 1964. "The Heritage of Latin America." In Louis Hartz, ed. *The Founding of New Societies.*

Moure García, José C. 1982. *La realidad económica y política argentina en el curso de la segunda guerra mundial, 1939–1945.* Buenos Aires: Macchi.

Moyano Llerena, Carlos. 1941. "La industria y el comercio internacional." *Revista de economía argentina* 40, no. 280: 314–18.

———. 1943. "Hacia la conquista del mercado olvidado." *Revista de economía argentina* 42, no. 296: 43–45.

———. 1945. "La desocupación después de la guerra." *Revista de economía argentina* 44, no. 322: 120–21.

Murmis, Miguel, and Juan C. Portantiero. 1971. *Estudios sobre los orígenes del peronismo.* Buenos Aires: Siglo XXI.

Murmis, Miguel, Mario Pérsico, and Carlos Ramil Cepeda. 1974. *Tipos de capitalismo y estructura de clases: La formación de la sociedad argentina, 1500–1800.* Buenos Aires: La Rosa Blindada.

Murphy, D. J., ed. 1975. *The State Labour Parties in Australia, 1880–1920.* St. Lucia, Queensland: University of Queensland Press.

Nadra, Fernando. 1972. *Perón hoy y ayer, 1971–1943.* Buenos Aires: Polémica.

Navarro Gerassi, Marysa. 1968. *Los nacionalistas.* Buenos Aires: Jorge Alvarez.

Niosi, Jorge. 1974. *Los empresarios y el estado argentino (1955–1969).* Buenos Aires: Siglo XXI.

Nolte, Ernst. 1965. *Three Faces of Fascism.* New York: Holt, Rinehart, and Winston.

Nordlinger, Eric. 1981. *On the Autonomy of the Democratic State.* Cambridge, Mass.: Harvard University Press.

Nunn, Frederick M. 1983. *Yesterday's Soldiers: European Military Professionalism in South America.* Lincoln: University of Nebraska Press.

O'Connell, Arturo. 1984. "La Argentina en la Depresión: los problemas de una economía abierta." *Desarrollo económico* 23, no. 92: 479–515.

Oddone, Jacinto. 1949. *Gremialismo proletario argentino.* Buenos Aires: La Vanguardia.

Oddone, Jacinto. 1975. *La burguesía terrateniente argentina,* 4th ed. Buenos Aires: Libera.

———. 1983. *Historia del socialismo argentino,* 2 vols. Buenos Aires: Centro Editor de América Latina.

O'Donnell, Guillermo A. 1973. *Modernization and Bureaucratic Authoritarianism: Studies in South American Politics.* Berkeley: Institute of International Studies.

———. 1977. "Estado y alianzas en la Argentina, 1956–1976." *Desarrollo económico* 16, no. 64: 523–54.

———. 1978a. "Permanent Crisis and the Failure to Create a Democratic Regime: Argentina, 1955–1966." In Juan J. Linz and Alfred Stepan, eds. *The Breakdown of Democratic Regimes: Latin America.*

———. 1978b. "Reflections on the Patterns of Change in the Bureaucratic Authoritarian Regime." *Latin American Research Review* 12, no. 1: 3–38.

———. 1979. "Tensions in the Bureaucratic Authoritarian State and the Question of Democracy." In David Collier, ed. *The New Authoritarianism in Latin America.*

———. 1982. *1966–1973: El estado burocrático autoritario.* Buenos Aires: Editorial de Belgrano.

Olson, Mancur. 1982. *The Rise and Decline of Nations: Economic Growth, Stagflation, and Social Rigidities.* New Haven: Yale University Press.

Organski, A.F.K. 1968. *The Stages of Political Development.* New York: Knopf.

Orona, Juan V. 1966. *La logia militar que derrocó a Castillo.* Buenos Aires: Imprenta López.

Ortiz, Ricardo M. 1964. *Historia económica de la Argentina.* 2 vols. Buenos Aires: Pampa y Cielo.

Oszlak, Oscar. 1982. *La formación del estado argentino.* Buenos Aires: Editorial de Belgrano.

Oved, Iaacov. 1978. *El anarquismo y el movimiento obrero en Argentina.* México: Siglo XXI.

Page, Joseph. 1983. *Perón: A Biography.* New York: Random House.

Panaia, Marta, and Ricardo Lesser. 1973. "Las estrategias militares frente al proceso de industrialización (1943–1947)." In Marta Panaia, Ricardo Lesser, and Pedro Skupch. *Estudios sobre los orígenes del peronismo,* vol. 2. Buenos Aires: Siglo XXI.

Panettieri, José. 1967. *Los trabajadores*. Buenos Aires: Jorge Alvarez.

Parsons, Talcott. 1964. *The Social System*. Glencoe: The Free Press.

———. 1966. *Societies: Evolutionary and Comparative Perspectives*. Englewood Cliffs: Prentice-Hall.

———. 1971a. *The System of Modern Societies*. Englewood Cliffs: Prentice-Hall.

———. 1971b. "Comparative Studies and Evolutionary Change." In Ivan Vallier, ed. *Comparative Methods in Sociology*. Berkeley and Los Angeles: University of California Press.

———. 1977. *The Evolution of Societies*. Englewood Cliffs: Prentice-Hall.

Partido Comunista. 1947. *Esbozo de historia del Partido Comunista de la Argentina*. Buenos Aires: Anteo.

Payá, Carlos, and Eduardo Cárdenas. 1978. *El primer nacionalismo argentino*. Buenos Aires: Peña Lillo.

Peicovich, Esteban. 1965. *Hola Perón*. Buenos Aires: Jorge Alvarez.

Pellegrini, Carlos. 1911. "Introduction" to Albert B. Martínez and Maurice Lewandowski, *The Argentine in the Twentieth Century*. London and Leipzig: T. Fisher Unwin.

Peña, Milcíades. 1972. *El peronismo: Selección de documentos para su historia*. Buenos Aires: Fichas.

———. 1973. *La clase dirigente argentina frente al imperialismo*. Buenos Aires: Ediciones Fichas.

Peña Guzmán, Solano. 1942. *La autarquía en la economía argentina*. Tucumán: La Raza.

Peralta-Ramos, Mónica. 1978. *Acumulación del capital y crisis política en Argentina (1930–1974)*. México: Siglo XXI.

———, and Carlos H. Waisman, eds. Forthcoming. *From Military Rule to Liberal Democracy in Argentina*. Boulder, Colorado: Westview Press.

Pereira Pinto, Juan Carlos. 1973. *Aspectos de la historia económica de la República Argentina durante los últimos setenta años, 1900–1971*. Buenos Aires: El Coloquio.

Perina, Rubén M. 1983. *Onganía, Levingston, Lanusse: Los militares en la política argentina*. Buenos Aires: Editorial de Belgrano.

Perón, Juan. 1944. *El pueblo quiere saber de qué se trata*. Buenos Aires.

———. n.d. [1946]. *El pueblo ya sabe de qué se trata: Discursos*. Buenos Aires.

Peter, José. 1968. *Crónicas proletarias*. Buenos Aires: Esfera.

Pike, Frederick B., and Thomas Stritch, eds. 1974. *The New Corporatism*. Notre Dame: University of Notre Dame Press.

Pinedo, Federico. 1943. *Argentina en la vorágine*. Buenos Aires: Editorial Mundo Forense.

―――. 1961. *Siglo y medio de economía argentina*. México: Centro de Estudios Monetarios Latinoamericanos.

Pinto, Aníbal. 1971. *Tres ensayos sobre Chile y América Latina*. Buenos Aires: Solar.

Platt, D.C.M. 1972. *Latin America and the British Trade, 1806–1914*. London: Adam and Charles Block.

Pont, Elena S. 1984. *Partido Laborista: Estado y sindicatos*. Buenos Aires: Centro Editor de América Latina.

Portnoy, Leopoldo. 1961. *Análisis crítico de la economía argentina*. México: Fondo de Cultura Económica.

Potash, Robert A. 1969. *The Army and Politics in Argentina, 1928– 1945: Yrigoyen to Perón*. Stanford: Stanford University Press.

―――. 1980. *The Army and Politics in Argentina, 1945–1962: Perón to Frondizi*. Stanford: Stanford University Press.

―――, ed. 1984. *Perón y el G.O.U.: Los documentos de una logia secreta*. Buenos Aires: Sudamericana.

Potter, Anne L. 1981. "The Failure of Democracy in Argentina, 1916– 1930: An Institutional Perspective." *Journal of Latin American Studies* 13, no. 1: 83–109.

―――. 1978. "Political Institutions, Political Decay, and the Argentine Crisis of 1930." Ph.D. diss., Stanford University.

Poulantzas, Nicos. 1973. *Political Power and Social Classes*. London: New Left Books.

―――. 1969. "The Problem of the Capitalist State." *New Left Review* 58: 67–78.

―――. 1974. *Fascism and Dictatorship*. London: New Left Books.

Prebisch, Raúl. 1950. *The Economic Development of Latin America and Its Principal Problems*. New York: United Nations.

―――. 1981. *El capitalismo periférico: Crisis y transformación*. México: Fondo de Cultura Económica.

Puiggrós, Rodolfo. 1969. *El Peronismo: Sus causas*. Buenos Aires: Jorge Alvarez.

Quesada, Ernesto. 1911. "La evolución social argentina." *Revista argentina de ciencias políticas* 2: 631–56.

Ramos, Jorge A. 1962. *El Partido Comunista en la política argentina.* Buenos Aires: Coyoacán.

———. 1970. *Revolución y contrarrevolución en la Argentina: Del patriciado a la oligarquía, 1862–1904.* Buenos Aires: Ediciones del Mar Dulce.

———. 1982. *La era del peronismo.* Buenos Aires: Ediciones del Mar Dulce.

Ramos Mejía, José M. 1977. *Las multitudes argentinas.* Buenos Aires: Editorial de Belgrano (originally published in 1910).

Randall, Laura. 1978. *An Economic History of Argentina in the Twentieth Century.* New York: Columbia University Press.

Ranis, Peter. 1966. "Peronismo without Perón: Ten Years after the Fall (1955–1965)." *Journal of Interamerican Studies* 8: 112–28.

———. 1979. "Early Peronism and the Post-Liberal Argentine State." *Journal of Interamerican Studies and World Affairs* 21, no. 3: 313–38.

Rapoport, Mario. 1981. *Gran Bretaña, Estados Unidos y las clases dirigentes argentinas, 1940–1945.* Buenos Aires: Editorial de Belgrano.

Real, Juan José. 1962. *Treinta años de historia argentina.* Buenos Aires: Ediciones Actualidad.

Remmer, Karen L. 1984. *Party Competition in Argentina and Chile: Political Recruitment and Public Policy, 1890–1930.* Lincoln: University of Nebraska Press.

Rennie, Ysabel F. 1945. *The Argentine Republic.* New York: Macmillan.

Repetto, Nicolás. 1957. *Mi paso por la política (de Roca a Yrigoyen).* Buenos Aires: Santiago Rueda.

Ribeiro, Darcy. 1971. *The Americas and Civilization.* New York: E. P. Dutton.

Rivarola, Rodolfo. 1908. *Del régimen federativo al unitario.* Buenos Aires: n.p.

Roca, Julio A. 1910. "Mensaje del Presidente de la República Julio A. Roca al abrir las sesiones del Congreso argentino." In H. Mabragaña, ed. *Los mensajes,* vol. 6. Buenos Aires: Comisión Nacional del Centenario.

Rock, David. 1972. "Lucha civil en la Argentina, la semana trágica de enero de 1919." *Desarrollo económico* 11, no. 42: 165–215.

Rock, David, ed. 1975a. *Argentina in the Twentieth Century*. Pittsburgh: University of Pittsburgh Press.

———. 1975b. *Politics in Argentina, 1890–1930: The Rise and Fall of Radicalism*. Cambridge: Cambridge University Press.

———. 1985. *Argentina 1516–1982: From the Spanish Colonization to the Falklands War*. Berkeley and Los Angeles: University of California Press.

Rodríguez, Octavio. 1980. *La teoría del subdesarrollo de la CEPAL*. México: Siglo XXI.

Rojas, Ricardo. 1916. *La argentinidad: Ensayo histórico sobre nuestra conciencia nacional en la gesta de emancipación, 1810–1816*. Buenos Aires: La Facultad.

Romero, José Luis. 1963. *A History of Argentine Political Thought*. Stanford: Stanford University Press.

Rosecrance, Richard N. 1964. "The Radical Culture of Australia." In Louis Hartz, ed. *The Founding of New Societies*.

Rotondaro, Rubén. 1971. *Realidad y cambio en el sindicalismo*. Buenos Aires: Pleamar.

Rouquié, Alain. 1978. *Pouvoir militaire et société politique en République Argentine*. Paris: Presses de la Fondation Nationale des Sciences Politiques.

———, ed. 1982. *Argentina, hoy*. México: Siglo XXI.

Rubinstein, Juan C. 1968. *Desarrollo y discontinuidad política en Argentina*. Buenos Aires: Siglo XXI.

Rueschemeyer, Dietrich, and Peter B. Evans. 1985. "The State and Economic Transformation: Toward an Analysis of the Conditions Underlying Effective Intervention." In Peter B. Evans, Dietrich Rueschemeyer, and Theda Skocpol, eds. *Bringing the State Back In*.

Sáenz Quesada, María, 1981. *Los estancieros*. Buenos Aires: Editorial de Belgrano.

Salera, Virgil. 1941. *Exchange Control and the Argentine Market*. New York: Columbia University Press.

Sánchez Sorondo, Marcelo. 1945. *La revolución que anunciamos*. Buenos Aires: Nueva Política.

Sánchez Sorondo, Matías G. 1937. *Represión del comunismo: Informe y réplica*. Buenos Aires: Senado de la Nación.

Sarmiento, Domingo F. 1868. *Life in the Argentine Republic in the*

*Days of the Tyrants.* New York: Hafner Press. (Translation of *Facundo*, originally published in 1848.)

————. 1980. "Educación popular." In Tulio Halperín Donghi, ed. *Proyecto y construcción de una nación (Argentina 1846–1880).*

Sarobe, José M. 1942. *Política económica argentina.* Buenos Aires: Unión Industrial Argentina.

Savio, Manuel N. 1942. *Política de la producción metalúrgica argentina.* Buenos Aires: Unión Industrial Argentina.

Scalabrini Ortiz, Raúl. 1957. *Política británica en el Río de la Plata.* Buenos Aires: Fernández Blanco (originally published in 1939).

————. 1958. *Historia de los ferrocarriles argentinos.* Buenos Aires: Devenir.

Scenna, Miguel A. 1980. *Los militares.* Buenos Aires: Editorial de Belgrano.

Schillizzi Moreno, Horacio A. 1973. *Argentina contemporánea: Fraude y entrega, 1930–1943.* Buenos Aires: Plus Ultra.

Schoultz, Lars. 1983. *The Populist Challenge: Argentine Electoral Behavior in the Postwar Era.* Chapel Hill: University of North Carolina Press.

Scobie, James R. 1964. *Revolution on the Pampas: A Social History of Argentine Wheat, 1860–1910.* Austin: University of Texas Press.

Shorter, Edward, and Charles Tilly. 1974. *Strikes in France, 1830–1968.* London: Cambridge University Press.

Sidicaro, Ricardo. 1981. "Consideraciones sociológicas sobre las relaciones entre el peronismo y la clase obrera en la Argentina." *Boletín de estudios latinoamericanos y del Caribe* (Amsterdam) 31: 43–61.

Sigaut, Lorenzo J. 1972. *Acerca de la distribución y niveles de ingreso en la Argentina, 1950–1972.* Buenos Aires: Macchi.

Silverman, Bertram. 1969. "Labor Ideology and Economic Development in the Peronist Epoch." *Studies in Comparative International Development* 4, no. 11: 243–58.

Skocpol, Theda. 1979. *States and Social Revolutions.* Cambridge, Engl.: Cambridge University Press.

————. 1980. "Political Responses to Capitalist Crises: Neo-Marxist Theories of the State and the Case of the New Deal." *Politics and Society* 10, no. 2: 155–201.

Smelser, Neil J. 1959. *Social Change in the Industrial Revolution.* Chicago: University of Chicago Press.

Smelser, Neil J. 1966. "Mechanisms of Change and Adjustment to Change." In Bert F. Hoselitz and Wilbert E. Moore, eds., *Industrialization and Society*. Paris: Unesco.

Smith, Adam. 1937 ed. *An Inquiry into the Nature and Causes of the Wealth of Nations*, Cannan ed. New York: Modern Library.

Smith, Brian H. 1982. *The Church and Politics in Chile*. Princeton: Princeton University Press.

Smith, Peter H. 1969. *Politics and Beef in Argentina*. New York: Columbia University Press.

————. 1974a. *Argentina and the Failure of Democracy*. Madison: University of Wisconsin Press.

————. 1974b. "The Breakdown of Democracy in Argentina." In Juan J. Linz and Alfred Stepan, eds. *The Breakdown of Democratic Regimes: Latin America*.

————. 1980a. "La base social del peronismo." In Manuel Mora y Araujo and Ignacio Llorente, eds. *El voto peronista*.

————. 1980b. "Las elecciones de 1946 y las inferencias ecológicas." In Manuel Mora y Araujo and Ignacio Llorente, eds. *El voto peronista*.

Smith, Tony. 1981. *The Pattern of Imperialism*. Cambridge: Cambridge University Press.

Smithies, Arthur. 1965. "Economic Growth: International Comparisons. Argentina and Australia." *American Economic Review* 55, 2: 17–30.

Snow, Peter. 1979. *Political Forces in Argentina*. New York: Praeger.

Solberg, Carl E. 1970. *Immigration and Nationalism: Argentina and Chile, 1890–1914*. Austin: University of Texas Press.

————. 1973. "Tariffs and Politics in Argentina, 1916–1930." *Hispanic American Historical Review* 53, no. 2: 260–84.

————. 1979. *Oil and Nationalism in Argentina*. Stanford: Stanford University Press.

————. 1981. "Argentina y Canadá: Una perspectiva comparada sobre su desarrollo económico, 1919–1939." *Desarrollo económico* 21, no. 82: 191–211.

Solomonoff, Jorge N. 1971. *Ideologías del movimiento obrero y conflicto social: De la Organización Nacional hasta la Primera Guerra Mundial*. Buenos Aires: Proyección.

Spalding, Hobart, ed. 1970. *La clase trabajadora argentina (documentos para su historia, 1890–1912)*. Buenos Aires: Editorial Galerna.

Stepan, Alfred. 1978. *The State and Society: Peru in Comparative Perspective*. Princeton: Princeton University Press.

Strassmann, W. Paul. 1964. "The Industrialist." In John J. Johnson, ed. *Continuity and Change in Latin America*. Stanford: Stanford University Press.

Sunkel, Osvaldo, and Pedro Paz. 1970. *El subdesarrollo latinoamericano y la teoría del desarrollo*. México: Siglo XXI.

Tamarin, David. 1985. *The Argentine Labor Movement, 1930–1945*. Albuquerque: University of New Mexico Press.

Taylor, Carl C. 1948. *Rural Life in Argentina*. Baton Rouge: Louisiana State University Press.

Taylor, Charles L., and Michael C. Hudson. 1972. *World Handbook of Political and Social Indicators*, 2nd ed. New Haven: Yale University Press.

Taylor, J. M. 1979. *Eva Perón: The Myths of a Woman*. Chicago: University of Chicago Press.

Teichman, Judith. 1981. "Interest Conflict and Entrepreneurial Support for Perón." *Latin American Research Review* 16, no. 1: 144–55.

Thailheimer, August. 1970. "Sul fascismo." In Renzo De Felice, ed. *Il Fascismo: Le interpretazioni dei contemporarei e degli storici*. Bari: Laterza.

Tilly, Charles. 1978. *From Mobilization to Revolution*. Reading, Mass.: Addison-Wesley.

Tilly, Charles, et al. 1975. *The Rebellious Century, 1830–1930*. Cambridge, Mass.: Harvard University Press.

Tocqueville, Alexis de. 1969. *Democracy in America*, Mayer ed. Garden City: Doubleday.

Tornquist, Ernesto & Co. 1919. *The Economic Development of the Argentine Republic in the Last Fifty Years*. Buenos Aires: Tornquist & Co.

Torres, José Luis. 1945. *La década infame*. Buenos Aires: Formación Patria.

———. 1953. *La oligarquía maléfica: Autopsia de un cadáver político*. Buenos Aires: Centro Antiperduélico Argentino.

Trimberger, Ellen K. 1978. *Revolution from Above*. New Brunswick: Transaction Books.

Trotsky, Leon. 1957. *The History of the Russian Revolution*. Ann Arbor: University of Michigan Press.

Trotsky, Leon. 1971. "Bonapartism and Fascism." In *Writings of Leon Trotsky (1934–35)*. New York: Pathfinder Press.

Turner, Frederick C., and José E. Miguens, eds. 1983. *Juan Perón and the Reshaping of Argentina*. Pittsburgh: University of Pittsburgh Press.

Turner, Frederick J. 1920. *The Frontier in American History*. New York: Henry Holt.

Turner, Ian. 1965. *Industrial Labour and Politics: The Dynamics of the Labour Movement in Eastern Australia, 1900–1921*. Canberra: Australian National University.

UCLA. 1980. *Statistical Abstract of Latin America*. vol. 20. Los Angeles: Latin American Center Publications.

Unión Industrial Argentina. 1944. *Un ciclo de veintidós conferencias radiotelefónicas*. Buenos Aires: Instituto de Estudios y Conferencias Industriales.

United Nations. 1959. *El desarrollo económico de la Argentina*, 3 vols. México: Naciones Unidas.

———. 1968. *El desarrollo económico y la distribución del ingreso en la Argentina*. New York: Naciones Unidas.

———, Economic Commission for Latin America (ECLA). 1981. *Statistical Yearbook for Latin America, 1979*. New York: United Nations.

———. 1985. *Statistical Yearbook for Latin America, 1984*. Santiago: United Nations.

United States, Department of State. 1946. *Consultation among the American Republics with Respect to the Argentine Situation*. Washington, D.C.

Vazeilles, José. 1967. *Los socialistas*. Buenos Aires: Jorge Alvarez.

Vázquez Presedo, Vicente. 1971. *El caso argentino: Migración de factores, comercio exterior y desarrollo, 1875–1914*. Buenos Aires: Eudeba.

———. 1971, 1976. *Estadísticas históricas argentinas (comparadas)*, 2 vols. Buenos Aires: Macchi.

———. 1978. *Crisis y retraso: Argentina y la economía internacional entre las dos guerras*. Buenos Aires: Eudeba.

Veblen, Thorstein. 1915. *Imperial Germany and the Industrial Revolution*. London: Macmillan.

Véliz, Claudio. 1980. *The Centralist Tradition in Latin America*. Princeton: Princeton University Press.

Villafañe, Benjamín. 1935. *Hora obscura*. Buenos Aires: n.p.

———. 1943. *La tragedia argentina*. Buenos Aires: n.p.

Villanueva, Javier. n.d. "La depresión y la segunda guerra mundial: sus efectos sobre el desarrollo económico argentino." Unpublished ms.

———. 1969. "Aspectos de la estrategia de industrialización argentina." In Torcuato S. Di Tella and Tulio Halperín Donghi, eds. *Los fragmentos del poder*.

———. 1972. "El origen de la industrialización argentina." *Desarrollo económico* 12, no. 47: 451–76.

———. 1975. "Economic Development." In Mark Falcoff and Ronald H. Dolkart, eds. *Prologue to Perón: Argentina in Depression and War, 1930–1943*.

———. 1981. "Evolución de las estrategias de desarrollo económico en el período de posguerra." *Desarrollo económico* 21, no. 81: 61–70.

Villarreal, Juan. 1978. *El capitalismo dependiente: Estudio sobre la estructura de clases en Argentina*. México: Siglo XXI.

Waisman, Carlos H. 1982. *Modernization and the Working Class: The Politics of Legitimacy*. Austin: University of Texas Press.

———. 1984. "The Transition to Democracy in Argentina: Constraints and Opportunities." *LASA Forum* (Bulletin of the Latin American Studies Association) 15, no. 2: 22–24.

———. Forthcoming. "The Legitimation of Democracy under Adverse Conditions: The Case of Argentina." In Mónica Peralta-Ramos and Carlos H. Waisman, eds. *The Transition from Military Rule to Liberal Democracy: The Case of Argentina*.

Waldmann, Peter. 1981. *El peronismo, 1943–1955*. Buenos Aires: Sudamericana.

Wallerstein, Immanuel. 1974. *The Modern World System: Capitalist Agriculture and the Origins of the European World-Economy in the Sixteenth Century*. New York: Academic Press.

———. 1979. *The Capitalist World-Economy*. Cambridge: Cambridge University Press, and Paris: Editions de la Maison des Sciences de l'Homme.

Walter, Richard J. 1977. *The Socialist Party of Argentina, 1890–1930*. Austin: University of Texas Press.

———. 1985. *The Province of Buenos Aires and Argentine Politics, 1912–1943*. Cambridge: Cambridge University Press.

Watkins, Melville H. 1963. "A Staple Theory of Economic Growth."

*The Canadian Journal of Economic and Political Science* 29, no. 2: 141–58.

Weil, Felix J. 1944. *The Argentine Riddle.* New York: John Day Co.

Whitaker, Arthur P. 1956. *Argentine Upheaval: Perón's Fall and the New Regime.* New York: Praeger.

Wiarda, Howard J. 1973. "Towards a Framework for the Study of Political Change in the Iberic-Latin Tradition: The Corporative Model." *World Politics* 25: 206–35.

―――. 1974. "Corporatism and Development in the Iberic-Latin World: Persistent Strains and New Variations." In Frederick B. Pike and Thomas Stritch, eds. *The New Corporatism.*

―――, ed. 1974. *Politics and Social Change in Latin America: The Distinct Tradition.* Amherst: University of Massachusetts Press.

―――. 1981. *Corporatism and National Development in Latin America.* Boulder, Colorado: Westview Press.

World Bank. 1971. *Trends in Developing Countries.* Washington, D.C.: World Bank.

―――. 1976. *World Tables 1976.* Baltimore: Johns Hopkins University Press.

―――. 1980. *Poverty and Human Development.* New York: Oxford University Press.

―――. 1984. *World Development Report.* New York: Oxford University Press.

Woytinsky, W. S. and E. S. Woytinsky. 1953. *World Population and Production: Trends and Outlook.* New York: The Twentieth Century Fund.

Wynia, Gary W. 1978. *Argentina in the Post-War Era: Politics and Economic Policymaking in a Divided Society.* Albuquerque: University of New Mexico Press.

Zulueta Alvarez, Enrique. 1975. *El nacionalismo argentino,* 2 vols. Buenos Aires: La Bastilla.

# Index

Library of Congress Cataloging-in-Publication Data

Waisman, Carlos H. (Carlos Horacio), 1943–
    Reversal of development in Argentina.

    Bibliography: p.
    Includes index.
    1. Argentina—Politics and government—1943–
2. Argentina—Economic conditions—1945–
3. Argentina—Social conditions—1945–      . I. Title.
JL2081.W35 1987      306'.2'0982      87–42738
ISBN 0–691–07740–1 (alk. paper)
ISBN 0–691–02266–6 (pbk.)